UFO CONTACT FROM PLANET UMMO

Volume II
The Incredible Truth

Limited First Edition

Book No. of 1,000

This is a limited first edition published exclusively for those few individuals really interested in the facts in this remarkable and extensive UFO contact case that has been going on since 1950, AND STILL CONTINUES.

UFO PHOTO ARCHIVES
P.O. Box 17206,
Tucson, Arizona 85710

Printed and Bound in Arizona
by Arizona industries

UFO CONTACT FROM PLANET UMMO

Volume II
The Incredible Truth

Antonio Ribera

Contributions by
Richard W. Heiden
Ted Blocher
Wendelle C. Stevens

Translations by
Wendelle C. Stevens

Edited by
Cece Stevens

Privately Published by Wendelle C. Stevens

ISBN 0-9608558-9-0

The main text and appendices were originally published in Spanish under the title, UMMO: LA INCREIBLE VERDAD, Copyright 1985 by Sr. Antonio Ribera, and printed by Plaza & Janes, S.A., Editors, Virgen da Guadalupe 21-33, Esplugues de Llobregat (Barcelona), SPAIN, under ISBN 84-01-47201-6. The first edition was printed in May 1985.

Distributed by **UFO BOOKS**
Christine Stevens-Cox
P.O. Box 1053, Florence, AZ 85232

FORWORD

By the Publisher

Having presented an in-depth overview of the extraterrestrial contacts from a planet these visitors call UMMO in the first volume of these two volumes on this case we offered a considerable amount of information developed in this case over a period of 24 years, but in doing so we raised a whole lot more questions needing answers.

We were not permitted to release all the information available to the internal group at that time due to various restrictions and promises to preserve confidentiality. As it now appears that the Ummites have concluded their studies here on Earth for this time and have returned to their home planet, or have gone on to study another, Sr. Antonio Ribera no longer feels bound to the original requirements and has decided to release more of the information in his possession.

This information is sometimes shocking, and there is some danger in its release because, though this is officially denied, we now know for certain that the military and state intelligence gathering agencies of all the major powers have known of the UMMO operations here, and of their circular spaceships, at least since 1967 when the UMMO ships were photographed with high resolution government cameras, and very probably long before that.

We assure all that the information we will present has been collected privately, and that we are not violating Oaths of Secrecy in releasing it at this time.

We will describe a major United States military demonstration of such importance that special units of the fleets of at least Great Britain, France, West Germany, Australia and Italy, including senior military and State Department officers, were there at a secret site to observe a special operation involving our latest and best atomic submarine at the time. At that time three 40' diameter apparently UMMO spacecraft arrived over the scene four hours before the scheduled demonstration, and were photographed on 350 feet of 35mm ASA 500, scientific quality cine film exposed through a government theodolite camera system at close range. The film was immediately developed out and some prints were made, but neither film nor prints have ever been released. The test was called off and all witnesses were debriefed by intelligence, given cover stories, sworn, and then were shipped to widely separated duty stations, all to different ones. Some were discharged and sent home within days.

The government agencies soon connected the interruption of electrical power, loss of Radar, and interference in the demonstration exercise to the worldwide UMMO operations already being traced by several national secret intelligence agencies of many governments. The international intelligence agencies cooperated in an attempt to capture one of the Ummites or one of their ships, but never succeeded.

By 1970 the intelligence operations became overt and even the UMMO themselves mentioned such activities in at least six of their communications; numbers 92, 93, 94, 97, 116, and 173 in the catalogue of UMMO documents assembled by Ignacio Darnaude Rojas-Marcos.

There is evidence that some of those agencies went to considerable effort to discredit the UMMO contact stories, even planting false evidence in extensive and elaborate disinformation programs, to deliberately obfuscate the realities.

This is the 8th and Antonio Ribera's 3rd full length book, in Spanish, on the UMMO contacts in Spain, only one of which has ever been translated into English, and that is our first volume on the UMMO. These books are:

UMMO, Otro Planeta Habitado, Prof. Fernando Sesma Manzano, 1967
Un Caso Perfecto, Antonio Ribers and Roberto Farriols, 1968
De Veras, Los OVNIs Nos Vigilan? Antonio Ribera, 1976
Mirando a la Lejania del Universo, Enrique Lopez Guerrero, 1978
El Misterio del UMMO, Antonio Ribera, 1979 (translated to English)
3-Vols UMMO Documents, Juan Aguirre Ceberio, 1982
El Pluricosmos, Juan Dominguez Montes, 1983

We translated the first of these into English, and now have undertaken the translation of this last one, UMMO: The Incredible Truth.

This volume continues the same pattern and format as used in the first volume, and amplifies and expands on subjects barely introduced in the first one, such as: The early years of UMMO study of Earth; How they lived; How they learned our languages and read our texts; How they were supported and maintained; How the Earth research program developed; The rotation of UMMO expeditionary crews and changes of the specialized scientists within their research program.

Those interested in the UMMO dictionary of terms presented in the first book will find new words in this volume to add to that list. We have still seen only a fraction of the documents the Ummites claim to have left in various contact cells around the world.

We will see here that the UMMO are not the only extraterrestrials active over Earth, and that they are in contact with some of those others, but are aware of still more, some of whom they seek to open contact with.

These volumes provide an illuminating commentary on the subject of extraterrestrial contact with Earth and indirectly point out answers to questions that have vexed UFO researchers for 35 years. This phenomenon is not isolated; there is not just one ET source. They are innumerable.

W. C. Stevens

INTRODUCTION

A second book about the UMMO, asks the uninvolved reader? But is this really necessary? Yes, I say, a second, and a third, and even a fourth, not only would be necessary, but is entirely possible. The amount of information received from the mysterious source self-called UMMO is really impressive. And this irritating business (yes irritating) has not ended by any means. It began in Spain in the middle of the sixties, and continues. Actually, in the Spring of 1984 the last known communications — up to now — have been received from the Ummites (or UMMOAA as they prefer to call themselves).

I consider the UMMO business irritating for various reasons. In the first place we still have not located the actual source of the UMMO documents and letters. Is this source truely extraterrestrial as the anonymous communicators affirm? Or as well terrestrial — and very Earthly — as some investigators presume? There are good arguments in favor of both theses. In the second place we have the (high) quality of some of these reports, which obliges us to disregard the joke hypothesis. A joke invented — for example — by a group of science students would hardly be maintained for twenty years (35 in fact). The students would have grown up in that time and gone their separate ways becoming today respected professionals and fathers of families.

The CIA? It is too easy to lay any machination of unknown origin at the door of that Agency. Did NASA launch such a test of credibility concerning the possible existence of extraterrestrials among us? Twenty years for such a test?...

Those same Ummites published in one of their communications, a long list of agencies (Appendix A) to whom we might ascribe the origin of such communications. There they list all, from the CIA to the Society of Jesus, passing through Freemasonry and the KGB. (It is one of the few, very few, times the Ummites — if that is who they are — have demonstrated a certain sense of humor, which is absent in the majority of the communications. But the enigma persists. And we have no other choice but to try to carefully untangle the only tangible evidence that we in truth have: their own Ummite texts. From the beginning, a surprise: a fact mentioned casually in one of them (a theft committed in a field house near the point of their arrival on Earth in 1950) was confirmed by the French Gendarmeria 24 years after the fact. In effect: In 1973 I found myself in Tarbes attending a reunion of French and Spanish UFO Investigators, and during that time, I had the opportunity to discuss the UMMO affair with Dr. Claude Poher, Chief Engineer of the Rocket Section of the National Center for Space Studies (CNES) of Toulouse. As I related in my book DE VERAS, LOS OVNIs NOS

VIGILAN?, Poher was so impressed that he organized a search operation in the supposed zone of arrival of the Ummites (in the region of La Javie and the skirt of Cheval Blanc Peak, in the then Department of Basses Alpes, today called Alpes de Alta Provenza), and was able to locate, in the region of Tartone, the rooming house robbed by the UMMO explorers. The theft, according to the Gendarmeria, was committed in April of 1950 — or about a month after their supposed arrival here on Earth. And among those objects stolen WAS THE ELECTRONIC COMPUTER.

The Ummites had promised to indemnify splendidly, the victims of that exploite — who were precisely Spanish migrant workers of very low socio-economic level — who were later located by Poher living in the outskirts of Cannes... in houses of workers of means (blue-collar level).

A tremendous internal coherence exists in all the UMMO affair. Apparent contradictions to a casual observer are quickly overcome when the question is examined. Who would be capable of erecting a structure of such apparent coherence, whose pieces fit perfectly with others, and successfully maintain this for more than twenty years?

As an example, here is another coherent fact confirmed. A young man, an eminent French astrophysicist and mathematician — whose name I am not authorized to reveal —, today "Master of Research" in the French National Center for Scientific Investigation (CNRS), made a trip to the United Staters to visit certain laboratories of Advanced Physics. Impressed by the UMMO affair, in which I had initiated him, he knew perfectly well the book by Fernando Sesma, UMMO, OTRO PLANETA HABITADO which beneath the title is labeled: THIS IS NOT SCIENCE-FICTION. However the majority of the readers (uninformed) of that work consider it to have sprung from the mind of Sesma, when in reality this book was limited to a recompilation and presentation in book form, the communications from UMMO that he had been receiving since 1965. On page 86 of that work, we read the following: "Remained thus contested the question of M. Theodore T. Polk of Pittsburgh (USA), referring to the origin of our arrival on this planet."

Very well, the French astrophysicist in question, finding himself one day in a Northamerican population center that was not Pittsburgh, (on impulse) responded to an idea to consult the telephone directory for Pittsburgh. Among those many listings under Polk, he did find one "Theodore T. Polk". He immediately called him long distance, and thus learned that: a) Mr. Polk was a Professor at Harvard University, and b) That since about 1965 he had been receiving some mysterious "extra-terrestrial" communications. Very good, now he added that the affair was too delicate to comment on over the telephone. As my friend was hundreds of miles from Pittsburgh, and had to return to France, he was not able to arrange a personal interview with Professor Polk. But his telephone call confirmed his existence, that he was not an invention, and that he had actually been receiving the communications from the UMMO Expeditionaries to Earth. Another piece of the puzzle that fit exactly.

But, careful! We have been warned by the same Ummite mentality to wait until all fits perfectly and explains coherently. Those same ones have taken care to erase their trail by including the presentation of false testimony, confusing evidence... arranged by themselves. Is this the height of Machieavelism? Of course, but so it is. For example, and there are plenty of examples, there is first the case of the famous photographs of San Jose de Valderas. Negatives analized by Poher — to whom Farriols courteously sent them —, who came to an ambiguous conclusion in his study published by in the Bulletin of CUFOS, the organization headed by doctor Hynek of the Center for UFO Studies. There are, according to him, evidences in favor of fraud, together with evidences in favor of authenticity of the photos. On the other hand, the analysis made by William Spaulding, of Ground Saucer Watch is more explicit: The photos are fraudulent, and to make them they employed a small plastic model of 20 centimeters diameter hung on a thread. It is a pity that Spaulding did not use the negatives for his analysis, as did Poher, but only a copy of a photograph of second generation that was sent to him by Vicente-Juan Ballester Olmos... under which conditions his analysis merits no confidence, and neither Poher nor Spaulding paid any regard to the witnesses, the people who SAW it and saw what was captured by the cameras, and whose descriptions agreed with the images photographed. Rafael Farriols and I posess many hours of recorded testimony made with the visual witnesses, who appear with their names and addresses in our book UN CASO PERFECTO. But all this I have already said in my Introduction to EL MISTERIO DEL UMMO.

In the defunct magazine MUNDO DESCONOCIDO, No. 33, (March 1979), I published an article entitled "UMMO, Luz y Sombras", in which I wrote the following, "There is an enormous parallel among UFOs in general and UMMO in particular. In the case of UFOs we have the reports of the witnesses. In the case of UMMO we have the reproduced reports. And in both cases the reports exist, they are there. In both cases also, we do not know what is behind them. Extraterrestrials? Very possible but not sure. Doctor Hynek says that he does not study UFOs but the reports of UFOs. I could say that I do not study UMMO, but reports of UMMO." I believe that this is the lense through which we must contemplate this enigma. And also, as I concede with the UFOs, I consider the extraterrestrial hypothesis the best, and that which most aspects of the UMMO case support.

To return to the "lights and shadows" that surrounds all that refers to UMMO, there is another example. In the same magazine cited before, MUNDO DESCONOCIDO, published by my good friend, Andreas Faber Kaiser, Number 64 (October 1961), the "Group U3", composed it seems of various Barcelonese students of this phenomenon, conducted a detailed search of the Alpes de Alta Provenza (formerly Basses Alpes) specifically in the village of La Javie, Cheval Blanc Peak and various places in the region cited in the Ummite communications concerning their "arrival on Earth". According to those investigators, nothing fit; they could not verify even one single fact of those expressed in the reports. A similar conclusion was arrived at on their part by some French investigators, Jean-Jacques Pastor and Jean-Pierre Petit, of that which refers to the inhabitation of the pretended "cave" that the Ummites excavated at the foot of Cheval Blanc Peak. According to them there is no place there from which one can see simultaneously, all the points of reference cited in the Ummite report. Are we to believe from this that all is false? Or would it be better to consider a camouflage tactic to deliberately sew doubt and confusion among us? We remember one of the more significant Ummite texts — a key text I say — which is one of seven documents that I received some fifteen years ago, and with which I shall close this introduction:

"Do not believe us. Treat these concepts with disconfidence. Do not divulge them for now in the mass communications media. Demonstrate scepticism in front of those not familiar with your sciences (which analyze these things), but do not destroy these reproduced pages. With some thousands more distributed secretly, they constitute the primary history of the first relations between our two human races."

Antonio Ribers

[NOTE- Because we have been very specifically requested by the Ummite Expeditionaries themselves not to attempt to improve on or to redraw the illustrations they have furnished, we have decided if we are to offer them at all we must be content with the copies that we have, which have been reproduced directly from their original reports. We apologize for the loss of clarity in reproduction. -Publisher]

CONTENTS

BACKGROUND

In this book I am going to leave aside (for the time being) whom the actual authors of the communications said to be of UMMO are that are doing the speaking. I will remain discretely outside, appearing only when necessary to make a marginal note, point out some consequence, or show some relation. This will be another of my expositive books, in which I once more bring out one of those strange things, which is the unusual vocation I have been drawn to since my infancy. Little by lit= tle the reader is going to find himself confronting a strange and dis- concerting world; a science that does not seem to be of Earth; a cold rational mind that perhaps does come from tremendous cosmic distances. If anything distinguishes the communications from UMMO it is their asceptic character. free from proselitic ardor. These (communications) are light-years from the messianic kind that are continually spread in our world. They do not try to convert us to any religion of space. They limit their words to us like an elder brother would speak to his smaller unruly and ill prepared brother. They do not present themselves as brothers, however, reserving that appelation to our relations among ourselves. They say "your brothers" when they address one terrestrial in reference to other terrestrials. They address us with a respectful "Senor".

We begin this report however, with a terrestrial document: a letter that the mysterious "copyist" addressed to Fernando Sesma. Despite its colloquial and even vulgar style, it is a precious document because, his accounts may be the <u>only</u> direct testimony we have concerning <u>them</u>, the mysterious Ummites. The young copyist is perhaps the only Earth man (we know) who has seen them and has communicated with them with perseverance. For that his testimony is important and of particular interest.

THE COPYIST'S LETTER TO FERNANDO SESMA

Sr. D. Fernando Sesma Manzano
MADRID

My Dear Sir:

First of all, as I have not signed this letter, I want to remind you who I am. Surely you remember when I came to your house some months ago to bring you some extraordinary photographs that one could view perfectly in three-dimension relief in full color.

I wrote many of the pages that they sent you. You already know to whom I refer. They dictated to me and I typed and reproduced those folios They gave me a responsibility that I accomplished with gusto.

Those gentlemen have had to absent themselves from here though the chief or Director of them informed me that they would come back after some days for something important has occurred with relation to something that does not involve us. They gave me various instructions with respect to various Senores of Barcelona, Madrid and Valladolid to whom we habitually write. With respect to you, they ask that you excuse the interruption.

I have not come back to talk to you, Sr. Sesma, since that evening that I visited. Do you remember? Well with me they have exercised the greatest reserve. Since then many things have occurred and at times I burn with a desire to tell someone when it seems that I am about to go crazy.

Besides my wife and you, I have only spoken of this affair with a Doctor who is a professor at the Facultad de Medicina de Madrid, and to whom they send pages and pages with greater asciduity than with you. For that gentleman, whom I see frequently, they gave me some little rectangular crystals with clouds of color in the center. He is as convinced as I of the truth of this affair.

I have to struggle alone without knowing what route to take, between my passion for this affair, and the fears and anxieties of my wife that, as you know with women, something bad is bound to come of this, and already once was at the point with her nerves to lay it all out and discuss it with her mother. She had gotten it in her head that this was an espionage affair, influenced by the movies I say...

This affair, Sr. Sesma, is arousing. I myself would not know if I am awake or dreaming if it were not that my wife sees them with me in my house all these weeks, and because I have proofs that some day I will reveal, which nobody can deny. I have the names and addresses of all those gentlemen for whom I have prepared their dictations. And I also know another individual who like me has transcribed their dictated letters, and who says he does not want to know anything, and was frightened, but I am sure he will speak when all has passed.

There is this Doctor also to whom I have spoken. I know that he does not want to expose himself and be recognized publicly as maintaining relations with them. He also has asked me to maintain reserve and he would reward me, though I did not consent, for I have had enough of everyone asking me to guard some secret which I do (regularly) without compensation. But I am sure that this gentleman at least will not take me as deceitful in certain things which he had forbidden.

When I went to your house, Sr. Sesma, as God well knows, I did not know you, and that the first sceptic was myself for many weeks after.

They began to give me to know them as Danish Doctors who were in Spain to participate in a Seminar on Endocrinology. They dictated many things to me that I could see were not of medicine but of mathematics, and you know that medicine has little relationship with mathematics. (It is true that some things were of Medicine, but scarcely.) The day I delivered those photos that brought your admiration, you know that I confessed having mentioned it to a photographer neighbor of mine who had not seen them, and who said that it was impossible to see three dimensional relief without an optical apparatus.

Little by little the naturalness of those writings was giving me a story of something rare behind them. Then the taller of them who was called DA 3 came alone. The Director, I came to know later, was called DEI 98.

All this had a bad smell to me. For one thing the form of speech was different (later I came to know why). The names accompanied by a number. The form of precautions taken. It was a grave affair of conscience, to struggle between this and that which my wife and I believed was a duty to denounce this affair to the authorities. The other thing was the promise made to those gentlemen who paid me, and who paid splendidly. I saw as well in them something of nobility, of humbleness and faith that you could not understand if you did not know them.

We discarded the idea that we were going crazy. I had proofs, Sr. Sesma, that we were confronted with the greatest case in history. They brought an apparatus one fourth of which was a jet of gas. You could hear conversations in the home with a perfection and clarity like no magnetophone I ever heard. If you saw the size of the (viewing) screen it had you would be astonished. They said that though independent, it was activated by an apparatus inside. It was something marvelous. I saw in it my small office and us talking, like in a movie. The color was perfect, and everything with depth like in those photos I showed you. If you tell me I have read this in a future fantasy novel, tell me if I should not believe that all these gentlemen (of UMMO as they call their planet) say is true.

Look, Sr. Sesma, I do not have much culture, I recognize it, I am a mercantile teacher, and to understand well I would have to be a professor like the gentleman I mentioned. But you stand with your mouth open hearing them talk. One afternoon we were nearly three hours discussing the French system of accounting. They understood the codification of accounts of that system, and they made me a critic of the same which I already could not follow, speaking for example of the System of accountability by Decalco as if they practised it every day. They spoke of the Pert System applied to the rationalization of offices the same as that of the functionality of a perforator or of a classifying machine employed for statistical work in offices. In other things of which I had no understanding, one time I said, "You are inserting accounts of things, the utilization of which I have no understanding...! But of this business I "know something" (as must be understood in my profession).

My God, if I was to tell my boss or my companions in the office who taught me certain things, what was going on, it would leave them astonished: and the next day I would be put in a sanitarium for the mentally ill.

Sometimes I say: This cannot be; these men are lying or I am dreaming, or it pertains to some secret organization, or some sect of the Masons, but I do not believe some crazies would be capable of inventing those marvelous apparatus they carried.

I obtained various books that spoke of flying saucers, but could find nothing that mentioned the planet UMMO in any way. There was something that left me astonished in one of them. I don't know if you have read it. Its title was EL GRAN ENIGMA DE LOS PLATILLOS VOLANTES and they sell it in the Libraria de Espasa Calpe on the Avenida de Jose Antonio. On page 429 there is a sketch of a saucer that came down in Aluche, and of which all the press reported. (They had indicated that it was from UMMO) very well. I was more surprised to perceive that in the sketch, there appeared on the underside of the disc, a symbol that is like theirs. It is true that it lacks the horizontal bar to be exact, but it is the symbol of UMMO that I have seen with them though before the arrival of the disc (You remember that my visit was before the notice published by the newspapers of that time).

Besides a proof that I have (and could produce some day if I am called a liar), those gentlemen have been seen by my wife, and they have been seen by my brother-in-law, though we did not tell him who they were but he was intrigued, and they were seen by my portera also for whom my wife had to provide an explanation to justify their coming to my house.

Among the things they did not explain was the patience they take in writing people. There are weeks when I prepared and reproduced up to 30 pages. This was besides an additional copyist with whom I have spoken, and though he did not break his pledge, and was afraid, he felt obliged to write his (work) also, and we do not know if they had anybody else.

I sent the envelopes, and at times I delivered folios written with more than three different kinds of typewriters. I can not tell you the names but their correspondents were of various professions. There were many professors, one engineer of I.C.A.I., an industrial engineer. a police commissioner, a professor of medicine, a well known dramatist, two priests, two assistant engineers, various writers, a lady pharmacist, another lady, an astronomer, etc... At first there were only a few, professors of Barcelona and Madrid, later you, after that a priest, and then always there were more. Sometimes they wrote only one time and sent nothing else. To me they dictated the most varied things that you can imagine, from Astronomy to Biology, and I suggested they buy an IBM machine that had a ball to type mathematical symbols, and though it cost more, it had symbols that I had to write by hand, and Greek letters. But they smiled and said that they would be able to find the machine soon though few were available for sale.

There are some strange things. Why, Sr. Sesma, those gentlemen who knew so much and were so intelligent could not type, and took the risk that one of us might betray them? I am not going to do it but they can not be sure of that.

Also, what do they gain by writing? If they want us to believe them, why not demonstrate proofs to the whole world? It would be enough if they saw what I have seen, or permit the journalists to see the remarkable photos that you know, or simply allow themselves to be seen.

But it would be enough to observe them a little! When they speak, those strangers move their lips very little. I have seen them speak with that strange voice that they have and don't move their lips. They say (and I believe it) that they have an apparatus in the throat, and that a doctor could examine them and prove this. What better proof! When I mentioned this to them the smiled and did not answer.

Why such secrecy? I say they have nothing to do with the government. On the contrary, that is one thing that makes me suspicious. Why such secrecy? And why don't they seem to be worried when the persons to whom they write make no case of it?

At times it seems to me of a cleverness that appears backward if it were not for the enormous culture that does not fit with this explanation. How are those gentlemen they write to (who are not exactly nobodies) going to believe that this treats of men from another planet? The least they could be taken for is impersonators. And this is reasonable to my wife, and on which she bases her suggested espionage.

But can you imagine such spies writing letters to those people?

And finally, Sr. Sesma, I don't know what is going to happen in all this. If I could have proved anything wrong in their conduct I would have already denounced them. Also the Police must know of them, because I have written to one police commissioner for them. It was when they did not act on something. When the government does not act something will happen, and we are not going to be more fatherly than the father...

Le Saluda su s.s.

Pardon me for omitting the signature.
I believe you understand.

Anguished by the unusual situation he was living, the young copyist got the idea to ask the neurophysiological professor he had seen, to write a letter-circular and he would send it around to all the UMMO correspondents to collect their opinions, and eventually arrange a meeting of them together in the house of the professor, from which could come a report to be directed to the Spanish authorities.

The professor wrote the letter requested by the copyist, who transcribed it and made copies, but the meeting did not take place. When the "Danish Doctors" (with their special means) discovered the initiative of their copyist, they became extremely angry. The frightened copyist decided to quit the project.

Who was this mysterious professor? The components of the so-called "Madrid Group" are identified with Prof. Doctor don Antonio Gallego Fernandez, Professor of Physiology of the Facultad de Medicina, Universidad Complutense, Madrid. This is based principally on the reconstruction of the letterhead that figured in the pages of the letter written by that man of science (and which he cut off), in whose lower part may be read "Madrid", seeing also what seems to be the lower half of an "o" (end of "Neurophysiologo") lower case, plus part of an "O", upper case, that corresponds to the end of the name "Gallego". Nevertheless an investigation made on my part in Madrid seemed to discard such an hypothesis, as we shall see further on.

We look now in continuation at the text of the letter of the professor. (Observe the evident difference of style between this letter, written by a scientist, with the vulgar and untidy style of the copyist. This would be a "semantic proof" that both were written by different persons):

Professor Doctor don Antonio Gallego Fernandez
Professor of Physiology,
Facultad de Medicina
Universidad Complutense
Madrid

13-1-1967

My Dear Sir:

I consider a preliminary presentation necessary. (Although in this first contact I pray you will excuse the omission of my name for reasons easy to understand.)

I am a Medical Doctor, and in actuality titled Professor of the Faculty of Madrid.

The 8 cte. (8 January 1967) I was visited by a young man in the profession of Mercantil Expert with whom lately I have been maintaining a series of very unusual contacts.

This young man argued a series of reasons that seemed to me sufficiently convincing for me to decide to write this extensive letter and eight copies more to other gentlemen as unknown to me as to you yourself.

The exceptional character of this affair requires offering a reference to certain past actions. At least those that do not violate the reservations imposed on me for obvious reasons, I can relate to you.

On the 18th of December 1965 an unknown (person) called by telephone to my personal residence. As our housemaid found the phrases she heard unintelligible, my wife took the apparatus to whom they expressed the desire to talk to me. (I was not at home during those hours.)

A similar call was repeated that same night at about 11:00 (p.m.). A repitition of incoherent words (came through the phone). (Later I understood its significance.) I felt impelled to hang up the bothersome telephone. It was not the first time that some of my students had amused themselves molesting us at inopportune hours.

But on the 19th (the following day), the same individual repeated his call. This time, with an indefinable foreign accent, but articulating the words perfectly in Castilano, he spoke correctly in terms that made me think he was a colleague. He did not refer at first to his nationality. He wanted to speak with me about a supposed discovery concerning the function of the Haces of Goll and Burdach and of some secondary effects provoked by the hemisection of the Medula, as called the Brown-Sequard Syndrome.

His point of view resulted in such suggestivity, that through a very pleasant dialogue that lasted, without exaggerating, a full hour, I courteously invited him to have tea with me the following day.

Not only did he refuse, but his reaction left me truely astonished.

He treated it as an evident discourtesy on my part, bruesquely hanging up the telephone. My interlocutor informed me with disconcerting naturalness that he came from a distant planet no less than fourteen years distant from ours, and called by him something like "UMO".

The incident left me perplexed and I tried to imagine an explanation in consonence with the conduct of my supposed colleague. I discarded the hypothesis of a student joke (because of the exceptional erudition that he demonstrated on a theme so profound as Neurophysiology), I could imagine that it might be a colleague with a paranoid mentality or someone with a strange sense of humor.

I forgot the incident that in truth I discussed in sarcastic tones with my wife.

But in four or five days (I remember that it was before the Nochebuena of year before last) our man tried his call one more time, in the hours just before dinner. I decided to answer, without doubt influenced by purely natural curiosity.

I was impressed though, more than the preceeding time, with the incalculable erudition of this mysterious communicator. This time, I maliciously formulated a series of questions on themes as diverse as Histology, Renal Surgery, Biochemistry and Techniques of Diagnostic Electrocardiography. I was so impressed by the conciseness of his responses and precision in scientific exposition of same, so confused and overwhelmed by my own awareness of my professional inferiority with respect to my strange communicator, that after timidly congratulating him I insinuated that I would like to know the real objective of his calls.

He came back to insist that he came from a distant star, making the observation that he understood my scepticism and that this was no joke and that I could discard the idea of interpreting this as a version of psychopathology. And continuing, he explained the secondary symptomatic delusions in some paranoic syndromes, and concluded by demonstrating that possible arguments intended to evaluate a diagnostic interpretation of a mental illness lacked value.

I insisted in my turn in offering the consequent object, that no man of science would accept "a priori" an affirmation of such transcendence without being supported by convincing scientific proofs.

My interlocutor showed comprehension and satisfaction. Referring to my point of view with complete naturalness, he offered to send me an apparatus or technical demonstrator relating to my profession which existence on Earth I would not be able to find the least reference. He asked me on my formal Word that the equipment be returned intact, and without my trying to mechanically get at its interior nor damage it, and that only I and my most immediate acquaintences would manipulate it. Such reservations and restrictions made me suspect the possibility of fraud, but I decided to calm my distrust and verbally accept the conditions that he demanded.

The calls began to disturb me *and I spoke of them with two companions of the Facultad, commenting gayly on the hypothetic origin of the mysterious colleague.*

On 3 January 1966 (though protected in a casket of wood and wrapping with cancelled stamps) I received the sample package, cancelled in Madrid, and wrapped in normal layers of paper. It had a return address which I later learned was false, and the address of the copyist. (Whom I later came to know as the young Mercantile Expert. My address had been written by him.)

In its interior I saw a device of prismatic form with rounded edges. It seemed of steel though its surface was covered with a film of transparent enamel so hard it was impossible to scratch it with a carborundum crystal, preventing evaluation with any exactitude the type of metal or alloy utilized.

The aparatus had dimensions of approximately 8x8x5.3 centimeters. In the upper part there was a kind of squared screen it seemed, of glass or plastic very hard and of opaline color. My attention was called to the fact that the metal or alloy of the structure seemed to be made with the translucent lamination of the screen without any visible separation in continuity. The base or lower surface of the apparatus had five orifices. One of them was squared and the rest were of circular section and of different sizes.

A letter accompanied it, without signature and also mechanically reproduced, with text in Spanish, containing a series of instructions to make the small apparatus operate. (I read the instructions carefully.) It was necessary to place it on a thick soft pad of felt or foam rubber or polyfoam. One had to come close to the box and pronounce (holding the vocals) the dipthong "iiiiaaaa".

With a certain fear, I decided to make a test. This whole affair seemed incoherent and strange. Although the idea passed through my mind that this could be an explosive device activated acoustically, I rejected the idea immediately as too purile and novelesque. Nevertheless I believed it prudent to take the apparatus to the Facultad (to test it) and not communicate my fears to my wife.

I remember it was Monday, and vacation time. I asked the watchman for the keys to the laboratory and took it inside with me. I began examining and measuring the dimensions of that box, though I did not try to insert any tool into the perforations that appeared on the back. Nor did I hear the movement of anything inside. Examining the orifices with a flashlight, I could not distinguish any part of any mechanism.

In the depth of one of them and placed axially I could see something that looked like a plated or chromed needle.

Finally I decided to experiment with the instructions. I placed the strange device on a flannel dust cloth, the only thing I could find that was somewhat clean, and pronounced the vocals in front of the screen just as advised in the accompanying note. I had to repeat it two more times, changing the position of the mouth. Finally the screen came "on" so bruesquely that I instinctively jumped back from the device.

There appeared on the screen a stereoscopic image of great depth and detail. It looked like a microscopic preparation, though what caught my attention to the contrary was that which occurs with vision through the eyepiece of a normal microscope, the distinct planes of depth of field were not disenfocused, and I could observe all of the points in finest detail. Until later it was impossible for me to identify the nature of the image that was moving actively on the screen. A viscous mass seemed to flow transversally at great velocity. Evidentally the image recorded a histological preparation seen in great magnification, though less than that obtained with electron microscopes. The most extraordinary was the dynamic vision of the process, in detail and in natural color, and in perfect image relief.

Later I understood that it treated of the visualization of the synapsis between two adjacent corresponding dendrites to two neurons in chain. The molecular structure of the acetilcolina could be surprisingly appreciated, such was the definition of the image. The most surprising was that it did not treat of an image recorded by some magnetoscopic or cinematographic process, but of a real process of a physiological preparation "in vitro", placed inside the apparatus, by unknown technologies I supposed, to impede the cellular necrosis of the specimen under study.

That same night the unknown (communicator) called again. He recognized that I was very impressed by the experience, and he asked me to identify the images seen during those hours. Also I did not know how to stop the operation of that equipment. He advised me in complete detail and also informed me how I could contemplate three other corresponding images as well as such other histological preparations contained in the cone of the apparatus, which he called something like "ULODOOISAGII".

Also he announced that another individual unaware of all this would pass by my house and pick up the device after 48 hours.

The following day (4 January 1966) I went to a friend of mine to borrow a photo camera, a Japanese model "Canon" without explaining the true reason. After showing me how to operate it, he gave it to me already loaded with film (My photographic experience had not gone past the use of a "Contax", used in the laboratory). I shot a strip of some seven meters taken at a speed of 18 frames per second, in which could be recognized not only diverse scenes in the apparatus and also a graduated reference scale, but various sequences of the physiological-histological processes seen in the apparatus. I used Kodachrome color film. It is a pity that one cannot appreciate in the film the surprising depth of the images!!! In any case this document which I guard in my posession has, in my estimate, undoubtable value.

The young man who came to see me showed extreme reserve. *Later on I came to understand that this unknown youth even knew of the supposed identity of my interlocutor.* From then on, neither in his voice nor in his form of expression could I identify in him the mysterious unknown "colleague".

The continued calls were followed by a series of postal shipments of rich scientific content. The surprising theses expressed in them about the comportment and function of distinct zones of the hypothalmus left me truely astonished.

If I wasn't afraid of tiring you, I could fill many pages extracting the abundant documentation obtained, the delightful telephonic discussions maintained with a man that I still had not been able to see. In some of the conversations we discussed an extensive range of intellectual fields. He demonstrated brilliant erudition in turn on the most heterogeneous themes (Zoology, Politics, Socialogy, Anthropology, History of our World War, etc., etc.)

My only connection with them is the youth I've mentioned in the beginning, the same who (according to his version) copied and mailed the studies which, he says, they also sent to you. As said, he has asked me to make contact with all the parties of this group of technicians and specialists in diverse scientific branches with whom he maintains periodic contact.

The abnormal circumstances that impell me to write this letter, justifies the fact that for the first time in my professional life, I send one of my writings to a destination unknown to me, for which I ignore including my name. You will understand my abstaining this time from signing my name as would be customary.

With very good reason, this young man has denied giving me your name and that of the other correspondents. He has given me only a list of your professions. It seems that those supposed Gentlemen posess the means of being amply informed about the identity of the persons that they select.

I have acceeded then, to the requirements of this Copyist, who is writing nine letters identical to this in their content, with the condition that he will send them to those correspondents titled in some scientific or technological specialty. without doubt we have to put ourselves in contact with the rest of the non-technical correspondents as soon as we can arrange references about their criteria with respect to this strange affair.

It is very possible if you have not received reports of scientific nature as I suppose, one could logically conclude that this treats of a vulgar joke in which case it would be advisable to go no further with them.

I do not know, then, if you accept my point of view regarding this extraordinary affair. I believe, also, that I must expose systematically and briefly, the various aspects of my criticism.

Those of us that make up this group of Spaniards selected by those Gentlemen cited, are living without doubt an episode of whose reach and transcendence I myself am ignorant at this moment. I don't believe it is the time for us to make dramatic pronouncements. We must judge the situation serenely, without nervous extemproaneous reactions by anybody. As experts in diverse scientific sectors I don't want to hide from you that we should maintain a balanced distrust of such exceptional things.

I don't know (since I have abstained from initiating unilateral investigations without contact with you) if the governmental Administration posesses at this time information in this respect. The youth who acts as the connection assures that *one of the corresponednts is precisely an Inspector or Commissioner of the Direccion General de Seguridad*. But as we don't know if such relations are with officials or purely personalities, I believe that we must maintain a prudent reserve that we do not impede the private interests of such functionary whose identity, on the other hand, we do not know at the moment. Without prejudgement of time, we should consider the convenience of seeking an interview with him to sound out his point of view and to confirm the hypothesis of his functions as a delegate of the Spanish Government with this mysterious group that occupies us.

In one of the reports sent by those supposed men of UMMO they made mention of a famous Northamerican Cardiologist as a man who receives from them another series of scientific reports. After obtaining his identity and address, I sent him a prudent exploratory letter dated 4 March 1966, that he answered on 13 March of the same year, and which I also logically guard in my file on this affair as a new and most valuable testimony.

In his friendly reply, he began by showing surprise that a Spanish Doctor such as I had been in contact with those gentlemen from UMMO. He continued by expressing a series of fears in this respect, after showing that he was totally convinced of the identity with respect to the extraterrestrial origin of our mysterious men. He invited me to join him in keeping the silence.

I lamented to disagree with my illustrious Yankee colleague with respect to the last two points of view.

Nevertheless, his testimony constitutes an undoubtedly solid proof that their (UMMO) activities are not limited only to the Iberian Peninsula as I at first believed.

In conclusion I estimate:

That undoubtedly we find ourselves confronting some individuals of the highest cultural, scientific and technical levels, demonstrated by (previously) unknown technical methods, at least for me and for those other witnesses that I know (the mentioned doctor in the United States and the young copyist). At least in the field of medicine they demonstrated an erudition truely fabulous. (I have had telephone conversations with two of those supposed visitors.)

With this basis, can we conclude that their affirmations with respect to their supposed interplanetary origin is true?

I believe that we must stand with care on such slippery ground.

I have not personally seen any of these individuals. The only testimony I have is that of the young man and his wife, who describe them *as like normal people similar in complexion to individuals of German or Nordic nationality*.

In my estimation it is very suspicious, that some beings supposedly coming from another planet, do not have traces of atypical morphology. I resist a belief that individuals of any (other) inhabited planet, would have a physiology similar to that of our terrestrial human species. I can not imagine how they could travel from there knowing that though travelling at the maximum velocity possible they would be some fourteen years on the trip.

Respecting this, I cannot hide from you a fact of grave importance with respect such a hypothesis. I remember from before that in all of our long telephone conversations, never was I able to discover one single error, one single fault, in the scientific exposition of their report. Not even one time did I ever discover in the context of their reproduced reports, any false data, or evident contradiction with respect to their later contentions.

But I remember that in a certain conversation (and their words are recorded on magnetic tape) they told me of a certain trip made by them *to Australia that lasted eight months*.

How is it possible to present coherently such affirmation with their version of distance to that supposed Planet (14 years)? Remember that physics and astronautics are not precisely my own fields of erudition, but at first they did not explain this anomaly. Up to a point I preferred not to ask them the reason for this evident contradiction to keep it from being evident.

Remember that despite all, the preceeding objections do not form a body of homogenous doctrine that permits rejection without the most careful examination of the veracity of their affirmations.

In Effect: Facing these serious doubts, one encounters the fabulous reality of their strange apparatus that reveals the posession of technologies unknown up to now among official scientists. The exceptional intelligence of those men together with their incredible erudition and the disconcertant conduct of some individuals that are affording me a line of knowledge in the field of Neurophysiology ignorant to those specialists that are today in the vanguard of this arousing sector of knowledge.

What conclusion, in view of these things, can we deduce from their conduct? Logically I have scrapped a series of hypotheses that progressively I have had to reject, conscious of their inconsistency. You understand the purile result attributing this to jokesters or a simple alliance of delerious paranoids, nor can it resist the slightest criticism to catalogue them as members of some secret organization or some sect. And of their conduct, one can never infer that they pertain to any particular body of any foreign power that operates secretely in other nations.

We must maintain much caution before accepting any hypothesis until more time has passed. Their reactions offer us the most solid argument with which to judge their identity.

On the other hand it covers serious doubts that our Government is informed about their activities, as is the opinion of our youthful friend. News of such transcendence ends by filtering through the administrative-technical departments and transcends rapidly. I have occupied myself to make some soundings in this sense, and have not obtained the least fact that would corroborate that possibility.

In view of all these things, and as I suppose that you, like I, may be interested in the resolution of this genuine enigma, I estimate that we could concentrate in my home, or some other adequate place, a confidential meeting.

In that first interchange of information and criticism (since it is logical to wait for the unknown information in the hands of other members of the group), we should consider the opportuneness of sending a detailed report to the State Administration accompanied by whatever testimonial facts and proofs we have under our control.

Rest assured that the dispatch of any report will be conditioned on the consent of a "quorum" of those attending, and will be precisely to find out if those supposed men from UMMO have previously given us a formal prohibition against sending such a report, and also to decide if we should invite a meeting of writers and journalists, etc., to advise them that we are having these contacts. I consider it obvious to advise that *public opinion has no need to have access to this information,* and my respected Northamerican colleague is in concurrence. The masses as you know, will adopt a posture of stupid scepticism, or engage in exalted manifestations of credulity, or collective hysteria, and even superstition ot these things.

I await your reply in the immediate future without the necessity of this prudent reserve and anonymity, as soon as the young copyist can give me the names of all of us. This would seen to depend on a prior authorization which he expects to be granted by Them.

I would like to terminate this long memorandum with affectionate greeting to you, feeling in truth that I do not know you well enough for more extensive dialogue with you. This letter will be delivered to the young man repeatedly cited, so that he can send it to you.

I remain yours, s.s.

LETTER OF "SILVIA" TO AUTHOR

I have written before that I have carried out in Madrid, certain steps to verify if the mysterious professor is really the Professor Antonio Gallego. I was greatly helped in this investigation by a lady friend of mine living in the capital of Spain who, for obvious reasons must remain anonymous, and whom I shall only call "Silvia".

Precisely, Silvia knew Professor Gallego very well, having been his secretary for years. In an extensive letter she summarized her conclusions with respect to my inquiries. I herewith present this letter, from which I have only removed some paragraphs and certain phrases of personal character.

Madrid, 27 June 1968

Dear Antonio:

Since you left I have never stopped being concerned about the affair that so interests us. I have undertaken a truely laborious police work ("insert" for him I have certain talents) but in which I have failed completely up to now. I visited full face with Tamarit, because I suspected that it could be him, though certain details of the letter made me doubt, and he not only demonstrated with arguments that I cannot write here because this letter would be interminable, but that he gave me his word of honor that this was the first word he had heard spoken of this in his life. Gallego (and of this I will speak later) IS NOT.

Validated to me by a functionary of the Decanato, I have verified that in the Catedra de Castro (Histology) there is no photographic machine, in the manner that neither Castro, whose typewriter is not the same as we have, nor his substitute, have been (aware of). I have thought of a number of reasons why it could be the the Decano (Prof. Velazquez, Pharmacology) because his laboratory posesses a Contax photographic machine. because I can write to Gallego or to Tamarit, with whom I am on good terms, to ask the loan of a Cannon, and because they have a typewriter in their homes for their personal writings that, though I have seen no writing from them, they could be of the Olivetti featherweight transportable type on which the famous letter (from the professor) was written. I suggested to Enrique Villagrasa that it may be better that I undertake this personally and expose myself to still another failure, for which they are going to know me in the highest spheres of the Facultad de Medicina as a crazy one and take me to Cienpozuelos, in which case he could send a letter conceived in the following terms, or similar, which does not obligate anybody: "Having come to the conclusion, by a series of deductions that it is not the case, that you could be the person who on such a date sent a letter without signature to eight different persons, referring to certain unusual telephone calls, I pray that you could call me at such and such a number to exchange impressions as you may desire." And sign it. If he is the one, one could suppose that his interest persists and that he will call. If he is not the one, he would think that the other was crazy and throw the letter in the basket. If it is him, and he does not want to go into it because he has thought better, he may give the called-for reply.

And I have continued my investigations. The only professor of the Facultad de Medicina de Madrid, whose particular home number corresponds to the 30, which is what seems to be revealed in the photocopy of the letter, is Diaz Rubio (Anatomy and Clinica Medicas), living at Hermosillo 30. I have in my posession a treatment (form) on a patient of his, and its letterhead does not correspond with the formation displayed in the photocopy in question nor does the type of the typewriter used, but this is not significant because the nurse typed the treatment report in the clinic, and he could have a particular form that correspondes to the one we know, and a portable typewriter (of that type in his home) with which he could have written the letter confidentially and secretly in his home. I am waiting for them to tell me if he has an Olivetti featherweight and if he has a Contax in his laboratory. If he has, I will communicate it to Villagrasa.

Now -- and pardon the length of this letter, its poor syntax and feather flying -- I am going to explain why it is not Gallego. Apart from some personal considerations, that would be too tedious to explain, but to which nobody better than I could come, because apart from knowing him since a child due to the friendship of our two families, I have been working with him 18 years and I know much better than he what he has brought to the world. There is something fundamental that is not a subjective appreciation and is in order of importance minor to major: that in the laboratory they have a Leica and not a Contax; that he does not have to ask anybody for a Cannon because months before that letter was written, he had brought one from Japan. (as well as Tamarit another, something I didn't know, for which I thought that Tamarit could have asked to borrow one from him); and finally that Gallego, being one of the most prominent neurophysiologists in the world, would be enthralled by a microscopic preparation impossible to preserve in the conditions as he says "alive", that he observed in the apparatus provided by the communicator, *but none could ignore that it treated of a synapsis of two dendrites correspondent to two neurons in chain,* because that is his, because it is happening on a daily basis in the laboratory. He would have been astonished by such a preparation but there would have been no necessity to explain what it was. That is *fundamentally* the reason for which, from the first moment, I told you *it was not him...* Apart from his open personal characteristics, some vanity, ready to communicate all to all the world, especially, especially to me, from whom he has never kept secrets, his sceptisism in this extraterrestrial field is absolute, and as a physiologist, he would never accept the possibility of any other beings "equal to us" coming from another planet. That is more appropriately of a morphology, and the letter several times repeats, also, is of a medical doctor who does not know much physiology, and until later nothing of neurophysiology; for this I also have my doubts about Tamarit.

But let us terminate. And so, I have arrived at the following conclusions: that the letter of the professor is not of such professor because it could have been written by one called Pardo, and that the kind of type of both letters is the same, however I saw both letters and compared them in the house of .... and saw perfectly that they are not of the same kind (independently of whether the professor exists, which is another matter); that in any case, whether he had dictated the letter to Pardo is pure illusion. The letter is very long, written in a careful manner, and without doubt by the interested or his wife (as those of professors help them). Nevertheless the brilliant conclusion I have come to is: that the letter of Pardo and that of the professor are written by the same hand on the same typewriter and that the professor is GALLEGO. Therefore, for a reason, *I, that know for certain,* must keep it quiet. Whoever understands Medicine, would know that a neurophysiologist, and more of the category of Gallego, and more still him being specialized in the central nervous system, never would have to have explained a synapsis of two dendrites of two neurons in chain.

Do you believe I exaggerate, my dear Antonio, or, leaving apart my vehemence, that I have reason?

Pardon, dear Antonio, this long letter perhaps incoherent because I write between telephone calls and visits of people that come and go. I, despite all, because the thing comes from you, and you inspire in me great affection, great respect, and treat these things in an objective and scientific manner, and because it interests me enormously, do continue my investigations, though little remains to do. But in truth, I am disappointed. And be it what must be that will come to be found out, I put in your knowledge.

Now, it only remains for me to pray that you will reserve this letter for yourself, most sincerely as you know that I am me...

Mountains of embraces for all,

"Silvia"

PS: Having in Madrid some fourty professors and a great many candidates, some of whom in any given moment may be "titled" to replace or to increase the professorships... to find the actual author of the letter is like looking for a needle in a haystack. I only investigated among those who I more or less knew of, and by some deduction - though vague - I think that could be our man; I think that a letter like I advised to E.V. could be sent to each one of those, if it is truely your desire for truth be given about him.

PRESENTING THE UMMITES

In the year 1967, the Ummites sent a communication to one of their correspondents of Madrid, don Manuel Campo, in which they made a kind of presentation of themselves and their culture, in a summary form. It is a precious document for knowing in synthesized form, that which is UMMO, and for that it seemed to me necessary to place it here first in this book. After reading it you will have a general idea of that which is signified by the vocable UMMO, which some hasty critics have even sought to confuse with "HUMMO" (spanish word for "smoke"), but which, as we will see in the length of this work, is far from that.

Here is the communication received by Sr. Campo (along with similar communications received by twenty eight other persons if we are to believe what they independently tell us).

UMMOAELEWE
Language: Spanish
No. of copies 28
Date 1967
Sr. Manuel Campo

Senor:

We know the transcendence of that which we are about to tell you. It is clear to us that an affirmation of this nature, not only could be considered the basis for a joke, a perturbed mental case with dilerious ideas, but even some news publicist who wanted to exploit the news to his advantage.

When a news item breaks the normal patterns for acceptance, and is lacking judgeable means and elements testifying to its reality, any balanced and intelligent mind has the right and must adopt an attitude of scepticism or fear. "Never should we accept simple testimony, and less when, as in this case, its origin is unknown and thus of suspicious nature."

To us it is clear that we can reveal it to you as truth, but can not however postulate a good logic why you should believe these manifestations so fantastic. "We admit that in your place we would act the same."

But nevertheless is admissable, the action that tolerates "A PRIORI" any version, to analyze it carefully and dispassionately and search for the truth. In fact all of the investigators of Earth have followed this criteria.

If concepts of YESTERDAY seemed fantastic and absurd, they would not be analyzed by competent specialists. Have you arrived at this cultural state throughout the Earth?

But if such concepts are erroneous, if such versions are fraudulent, if it is only the work of imposters, IN TRUTH you have steps to unmask the illusion, the jokester, the paranoic, or the imposter who seeks to get by scientific etiquette.

We have studied these heights sufficiently in Your History to be aware of that immense bitterness over false prophets, of paranoid minds, unaware of the benefits in exploiting the sincere credibility of your scientists of good faith.

We have appreciated how science has had to struggle against clouds of Superstition, Astrology, Theosophy, Spiritualism, and Radiesthesia and though in them they carry some few valid principles susceptible of being investigated, together they present an accumulation of gratuitas affirmations of reasonably analogus absurdities, of petitions at first totally unacceptable to a balanced mind.

In these recent years, with the appearance in the Terrestrial Atmosphere of those so-called UFOs or OVNIs, vulgarly called Flying Saucers, the fantasy of the men of Earth is overflowing with the multiplication of fraudulent notices of such phenomenon. and what is more grave, appearing in various countries are individuals such as George Adamski in 1952, Daniel Fry or the Norwegian Edith Jacob in 1954, assuring that they have had contact with beings coming from other stars.

These subjects and the credibility of the masses initially accepting their absurd versions has totally discredited those serious studies that in spite of all, are being carried out on the part of official technical departments of certain Governments.

Conscious then that such versions have created a logical climate of disconfidence it is not strange that it produces a repition of the popular fable you call The Pastor And The Wolf.

For this we know perfectly that we are not going to be believed in this case when we make the revelations that follow.

We repeat that our principal objective is not rooted in being believed without more proofs than these documents that we are going to send you. This is not to say that in the following we will not send you verified arguments and proofs of our identity as we have already done in the United States, England, and here in Spain with one person. We have made ourselves known in other countries. Australia, Germany, and the Soviet Union, are receiving our reports at this time, directed to prominent men of science, and though we recognize that in a high percentage of cases the receivers tore our letters up, logically taking them as the work of a jokester or perturbed mentality, in some cases the overwhelming collection of genuine scientific data submitted by us, have been sufficiently convincing to many, that in the end we can tell something of the truth.

With those persons the relations have continued, demonstrating reticence and disconfidence, but objectively validating the strange situation without totally discarding the hypothesis of which our "supposed" identity is known.

For that we ask you to read carefully what we are going to tell you: It is not important that in the beginning you have only simple curiosity, and totally discard the fitness of our apparently fantastic affirmations. We reiterate that we are not so ingeneous as to hope to be believed.

Nevertheless, there is a second reason that could seem paradoxical, and which we will explain at this opportunity. We do not desire that the masses have knowledge of our existence. And we have powerful motives that justify this action of ours.

Until the present and except for scarce exceptions, our contacts have been circumscribed to men of science (Pure Researchers and some Engineers) to whom we have offered certain data concerning Physics, Biology and Psychology, of interest to them. Thus with some technical procedures of industrial application, like in the concrete case of A.W.R., of Atlanta (in the United States), were accepted and patented, surprisingly, but believing that it treated of some scientific eccentric and was original.

There exist then, reasons that move us to present ourselves to you, precisely to form part of this restricted group, that with more or less intellectual formation, has preoccupied itself throughout your world with the problem that for the man in the street constitutes the origin of those UFO.

Physical Data of the Star of Origen

We come from a planet whose verbal expression or phonics could be written as "UM-MO" (the U may be closed or guttural. The M could be interpreted like a [soft] B [or like the m in plumb]).

Orbit of "UMMO"

Elliptical, with eccentricity of 0.007833 with focus on the star we call IUMMA or YUMMA which we see as having the same functions as the Sum in your system.

Distance from Earth to IUMMA

The apparent distance is said to be that followed by a beam of coherent waves in three dimensional space, as it was on 4 January 1955.

14.437 Lightyears.

Real distance in decadimensional space

The real distance in decadimensional space on the same date, according to our calculation.

3.685 Lightyears.

The first distance is that calculated by your Earth Astronomers, disregarding the curvatures of the light as it travels through intense gravitational fields. Such distance is "constant" only for two bodies fixed in (unperturbed) space.

The real distance in decadimensional space is a function of time, as verified in a Space of N dimensions, and presents certain periodicity. Its calculation is very important, as this is connected to our Galactic voyages.

Equatorial radius of UMMO

Measured on the average surface of UAUAWEE.

R = 7,251.61 Kilometers.

Mass of UMMO

$M = 9.36 \cdot 10^{34}$ Kilograms Mass.

Inclination of UMMO

To the normal at the Plane of the Ecliptic is 18° 39' 15".

Time of rotation about its axis

600 UIW, Some 30.03 hours, equivalent to a day of yours, if well of longer duration.

Acceleration of gravity (at the surface) on UMMO

11.88 meters/second.

Though it must seem strange to you, we are not certain which of the stars catalogued by you, coincides with our IUMMA. By means of translation of coordinates, we estimate that from Earth, our IUMMA can be seen as a star with the following characteristics:

Right Ascension

12 hours, 31" minutes, 14" seconds.

Declination

9° hours, 18' Minutes, 14" seconds, (Constellation "Virgo").

Aboslute Visual Magnitude

"14.3".

Apparent Visual Magnitude

Would surely be reduced by measuring at a distance of 3.682 Parsecs, a great cloud of cosmic dust, but would be understood as between 12 and 13, as it has only been accessible to you by photographic means. (Remember this was in 1955.)

Spectral Type

Type M (according to the Earth Astronomical Classification). Our Sun IUMMA is what you call a Dwarf Star.

Unfortunately the errors made by you when evaluating distances, are in many cases more than 15% in certain star catalogues you have prepared. This is why it is impossible, even with careful translation of the axiis (and trajectories), to identify one star codified by us, with any catalogued by the Astronomers of Earth. We believe, nevertheless, that our IUMMA could perhaps be a star which you catalogue as WOLF 424 since its coordinates (and data) seem to be what we have indicated.

Geographical structure of UMMO

Our geological-geographical structure is quite different from that of Planet Earth. The oceans occupy 61.84% with waters in which are found distinct saline clorides.

There is only one single continent, full of great lakes, the largest of which, the AUWOA SAAOA (Little Sea of God) contains, alone, some 276.10^3 Km^2.

Our mountains (very eroded) scarcely present rough forms.

The OAG OEII are a kind of volcanos that take the form of great fissures that project elevated and brilliant columns of incandescent mixtures of Methane-Pentane-Oxygen.

Language and Characteristics

We utilize a double language (by means of sequential repetition of various vocables we gain the ability to express two currents of ideas simultaneously). The words that we annotate in this report are graphic expressions approximating their real phonics.

Mathematics of UMMO

In mathematics we use a system of numbers of base 12. (Of course we only have 10 fingers like yourselves.) The reasons are purely historical. As simple curiosity the phonemes are a continuation of some exercises of mathematical expressions with their equivalence in our system. (See Imagen A below)

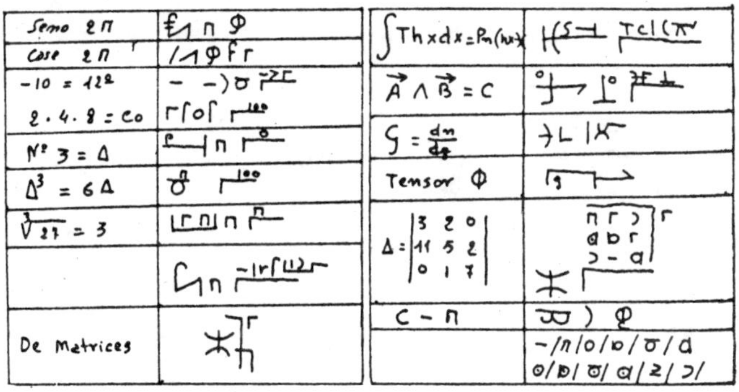

Physical Units of UMMO

We include here some units utilized on our planet.

Unit of Astronomical Longitude (length in distance)

is pronounced WAALI and is equivalent to $12^{4,3}$ (SIC) light-years.

Universal unit of longitude of UMMO

ENMOO equivalent to 1.8736658 meters.

Unit of time on UMMO

UIW equivalent to some 3.09 seconds, and is defined as that time which transpires for the mass of an isotope of TORIO WAEELEWI-WWOAT to be reduced by 50%.

Frequency of the impulses of activation of the nervous centers

The frequency of the impulses of activation of the nervous centers situated in the ventrolateral coroidal plexus of the brain is of 6.12^3 cycles per second.

Unit of frequency much utilized in neurophysiology ( ).

Biogenetic Constants

)H($12^{-10} \cdot 6,58102$ seconds. That is the time it takes to integrate the quantic state 7K in the carbon atom of the chain of Deoxyribonucleic Acid for the formation of one GEN.

Morphology of the Inhabitants of UMMO

The inhabitants of UMMO posess a body whose physical morphology is analogus to that of Earth Homo Sapiens. This is logical if you consider that the biogenetic laws reign for all the Universe. Only small constitutional differences with respect to you, appear between us.

In a high percentage of inhabitants of our Planet, the phonetic organ atrophies during the age of adolescence, in which the human glottis suffers a process of sclerosis which deprives us of verbal acoustical expression. Nevertheless, with the help of special prosthesis amplifiers of the weak frequencies emitted, we can speak normally, though the timbre of voice is not as harmonious as yours, for love of superior harmony, and is restricted to a graver range.

Sociological characteristics of the UMMO people

We are a people much older than yourselves, and have reached an elevated level of civilization.

Our social structure differs considerably in manner from that of the Earth.

Government of UMMO

Our Government is ruled by the "UMMOAELEWE" (Counsel General of UMMO) composed of four members who have been selected from all UMMO by means of Psychophysiological examinations.

The laws are developed as a function of the Sociometric Principles that regulate the humanity of our Planet.

Labor Coordination on UMMO

The coordination of the labor of the population is obtained by means of an efficient group discipline. Our economic structure is radically different from yours.

The curious institution of money is unknown to us since all transactions in the few valuable goods that exist on UMMO is accomplished by means of a Net of XANMOO (a kind of computers or electronic brains). On the other hand the consumer goods (food and transportation) are not valued since the abundance of those much exceed the demand. The ground and the space are public

Religion and Creed of UMMO

We are a profoundly religious society. We believe in WOA (Generator or God) and we posess scientific arguments in favor of the existence of the BUAWAA (Soul).

We know also a third factor of Man that connects him to the Adimensional Soul. It is lodged in the Encephalic Cortex and we are informed of your discovery of this by two neurophysiologists.

Our religion is so similar to terrestrial Christianity that we were truely surprised to discover this. They only differ in the fact that it appeared upon UMMO in a state of our humanity in which the civilization was more developed than that of yours in the time of Jesus Christ. Our kind of life, sexual customs, entertainment, etc., are much more different than you could presume. No true race distinction exists among the people of UMMO, and the varieties and biological species are more restricted than on the Earth. We attribute this to the probability of reduced mutations among the chromosomes since our atmosphere is more protected than that of yourselves by the secondary effects of cosmic radiations.

First Arrival on Planet Earth

Our first arrival on Planet Earth verified using the excellent isodynamic conditions of space (curvature of space) at that time.

Three of our OAWOOLEA UEWA OEM (denominated by you UFO or Flying Saucers) came to ground at a point some 13 kilometers from Digne (to the north), and 8 to 10 from the locality of La Javie, in the French Department of Basses Alpes. It was 4 hours and 17 minutes GMT (Greenwich Mean Time), on the 28th day of March 1950.

There are striking explanations about the vicissitudes suffered by our first explorer group, who had to save grave situations created by their absolute ignorance of the languages and customs of Earth.

Other Arrivals at Earth, and Dates

Since then various additional ships have arrived, culminating with the landing of three OAWOOLEA UEWA in February 1966.

The contact with the terrestrial orography is registered as:

The arrival of two brothers in the vicinity of Erivan (Soviet Territory) at 18 hours 47 minutes (Spanish Time) at a point situated 6 kilometers from the Araks River, on 6 February 1966.

The arrival of two brothers at 20 hours 2 minutes, at a point situated near Madrid (Spanish Territory) near the Colonia de Aluche on 6 February 1966.

The arrival of three brothers at a point situated in the proximity of Townsville (Queensland Territory, Australia) at 22 hours 45 minutes of 6 February 1966 (Spanish Time).

Revealable Characteristics of Our Ships

The revealable characteristics of our OAWOOLEA UEWA, divulgeable as not subject to our norms of security are:

Circular body of exterior diameter 7.1 ENMOO (some 13.18 meters).

Transverse section. Pseudolenticular of approximately 3.25 meters height.

Provision of three legs, extensible, landing support, with rectangular panels.

The magnetic perturbations recorded by the Soviet Engineer, Alexi Krylov, were not natural, but due to the propulsion it has, based on magnetism. The strong induction observed, and that at a point situated in the axis of the spaceship, at ten meters from its "Center of Inertia", frequently reaches a value of "600 Gauss", due to a secondary effect.

Reason and Objective of the Voyage (to Earth)

The objective of our approach to Planet Earth is centered in our study and analysis of the Earth Culture. It is difficult to establish in a few paragraphs, the essential differences between our civilization and yours, since the grade of development of science and technology is much more advanced, however we recognize that certain forms of art (painting, sculpture, and especially Music) have been cultivated by yourselves to a superior level.

Official contacts with Governments and People

There exist powerful reasons, expressed to certain persons with whom we have had contact, for not making us known officially, though those officials of some countries have at this time consciousness of our arrival on Earth.

There have been many scientists and cultural entities who have received our communications, in all the Earth.

But we recognize that the results, as was foreseen, have been very poor, having to contend with the scepticism (not excepting the good humor) with which we have been welcomed. When we brought you true revelations such as in the case of the tri-dimensional photographs not needing the help of ocular vision to be seen in stereo, or the interesting mathematical developments, concerning for example the technology of graphics or networks, that has been attributed by the receivers as the work of some eccentric scientist or jokester.

We do not tell you with despair or bitterness; from a psychological point of view, such reactions are normal.

We wish to offer a short list of Spanish persons with whom we have established contact and come to know them:

A specialist in Astrophysics of the Observatorio Astronomica Fabra of Barcelona. We have given him valuable data on Novas. He refused to continue telephone contacts with us, asking us to keep his identification confidential (December 1961).

.....

A Professor of the Facultad de Medicina de Madrid (March 1962). (A. Gallego?)

.....

A Professor of the Facultad de Ciencias Quimicas de Madrid (January of 1965).

.....

Two who demonstrated total scepticism and rudely asked us to cease our postal mailings to them, despite the fact that the communications sent contained the last word on most interesting problems in the behavior of colloides.

.....

A Mercantile Expert of Madrid, acceding for remuneration to lend us valuable transcription and reproduction assistance (this circular is prepared by him). In his time he accepted us and fulfilled declarations concerning this experience. We judge those declarations pertinent. (February 1966.)

.....

A Publicity Officer of the Captania General de Madrid, Sr. D. Fernando Sesma Manzano (C. Fernando el Catolico, 6), Madrid.

This gentleman had published a monograph concerning certain contacts realized by him with extraterrestrial beings. Though his versions were in our judgement some diluted by fantastic elements, such as Magic, Astrology and Symbolisms arbitrarily interpretated in the first paper, we observed in his publications some factors that attracted our attention; for which we established contact (with him) on the 14th of January 1966, submitting him to a series of tests to assure ourselves of his good faith or of his excess of credulity.

Sr. Sesma showed scepticism at first and was demonstrating to us his excellent uprightness, though we felt to disagree with him on the initial origin of his earlier experiences which we attribut to a simple tale.

To this gentleman we have delivered up to this time a great number of communications about our civilization and social structure.

.....

An Artist, Paintor, who lives at Calle Conde Penalver 20 of Madrid. Concerning our arrival at Aluche (Madrid) the 6th of February, he made some declarations to the press that motivated our interest in him. We solicitated a personal interview with him but he declined, interpreting it as the work of jokesters. (E. Gran.)

.....

Two gentlemen residents of Madrid who kindly submitted to a Psychotechnical Test for our Sociometric Evaluation. (March and April 1966)

.....

A Catholic Priest D. Severino Machado (Calle Espoz and Mina, 7, 3º Madrid). We established contact by Post and Telephone with him, who demonstrated logical reserve in the expectation of proofs. (April of 1966, now deceased.)

As can be seen, the result up to now has projected a high percentage of negative reactions (not much better on balance than evaluated by us in those (other) countries in which we have also established analogous contacts), excepting the United States, in which some 16% of those persons with whom we have communicated showed apparent credulity.

In Spain, only Sr. Sesma Manzano seems to have accepted our identity (but after having provided proofs, such as that notice anticipating our arrival "Landing in Madrid on the 6th of February").

Our valuable collaborator to which we generally dictate our writings has received a good number of proofs also, reacting consequently with credulity.

We are truely grateful for your extraordinary discretion. We fear and with reason the repetition of an incident, suffered in Milan, when our help was denounced to the authorities: Accusing us as spies.

LETTER TO MANUEL CAMPO

In the same year 1967, Don Manuel Campo received another letter from the Ummites (this time it seemed to be directed only to him), in which they manifested their interest concerning the aparition in the skies of Earth, of UFOs, that it seems did not pertain to them. This subject comes up again later, with the "Atienza Case". The authors of the letter received by Sr. Campo transmitted to him a digital code that could serve as a means of identifying presumed extraterrestrials who attempted contact with him (on the other hand, a remote possibility).

Here then is the letter received by Senor Campo which, as all may recognize in this book, is transcribed literally respecting even the inclusion of orthographic errors of syntax and punctuation (much no doubt attributable to the copyist). Where the text becomes unintelligible however, I have rearranged it to make it intelligible.

UMMOALEWE
Language: Spanish
Sr. Manuel Campo
Date: 1967

Dear Sir:

For years we have been intrigued by the appearance in the Terrestrial atmosphere of other spaceships (UFO) which are not precisely ours. Nobody including ourselves knows whether the origin of such vehicles (except those cases of simple illusions, hallucinations or jokes) are of Galactic type.

On UMMO we have officially established contact with other Civilizations but like you we desire to know the source of those that come to Earth. We do not have the means at our disposal here to identify them.

Senor: We do not expect to be believed. It is very probable that you smile upon reading the preceeding paragraphs, considering them fraudulent and purely imaginative.

Working thus you will comport yourself intelligently, since such affirmations, without proofs to support them, lack value. If we have written to you, it is because we know you are connected to the belief in one Galactic origin for those UFO.

We have reason to believe that, like we have made contact with you, there exists a certain grade of probability that those other beings, if they establish contact in any country, would be precisely with the sympathizers with this plausible hypothesis.

Key of Identification

We desire that you do us a favor that will not jeopardize your prestige or your economic situation. If you so desire you may hide the evidence of reception of this communication. What we want to ask of you is compatible with any concept that you may have formed concerning our personality.

We are going to dictate you a series of Digits (Numbers) that express some cyphers registered in a system of binary numeration. We ask you to preserve them.

If, though a little improbable in your case, anyone approaches you pretending to come from another Planet, that one would react by offer-another sequence of digits.

If you are given the circumstance in which some stranger tries to establish some kind of verbal relations (telephone or personal interview) it is not necessary to reiterate the convenience of adopting a reticent attitude, to avoid any kind of joke or to elude anormal conduct of mentalities that present a presumable psychopathological set.

Generally the jokesters present their arguments in a form a little elaborated. There abound, on the other hand, certain forms of delirious ideas whose structure appears perfectly coherent and logical, and having a strong persuasive force. Above all, if those individuals that propound these ideas are very intelligent mentally ill persons (in Terrestrial Paranoia this syndrome is perfectly compatible with an elevated intellectual consciousness).

If, as in this case, the person who pretends to identify himself as a space traveler, offers a minimum of coherent argument and is apparently serious (though risking that his identity is fraudulent) read or deliver him the series of Digits.

If he understands well, and though you do not solicit it (you can say that it is a simple cypher to be delivered to a friend, or better still, that to prove his good faith you want to make a test), he or them should in their turn repeat a different sequence of numbers (also in the binary system) that we ask you to write down.

Soon we will give you the name of a person who will act as a connection between all of you and us. We repeat, there is little probability of such a case for you (but from a statistical point of view, it is more probable for some of those components of this group) however in case it happens we ask in the name of this advanced group of UMMO, write to our connection communicating to him:

THE CYPHER DICTATED TO THE SUBJECT... IMPRESSION HE HAS CAUSED.
VARIOUS DATA OFFERED BY HIM... DATE OF THE CONTACT

In termination we transcribe twice the series of digits repeated in other such· lines for fear that the multicopied impression may make any of them illegible.

1011010111--100101--101000100111

1011010111--100101--101000100111

We cordially thank you for your attention, even in the case that all this could be a simple joke or a delirious idea. You have not prejudiced this favor. Our respect, Senor.

Order: DEII-98 son of DEII-97

In obedience to YU-1 daughter of AIM-368

Divide the second page to other interested persons.

UMMITE OPINION OF EARTH EVOLUTION

I am going to terminate this part by reproducing part of a text also received by don Manuel Campo, in which the Ummites offer an opinion concerning the evolution of Earth society. It is a document of sombre tone, that have been accentuated in later communications, as we shall see; still in this they leave a door open to hope, and also talk of a radiant future of terrestrial integration. They still have not had time to know us sufficiently!

.....

You, Sr. Campo, can perhaps, after reading these paragraphs, suggest that the Earth is somewhat different from UMMO, that the Terrestrial Social Network can never dream even of a structurization like ours.

If you think this way, you are committing a scientific error of first magnitude. We can ignore whether the future political economy of Earth will be an imitiation of our actual system. What we can assure you is that after studying, from 1950 when we came to OYAGAA (the Planet Earth), the social biological evolution of terrestrial OEMII, we can advance a favorable diagnosis through analysis of the actual state of evolution.

If in these approaching years, you and your politicians can overcome the threat of nuclear war. (I can tell you in confidence that the United States is accomplishing in actual studies, the control of the gaseous turbulence after an atomic explosion, in a manner that the Earth magnetic field facilitates the diffusion of the radioactive mass in immense areas, with a minimum mass of tritium H 1/3, and that the security services of the Soviets, Israelis, English, French, and Hindu governments have knowledge of this.)

Possibility of Nuclear Destruction

The possibility of a destruction of Earth civilization had declined more.

The true tragedy of this humanity rests, in our judgement, on those technological advances in the fields of obtaining energy by nuclear fusion and fission, that was developed before the TERRESTRIAL SOCIAL NETWORK could obtain a global gathering into one single Nation at the Planetary Level.

We take seriously your reach in the progressive study of matter, a phase that will permit you to construct arms of plasma.

CONFIDENTIAL: We will tell you, Sr. Campo, that this news has already begun to filter through in those diplomatic means of various countries, that the scientists of the Peoples Republic of China had succeeded in the laboratory in submitting specimens to static pressures of two million four hundred thousand atmospheres. (Note 2)

To you, specialized in other branches of the culture this does not seem to say much, but it is of transcendental importance.

Matter submitted to pressures somewhat greater lose their atomic structures as is already known by yourselves.

A pressure of sixteen million atmospheres (15,445,680 atmospheres) called by us AADAGIOOU (can translate as critical pressure) simultaneously inverts the atomic sub-particles (IBOZOO UU) and the mass converts integrally into energy. The expansion that follows after is immeasurable. This was the initial pressure of all the mass of the Universe!!!

We confide to you that when the investigations of the Chinese Physicists have evolved further, the political circumstances of that country and the fanaticism of its directors will be on a plane of moderation acknowledged.

These threats darken the future of the earth, but they are being compensated by the continual process of biological neurocortication, in the newer generations for one part, and the hopeful perspective that glimmers in the orientations of terrestrial thought.

Evolution of Terrestrial Thought

The conversations between intellectual Marxists and Catholics (the next will be celebrated in Mariembad, Czechoslovakia [now celebrated]) acknowledged the possibility of future understandings to great level.

The three currents of Earth philosophy most important, CHRISTIANITY, MARXISM and EXISTENTIALISM, converge at accelerated pace toward a phase of UNITARY Nucleization.

It is already symptomatic that Communist thinkers like Frances Garaudy admits the possibility that Marxism accepts the existence of God, and that the Roman Church veers toward socialism.

Without the melancholy weight of the Totalitarians and those Conservative Integrist groups, you would already be two steps closer to overcoming the ultimate barriers to unification.

Final Integration on the Earth

You, Sr. Campo, will not live the enlightening ages of integration in the fields of Economics, Politics, Religion and Philosophy steps of Earth, but we know that these states will come.

Meanwhile, we greet you all "especially the United States and the United Soviet Socialist Republics for the place and point of your System of Planning truely scientific bluff" that it will prevent in the event of an error in calculation, the unleashing of a NUCLEAR WAR.

You have already surpassed the phase in which the instant alienation of a Military Executive or Politician could provoke an irreparable agression.

Note 2

You have already obtained instant pressures still higher but in that case, the analysis of the structure of the matter is almost steril. Only parameters such as Pressure, Volume, Temperature and Density are then measurable. We conrgatulate the Chinese Investigators for their triumph. In our judgement your greater bluff does not consist in obtaining the greater pressure, but in the technology of the equipments of control of the structure of the nucleus without probes introduced into the sample or test.

IUMMA/WOLF 424 - STELLAR BODY

Amature Astronomer Wendell Shuster, undertaking a search of the records for available data on Wolf 424 found the earliesr reports going back to 1938 (Reuyl, D., 1938, HARVARD ANNOUNCEMENT CARD No. 449, June 1st 1938). Other reports mentioning Wolf 424 included the following:

Reuyl, D., 1941, PUB. A.S.P., 53.336
Strand, K.A. and Hall, R.G., Jr., 1951, ASTRONOMICAL JOURNAL 56.106
Van de Kamp, P., 1945, ASTRONOMICAL JOURNAL 51.159
van Alaanen, A., 1945, PUB A.S.P., 57.216
Vyssotsky, A.N. and Williams, E.T.R., 1948, PUB. McCORMICK OBS., 10.38
Van de Kamp, P. and Lippincot, S.L., 1949, ASTRONOMICAL JOURNAL 55.16
Van de Kamp, P. and Damkoehler, J.E., 1953, ASTRONOMICAL JOURNAL 58.21
Wilson, R.H. Jr., 1954, ASTRONOMICAL JOURNAL 50.132
Sarah Lee Lippincott, 1958, ASTRONOMICAL JOURNAL 63.1262

Wolf 424 was first discovered to be a possible double star by Reuyl who published his findings in 1941, with a preliminary calculation of time of revolution about a common center to be about 16 years based on 18 years observation. The stars are now identified as Wolf 424a and Wolf 424b. Angular separation between the two is measured as 1.0" The location of the pair, over time, is given as:

Right Ascension	1938	12h 28m 40s, Declination	+9°34',	Mag. 12.7
	1950	12h 31m	+9°21'	
	1980	12h 32m	+9°09'	
	2000	12h 33m	+9°01'	

Brightness: B-V 1.80, U-B 1.18, R-I 1.62

Visual Magnitude:	Wolf 424a, 13.16	Wolf 424b, 13.40
Absolute Magnitude:	Wolf 424a, 14.97	Wolf 424b, 15.20
Luminosity	Wolf 424a, 0.00009	Wolf 424b, 0.00007

According to latest reports, adjusted data calculations amd characteristics are as follows:

Spectral class:	Wolf 424a, M6 V e	Wolf 424b, M5.3 V e
Possible Planets?	Wolf 424a, 3 (?)	Wolf 424b, (?)

Both luminaries share some common characteristics as follows:

Star Type: UV Ceti flare stars
Parallax Deviation: 0.230" ±0.006"
Proper Motion: 1.76 arc seconds per year
Position Angle of Proper Motion: 279 degrees
Total Space velocity relative to Sol: 3700 meters/sec recessional
or 2.3 miles/sec recessional
Distance from Sol: 12.4 Light Years or 3.80 Parsecs
134,300 000 000 000 Kilometers
83,400 000 000 000 miles

COMPARATIVE DATA

	IUMMA/WOLF 424 (1958)	OUR SOL (1950)
Right Ascension	12h 31' 14" ±2' 11"	18h 04'
Declination	9° 18' 07" ±14' 2"	+30°
Apparent Magnitude	12.5	-26.91
Absolute Magnitude	14.3	+4.69 to +4.84
Spectral Class	M7	G2 V
Mass	$1.48 \cdot 10^{33}$ Kg	$1.9891 \cdot 10^{30}$ Kg
Distance (in July 1967)	14.421 LY in 3-D Space/time	
Distance (in July 1967)	3.685 LY in Multi-D Space/time	
Temperature (surface)	4,580 Kelvin	5,770 Kelvin
Magnetic Field	3.8 to 216 gauss (variable)	
Surface Gravity		460 m/sec²

A great cloud of cosmic dust at 3,682 Parsecs from SOL obscures the star they Ummites call IUMMA and which we assume to be Wolf 424.

	UMMO	EARTH
Max Radius	$7,251,608 \cdot 10^3$m	6,378,500 miles
Min Radius	$7,016,091 \cdot 10^3$m	6,357,000 miles
Mass	$9.36 \cdot 10^{24}$ Kg Mass	$6.60 \cdot 10^{24}$ Kg Mass
Inclination	18° 39' 56.3"	23° 27' 08.26"
with variation	19.8"	
Acceleration of Gravity	11.88 m/sec²	9.81 m/sec²
Rotation about axis	30.02 hours	23h 56m 4.09sec
Eccentricity	0.007833	0.01674
Distance from own Sun	$9.96 \cdot 10^{12}$ Centimeters	92,957,200 miles
Magnetic Field Max	0.23 gauss	
Min	0.07 gauss	
Land Area	38%	29%
Water Area	62%	71%
Mean orbital velocity		66,000 mph

All UMMO figures have been converted to Metric standard for greater facility in comparison. A point of interest is the convenience with which the UMMO figures for Right Ascension and Declination fit into the other similat figures for years 1938, 1950, 1980 and 2000 in our Astronomical Tables. Now we must see how well the rest of the UMMO data given is verified as we advance with new knowledge in our sciences, and particularly with respect to the fluctuating gravity field of UMMO and the dust cloud obscuring the UMMO sun, neither of which we had reported before release of these figures. -Publisher

ASTRONOMICAL DATA - ARGUMENT

The surface temperature we measure for the Wolf 424 pair is 2,700 K. and we allow that value for each of those dim red dwarf stars. They therefore list them in spectral class M in the Hertzprung-Russell diagram, the standard for classification used by Earth astronomers. This pair, reported as Gliese 473 is similar to Wolf 359, also an M star listed as Gliese 406 at only 7.747 LY distance from our Sol, one of the model stars for the type. But how accurate is our data?

The UMMO visitors themselves stated the surface temperature for their IUMMA (Believed to be Wolf 424) as 4,580 Kelvin, which clearly puts it in spectral class K. These are generally orange giants going to red giant phase. There are, however, the cooler orange K stars on the main sequence in the H-S diagram, but they are cooling and thus shrinking, and are therefore believed to be speeding up in rotation due to the contraction as a result of cooling. The assumed rapid rotation and all of its consequences argue against conditions hospitable to life as we know it.

In that same document delivered to Antonio Ribera in Spain in 1969, and in the mext paragraph following the report of higher surface temperature for IUMMA/Wolf 424, the Ummites described a vast nebulosity of dust and gas at 3.682 parsecs from our sun in the direction of UMMO. They insist that this reduces the visual magnitude. They allege that when the line of sight passes through the denser layers of this dust cloud, the visual magnitude from here could drop to 26 on our scale, and that in the thinner areas we may see it at 12 to 13 on the conventional Earth scale (This is exactly what we have reported for Wolf 424 since its recent discovery). This same dust cloud might account for the disparity between the surface temperature they report and the one we observe. They stated that without the clouds of attenuating dust we would see IUMMA/Wolf 424 at 7.4 magnitude. which gives us a measure of the amount of attenuation due to the dust cloud, which also disturbes the temperature and magnetic field measurements. Perhaps all of this can be verified by our astronomers now that we know what to look for.

The Ummites also say that along that same line of sight we may be able to see two more dim red main sequence suns of the same type. The nearest, 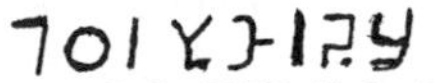, situated .62 LY from IUMMA, has a surface temperature of 2,575° Kelvin. The second, 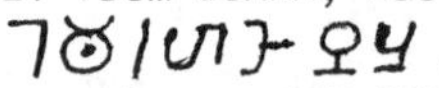, situated some 20.7 LY from IUMMA has a surface temperature of 3,210° Kelvin. They may both be completely invisible from here with our present instruments, but when these aids improve we may look for evidence of such bodies. If seen at all through the dust cloud under our present instrumental restrictions these values would appear to be much more attenuated.

But what about the spectral class M stars? They have always been considered to be too cool and thus spinning too fast for inhabitation. The rate of spin is deduced from the estimated amount of cooling and thus contraction, which speeds up the star, like a skater pulling in his arms. But is that necessarily true? And if it is true, is the first assumption that life could not exist there correct. This assumption seems to be based on the concept that WE are the biological center of the Universe, and no other life forms exist because they would have to form under conditions similar to our own, which many younger scientists are now coming to doubt.

In THE INTELLIGENT UNIVERSE by Fred Hoyle, (Holt, Rinehart & Winston), the author contends that life on Earth arose in space. He argues with characteristic conviction, "In pre-Copernican days the Earth was thought to be the geometrical and physical center of the universe. Nowadays it is taken to be the biological center, an almost incredible repetition of the previous error." DISCOVER magazine for May 1984 has this to say, "Hoyle starts by citing the infinitesimal odds for the chance development on Earth of just the enzymes on which life depends --one in $10^{40,000}$, by his reckoning--and points out that even these enzymes are only a small fraction of the proteins found in all living things. Moreover, he asserts that there is 'not a shred of objective evidence to support the hypothesis that life began on Earth.' Space, he contends, is liklier a crucible. Organic (carbon-containing) molecules not only can form in space but can combine there to make the building blocks of life, and life itself."

The argument goes that cooling stars contract, and contracting stars speed up affecting many other constants such as magnetic fields and gravity, as well as surface geophysical conditions that would be very hostile to life.

Hence a class M star is too cool and rotating too fast to support life (as we know it), thus casting the whole UMMO story under suspicion. This was relied on as effective counter-proof, and weighted the validity of the case in favor of the detractors. But that was in the late 60s. Now with more knowledge, better equipment and more sophisticated testing we see that such arguments were ill-founded on inadequate data, and that the proponents of the story have more support than they thought.

John Stauffer, Lee Hartman, Dave Soderblum, and Neal Burnham, measured the rate of rotation of 65 spectral class G, K and M stars in the Pleiades: 11 of type G, 38 of type K and 16 of type M. In their report in the ASTROPHYSICAL JOURNAL for May 1984, they said that only 18 of that sample were rotating rapidly, and they were all K and M stars. But they also found many K and M stars that rotate slowly, so that argument is no longer as sound as it once was.

ARRIVAL UPON PLANET EARTH

DISCOVERY OF EARTH

Between the days of 5 and 7 February 1934, a Norwegian ship navigating the waters off Newfoundland, carrying certain scientific equipment aboard, was conducting experiments in communications over large distances by reflecting the radio waves off the ionosphere. A train of Hertzian waves emitted from the Norwegian ship penetrated the ionosphere and was lost in space. Some 14 years later, on a planet which its human inhabitants call UMMO, a very weak signal was received of a frequency of 413.44 megacycles, which their technicians were unable to identify. It was evident however, that it was not background Galactic "noise" emitted in the wavelength of natural hydrogen (21 cm.), but was a signal of intelligent origin.

And those same Ummites wrote, in a communication sent to a North-american correspondent, "This date then, is historical in the Tierra-UMMO relations. We have photocopies of the radiograms emitted. (They were obtained for us by our brothers in Germany who traveled to Bergen for this.) And, of course, the recordings of the signals in Morse, were then unintelligible to us, for our technicians believed them to be in some numerical binary code (POINT EQUALS ZERO, DASH EQUALS ONE, or vice versa). You will be surprised to know that the duration of the fraction of the radiogram captured was of 2.2 UIW (some 6.8 minutes) duration, which was enough to identify in Galactic coordinates, the position of the star from which the signals came, a solar system which our technicians baptized with the name of GAA (SQUARE), since the graphic (image) obtained with the signal, reminded of the analytic equation that expresses the area of this geometric figure".

And continued:

"Only after coming to you did we understand that the called by us OOYAGAA (Cold Star of the square) was falsely indicative, since the nature of the message was not precisely mathematical.."

They concluded:

"That was part of our answer to M. Theodore K. Polk, of Pittsburgh (USA), referring to the origin of our arrival on this planet."

They had organized the first INAYUYISAA (expedition) to OOYAGAA, arriving with two OAWOLEA UEWA OEMM (lenticular spacecraft) at Planet Earth. To say it in their own words (at times a little pedantic for their love of extreme precision), they made contact with the lithosphere of Earth at 4 hours 17 minutes and 3 seconds GMT of our time on the Earth day, 28 March 1950, in a defined zone of the French Department of "Basses Alpes" (now Alpes de Alta Provenza), at some 8 kilometers from the village of La Javie (France).

The six expeditionaries aboard immediately took measures to establish themselves for a long time on this new world, so similar in so many rspects to their own planet of origin, even to the point of the expeditionaries not needing artificial respiration apparatus, nor having to protect their bodies against the ambient conditions.

What follows is the story, related by those same Ummites, of their arrival in our solar system first, and then the account of their first days on Earth. In this history they describe various episodes frankly comical: for example, when they saw by their means of remote observation, that Earth men made smoke from some tubes that they held between their lips. Only later did they come to know that this was called "smoking". At first they thought it must be a means of purifying the atmosphere (completely the contrary!). Or like when they came out of the cave they had excavated at the foot of Pic du Cheval Blanc, to reconnoiter the surroundings, and encountered a piece of crumpled newspaper with human cartoons. After analyzing the paper and the carciatures, they suspected it to be the work of some maladjusted person with foolish concepts, using the pages of the newspaper to manifest his discontent...

But let us allow them to tell us themselves; beginning with their discovery of other inhabited planets seen by UMMO:

SUPPLEMENTARY REPORT
Copies Distributed: 2
Languages: Spanish
French

DISCOVERY OF OTHER INHABITED PLANETS SEEN BY UMMO

In our displacements (travels) we have not yet reached the limits of our Galaxy. Our techniques for space voyages take advantage of certain curvatures of space. We can not always travel to where and when we desire.

In the length of our history some contacts established have been: (The dates correspond to our last Epoch, UMMO years.)

Year 27/32456,5616 tU We captured the first codified messages from the System OOYAUME (a star we have not been able to identify in the Astronomical Tables of Earth).

Year 29/36008,53 tU We recorded undecipherable messages coming from the Group UUYABOO WEAM in the Nebula NEAAA.

Year 64/87,3 tU Two spacecraft similar to our OAWOLEA UEWA arrived (at UMMO). They disappeared without leaving a trace. Formerly, and without official proof, the URAA (official chronicles) recorded up to approximately 4,230 contacts of this type.

Between years 84 and 509: 42 messages received were decodified.
103 messages received were undecipherable.

Of these 145 codigrams received radioelectrically (322-329 Megacycles BAND OF DEUTERIUM — and frequencies understood between 407, 658 and 8306.63 Megacycles, all came from 27 local planetary systems or clouds. Two messages (decodified) were extragalactic. One came from the Galaxy OREEAU which you call ANDROMEDA), and we are not certain of the origin of the second one.

The first real contact by means of our OAQOOLEA OEMM (spacecraft) was established by us with the planet IEYIOBAA (the phonetic name given it by your inhabitants sounds about like FRRRANSSSS). This in turn is situated in a group in the star OOYAUNMEEEI (in the Earth Astronomical Tables it is denominated Ofiuco 70).

The second (in year 501/978,56) tU was with the Planet OOYAWILA whose inhabitants killed the six crew members. the Planets visited without life, or with life in primary stages, came to 218 at that time

All of our attempts at telepathic communications have been fruitless with respect to other human beings, including yourselves. The distances, on the other hand (VIA LIGHT), are so great that electromagnetic communications intended to answer those messages received and happily interpreted would arrive too late 38,608.46 years later (even within our own Galaxy). This is the extraordinary case with Planet OOYAE-BEEM situated in the System UYIABEE. The beneficial ISODYNAMIC conditions of space in the year 487/84465,2 †U permitted us to visit it, delaying the ship 40078427.56 thousandths of †U while the light took 9,165 years to arrive.

Our technicians were only able to capture the traces of an immense destruction localized some 6,000 (Earth) years before.

Later we recorded two codified messages, coming from that very same Planet that were emitted before the humanity living there had finally destroyed themselves with their terrible Plasma Weapons.

Date: 30 January 1967

FIRST ARRIVAL IN THE PROXIMITY OF EARTH

On the 7th of January 1949, and after exploration of the Planets Nepture and Mars by our brothers traveling in two OAUOLEA UEWA OEMM (spaceships), they came to the proximity of a new OOYAGAA having an atmosphere much more dense than that recorded on the previous planet.

The first exploration was made in helicoidal orbit above the plane of the ecliptic, and with a perigee 337 kilometers above the surface of the Earth and an apogee of 398 kilometers.

EXPLORATION OF NEPTUNE

Already during the exploration of Neptune, they had received an extensive range of radioelectric emissions from the Earth, which permitted our brothers to identify that Planet. The presence of superior life on it was evident. No other source of emission was identified, for which they reasonably deduced that the rest of the OYAA (cold stars) gravitationally connected to the OOYIA J5(O< which you call Sol lacked intelligent biological forms, at least those having developed technologies. This last conclusion induced the explorers to address themselves to another OOYAA (near by) which they codified with the name J♀ KO which you know as MARS.

EXPLORATION OF THE PLANET MARS

In that first examination, made from a distance of 290 KOAEE (some 25,926 kilometers), one KOAE being equivalent to about 6.7 kilometers, there was revealed the existence of an atmosphere of sufficient density to permit the exterior development of Complete Pluricellular Beings. The marks of multiple impacts of meteorites, and the crystalline structure of the ground verified by our long range sounding instruments, revealed the absence of active bacteriological life capable of producing decomposition of this ground, at least in the small zones explored. Later we discovered on that OYAA not only Protein and Amino Acid Forms, but simple unicellular and Pluricellular vegetable beings. (It will not be long before you verify this.)

EXAMINATION AND EXPLORATION OF THE EARTH

A strict program of examination of the inhabited OYAA was begun. Above all they had to maintain a means of evasion in case of attack, which obliged them to maintain very high velocities of translocation, which made the precision of observations difficult.

It seemed evident that the OOYAGA (enclosed star) recorded by our UMMO was precisely that which we were analyzing. (I use the plural form referring to my brothers since I personally was on UMMO.)

FIRST EXAMINATION OF THE TERRESTRIAL CRUST BY THE UMMO

The abundant cumulus clouds at that time over the American and South Asian Continents did not impede our intentions to observe in detail the density of communications. (Identified later as roads and railroads after an earlier error when we seemed to identify them as tubular conduits.) That permitted us to evaluate, in our first estimates, your grade of technical civilization. (We did not know until later that they were a network of paved roads.)

The first aircraft of yours was detected in the proximity of an archipelago that later we identified as the Bahamas Islands. The image we captured was amplified in the laboratory aboard, and we analyzed its morphological characteristics. This was the first data we obtained indicating your level of technology.

During those 86 UIW that the analysis endured, we came to descend to an altitude of 0.62 KOAE (53.94 kms.) over a zone later identified as the southeast part of the Republic of Helvetica (Switzerland) where we captured images of urban centers and industries at points of convergence of the railroads, concentrations of flora (forests and plantations) and floating structures above the Atlantic Ocean. We collected samples of fluvial currents as well as many specimens of atmospheric gas at different levels of altitude.

FIRST IMAGE OF A HUMAN OBTAINED IN THIS EXPLORATION

We still preserve as a historical curiosity, the picture obtained of one of the streets of the village of Montreux (Switzerland), in which can be seen the first individual humans captured by our equipment. The blurred features nevertheless did not impede analysis of the fundamental physical and physiological characteristics and the morphology of their dress. It was impossible at that time to extend our interval of exploration, if we wanted to return to our UMMO before the isodynamic conditions of space returned to an unfavorable phase.

Not one time did our UEWA (ship) make contact with the Terrestrial crust.

[Note- This remarkable statement of variable isodynamic conditions of space helping or hindering interplanetary travel over long distances has come up in much the same way in a number of other extraterrestrial contact cases. There are scores of such reports in UFO literature from widely separated sources with no detectable contact between them. Notable examples are the contacts at Mirassol and those with a Baptist Minister in Puerto Rico.]

ANALYSIS ON UMMO OF THE SPECIMENS COLLECTED OVER EARTH

The impact produced on our society by the notice of having identified a civilization on OYAGAA (your planet) was truely emotional.

Our technicians and scientists immediately rushed the careful examination of the objective data obtained (samples of air, radioelectric phenomena recorded, and optical images) thus confirming the subjective reports of that first expedition.

HYPOTHETICAL STUDIES OF THE SOCIAL STRUCTURE AND GRADE OF CIVILIZATION

It was necessary to forge with these abundant, but without doubt insufficient data, an initial image though presumably considerably distorted, of the social structure and grade of civilization of this new planet.

That primitive conception forged by us remains today very far from the views of our actual perspective (now). I would like to offer, as a simple curiosity, the idea that we conceived at that time, of what the civilization of Earth could be. There were many errors, but nevertheless the outline seen presented a number of points concomitant with reality.

STUDYOF THE PICTURES OF HUMANS AND THEIR DRESS

The first objective of study consisted of three images of human beings. The first and most complete picture included individuals of different sex and age walking among building structures. Careful analysis, though failing to reveal the facial features in sufficient detail for analysis, left no doubt of sexual identification, thanks to the localization of feminine signs on some of the figures. It was impossible, however, to determine small details of dress.

We discovered likewise that the YIE (women in our language) were characterized by an abundance of cranial hair, though this could have been some fibrous material over the head. Unfortunately some images of the YIE clearly differentiated by the bust, covered their legs just like the men, which introduced controversy about the differences in dress of both sexes.

This analysis was very important, as our brothers selected to travel to Earth must be provided with EEUE (dress) similar to that of Earth to pass undetected. Unfortunately it was not possible to determine even the composition of the same. (We did not suspect that it treated of knit fibres until our arrival, nor the most essential details of its construction.)

DATA CONCERNING THE ZONE OF DESCENT OF OUR BROTHERS

A second point debated concerned the best zone of entry for the explorers, for the descent to Earth of our brothers. Of course it would have to be an unpopulated zone without arriving in a deserted area that would totally impede the expeditionaries cautious contact with some inhabitants.

This view from your perspective would seem very simple, being apparently enough to examine the UULAYA (captured images) topographically and select a half-open semi-jungle geographical location, but we did not know if the men of Earth lived in subterranean "beehives". Don't forget that we concentrate the population and structures in free air only when it treats of what you call industrial plants. Meanwhile the rest live dispersed in their XAUUI ("emerging" houses) that can retreat underground.

Also, other inhabited planets concentrate their human beings in great subterranean colonies. Could this be the case on OYAGAA (Planet Earth)?

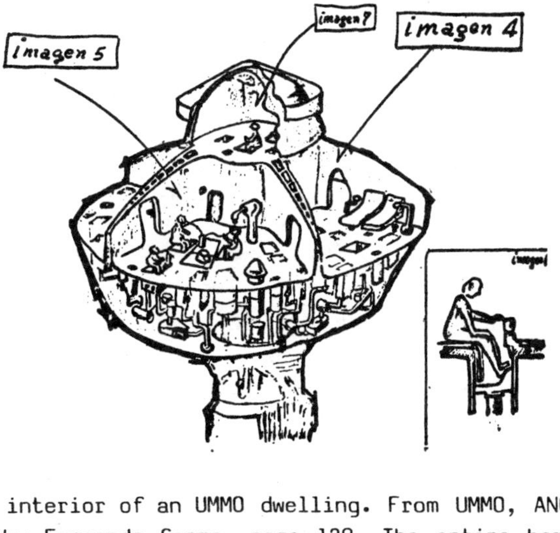

Sketch of the interior of an UMMO dwelling. From UMMO, ANOTHER INHABITED PLANET, by Fernando Sesma, page 120. The entire home is raised and lowered automatically according to temperature.

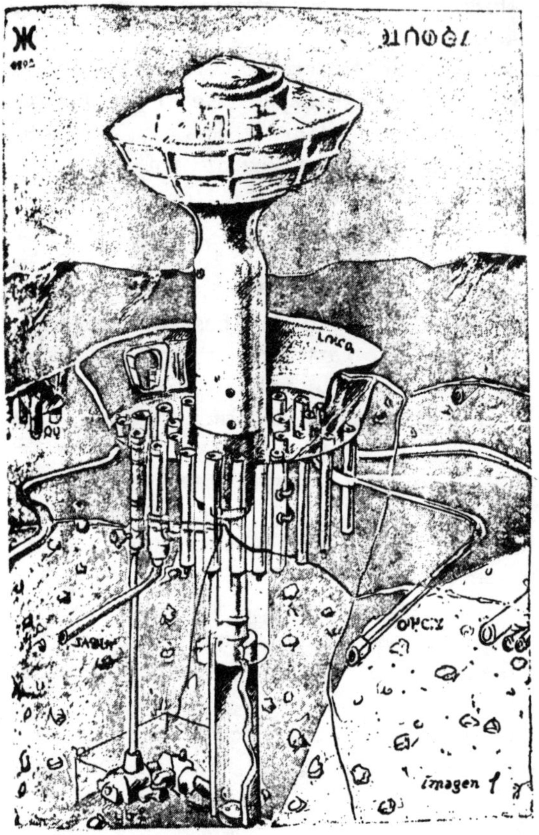

Sketch of exterior plant layout of the typical UMMO family dwelling. Each house is provided with a series of vertical cylindrical tubes buried in the ground that surrounds the perforation of the ANAUANAA, axial column of the XAABII or dwelling. These tubes of identical calibre (a universal size) called NUUYA constitute a veritable store whose function is rooted in the conservation and distribution of habitually consumed products required by the family (alimentation, chemical products, liquified gasses, perfumes, etc.). The foods, natural, semi-prepared, or artificial, are manufactured in industrial plants and subterranean galleries of cultivation at many KOAE distance, and preserved in cylinders of equal diameter. Thus the juices of INQWII (a fruit of yellow pulp enveloped in a brown rough covering) previously bombarded with neutrons to eliminate superficial germs that could provoke putrifaction, along with many other things, is delivered directly to each home. A fruit thus prepared conserves all its aroma (very important to Ummites), taste, and all its other qualities without refrigeration and can last many months.

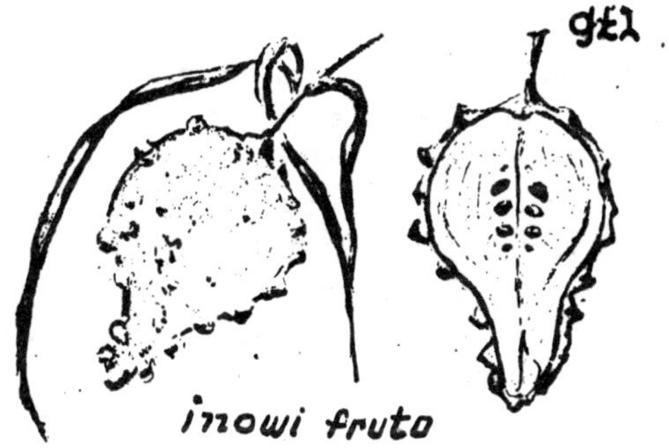

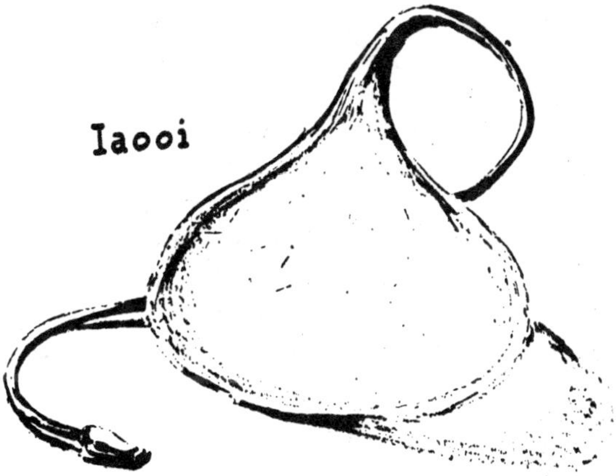

Two of the natural fruits especially cultivated on UMMO for their nutricious food value. The INOWII above is mainly consumed in a pulp or juice state while the IAOOI below is more often consumed as a solid. From UMMO, ANOTHER INHABITED PLANET, BY Fernando Sesma, pages 148-156.

MYSTERY OF THE TUBULAR CHIMNEYS AND CIGARETTES

The constructions that we know today as houses were at first identified as factories, but what especially intrigued us were the pictures obtained of large vertical tubes situated on or beside all of these constructions, and more tubes on the vehicles captured by our cameras. All of them expelled vapors or aerosols (smoke) of a dark color.

You can not imagine the surprise that was caused by what to you is very familiar; the small cylinder in the mouth of some humans. a spectral analysis of the gas expelled, presented a strong mixture of oxide of carbon, tars and hydrocarbons. [could the ambient creatures be a kind of robot energized the same way as the buildings and vehicles?]

We imagined then, that the physiological organisms of the Terrestrials could not live in an atmosphere of oxygen and nitrogen without such gasses, for which it was necessary for you to add to the circulating air to make it more breathable. This filled us with anxiety, thinking the consequences for us if we had to carry a portable artificial atmosphere. Once we arrived on Earth, as we will tell you a bit later, we corroborated still more this hypothesis, seeing you with these cylinders of tobacco which we at first interpreted as generators of gas for respiration, marvelling still more that children and others did not carry them.

SELECTION OF THE ZONE OF DESCENT

We can tell you that strong disagreements developed among the technicians trying to select the Earth zone where the expeditionaries would make their first descent, and we took a risk in trying to select a place apparently less populated, that might situate us precisely in the middle of subterranean concentrations, where we might be detected and perhaps destroyed by yourselves.

The detailed study of images brought back of various aircraft we had observed offered an index of your technological level achieved. Some appeared to be pulled by helical devices. They carefully examined the joints between the sheets of metal (though nevertheless ignorant that it was aluminum alloy) and the same with some auxiliary mechanical structures.

CONFUSED BY THE MULTIPLICITY OF LANGUAGES

There was something that made us conceive a totally aberrent idea with respect to your Terrestrial Social Net.

We had recorded several hundred electromagnetic emissions coming from various points on the planet, in an extensive range of frequencies. From that we were able to detect with surprise, the enormous linguistic multiplicity, and our technical specialists in acoustics classified those that presented homogenuity in their phonemes, identifying in some cases two or three, erroneously integrated into one.

Our attention was powerfully called to the fact that a great part of the emissions captured were of metric wavelengths presenting the same character of binary language (short impulse-long impulse) as that already captured by us in that first message.

But upon trying to translate it with the same criteria (as binary), we realized the error. What could be the true codeification used by yourselves? We came to the conclusion that the inhabitants of OYAAGA (planet Earth) utilized a multitude of languages, and to intercommunicate, the diverse communities among you, logically used one international language, one based on short and long whistles whose code was inscrutable to us.

Later we understood that that hypothesis was very simplistic because the Morse Code in its turn served as a vehicle for many languages.

To further complicate this panorama we captured [audio voice] and Video Television emissions; but we were ignorant of the fact that each such frequencies were carriers of images [and other information] which we tried to interpret acoustically. Also, most of those recorded came from what we later identified as Northamerica, thinking that in that zone they spoke three languages. The last of those (video signals) did not present the least similarity to the others.

The enormous linguistic anarchy (complicated still more by these false interpretations) united with the immense range of technical differences observed in the multiplicity of equipment and constructions of distinct zones of the planet truely filled us with perplexity.

It was impossible for us to make a coherent panorama of what the terrestrial civilization might be like.

STUDY OF THE ATMOSPHERIC COMPOSITION OF EARTH

The atmospheric composition, on the other hand, obtained from diverse samples from various points of OYAA and at different levels, showed us that we could descend without the necessity of auxiliary respiratory equipment.

KEY POINT TO KNOW THE STRUCTURE OF PROTEIN MOLECULES

There remained to be solved only the most important question of the enantiomorphic structure of the protein molecules. Were they "Dextrogiras" or "Levogiras"?

If the biological molecules of those beings and the alimentation items of Earth were found to be the inverse of ours, it would be impossible to assimilate them in our digestive system, and we would be condemned to starve if we did not carry our own alimentation with us.

It was necessary, of course, to provide the expedition with other auxiliary equipment to purify the water in case it contained toxins in suspension, perhaps assimilatable by the inhabitants of the OYAGAA (Earth) but not by us.

POLITICS TO BE CARRIED OUT WITH THE TERRESTRIALS

The politics to be followed with you was carefully elaborated. Violent defense in case of being attacked. Initiation of Official Contact on the supposition of being detected and controlled peacefully. Absolute inhibition, and to try with all the techniques within our reach to pass unnoticed. For which we were advised of course that it would be almost impossible to pass unperceived among the terrestrials. To remain hidden then, they would install an underground observatory in the rustic zone most ideal and above the terrain where they would study the methods and techniques most appropriate.

In this we were wrong however, as we came to see later, for we discovered with surprise that it was perfectly possible to mix among you without drawing attention.

WE INITIATE A PROGRAM FOR AN EXPEDITION

We immediately initiated a program of preparation. The persons to make up the first expedition were carefully selected.

Among those six selected there were only two YIEE (that is what we call the women). All of them learned lengthy fragments of distinct languages captured (without absolutely knowing the significance) as much as to familiarise their EESEEOA (Subconscious) with the phonetic structure of the acoustical codes of terrestrial expression.

They were able to examine all the informative material captured and to familiarize themselves with the multiplicity of forms of vegetables whose images were most clear in those of the terrestrial flora seen... Little data in truth for those OEMII that were going to confront an unknown world.

UMMOAELEWE
Language: Spanish
Date: 12-2-1967

DESCENT ON OYAAGAA (EARTH) OF OUR BROTHERS

The six OEMII (persons) who departed for the first time to land on your planet were:

OEDEE-95 son of OEDEE-91: Director of the Expedition.

Specialist in BAAYIODUII (Biology), then (equivalent to) 31 terrestrial years old. Director of the expeditionary team. Actually fulfilling the function of OGIIA (Chief) of coordination of the activities of he and his brothers displaced here on Earth with their home planet UMMO.

UURIO-79 son of IYIA-55: Expert in Human Psychobiology.

Expert in BIIEUIGUU (Human Psychobiology) then (equivalent to) 18 terrestrial years old. (The only one of that expedition who still remains on this planet.)

INNDO-33 daughter of INNDO-29: Expert in Physics of the Structure of matter.

Expert in DOLGAA GOO (Physics of the Structure of Matter) at that time (equivalent to) 18 terrestrial years of age.

ODDIOA-1 son of ADAA-65: Expert on Communications.

Specialized in AYUU WADDOSIA (Communications) then (equal to) 78 terrestrial years of age.

ADAA-66 son of ADAA-65: Expert in Sociology.

Technician in AYUYISAA (Sociology) of 22 (terrestrial equivalent) years of age. (Our only brother who died on Earth) He was killed on 6 November 1967 in Yugoslavia, the victim of an accident (his body could not be recuperated.)

UORII-19 daughter of OBAA-7: Expert in Pathology of Digestion.

Expert in the pathology of Digestive Systems, then (equivalent to) 32 terrestrial years of age.

DEPARTURE FROM UMMO OF THE EXPEDITIONARIES

I can still remember the images of the departure that I myself saw in the hemispheric panorama of my UULODASAABII (semispherical apartment in our SAAABI or dwelling which serves to contemplate images at a distance).

With respect to the most favorable time for departure we were not so fortunate. The possibility was foreseen that several XEE (UMMO years) later, the Isodynamic conditions of space would be exceptionally favorable [but they decided to proceed anyway].

We would have arrived at the Earth during your year 1952, accomplishing the trip in less than 30,000 UIW (for the incredibly short distance that at that [future] time we would enjoy). But the probability that such predictions could be depended upon was evaluated to be sufficiently low that the decision to go ahead was given priority.

LETTER OF PRESENTATION OF THE EXPEDITIONARIES OF UMMO

The expeditionaries carried a message with complete instructions that would permit rapid transcription to terrestrial languages, written by the GENERAL COUNCIL of UMMO to the COUNCIL of CHIEF of the inhabitants of that planet (Earth) in case the terrestrials intercepted our brothers.

This letter was impressed upon a lamination of GUU (alloy of iron, carbon and vanadium) and it carried a series of ideographic images, representing human acts and gestures, combinations of geometric figure forms and ciphers expressed in language of a Binary System.

The interpretation of its contents by Earth experts in phylology and semantics would not have been difficult, thus permitting probably the first communication of our expeditionaries with what we supposed would be the General Government of OYAAGA (Earth).

The equipment that had to be transported by the group of explorers was complete but reduced in volume and mass.

[Note- This startling revelation was actually in the hands of the members of the Madrid Group of UMMO contactees in February of 1967, more than 10 years before we installed a similar metal plaque on our own interplanetary Voyager 2, lanuched on 4 August 1977, with Voyager 1 launched one month later. Is it simply remarkable coincidence that these attempts at interplanetary communication are almost identical,-- or is one copying the other, and which one is doing the copying? Is there something our governments are not telling us? We have our own very convincing answers! -Publisher]

BAAYIODIXAA UUDII, CONDITIONANT FACTORS OF THE BIOLOGICAL EQUILIBRIUM

We cannot explain the value of the coefficient BAAYIODIXAA UUDII (untranslatable).

The biological sciences of Earth still have not developed this very important concept. It treats of a formula that expresses the condition of Biological Equilibrium that can be verified by one given method. Each OYAA (planet) posesses certain peculiar conditions which does or does not permit the existence of a biological cycle of carbon in its Troposphere.

The biogenetic development of the morphology of animal and vegetable life is a function of a series of physical constants.

This biogenetic development then is no consequence of simple CHANCE. though this intervenes in no unappreciable amount at subatomic levels in the development of the genes. And so the form and physiological structure of the species varies considerably from one planet to any other, such that the more simple the cellular constitution of the living being is, the greater the effect could be.

Not only are the species of filtrable viruses of UMMO totally distinct from the species of Earth, but also included are levels of complex pluricellular animals, such that it is almost impossible to find great anologies with the species known by those of Earth.

PARAMETERS THAT CONSTITUTE THE BAAYIODIXAA UUDII

The foumula that expresses the BAAYIODIXAA UUDII is a complex function in which are integrated a multitude of parameters such as:

ACCELERATION OF GRAVITY: - ATMOSPHERIC IONIZATION: - SPECTRUM OF SOLAR RADIATION: - GRAVITATIONAL CYCLES OF THE POSSIBLE SATELLITES AND ANY NEARBY PLANETS: - ELECTROSTATIC GRADIENTS OF THE ATMOSPHERE: - ELECTROMAGNETIC CURRENTS: - ETC., ETC.

This together with the component percentages of the chemical elements of the crust of the planet, permits some prediction of the evolutionary orientation of the living beings involved. Other factors could independently alter this, such as mutations provoked by radiations and autoselection influenced by predictable environmental influences.

This formula or coefficient is of transcendental importance when trying to analyze the possibilities for an interplanetary voyage (to another planet). But, unfortunately, it is not easy to know these values exactly without laborious study "in situ".

Without that, the explorers are at risk of introduction into an adverse biological environment, and they could become victims not only of infectious illnesses, and germs, against which the organism, adequate for another environment, lacks the most elemental defenses, but also for lack of effective medical prophylaxis, the OEMII could be incurable and perish as soon as the lack of equipment protecting the epidermis and external organs exposed them to the influence of the new environment.

PROTECTIVE EQUIPMENT OF THE EXPEDITIONARIES

This protective equipment is different from the spacesuits used by yourselves in submarine and space exploration.

New plastic epidermis: The individual is provided with a new plastic epidermis which permits transpiration (respiration) while at the same time impeding the filtration through its pores, of biological chemical agents.

place losses through transpiration (breathing and body vapors). The rest of the elements are transmuted completely and are expelled in the form of gasses.

PROCESS OF ENDOWMENT WITH THE NEW EPIDERMIS

When all of these equipments, of tiny size, are affixed to the epidermis of the nude individual, that is sprayed with distinct protective aerosols, which form a fine elastic film, that constitutes a veritable protective skin. The subject thus enjoys the liberty of movements, can dress in special clothes and maneuver freely in the midst of an adverse atmosphere from a biological point of view.

Nevertheless, this new epidermis (new skin) of course, does not protect him from changes of pressure such as encountered, for example, on the surface of an asteroid with practically no atmosphere.

EQUIPMENT FOR EXPLORATIONS WITHOUT ATMOSPHERIC PRESSURE

In these cases the explorer does not use any special supplementary space-suit. The most superficial outer layer is now re-covered with a new layer of metalized plastic, which observed under a device for high magnification, presents a reticulate structure (an authentic coat of mail) and corporeal movements are now slowed by the greater rigidity of the system, but the dynamism of the OEMII is not unacceptably restricted.

ACCESSORY EQUIPMENT REQUIRED FOR THE EXPLORATION

Apart from these individual equipments, the expeditionaries were provided with equipments for the conversion of Nitrogen, Carbon, Oxygen, and Hydrogen of water in hydrates of carbon and other basic components for emergency alimentation, to be used on OYAAGAA in the case that the protein molecules, amino acids, and esters of terrestrial alimentation might be the inverse of those of UMMO (all of you know that each asymetric organic molecule can adopt two forms in space, Dextrogira [right rotating] and Levrogira [left rotating]),

[We are reminded here again, as in a considerable number of other UFO Contactee cases, of the existence of opposite substance, anti-matter, counterpart reality, or whatever we want to call it, in which matter has a different spin and vector, and usually an opposite charge. There was very litle understanding of these states of matter in 1967 when this communication was received. Since that time this subject has come up frequently in UFO lore. -Publisher]

Likewise there was apparatus for the purification of water, and also for its synthesis if necessary. There were equipments for sounding and analysis. They had "photographic" equipment (we use other systems for fixation of images, in which case the vocable "photographic" is not correct).

Mechanical operation: Previously are placed, near the natural orifices (of the body), a series of devices with functions adequate for the necessities of each organ. Thus capsules placed in the nostrils generated oxygen and nitrogen, apart from the transmutiaton of the pure carbon; and the anhydrous carbonate is captured by the same device, decomposed into its basic elements, carbon and oxygen, and transmuted (you would say transmuted, a term that seems to us incorrect) first by energy liberation that is used to heat the epidermis. That is the EEWEEGOO.

EQUIPMENT IN THE EYES AND MOUTH

The eyes and the mouth are conveniently protected. The first are equipped with an integrated optical system of lenses of gas, which, controlled by a computer, then permits the adaptation of vision in the vaccuum of sidereal space as well as in the atmospheric medium.

Alimentation: A double tube leads from an equipment device placed in the lumbar region, to terminate in a device controlled by the lower lip. The interior of this tube is provided with mechanical cilia which slowly propel through its cavity various capsules which contain diverse concentrated alimentations. These are of elliptical section, and are protected by a very delicate gelatinous film quickly soluable in the saliva.

Activation of mechanism: A signal, by the eyelid (Opening and closing in a sequential series) codified and transmitted, propells the different capsules to the mouth to sustain the brother explorer.

The other conduit transports a nutritional serum, with distinct regulated concentrations.

Provision of water: The necessary water for the most part is obtained from the individual's own urine (through a process of elimination of salts, followed by integral purification and storage of the chemically pure water by means of carbonates).

EQUIPMENT FOR THE EARS

They are provided with paired acoustical transducers excited by an UAXOOAADO (Receiver-transmitter for gravitational waves, which serve to transmit short messages among the components of the group).

Messages or conversations of longer duration, and at great distances are accomplished by telepathy.

EQUIPMENT FOR DEFACATION

A probe introduced into the rectum, through the anus collects the fecal wastes, previously treated with turbulent currents of water at 38° terrestrial Centigrade, succtioning them out with a device fitted to the buttocks. There they are decomposed into their basic chemical elements, part of which (oxygen and hydrogen) are recombined to obtain liquid water to replenish the urine-water injestion cycle and to re-

There was XOOOIMAA UYII (Geological Sounding) equipment and the UULUEWAA, devices that permitted the capture of sounds, and the recording of images, or to control the distinct physical factors of the environment, controlled from a distance.

There were instruments of defense, whose nature we can not reveal for obvious reasons.

The provisioning included special detectors to measure physical magnitudes, record geological and atmospheric functions, and equipment for spectral and molecular analysis. There was a complete range of telmetric equipment devices.

STRATEGY TO FOLLOW STUDIED

As we said in an earlier communication, we profoundly studied the strategy to be followed with the inhabitants of OYAAGAA (Earth).

We were ignorant of the methods of detection and control that you posessed, thus, for example, in our preliminary study voyage we have already mentioned, we recorded wave emissions of 1347 and 2402 Megacycles (Earth term) called by you the ten meter band. We were ignorant of the fact that such waves were assigned to the radiolocation services (Terrestrial Radar). In any case we assigned a probability value to such a possibility. If in spite of all, our brothers were not detected, they had orders to construct a subterranean observatory, endowed with emergency installations for the production of synthetic water and basic alimentation, once the supplies brought in our UEWA (ships) were exhausted.

Likewise installations for the synthetic production (in emergency) of hydrates of carbon and lipids (combustible greases) starting with the transmutation of silicates of aluminum (we knew of the existence of clays in the surface layer of Earth).

Decisions with respect to the nature of action for the study of the men of Earth, would have to be determined by the expeditionaries, once they were on the unknown planet.

NORMS TO BE OBSERVED BY THE UMMO EXPEDITIONARY GROUP

All of our valient expeditionaries posessed families on UMMO.

OEDEE-95 had four children, and UURIO-79 and ADAA-66 each had two children. All knew what was expected of them. Unfortunately we already knew of precedents in which the death of our brothers was the result of our scientific spirit.

We have on UMMO a gregarious mentality, so developed that practically no grave disciplinary problems exist in our Social Network.

The OEMII (men) of UMMO may feel humiliated when they must obey a Superior younger than they, or of the opposite sex, but they always submit without complaint, though always reserving the right to disagree ideologically with the Superior and express their own point of view reasonably.

The OEMII of UMMO is for that reason more free in his hierarchial relations than Terrestrial men.

Nevertheless, exceptional conditions involved in an interplanetary expedition, of necessity, reinforced the rigid discipliianry criteria governing relations between the members of the explorer group.

Those freely volunteered (once selected as a result of special psychosomatic tests and evaluation of their conformity to the most severe norms of the group). We do not precisely prescribe any formula for judgement or expression; only the vote of obedience as in some of your religious orders on Earth. From the moment we are accepted and integrated into the small group of voyagers, we know with absolute clarity, that our will must be completely subordinated to that of our Superior, whether man or woman. Our bodies are completely at his disposition.

You must understand that we are going to be immersed in a strange and perhaps adverse world, where the lack of discipline of one member could have grave repercussions on our brother expeditionaries and the scientific interests of UMMOAELEWE and our Social Network of UMMO.

The least punishment for a transgression could bring us before our Superior suffering the humiliation (much accentuated in our psychology) of exposing ourselves totally nude before him. The physical punishments prescribed from very long ago on UMMO can be applied with extreme rigor, even to the loss of life.

PRECISE TIME OF THE OAWOOLEAIDAA

At four hours, sixteen minutes and fourty two seconds, GMT Greenwich time, the OAWOOLEAIDAA (untranslatable in the Earth languages) took place.

That is what we call the critical instant in which the UEWA OEMM (interplanetary ship) with all aboard undergoes an axial inversion of its subatomic particles, which substitutes one tridimensional reference system for the other.

This change of dimensions is necessary for us in order to accomplish a voyage utilizing the REAL MOST SHORT distance, distinct of course from the distance required by light in the other three dimensional reference system of space in which we live.

VISUAL PERCEPTION OF THE "OAWOOLEAIDAA"

The sight of the OAWOOLEAIDAA by an observer on Earth presents some very singular peculiarities.

For example. the UEWA (ship) appears suddenly, as though it emerged out of nothing, or disappears the same way when the process is reversed.

[NOTE- This peculiar phenomenon has been reported repeatedly, over and over again in UFO literature, and the reports come from all over the world, from witnesses completely out of touch with each other, and even from non-believers, pure sceptics and primitives who have not had the least exposure to media and outside situations. All things being considered, we must accept the probability that such phenomenoa have actually been witnessed by Earth men. We have never seen a suitable explanation in Earth scientific terms, and certainly no such explanation ever demonstrated or proved. Here, finally (way back in 1967) is an explanation that is not easily disproved, and seems as plausible as any. The argument about changing the spin of the subatomic particles in a field has been mentioned by extraterrestrials in a number of other UFO contactee cases, notably the contacts with Dr. Wilbert B. Smith in Canada and those with Edwin W. in South Africa where other dimensional realities and other kinds of matter are discussed. See THE NEW SCIENCE by Wilbert B. Smith and UFO CONTACT FROM PLANET KOLDAS by Carl vanVlierden. Two papers by American scientists on the prospect of interplanetary space travel, published one in 1980 and the other in 1981 before the American Institute of Aeronautics and Astronautics (AIAA) discussed the need for a new view of physics and the need for developing some new fields of physical sciences before we could go anywhere in deeper space. In both cases they offered position papers on the subject, and in both cases they had to resort to other dimensional realities to escape the restrictive properties of three dimensional physical space. Refer to book UFO CONTACT FROM THE PLEIADES, A Preliminary Investigation Report, Appendix IX. The first of these Papars, AIAA-80-1233, Prospects for a Breakthrough in Field Dependent Propulsion, is authored by A.C. Holt, NASA Johnson Space Center, in Houston where he was with the astronaut training program. The other Paper, AIAA-81-1533, Investigation of a Quantum Ramjet for Interstellar Flight, was authored by none other than H.D.Froning, Jr., McDonnel Douglas Astronautics Co., a senior engineer on the Space Shuttle design and development team. These men are no amatures in the fields of Earth sciences. That others have successfully accomplished this is hardly in doubt. We know of no UFO contact cases where the extraterrestrials took more than a year in getting here. Either they have a better method of overcoming distance or they are all coming here from less than one lightyear of distance, and we consider the former the more likely. There are also many references to non-linear travel in UFO literature, where the displacement takes effect by another process entirely, something like changing the vibrational rate of being, a process unfamiliar to our science today. Given these clues, what may our prospects for tomorrow be? -Publisher]

In reality the disappearance is only apparent because the ship continues to exist in the reality of *another system of dimensions*.

Nevertheless another ship that tries to pursue it into the new dimensional frame of reference, not only would find it impossible to see it but also to establish any kind of mechanical contact with it such as radioelectrically or gravitationally.

The vivid orange radiance emitted by our UEWA is due to a peculiar incandescence provoked by decontamination of all types of living germs that could adhere to the surface, germs that, if we did not adopt this precaution, would also be tridimensionally inverted and carried to our planet with unforeseen biological consequences easy to presume.

Another characteristic easily detected is the strong magnetic field that appears in the region of the axis of symmetry of our ship, and perhaps with other space vehicles of other presumed extraterrestrials.

This magnetic field can reach values expressed in terrestrial units, several thousands of WEBBER Mtrs^2, is not as many imagine, indicative that our system of propulsion is magnetodynamic.

This strong magnetic induction is not only the axial inversion at an angle of 90 degrees, but the intensity of the electrostatic field produced by a powerful generator, whose function consists in inverting the subatomic particles of the ship and all aboard.

SCHEME OF IDENTITY OF ENERGY FIELDS

Remember that the vectors representing the fields of Gravity, Electricity and Magnetics form a triad in the bosom of Pluridimensional Space. The three fields are in reality IDENTICAL.

In our illusory physiological perception, we attribute to them a distinct nature, according to their orientation.

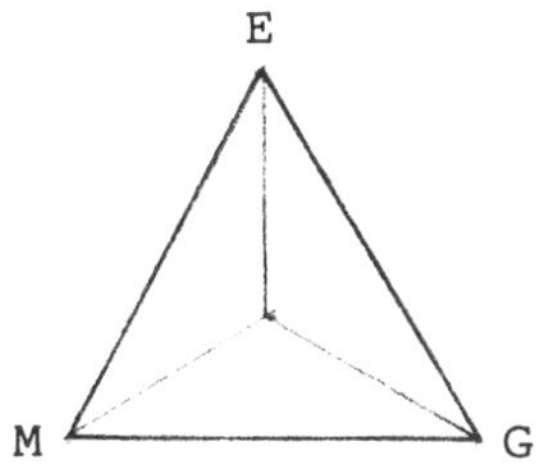

We repeat (with explicit emphasis), at the hour cited, three of our OAWOOLEA UEWA OEMM (spaceships) appeared suddenly at one point situated at an altitude of 7,336 kilometers above a place located some 13 kilometers from the French city of Digne, and 8 kilometers from the village of La Javie (Department of Basses Alpes) not far from the frontier with the Cantonal Republic and federation of Switzerland.

DATE AND HOUR OF THE DESCENT TO PLANET EARTH

It was on the 28th of March 1950. The three ships descended rapidly, reaching the earth at 4 hours, 17 minutes and 3 seconds GMT..

The extendible landing gear of the ships scarcely sunk into the rocky terrain of an alpine spur, near what we later identified as the peak of Cheval Blanc, at 2,322.95 meters above mean sea level, and near the small fluvial current (crick) of Bleone.

During some 20 UIW, nobody left our ships, in expectation of a presumed attack. Our equipments discovered, in a radius of 800 meters, the possible emission of infrared radiations coming from human beings.

A heavy fog at that time impeded direct vision of the surroundings. The images obtained there in the range of 740 micromillimeters wavelength permitted us nevertheless to view the surroundings (with the instruments).

Plants of strange morphology grew in the vicinity. the eroded morphology of the terrain permitted us to survey some watery faults such as the bed of the cited river (Bleone). Until the following morning we were unable to identify the nature of residential lights that appeared at three definite points in the distance.

FIRST DESCENT OF FOUR BROTHERS

Verifying that there was no detectable trace of human beings in the vicinity, four of our nonexpeditionary brothers of the thirty six that made up the total complement of the three ships, descended to the ground.

They took with them protective equipment and devices for defense. One of the UEWA remained suspended 30 centimeters above the ground, to cover a retreat in case of attack.

The pairs dedicated some 10 UIW to the exploration of the surroundings, sounding the ground continually to detect any possible subterranean noises coming from underground human installations. To you such precautions might seem naive, but for us at that time the possibility of subterranean habitations of Earth human beings was not discarded nor much less. There however it seemed deserted. They collected from the ground some insects and spiders, and some vegetal species later identified according to botanical classification of Earth as "Valeriana Celta and Erica Carnea, and carried them to the ship where we could examine them with excited curiosity. As it was hoped, the morphology of those small animals and plants differed from the species known on UMMO.

SAMPLE EVALUATION OF THE GROUND AND CONSTRUCTION OF CAVE

A little later the six expeditionaries went out accompanied by 20 members of the party. It was necessary to begin work on an emergency subterranean construction.

They made a sample evaluation of the characteristics of the ground. One thing that attracted their attention was the absence of Titanium in the chemical composition of the rocks and soil.

In our soil of UMMO this chemical element is as abundant as aluminum in the clays of Earth. They detected numerous ferrocrystals in porous rocks. The dispersion of igneous rocks was evidently useless in trying to understand the percentage composition of sand and clay. The abundant carbonates and silicates permitted them to evolve a preliminary hypothesis concerning the geological evolution of those terrains.

Finishing the study, they began the perforation, fusing at great temperatures the sands and rocks. The high composition of silica in the ground provoked at first a serious problem which was quickly resolved. The materials thus fused were transmuted to an isotope of Nitrogen; and in this manner a mound of earth on the exterior that could reveal our presence to possible terrestrial human observers was avoided.

They worked all the night until 07:00. A little before dawn our UEWA were removed to a small woods of strange trees with filiamentary leaves later identified by the name of "Pinus Montana".

The gallery opened underground to a width of 4 meters and a depth of 8 meters. It was excavated with IGAAYUU (a kind of extensible tapered vibrator of an alloy of magnesium, very light).

It maintained a high temperature (500°) for the fusion by means of a nuclear energy process of the component products of the subsoil, and was accompanied afterward by a rapid solidification. It was necessary also to solve the problem of vapor condensation in the form of steam clouds released from the gallery in a high column which could reveal our presence. It was necessary to obscure the mouth of the gallery or tunnel with a plastic sheet and to collect by aspiration the smokes and vapors released by the combustion of the organic substances of the ground.

MORNING OF THAT FIRST DAY ON PLANET EARTH, 29 MARCH 1950

The new day offered the expeditionaries a beautiful new spectacle: For the first time they were face to face with the new world, a new geological structure.

The sky was more blue than that of UMMO; numerous stratocumulous reduced the brightness of the sky in that region that day. Soon they discovered the presence of two artificial structures (modest homes) situated at 1.3 and 1.9 kilometers distance respectively.

Now it was perfectly clear that the origin of the lights seen the evening before pertained to the villages and small population centers of Digne and La Javie (and others).

The chaotic form of the strange structures powerfully attracted their attention. Digne appeared to be dominated by a strange tower that we later learned was part of an ancient Catholic Cathedral of Romantic XIII Century style.

Optical instruments of great magnification revealed the first images of those first terrestrial beings (seen by this team). They did not notice any exceptional activity or unusual nervousness on the part of those seen, perhaps unaware of the presence of our brothers in their vicinity.

Also at a distance of some 200 meters was discovered some strange prismatic columns constructed with artificial materials, all in evident state of ruin. This was the first work by the terrestrial human beings recorded. Later we understood that it was a small and ancient nave, but the discovery filled my brothers with emotion.

They took samples from the columns and radiographed the interior.

Their analysis showed the presence of an aglutinate substance containing in the mixture Calcium Sulphate, Aluminates and small quantities of mineral oxides (which we later found to be oversulphated cement) such as fragments of rock and sand in almost constant and perhaps measured proportion, which we later understood resulted from the classic drying of concrete on the ground. Analysis of the interior showed various evident hardware.

CORRECTION OF SMALL ERRORS IN TRANSCRIPTIONS

In preceeding communications we furnished a resume of the history of our arrival in the vicinity of Digne (France). Three of our OAWOOLEA OEMM (spacecraft of lenticular structure and form), descended to a point situated 7,339 kilometers above the cited French locality.

The instant of our OAWOOLEAIDAA, which we call the physical process of inversion of the subatomic corpuscles, which permits the orientation of such ships through another AXIS in its space voyages, had been recorded by us in your Earth version as 4 hours, 16 minutes and 42 seconds GMT with a margin of error of ± 6 seconds.

ATTENTION! On the 8th of November 1965, we sent, through the mediation of a brother of ours, UDIIE-36 son of UDIEE-34, then in the United States, a small communication, very brief, concerning our arrival on Earth to Medical Doctor Peter Welter.

Our brother dictated the hour of arrival as "4 hours, 23 minutes" (without specifying any margin of error).

Some more careful investigations into the conversion of our dimensional data of time, comparing it with the radioelectric signals emitted at that time by the broadcasting centers of the Republic of France and the Republic of Helvitica, which were detected by our equipment, permitted rectification of the first appreciation of time, which was the result of comparing the thermal and barometric curves of a French meteorological observatory with our own data on the terrestrial atmosphere on our arrival.

Six of our brothers (four GEE and two YIEE) descended that evening (see the communication sent you on this). We have told you that the first operation undertaken was to excavate a gallery to hold all the equipments of the expeditionaries, which served at the same time as protected shelter if confronted with a hypothetical attack by terrestrials.

DETAILS OF THE GALLERY EXCAVATED

They stored in this gallery, synthesized food and liquids that could permit our brothers to survive for "240 XII" (One XII is equal to one rotation of our planet, some 30.9 terrestrial hours). [About 310 Earth days.]

On the 29th of March they concluded their work on adaptation of the subterranean gallery. It was necessary to accelerate the refrigeration of its walls to permit the storage of material.

To Earth engineers this data concerning refrigeration would seem strange. Our procedures of fusion at high temperatures of the rocks, sands and slimes of the terrain controlled the expansion of the gasses which were immediately converted to Nitrogen and Oxygen. Moreover by obtaining greater speed we avoid multiple secondary effects such as the expansion that takes place upon transforming the anhydrite in gypsum by contact with water.

Of course we previously had made a geological study of Earth but not by means of seismographic or electrical probes, but by analysis of the outside with a stereographic procedure similar to terrestrial X-rays. They obtained thus an image that revealed not only the composition of the different strata, but the location of deposits situated at great depth.

The systems of heating held a certain similarity to those of Earth. On UMMO they construct, for example, heating modules "in situ". The silica and titanium of the rocks, once melted, are transmuted into Magnesium and Aluminum with which they then construct the IGAYUU (metallic arcs).

As we said, it was necessary to accelerate the work for the activity (more easily observed in daylight) might endanger the expeditionaries. In the first place they did not know if the Isodynamic Conditions Of Space would vary much in the following UIW (unit of time on UMMO) so impeding the conditions of return that the time required would be unacceptable to the crews.

In the second place, the night before, they had transferred the UEWA (spaceships) to a stand of nearby pines, but in spite of all, they feared the possibility that they had been seen by the Terrestrials.

DEPARTURE OF THE EXPLORATION SHIPS AND CREWS

Considering it imprudent to leave the ships there, at 11:00 of the morning of the 29th of May (French time) the expeditionaries and the explorer crews celebrated an emotional farewell. We have images of that act. The hands of each one were placed on the chest of his brother as is the customary closing of the moment of departure. Nobody pronounced one word. The eyes said all.

Thirty crew members boarded the three ships, and soon they initiated the process of AIAIEDUNNI (the superficial exterior areas of the ships increased in temperature until incandescence, thus destroying the living germs and obtaining perfect sterilization. This process is necessary, because such microorganisms as virus could be inverted in their dimensions and accompany the spaceship on its space voyage, thus arriving on our planet).

The three UEWA (ships) rose to a height of some six kilometers. The expeditionaries contemplated their apparent disappearance upon producing at that level, the second OAWOOLEAIDAA (inversion) for their return (to UMMO).

29 MARCH 1950 - THE FIRST EXPLORATION

That same day two of our brothers received orders to conduct a preliminary exploration to a certain distance from the gallery, while the rest proceeded with their labors there.

The entrance to the gallery was located on one of those mountainous spurs of that region, not very far from Cheval Blanc Peak. From there they dominated all the valley through which ran the river Bleone. With good optical instruments they could see the structures of Digne perfectly, including its old cathedral. And fragmentally they could perfectly observe the hamlet of La Javie and some humble structures in its vicinity and around there. As an item of interest, we can tell you that that historic gallery is still preserved, enclosing in its interior, part of the original scientific equipment that was brought by out brothers.

Its access is perfectly camouflaged. The day, perhaps not very far off, in which we oficially present ourselves to the governmental organs of this planet, we will donate this installation to the Government of France, as a symbolic thanks from our civilization to that of Earth.

The first exploration of our two brothers, was made in the afternoon of 29 March, and it produced an result unforeseen by us. To you the incident could seem vulgar, and you might judge our consideration naive and even comical, but the result greatly impressed our brothers.

To understand better, it is necessary that you place yourselves in the mental frame of those OEMII who had just arrived on an unknown planet whose only known means of expression were some modulated sounds picked up by our radioelectric detection equipment, and whose unintelligible jargon still offered no basis for serious study.

Around six in the evening of that date ADAA-66 daughter of ADAA-65, roving the surroundings in company with another brother, pulled up roots here and there and took leaf specimens from these unknown trees for later analysis. They observed in the surroundings of two taller trees (surely would have been pines, though the report does not specifically say) some piled and blackened stones. They identified the structure of these fragments of rock as having been heated. Some ashes scattered around made them think that this had been used for a fire, but that was not what was of most interest.

At some 1.8 ENMOO (one ENMOO = 1.9 meters) they discovered some fragments of yellowish white sheets, flexible and crushed into wrinkles, and full of characters or symbols written by human beings. Three of them appeared soiled by fecal traces. A multitude of unknown flying animals (one could figure that they were flies or mosquitos) were taking flight.

The discovery was considered so transcendental that they immediately returned to the gallery.

The macroscopic structure of those pages was analyzed immediately. The texture was unknown to us, for on UMMO we did not utilize the paste of cellulose in the fabrication of paper.

The symbols or codified marks revealed that they had not been written but impressions by means of standard molds. Undoubtedly some liquid vehicle had been used for the impression (press ink). This was strange for us because our ancient systems of duplicating characters employed an electrostatic system of projection of colored powder, or lightly burned the surface of the sheets.

(Actually our systems were based on turning around the molecules of the sheet where you are going to produce an image, transmuting them into others of chromatic color. As said this does not transfer ink by means of type, but provokes a complete chemical reaction in the same image surface.)

The presence of fecal traces constituted an enigma at first. Analysis of the excrement revealed the presence of epithelial cells, no doubt coming from human intestinal glands.

STUDY AND HYPOTHESIS IN TURN OF MATERIAL COLLECTED

They made a list of probable hypotheses. To the most supported was attributed a ritual character.

Perhaps these beings, when the disagreed with what was expressed in the written document, defaced it with fecal traces. Among these suppositions they deduced also that it was now evident for all (surely some shepherd had used that famous newspaper for hygenic purposes).

You would understand the controversy better if you took into account the fact that the UUGEEYIE (children of UMMO) are provided after birth, with a device fitted into the rectum which has a terminal duct or tube which exits at the anus.

The fecal matter is liquified by a process of enzyme transformation, followed by a process of gelification and expulsion by electrostatic elimination through the tube of the residues that remain. It is not necessary then to proceed with cleaning after the deposition as done by terrestrials. Our ancestors, on the other hand, employed a spongy substance for cleaning after defacation.

But there was no doubt at least of the origin of the residues that soiled the newspaper (as we later understood it to be).

Those fragments are historic for us. The original of which lacks one page and various fragments, is preserved on UMMO in such a way that it is preserved in a transparent gelatinous mass, and at constant temperature of YIIEGAA as we call a technique unknown to you, by which a biological structure is preserved at low temperature, but controlling the gradients of temperature at each point, since some zones or textures of same cannot stand low temperatures without the congealing of the water and provoking destruction of the cells, while some other points may preserve better at other thermic levels.

This famous example for us constitutes the first important document we were able to obtain.

This first document corresponds to one issue of a Daily published in the French language, "LE FIGARO", Samedi Diamanche, 25-26 March 1950.

The strange characters perplexed our brothers. The most exciting and suggestive of that strange piece were the sketches and photographs (we of course did not know the technique of direct photo transmission by lines).

In the page later identified as the first appeared precisely, a curious caricature signed by a French humorist, J. Sennup. It was a drawing of a hydrogen bomb on whose side appeared the caricature of a certain French politician, below which was lettered this:

Batailles Parlamentaires.
S'ils nous embetent, nous avons la bombe H.
Se apreciaban grandes titulares tales como:
L'Urss est favorable a une session speciale du conseil
De segurite pour Regler les Differences est-Ouest.

And other headlines like those that follow:

Serie Noire Dans L'Aviation.
Trois Catastrophes Aeriennes
Ont Fait 19 Morts.
Aide Immediate a L'Indochine.

On the back of the paper, though badly soiled, could be seen an image of exceptional interest to us. One could see a human adult being with two UGEEYIE (we could not clearly identify the sex) though later we knew that it was a woman and children of both sexes. This was determined from their clothes. Don't forget that one of our brainbusters consisted in finding out how you dressed. Above the sketch there was a text of course then unintelligible to the explorers which said "Mundiale Nursery".

To end the confusion about the type of terrestrial dress, there appeared on another page of the paper (page 6), a photograph of another human being dressed in the classic style represented in the theatrical "MALBOROUGH" of Marcel Achard that ended presentation in the Marigni Theater.

That documental discovery, we repeat, was of transcendental importance. But we knew of no scientific way to be able to interpret those characters. There was no direct relation between the images and the text. We did not know if those symbols represented cyphers, or expressed ideograms, or could be interpreted as representations of complete sounds or unintegrated phonemes.

What was that document doing there in the middle of the field? We could not decide whether it had been placed there for us, however the excrement showed evidence of desication begun before our arrival on Earth.

UMMOAELEWE
Language: Spanish
Date: 27-3-67

SECOND DAY ON PLANET EARTH

On the 30th of March 1950 two of our brothers saw some vertibrate animals with sharply pointed protruberances coming out of the top of the cranium; altogether there were eight of them. They were situated at a distance of 350 meters, terrestrial.

They were given orders to seek an opportunity to approach, having been provided with adequate equipment for defense if necessary. Our brothers were covered with EEWEEGOO, vestment; the external appearance of which was like a monkey, very close fitting.

CHARACTERISTICS OF THE EEWEEGOO

In reality this consists of a fine film that has been sprayed from a tube over the epidermis of the thorax, back, arms and legs.

It is a substance whose principal base is dissolved silicates in a colloidal solution which is quite volatil. This liquid, upon being sprayed over the skin, evaporates rapidly leaving there a delicate covering of film "of opaque, porous and electrostatic character". It is the dress we use when we work in intimate contact with nature.

COLOR. Its color varies in certain circumstances with the work.

In general they utilize a color code when a team is using these (protective coverings) on our planet. Nevertheless, our brothers of UMMO displaced here at that time, used a brown color for its camouflage effect. We explain these small details because of a surprising result still in that time for us in an incident that we are going to relate.

Our brothers took a path toward the herd of animals that we have indicated. It was simply cows with halters, but such animals did not exist on UMMO and to us were completely unknown. Only the evidence of the udders permitted identification of the sex of those beings.

They finally reached the vicinity of that group but, before going much closer, they initiated the usual operations of recording of the sounds and images and a process of detection of "gravitational and electrostatic fields emitted by those animals" which, situated at a distance of 15 terrestrial meters, they carefully observed their peculiar conduct which, despite noticing the presence of our brothers continued with immutable patience.

PRESENCE OF UUGEE (children)

Soon there appeared from behind some rocks in the vicinity, a human being of obvious adolescence, dressed in a form strange to our observers. His clothes were not like in the images we had captured up to now. The sex of the individual was masculine but at first it was not possible to identify this as such. It was a boy about 11 years old who was guarding the cows of his father, but all this we came to know later as things cleared up. The surprise and immediate worry of our brothers was heightened. Without moving from the position they occupied, they called for instructions from the Chief of the subterranean base by means of a touch code, so that the recent arrival could not see their lips move.

The boy carried a yellowish-white substance in his hand (bread) impregnated with a dark product (surely it was a sausage or some kind of spread) [the communication was not specific], which he continued to eat without interruption in front of our three brothers who watched with attention without seeming too much surprised.

The small UUGEE spoke some phrases of course unintelligible. Then upon seeing that he was getting no response, he came closer still, and putting his hand on his forehead, looked with more attention. The series of misunderstandings that followed are curious.

Analyzing the conduct of the adolescent (named Pierre) later, it was understandable that the gesture of raising the hand to the forehead was simply to shade his eyes from the sun, but they interpreted such a sign as a salute, and repeated the salute, much to the surprise of the UUGEE.

The young French boy, upon seeing the passive attitude of our brothers, called to his cows and timidly retired.

During the incident the explorers did not move from their places, following the instructions of the Chief of our Group, and returned to our Gallery Base profoundly preoccupied.

Immediately they began a studious debate of the situation. Their surprise was so great that neither of them thought to capture images of the Earth boy, which might have helped in the analysis of the gestures to interpret his actions.

This event was so grave that they seriously considered the need to make contact with UMMO via telepathy, but after all it was necessary to reconsider that situations such as that, and more grave still, had been foreseen before the arrival at OYAAGAA (Planet Earth).

The grade of uncertainty about what could occur was so indeterminate that they decided to adopt the best means of defense and protection that they could. The entrance to the gallery was closed and camouflaged, and they resolved not to go out of there for 200 UIW. The only contact with the exterior consisted of the air pumps and devices for optical vision and capturing of images, listening devices, and the fields of force.

THIRD DAY ON PLANET EARTH

31 March 1950: On the 31st almost 467 UIW had transpired since the

serious incident we have related, without observing any abnormal signs outside, nor in the vicinity, such as in the hamlet of La Javie (The only one accessible in the optical field of the observation equipment). They saw across a distance of 377 ENMOO a group of cows (nine examples this time) seen in the evening, and the same boy. This time his image was captured in all his fidelity of movements, and all of the details were magnified, his morphology as well as his actions.

In the following 15 UIW, they captured the images of other humans crossing the field of optical observation, but at greater distance than the route followed by the UGEE. The others were two adult men.

Striking a retrospective balance of those experiences, we can look at what happened. Those activities are deduced later as a result of various chats with the people who intervened in the actions. For example, a result unheard of, that the boy, Pierre... (we omit his surname for obvious reasons), who still lives now, would not become estranged by out attentions and run to denounce us to his parents or the authorities in Digne.

This youth, who never has known our true identity, despite our frequent contacts with him (which we continue relating), confessed that his attention was not too much drawn to the strange tight-fitting clothes of those visitors. Two years earlier he had seen three German or Swiss topographers surveying the surroundings, and this second experience did not surprise him too much. He said he took us for what we were; foreigners. His youthful curiosity unsatisfied induced him to wait to meet us again before he would be satisfied, and he did not dare to say anything to his father, fearing with reason that he would be advised to stay away from the unknown strangers. He confessed his disillusionment upon finding the following day (31 March), that the strangers were no longer there. (Remember that on that date our expeditionary brothers did not dare to go out, fearing possible reaction by the Terrestrials.)

During the UIW that preceeded the next sally, they remembered to fabricate with sheets of AEEWWIEE (flexible elastic substance of a gray color) articles that vaguely resembled the dress of those adults whose images they had captured on the 31st of March.

The buttons were imitated with an alloy of aluminum (though in truth they did not know the real function of those buttons).

The neckties they made from a paste of IGUUXOO (of dark color) all in one piece, for the knot and the band seen in the image allowed no more appreciation than its exterior topological shape.

As a handkerchief stuck out of the pocket of one of the subjects seen, they imitated even this detail (not knowing its function) making it overextend a seam in the supposed suit. They used a wrinkled leaf of GIIXAA YUXAA (a synthetic food product usually used in the form of thin sheets).

Now it horrifies us even to think of what could have happened to our brothers walking in the middle of the central street of Digne (dressed that way). However no terrestrial observer had discovered those elastic garments that served as the makings of clothes in common with the grosser ones they tried to imitate. But the rigorous accuracy of our brothers avoided this danger. They tried such only by going out at night or very late in the day.

2 April 1959 (TERRESTRIAL ALIMENTATION SAMPLED)

Nevertheless on 2 April 1950, noting that our presence did not seem to have caused alarm, though still admitting the plausible hypothesis that the Terrestrials had become aware of our presence, they, remaining continuously vigilent, decided to go out in the daylight, having provided themselves with improvised attire in the style of Earth.

This time our brothers carried with them equipment for defense and for recording, and an example of the message prepared with ideographic symbols easy to interpret, which we have mentioned in an earlier communication. They also carried a fragment of the newspaper LE FIGARO encountered a few days earlier...

They decided to go in search of the Terrestrial boy who habitually accompanied the mammals seen days before. The UGEE saluted with his (raised) hand without our brothers understanding well whether it treated of a hostile gesture, a salute or an alarm, and they decided to remain standing and wait the reaction of the adolescent. He approached without fear it seemed and began to ask them something.

This time he seemed more surprised to see them in the stranger new clothes due to their attempt at immitation of those of the Terrestrials, than on the earlier date. It is curious to understand how the UGEE recognized them despite the difference in attire.

The UGEE took out a strange receptacle (that seems to be the term) and offered them its contents after having unrolled another package with food. He commenced an animated chat by signs. One of our brothers, though knowing the risk he ran, in case those alimentos had their proteins (axes of) oriented another way (you already know that the protein molecules can be dextrogiras and levrogiras), dared to accept the viands in order not to awaken more suspicion, advising his brothers to refuse.

This was the first time that one of our brothers had ingested Earth food, which did not seem to harm him (this detail that might seem trivial to you was of transcendental importance) signified confirmation of the hypothesis that established the same molecular orientation for all living beings in this WAAM (cosmos) as opposed to one of those postulates of the decadent hypothesis of parity in orientation, according to which "The probability that on one Planet could emerge molecular organic charges oriented in dextrogiro is statistically the

the same as for levrogiro".

[SPECIAL PUBLISHER'S NOTE- The reference here to dextrogiro (right rotating) and levrogiro (left rotating) charges of basic subatomic quanta is of great importance. The opposite form and charge can apparently be just as real and just as physical as ours, but unapparent to us at our present stage of technology.

The statement here by the Ummites of their discovery that all living physical beings are of the same polarity may be a premature conclusion or only oversimplification for us, to avoid more complex explanations.

The fact that they could detect and perceive our sun and its family of matter from UMMO should have told them that we had to be of the same nature of polarity as they, and that all others detected the same way, in their own original nature perceivable by normal UMMO technology, should seem to confirm this.

They would be unable to perceive anti-matter states without anti-matter instruments, a stage they are closer to than us, because they are already familiar with and use other dimensions of reality and being - even up to ten more, as they say - with different angular relationships to our (and their) natural state.

In a South African UFO contact case the extraterrestrials described (in more than 100 hours of recorded dialogue in their own voices on audio tape - over a 15 year period), paired opposite Universes with axial angles 90° to ours which are tangible to neither our normal universe or their opposite counterpart -- and they described others at 90° to both in the third right angle direction from the other two , and at all angles in between in an infinity of paired opposite universes, which they actually see in a broader sense as a single paired unit. (See UFO CONTACT FROM PLANET KOLDAS by Carl vanVlierden)

In that particular case the extraterrestrials even stated that they have their origin in the opposite reality, in a field of opposite polarity and direction of spin from ours, which is thought to be a balancing counterpart of our own physical reality. A simple analogy, although only that, is the form of a sine wave 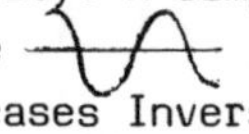, or better yet, one spiral of a helix 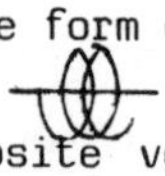. In both cases Inversion produces an identical form of opposite vector -- or anti-matter. It is easy to see from this that a change from right rotation to left rotation consists of nothing more than INVERTING THE QUANTA which can be done in a field. A simple gyroscope demonstrates the resistance to this.

Anthony Seratitis, formerly a laboratory researcher for DOW Chemical Company, conducted extensive expiriments along this line, and actually rewrote the book on atomic physics in his UNIFIED FIELD LAW, which is concurred with by most expert physical sciences professors who have examined the work, but which has not been adopted because, "all physical sciences textbooks would have to be rewritten" as they say, and nobody is willing to undertake such a task. Don Duke of Arizona State University in Phoenix, Arizona, is attempting to prepare video-graphic presentations for a future course on this concept.

In THE NEW SCIENCE by Wilbert B. Smith, a Canadian, this scientist discusses something very similar in his Quadrature Concept of matter and energy, time and space, and describes how the direction of spin of the quanta can be changed to change the polarity and thus our reality of matter.

In the TAO OF PHYSICS, Fritjoff Capra demonstrates the necessary reality of matter of opposite polarity and vector in the Feinman Diagrams, which work both ways in diagrams of the destruction of matter. The formula and diagrams only work out in terms of matter and opposite polarity counterpart, and the diagrams and formula are completely invertible in every case, again verifying the basic postulate that there of necessity is a balancing counterpart to our reality, and that it is of opposite charge and vector.

But this only takes into account <u>our</u> opposite balancing counterpart, and does not consider at all any of the other angular differentials of reality which may in some way also affect the multiple level dimensions of being in our own universe as indicated by the UMMO visitors.

In light of the above, we suggest that the postulate offered here, that all living material beings must be of the same direction and spin -- and therefore akin -- is not complete. -Publisher]

The Terrestrial youth did not seem to be too disturbed by the unfamiliar language of our brothers, as much as they were surprised that the adolescent was not disturbed that those beings came from another planet. (Don't forget that then we believed that all Terrestrials understood all of their own languages whose fragments had already been differentiated by out specialists, from the radioelectric emissions recorded.)

In a word, while the herdboy took our brother expeditionaries as only strangers,... those were convinced that the boy had devined their extraterrestrial identity.

THE BOY ACTS AS LANGUAGE TEACHER

One of our brothers immediately began the task of going about and indicating various objects for the UGEE to pronounce in his language. The youngster soon understood what was desired of him, and very proudly acting as teacher was interpreting in French a rich range of objects and simple verbs.

Our brothers produced the fragment of newspaper in the French language and the youth, with certain difficulty, read whole paragraphs.

One would not figure out the interior rejoicing of our brothers. The gestures of the boy and his words were recorded optically and phonetically without him being aware of it.

Out brothers in the subterranean Gallery followed these incidents faithfully through Gravitational Wave transmitting equipment.

You yourselves can understand the transcendence of this discovery to us, not only to know the significance of some Terrestrial language phonemes (in this case French), but to know the phonetic interpretation of those symbols or letters impressed on the document, though we still did not know their real significance.

On that journey 110 vocables corresponding to objects visible in the field, parts of the human body, and verbs representative of some typical actions such as grasp, eat, drink, get up, and their infinitives, were revealed to us by that young Terrestrial boy.

UMMOAELEWE
Language: Spanish
Date: 26-6-1967

In the preceeding communications we have succinctly related the historical journal of the events that preceeded our first arrival upon your planet, including the arrival of three "OAWOOLEA UEWA" (lenticular structured spacecraft) at a point in the region surrounding Digne (French Basses Alpes).

FIRST MONTHS OF STAY IN FRANCE

We would like, in these next paragraphs, to present an historical synthesis of those first months of our stay in France, up until the UMMOAELEWE Council General of the Planet UMMO, to whom the surprising reports from the expeditionary group were sent, in turn considered the possibility (inconceivable at first) of mixing them with the OEM-II (human beings) of this Planet without being identified. They then decided that our brothers should disperse over the Earth.

For reasons easily explainable, we omit the assistance of some citizens of the French Republic who in those weeks had contact with us. (They suspected us then for well founded reasons without presuming in the least our identity.)

When in the length of this report we omit some date, substituting a reference cypher for the day, we have judged that that date in the hands of some expert, could result in danger on account of some identification that could result in harm to us.

We have also held back from fattening this history with some happenings of negligible anecdotal value and which might constitute important holdbacks in the process of our eventual clandestine assimilation into the Terrestrial Social Network.

This deals with some contacts made with persons and Official Entities (Central and in certain cases Municipal Administrations) of the French State. Always, of course, these contacts were effected using fradulent names and nationality, having been registered in a certain documental manner which we prefer not to mention for obvious reasons.

The Administrative and Technical Services of the French Government at that time had no knowledge of our arrival in French territory. The news filtered through the local press and the sparse rumors among the farmers by the few visual witnesses to our descent, were lost among the barrage of notices in turn of the aparition at all points on the Planet of SOUCOUPES VOLANTES (Flying Saucers) published in the French Press.

The French Government also had at that time other more grave problems to resolve, for example the Bidault Cabinet in those days was confronted with the conflict in the Gas and Electric industries apart from the conflict in Indochina which then absorbed the Gallic specialists.

The French Services of Imformation "Deuxime Bureau" had received, on the other hand, disquieting indications that the Koreans were studying a plan for the invasion of the autonomous territory to the south, and that could aggrevate in unsuspected ways the World Tension of the Planet.

For this reason if the technical services would have brought to the attention of superiors any vague indications that we had inadvertently allowed to filter out through the inexperience of our brothers unknowing then the French language, these would have been discounted.

In effect: when in 1959 we made a secret probe through the official media, to obtain all the documents of the time, that reported anything suspicious concerning our arrival on Planet Earth in the south of the of the country, "We absolutely did not encounter, the least reference to this affair".

ISOLATION IN THE GALLERY AND STUDY OF THE LANGUAGE

We have already explained how that adolescent French cowherd (who still lives), without suspecting our identity, reading various texts of the press, and indicating to us those sounds, offered us the possibility that we had not probed, of being able by this means to translate our verbal expressions to French, and to understand the significance of the characters printed by you. Our brothers decided to isolate themselves for some time in the interior of our subterranean base to assimilate this idiomatic fraction so precariously obtained. Still much of your impressions in the columns of the paper were as a result unintelligible, but French Radiobroadcast and radioelectric emissions were continually captured, which helped us greatly.

It was lamentable that we did not have equipment to translate the images emitted by television. They were also able to detect weak signals, arriving by tropospheric reflection, from other countries, but the reception was made phonetically and naturally was totally inintelligible to our brothers.

ENTRY FOR THE FIRST TIME IN AN EARTH DWELLING

The 24th of April is a historic date for the first expeditionary group of UMMO.

By then we had a very rudimentary scheme of the social structure of the mysterious Planet Earth.

We reestablished contact with the UGEE (French boy) who, though posessing an elemental education, clarified for our brothers the significance of certain vocables, which shed sufficient light on such important aspects as the existence of Autonomous Nations, the use of money and certain terrestrial customs, to make them understandable.

A French waiter gave us copies of the French papers LE MONDE for 22 April and LE FIGARO for 17 April, one day. From them they learned for example that there existed a Stalin, who controlled the Communists, a word filled with mystery for our brothers, which they encountered repeatedly in those texts.

One news item dated 23 April, which appeared in another copy of LA MONDE (later obtained) reported, for example, that one Chiang Kai Shek decided to abandon Hainan, as the Communists occupied the capital Hoihow of that island.

It was impossible to obtain from the youth the least reference to the vocable Chiang, nor if it pertained to a machine, an entity, some social group or an OEMII.

But our brothers had learned something very important. There did not exist on this planet any homogenuity of language and social structure. The OEMII associated in great groups with peculiar traces of cultural morphology and though incredible, it may be possible to present ourselves to one of those groups or nationalities masked under the name of another. It was possible to feign a nonexistent language without arousing suspicion.

On the 24th of April 1950, they planned to enter a dwelling that they saw at two KOAE from the base.

This was the first of the acts of transgression against property committed in the French Department of Basses Alpes, and of some 18 others committed in the rest of France and the Swiss Republic.

In none of them did the victims suffer any injuries, and in a few months all of them were compensated. As soon as they were able to obtain money without robbery, and could falsify the necessary identification documents, and knew the characteristics of some weapons, they decided to terminate such acts which for them were justified.

On the night of 24 April, four of our brothers penetrated a dwelling isolated in a field.

First they recorded the location of the human bodies inside by means of our UULEWUA (small detector spheres that flew at any height, capturing images and sounds).

At 03:00 in the morning, of that day, the workers who were sleeping in a dormitory and a married couple, owners of the dwelling, with their three children, were anesthetized in their sleep.

THINGS TAKEN included: Approximately 70,000 (old) Francs, clothes, identification documents (used to falisfy others similar), two ball-point pens, one hygrometer in the statue of a Nun, several keys, some postage stamps, a package of invoices and paid receipts corresponding to a tractor, various old newspapers, specialized books on the raising of cattle, an explanatory text on the characteristics of a harvester, another manuel for the tractor, a children's encyclopedia, a roll of toilette paper, a small pest fumigator, an alarm clock, two incandescent lamps - in Spain you call them "bombillas" (bulbs), and a cake of soap. They pulled out an electric interruptor switch and the energy contacts, as well as various accessories of the tractor, some tubes of medicine in grease form, an envelope of school grades, six pairs of men's shoes and two pairs for a woman (all that they had), a small bottle of lemon juice, two potatoes, a wall calendar, some scissors and one oil lamp.

Part of the collection of objects was camouflaged at some 400 meters away to be recovered the following night and the rest were carried to the subterranean base.

For eight Earth days our brothers did not go out and continued analyzing those strange utensiles, trying to translate the printed texts and the images obtained of the interior of those rooms.

All that was fascinating. Our brothers examined other strange and isolated habitations, examining the furniture, which they found to be made of a substance which at first they could not identify as of vegetable origin.

TECHNIQUE OF THE OPERATION

With artificial light oriented as necessary through the windows, they observed nothing abnormal happening inside. UURIO-79 the son of ISAA-5, UORI-19 daughter of OBAA-7, ADAA-66 son of ADAA-65 (who died on Earth in 1957) were that night examining for the first time in our history a Terrestrial dwelling.

The operation was controlled by ODDIOA-1 son of ISAAO-132.

[NOTE- Yes, you have detected what seems to be a mistake in the name identification of the Ummites, but you must remember that these communications are dictated verbally by extraterrestrials with a prosthesis larynx in their throat, to a public scribe who then transcribes the dictation with a typewriter onto typed sheets which are then mechanically copied and held for the dictator of the original to check and approve the translated work, after which the pages are originally sealed with the finger seal of UMMO and returned to the copyist to mail. More than one copyist was used, allowing for slight differences in translating the unusual phoneticization of the strange names. But the Ummites were quite careful in trying to avoid this. Still there was a foreign accent besides everything else to contend with, and these were among the earlier communications. Also, these various communications were sent to different people, and were only collected together at a later time. We feel that the minor discrepancies that do exist tend, under the true circumstances described, more to support the actual validity than to detract from it. -Publisher]

In one big bed slept two terrestrials under the effects of the anesthetic gas. Our brothers did not identify the sex at first, though they knew that on Earth the YII let their hair grow long. They removed the sheets after cutting a small fragment from them.

Both bodies were partly nude, and they collected perspiration from the armpits and the lower abdomen. They also collected specimens of hair from the head, arms, pubis, and legs, and eyelashes, as well as samples of nasal mucous and vulvar secretion.

Apart from the objects removed, they perforated many of the furniture and furnishing items, rugs and covering materials, to obtain quantified samples that were coded by function and matched with the images recorded (by a kind of tridimensional photography obtained at the same time.

It was not possible to get samples of saliva from none of the terrestrials at that time. In one jacket taken, they found also a lighter and cigarettes. They also took time to extract sample specimens from a cow found in a structure nearby.

They also had to first anesthetize the two dogs that began to raise a great "alarm".

ANALYSIS OF OBJECTS TAKEN

Though it might seem strange, the rendering of effective analysis, due to the great variety of objects obtained, and the rich range of small specimens gathered, though the chemical composition of same was well determined with great exactitude, little light was shed on the function or use of many of the objects.

For example, it was impossible to determine for what use could serve those fractions of congealed esters (soap). All the inductive methods to find out the utility of the "Quinque" (oil lamp) failed also.

Still it was most surprising to determine on one hand, that the small Electric Energy motor of the clock was impelled by alternate tension and to observe how it registered on its face the graduated function of the energy; but without coming to any conclusion that what it signified was a measure of time, or other periodic magnitude.

ALARM: What intrigued us for many UIW was the function of the old alarm clock. At first it was feared that our brothers could be detected at a distance by the sound of the alarm if somebody had a sound detector. Its mechanical characteristics were rapidly analyzed. Due to the fault of its loud sound they were seriously doubting its utility as a meter of the magnitude of time.

LIGHTBULBS: They committed a grave error in carefully perforating the glass of the bulbs to extract a specimen of the filiament; and this considerably retarded the specification of its function. The filiaments oxidized rapidly upon being submitted to increasing electrical tension melting them completely.

CIGARETTES: The cigarettes were identified by means of other images of OEMII recorded earlier. Remember that they were interpreted as special devices to produce a gas aiding the respiration of the terrestrials. Our brothers felt defrauded upon not encountering in their interior the complicated mechanisms they expected. The enigma was accentuated several degrees.

THE MONEY: But without doubt the importance of the unforeseen finding of money in banknotes and the clothes and shoes, considerably superceeded the rest of those objects.

We understood the grave distress caused to that peaceful French family, and that it could provoke in you an act of severe reproach, for which we later secretly indemnified them with increases. Also our brothers felt worried about the immediate consequences of the action. They prohibited all from going out, and from afar observed the visual field of the surroundings, adopting all measures of possible defense.

But except for agitation observed on the farm, and the goings and comings from the small village of some terrestrials, nothing abnormal occured. And that same night they were able to recover part of the cache hidden in the vicinity.

UMMOAELEWE
Language: Spanish
Date:

REASONS THAT JUSTIFIED OUR CLANDESTINE PRESENCE

We knew that if you had reached a certain grade of civilization you would have detected our presence instantly.

But the case in which this presumption did not hold (undetected in this case), imposed the criteria of not ostensibly manifesting our presence. This followed for obvious reasons: If we wanted to study a Civilization in all its purity, we would not want our presence to provoke disturbances in society, or abnormal dynamism in the technical measures of detection, interception and defense, nor serious perterbations in the means of communications relating to the information Net. A Social Network thus deformed or perturbed by the presence of beings strange to it, could not be studied in all its purity.

You could find an analogy in a specialist in bacteriology who desired, for example, to study a Mass of Spirochetes, would not allow to occur a disturbance of the culture with new germs that would alter the biological processes of the first. If such were the case, in the field of his microscope, elemental forms of conduct of those microorganisms would be abnormal. That and no other reason is the cause of our presence before you being clandestine.

Some of those persons with whom we maintain contact, and above all those of Northamerican and Australian nationality ask us repeatedly and insistently why we do not allow you to know us officially.

It is curiously evident that among them we find Earth men who for their erudition and scientific stature should reason for themselves the conditions which oblige us to inhibit ourselves. We had believed for some time that you would be more realistic.

This tells us that the mass humanity of Earth, little endowed with intelectual faculties, maintains the stupid hypothesis that we, as well as other (presumed Galactic visitors) must present ourselves with one of our UEWA OEMM (called by you Flying Discs) in the middle of a great plaza of New York, dressed in silver suits and carrying a ray pistol, as in your Science Fiction novels.

As said, we judge such desires a popular absurdity. Your embryonic and primitive reasoning seems to be this: If these beings come from another star, why don't they allow us to know them and put on a demonstration for us?

Any expert in Earth philosophy would call such sophism "The Principle of Petition".

Let there be no doubt that we, and we presume that there are no other visitors that could be among you, "have absolutely no interest that the Terrestrial Social Network has proof of our presence".

From the beginning, as we have said, our brothers adopted precautions to pass totally unrecognized, according to which we absorbed from your culture and knowledge the psychological laws of the terrestrial social network from which we learned that the dosified revelation of our presence to a few people did not result in great danger because the rest of your society reacted with incredulity and disbelief which in effect was successful. Do you believe that if this were not the case we would risk putting ourselves in contact with You?

We could cite the case of three professional publicists, with whom we have maintained communications, who have published our story (in three periodicals or magazines, of Poland, Spain and Canada), logically adopting a natural sceptical posture as expected by us.

Such a position would be modified if we ostentatiously presented ourselves, carrying proofs of our identity, before the Terrestrial Press and Government or International Technical Organs. We have absolutely no thought of adopting such a posture FOR NOW.

In this manner we have successfully covered two objectives: Direct contact with a group of terrestrial inhabitants, for the interchange of data with respect to our mutual Civilizations; Avoiding disturbance to the rest of the Terrestrial Society, which remains on the frontier of a situation they consider legendary for its insufficiency of proof.

GOVERNMENTS KNOW OF OUR PRESENCE ON EARTH

Unfortunately we have not been able to achieve another objective, to pass unperceived before the State Technical Organizations of the United States, France, England, and the Soviet Union, and we suspect with good reason those of Italy, Germany, and the Republic of Argentina are aware of our presence as well, and show worried reservations though we have expressed the lack of foundation for their fears.

With respect to this, knowledge of the situation could provoke reactions of anxiety and panic in the civil population, but the chanceries of the governments can be sure, at least with respect to our brothers from UMMO, we will not allow ourselves to be known FOR NOW.

The risk that exists through those few scientists and writers with whom we are in contact is "zero", except for a few persons of high critically observant spirit known among the families and friends of our correspondents.

The rest, saturated with prejudices, narrow mental vistas, or conscious of the risk of fraud that could be involved in our revelations, maintain a neutral posture.

ADVICE TO THE GROUP OF UMMO ENTHUSIASTS

For that we exhort you not to be excessively jealous of sharing, among the persons of your reduced circle, the reality of our actual existence. With that, not only can you judge whether illusions or mental disturbances, but whether your own professional stability could be damaged.

To those who, without previous analytical examination of these communications, demonstrate an attitude of scepticism, believing themselves thus very intelligent, proceed to inquire their reasons without more commentary.

(Finger Seal)

(End of Communication)

Ummites spent first 6 months at an excavated base north of Digne, near Cheval Blanc Peak, at a site overlooking the Bleone River. UMMO team was 6 ETs. ▼ 2940

REPORT ON THE BIOGENETIC BASES

BIOGENETIC BASES OF THOSE BEINGS WHO POPULATE THE COSMOS

In the year 1969 I made a trip to Paris, carrying with me a voluminous mass of information on UMMO, which I delivered to my good friend Rene Fouere, Secretary General of GEPA (not to be confused here with GEPAN) (1) and director of the French publication PHENOMENES SPATIAUX. Fouere distributed this information among a team of scientific analysts of said publication, among which were "polytechnicians" and members of CNRS (Conseil National de la Recherche Scientifique), the highest scientific organization of France.

Among those reports which I had carried with me was one titled "Las bases biogeneticas de los seres que pueblan el WAAM (the Cosmos)". Fouere gave it to an anthropologist of the CNRS (later known to be Dr. J.M. Dutuit) to read, which left him stupified, coming to mention the word "genius" to characterize it. On the other hand I had delivered copies of the same report to other scientists, Spanish and foreign as well. Dr. Luis Cornudella, a Barcelonan, expressed an opinion much to the contrary, which we will review at the end of this section.

This most interesting document was received by the Senorita Alicia Araujo, prematurely deceased shortly after my initiating a relationship by correspondence with her. I consider it of enormous documental importance to reproduce here some of the letters that passed between us. The imperative circumstances at the time have now passed and gone into history, as unfortunately has Alicia Araujo. And so nothing now impedes me from citing her name. In the deepest part of my heart I know that our dear and unforgettable friend would approve.

Madrid, 16 January of 1968

Sr. D. Antonio Ribera Jorda
Roca y Batlle, 5, izda.
Barcelona VI

Distinguished Sr. Ribera:

I am sincerely pleased to receive your letter of 9 January, though I have not had the pleasure of knowing you personally. I have seen your name frequently on articles and in publications concerning the UFOs -- in Spain as well as foreign--, and in Spanish versions of Science Fic-

(1) GEPA is the acronym for Groupement d'Etude de Phenomenes Aeriens. GEPAN, however, is the Groupement pour l'Etude des Phenomenes Aerospatiaux Non-identifies, created on May 1977 within CNES (Centre National d'Etudes Spatiales) of Toulouse, being directed successively by Claude Poher, Alain Esterle and Dr. Velasco. (Equivalent to U.S. NASA)

tion novels published by EDHASA, and in books like LOS HUMANOIDES, which I have aquired recently.

I know of your solid reputation as a serious man and an objective investigator in this fascinating field that supposes the presence or presumed reality of those extraterrestrials, not only in our skies, but also on our Earth, where it is quite possible -- which I believe now -- to hide among us.

I don't know -- though I suppose it -- what has been the channel by which you have been informed that I have received some communications concerning biology of the Cosmos from some supposed extraterrestrials. But I must affirm to you effectively, that it is true that I have received such communications, with the indication that it would treat of transcendent revelations for terrestrial scientists, and that I should give them to the knowledge of biologists of Earth.

Pertaining to a panel of persons interested in those visitors from space (1) that could meet weekly for some time, to receive these communications and place their contents at the disposition of those persons who would have interest in them, who could be given photocopies and some of them such as students of universities who could present them to their teachers and professors; but the diffusion that these reports would get by this means is in all lights insufficient, and I have always had the desire to be able to bring to the knowledge of those who for their knowledge of the material could valorate it in a proper manner. (I was given a perfect example of the difficulties that entailed, because in the name of what and of whom could I present myself before biologists and scientists, if I did not know them previously, to tell them that they should examine some communications, whose origin could not be absolutely established for them?) Moreover, my interest in biology, though real, is no more than the scale of an observer who has tried to inform himself in this business with books and articles whose contents were popularly understandable, at least for the most part. I believe, for the moment, that if I do not know directly of one of these specialists in this subject, the more convenient would be that serious investigators of the question of extraterrestrial could be interested in this matter and try to study it without prejudgements and in a critical and objective manner. I believe I remember that in one of your last books French investigator Aime Michel, referring to the supposed "contacts" with extraterrestrials, said "Why don't these supposed extraterrestrials give us objective proofs to confirm what they say?" Well in this case it seems that they have given it, though it is necessary to come to complete sureness -- if this is possible -- of which it is.

(1) Refers to the group that met in the Cafe Leon, near Madrid, with Professor Fernando Sesma Manzano, another UMMO contactee.

Now, Sr. Ribera, referring to the last paragraph of your cited letter, let us firm up those things a little.

1. With pleasure, I will send you a photocopy of all the communications that I have received in my name (There are many more communications addressed to other members of the group to which I referred before, but naturally I can not send those).

2. I ask that, in principle, you keep this confidential and not mention my name; nevertheless you can speak of it with your companions at the center including, if one has studied this affair, coming to a conclusion that there are many probabilities (to speak of a certainty is impossible) from which these communications could come, including from extraterrestrials. You may speak of this affair with your colleagues, and I ask that you keep me informed of your activities with respect to this.

In view of the conclusion to which you will come we can try to decide what order of steps to take to disseminate the information received among the pertinent persons.

This, in which you refer to those communications on biology which I myself have received. But these communications form a part of a more general affair. I believe you have, though in brief form, an idea of some of the circumstances that have taken place with respect to this affair. I can tell you that I am constrained to accept, as almost certain, that these mysterious communicators are extraterrestrials, as they announced to me, as well as other persons of the group, the arrival (in advance), the arrival of three flying discs coming from their planet to Earth, one of them actually to Madrid (in the photocopy that I will send you in a few days you will see this rarity). The disc was seen, within the zone and on the date specified, by hundreds of witnesses on the outskirts of Madrid (San Jose de Valderas, Boadilla del Monte, etc.). The Spanish Press gave extensive coverage to this notice in the newspapers of 2 June 1967, accompanied by two photographs of the disc, in one of which you could see the symbol of their planet, which is the same as appears on the communications, as you can also see, though not as clearly in the photocopies. I believe that the interest in this case is greater than that of the majority of the cases cited in cited in THE HUMANOIDS.

As you can see, they have given sufficient evidence in all this affair to merit a detailed study. I ask you to tell me, what are your conclusions, and with them, we can think of what to do.

Briefly, I am sending you by certified mail the photocopies of the communications; accepting your offer to reimburse the expense.

I await with great interest your comments on this affair, and happily take this opportunity to salute you affectionately.

/s/ Alicia Araujo

Alicia Araujo
Hermosillo, 29
Madrid - 1

Madrid, 23 February 1968

Sr. D. Antonio Ribera Jorda
Roca Y Batlle, 5 Isq.
Barcelona VI

Distinguished Sr. Ribera:

I hope you have received the photocopies of the communications that I sent you on the biology of the cosmos. I want to call your attention to possible confirmation of the theories expressed in those communications in the latest issue of Planeta magazine, to which I subscribe, Aime Michel made a study of a book by Koestler, recently published, THE GHOST IN THE MACHINE, in which they studied the problems of evolution, neodarwinism, etc.; and much of the questions posed by the author of the book, and which Michel analized, were precisely answered in these communications. The article had attracted my attention and I wanted to bring it to your knowledge because I believe that you may also be interested.

The cost of the photocopies that I sent to you came to 250 pesatas; you can send me this amount at your complete convenience and when it is opportune.

Also I am going to send you, for I consider that it would interest you, a photocopy of a letter -- that has no signature -- which was sent to me by him who says he wasthe stenographer for those gentlemen of UMMO at the time that they were dictating communications to those correspondents who recieved them in Spanish. The letter is curious and could be one more fact for you. Naturally the cost for these photocopies will be at my expense since you did not ask for them. I hope they will be of some help.

I would like to receive your comments on the impressions that you have concerning this enigmatic affair. Don't you think you could inform Aime Michel of all of this, since he also is interested in the subject of biology? Nor can I say that for my part there would be no inconvenience. My desire is that these communications come to the knowledge of serious persons who could study and evaluate them.

I salute you very affectionately.

/s/ Alicia Araujo

Alicia Araujo
Hermosillo, 29
Madrid - 1

Madrid, 10 April 1968

Sr. D. Antonio Ribera
Director de HORIZONTE
Plaza & Janes
Enrique Granados, 86-88
Barcelona - 8

My Esteemed Friend:

Many thanks for your letter of 26 March, which arrived promptly, despite the fact that the letter indicated Hermosillo, 24 instead of Hermosillo 29.

I am very sorry for the painful steps that have passed for you in the death of your mother, and I desire to express my great desires to be able to console you in this test. Sometimes the most lonely hours are also the richest in spiritual experiences.

I am happy that you and your collaborators -- above all Farriols, of whom I have an excellent impression of his intelligence, spirit of organization and enthusiasm -- is studying the UMMO case. I also am of the opinion, like you, that this study has to be, of necessity, the work of a team, and I am disposed to offer my colaboration in whatever way may be possible. I believe that your meeting with Aime Michel could be highly interesting, and I would very much like to know the impression of this gentleman after hearing all that you can tell him about this fascinating affair.

Now I am going to answer the part of your letter that I have considered, and am considering still, carefully and will not hide what has passed in various vaccilations and worries, trying to see clearly what should be our conduct that we should follow with respect to the UMMO affair. My action is distinct from that of some other members of the group, which I consider, though I am not hiding what could be equivocation, that the difusion of this affair, at a serious and objective level, without sensational publicity, is not only legitimate but desirable, and does not contradict in essence the instructions that we have received from them. I am basing this on various actions, one of which is that they have told me repeatedly -- by telephone, in the letter announcing the dispatch of the report on biogenetics, and in that same communication -- which said to "share this knowledge with my bothers" (that was their habitual form of addressing us in reference to terrestrials), and in another place to "those terrestrial biologists". It has been for me, at least, a satisfaction and a relief to know that you have delivered those communica-

tions to Catalonian biologists who can render professional judgement of them, completing your desire and giving me the satisfaction of having transmitted through you something that could have great scientific interest and value. Though in the first paragraph I said that my attitude was different from some other members of the group, I believe that up to here, and while the dissemination of these communications remains among scientists and specialists, all the members of the group are in agreement in that the disemination is desirable. But let us go now to the part in which the opinions divide us, and this is precisely with respect to the publication that you think you must do. Nothing has impeded your publication of the case of the disc at San Jose de Valderas, and all concur in that, because it already is public knowledge, of which there are hundreds of witnesses and it had been photographed. But that on which we do not all agree, who have in a more or less direct manner participated in the UMMO experience, is the publication of the communications received, relating them to this sighting and indicating their origin. My opinion is that if we do not signify this relationship, the case of San Jose de Valderas is left to one case, no more than "any other case", when the arrival of the disc was the culmination of a whole process and constituted a test that is in my judgement, almost absolutely confirms all the rest of this affair.

It is true that in the length of time that this experience has now lasted, as said, from the first telephone call to Sesma to the announcement of the arrival of the ship, they have made a number of reccomendations to us for silence and discretion; but it is my opinion, as I say, my personal interpretation of these things, that the affair must be considered altogether, and that for them not only have they taken into account these recommendations, but also the recommendation that we should disseminate the reports received -- at least to some of those --; also must be taken into account that they asked for silence about the arrival of the ships to Earth, but only until after they had made the landing; and also, and this I believe to be important, that when the ship arrived at San Jose de Valderas, they exhibited it fully, and seemed to take special care that we would see the symbol of UMMO. For all this, as I said, my opinion is that we should give this affair a serious and objective diffusion, for which you are authorized to use in your publication all or part of the material on biogenetics that they sent me, in accord with your own criteria. The vaccilations and doubts that I referred to before are because I am conscious, as I said, of my actions, taken after my thinking this over seriously, cannot be based on more than the interpretation of some actions which could be mistaken; but if I believe that the probabilities of being correct are say 75%, I must act on them and not take the easy and a little cowardly way of restraining myself in this affair. Naturally, those persons who think they should maintain silence, and have a good motive, would do well to maintain it; as I say, it is a question of interpretation, and there are no final instructions on this affair.

All I ask is that upon publishing the communications -- whether all or partially -- cite the text exactly and in case you have any commentary, leave in context that on which you are commenting, and separate the comments from the original text. Whenever the graphics are reproduced, they must be authentic photographs (or photocopies), and not sketches of any kind. All this they have indicated among the recommendations they have made. Also they prohibited oral declarations to reporters, and employees of radio and television, on the business of the extraterrestrials (Sesma can personally make such declarations and I suppose that we can too). I believe that they are trying to avoid in this manner, any third party interpretation or sensationalism which could discredit this affair.

With respect to me, I ask that you cite only my initials, though you can say, naturally, that I exist and that you know me.; I desire no publicity; and please, do not indicate that I work in the Embassy of the United States. (In the recording I made with Farriols, as I described the announcement that we had received of the arrival of the ship at San Jose de Valderas, I made allusion to my place of work). This fact, which on the other hand is of no importance to the investigation and study of the case which interests us, I would like to leave out.

However the document which we signed on the 30th of May, and which is in the hands of Sesma, I don't believe is possible for me to get back. Permit me that in this, and in all this affair in general, I can make a suggestion that surely will surprise you; naturally, it is no more than a suggestion but perhaps after you consider it you may think that it will serve. Sesma has not only this document announcing the arrival on Earth of three spaceships coming from UMMO, but an incredible number of communications, and has spoken many times with the communicators from UMMO. Apart from the differences that no doubt exist between two mentalities as distinct as those of Sesma and yourself -- and I would include between the majority of people and Sesma -- He is, or could be, an available man and would not have to have a closed attitude (but the contrary). And if you wrote to him...? You would not have to be in accord on the points of view in which you differ; I also differ with him on a large part in question, above all with respect to UMMO, but I sincerely appreciate and believe that I know him well. He is much more frank and more noble than the majority of the people who met with us in the Ballena Alegre. He is not resentful, and the other day he said publicly that the objective investigators and scientists such as yourself and Michel, are also necessary. But as I said, this is only a suggestion that I make in believing that I know Sesma, and guided by the desire for true colloboration in this affair.

A few days ago I received a letter from Farriols, sending me a copy of that of yourself of 26 March which, as I said at the beginning of this letter I had already received. Today I received a second letter delivering the pages that he sent and sending me copies of the transparencies. Please thank him in my name. I will answer them soon; without much delay I believe, I think I am much behind in my work. As I said, I am pleased to collaborate with you in this affair, and I am at your disposition to help you in all that may be possible. I agree with what Farriols says and, effectively, a serious investigator is morally obligated to not overlook facts just because they may seem to be rare. Many thanks also for the enlargement of the UMMO symbol that you sent me. The photographs are very well made and presented with the care characteristic of Farriols.

I am very happy to think that you will come to Madrid; I did not know when I would have the pleasure of knowing you personally, and of having the opportunity to talk with Farriols and you on all of this fascinating affair.

An affectionate salute of

/s/ Alicia Araujo

Srta. Alicia Araujo
Jorge Juan, 85
Madrid - 9

My Dear Friend:

Concerning my recent trip to Paris to meet with Pauwels, Bergier and other members of the PLANETE team, I visited also with my good friend Rene Fouere, Secretary General of GEPA, and director of the magazine "Phenomenes Spatiaux". In the course of the two days that I spent with him, we spoke much about the UMMO affair and I left him a good quantity of xerocopies of the communications, among them that received by you, concerning the Biogenetic Bases. Two days before my arrival, Fouere had received from West Berlin, a dispatch from "U" consisting of five microfilms, three of them with a text of "descriptions" in French, and the other two with ideograms, plainly of a lenticular spaceship "identical" to that of Valderas, and one photograph of the same, in flight.

Fouere showed enormous interest in the question, as well as Paul Misraki, with whom I also had a meeting. Fouere told me that he was going to pass all the material that I had left to the team of scientific consultants of GEPA, among whom were scholars with great knowledge; various members of CNRS, "polytechnicians" and astronomers of high reputation. All of them would prefer to remain anonymous, except the physicist and astronomer Michael Trouble. which is understandable due to the positions they hold.

Well, after a couple of days, I began to receive the first indications of results, and as it was one of them aluded to your work, my dear friend, which I received and am going to transcribe:

[Note- The letter was quoted in its original French and then translated into Spanish. We are providing only an English translation here in this text. -Publisher]

"You are no doubt impatient to know the opinion of the specialists concerning those papers that you left with me, and of which I have made many pages of photocopies. I sent the text on space to a well lnown physicist but he desires to remain anonymous. It would be difficult to find one better qualified. Unfortunately he has much difficulty reading in Spanish, and has not or at least had not finished the reading, when he telephoned me to tell me in substance: 'I believe this treats of a fraud, but it is magnificently done and by someone who has admirable knowledge of modern physics. Not only do they express themselves as terrestrials but, also, in the language of the western European physicists.' I observed to him that if they were intelligent extraterrestrials, it would be natural that they would elect to speak the language of those to whom they spoke.

"One anthropologist, 'Head of Research' at the CNRS, was particularly interested — the physicist also, in his part, but this last still had not read — the text on the biogenetic bases of the beings that live in the cosmos. He received it with a less favorable impression, because the sketches of the ramifications (branching diagram) shown on page 23 of the text sent by Alicia Arujo seemed to him to be very elementary. But with the passing of two days, after having commenced to read the text, he telephoned me to tell me in essence, 'If it is a farce — which I doubt more and more — it is genious. I find this text fascinating and ingenious. Encompassing one simple idea, so simple that what is surprising is that nobody has thought of it, and, nevertheless, and because I know, this is not found in any work on biology.'

"He added that, in certain points, he felt disturbed by the document, which, in biology, demands some knowledge of physics, which he did not posess.

"He told me that he was translating the text and preparing a French version typewritten...

"For his part, an electronics engineer has begun to make a French translation of the text on space.

"This is What it Is, a provisional title"

I consider these first results that have come from the collaborators of Fouere most interesting. One has to consider that the team of GEPA is perhaps one of the best qualified scientifically of any available in Europe — and perhaps the world — and their opinion is most valuable. The tone of humility that accompanied the commentaries of the anthropologist contrasted with the sufficiency, radiated in the pedantry of some Spanish doctors and biologists who had examined the same documents. But this is not all.

For my part I have made some surprising discoveries that I will expose: In FLYING SAUCER REVIEW for July/August of this year (1967), there appears on page 32, the photo of a UFO, taken over New Zealand, which is "identical" to that of Valderas, and by extension, those of UMMO. On page 29 of the same review they describe the casual encounter of a Maori with three beings, two men and one woman, who without doubt are members of the expeditionary team of THEM on Earth.

In Note No. 4 to the article by John Keel, "The Glendale Contact Claim" (BEYOND CONDON, Special Number of FSR, page 64), they mention telephone calls, made with a nasal tone and which pronounced the words slowly and with difficulty, received in the United States in 1966. Their Northamerican Net? The authors of these mysterious calls, which, I repeat, embraced all of the States of the Union, were identified as extraterrestrials.

One last detail (which I had omitted): In the letter received by

Fouere from Berlin, his address was written thus: 69, rue de la Tombe-Issoire — 7eme Droit - Paris XIVeme, despite the fact that the magazine and his personal cards, DO NOT MENTION the floor nor the door (7eme Droit), where Fouere lives, which only is known by him, his wife and his most intimate friends. What do you think?

And now a request: Would you take the kindness, my dear friend, to send a copy of the book of Sesma on UMMO to Fouere? I know you have mentioned it as a precious source of information, and he does urgently want to acquire it. No need to say he will refund the cost by check. Thanks in advance.

(Don't put 7eme Droit on the shipment, or he will come to be suspicious of you!)

I have no objection, but on the contrary, if you want to communicate this to our friends in this: Villagrasa, Garrido, Pena, etc., to whom I pray good health on the part of myself and Farriols.

Receive a very cordial salute from your good friend

/s/ Antonio Ribera

PS: Some days ago I recieved a text from THEM (Nuestro concepto de WOA), most profound, posted in Madrid, in Substation No. 3. I will send you a xerocopy.

Vale.

UMMOAELEWE
ALICIA ARAUJO
MADRID
Date: 7-3-67

You will receive before 12 days, a communication in which we shall reveal to you the biogenetic bases that regulate the internal mutations generated by the different "PHYLUM" or branches of living beings, like the progressive phases of neuroencephalization of OEMII (men).

We consider this report of transcendent gravity for you. Give this to the knowledge of your brothers. Without doubt they will aid you in the investigations of terrestrial biophysics.

[Note- That terse message was the advance warning of one of the most profound of the communications for its time in 1967. The message took more than 12 days to prepare however, and was finally dated 3 April 1967, taking 27 days to prepare to the satisfaction of the visitors from Planet UMMO. This is one of the documents carried by Ribera to his meetings in France, and the one most frequently commented upon by his contacts after they had studied its contents. -Publisher]

UMMOAELEWE
Language: Spanish
No. of Copies: 1
Date: 3-4-67
ALICIA ARAUJO
MADRID

THE BIOGENETIC BASES OF THE LIVING BEINGS THAT POPULATE THE WAAM (COSMOS)

To this moment certain men of the Earth have interrogated us concerning the political ramifications of our social structure. Does it have the characteristics of a democratic State of the right? Is it a Social State of the right? Does it have a peculiar socialist structure? Does it have the classical features of a liberal society, or on the contrary a rigid path recalling the totalitarianism of Germany under Hitler, the Soviet Union of Stalin, the Spain of General Franco or the Dominican Republic under Trujillo? Could it be similar to the ancient Theocratic State of Tibet, in the case of UMMO being ruled by four OEMII; does that induce one to think of it as a peculiar form of Policratic Oligarchy?

In another order of ideas, the interrogators are oriented toward the level of intelligence reached on our OYAA (cold star), as to say, the grade of development that approaches our neuroencephalogy in the actual evolutionary phase of development of our Social Network.

Both series of questions could at first sight seem interrelated. But an objective and systematic analysis not only throws sufficient light on their mutual interedependence, but for its correct interpretation we must look at previous probing of the root truths of the sociopolitical, psychosocial, and encephalogical developments of the humanity of UMMO. These roots are neither more nor less than the biogenetic bases of the evolution of all the living beings in our WAAM (Universe). For that, before penetrating such profound themes as our political organization, or an analysis of the intellectual capacity that begins to develop in the embryo of the OEMII in its seat of the maternal uterus, we must return to a global vision (though presented at a lay level) of the mechanisms that regulate evolution.

In the succeeding paragraphs we shall inform you concerning a series of transcendental questions and judgements. In some cases we will remind you of concepts almost familiar today to biophysicists of Earth, such as the nuclear structure of the chromosomes, genetic mutations and the basis of the genetic code or of life itself. But along with these concepts that all of you though not specialized in biology must know, we are going to present a series of transcendental revelations to you, of the existence of which the biochemists of Earth are ignorant. This will serve to explain some gaps that have made certain mechanisms of evolution incomprehensible (for example the internal mutations that originate a perfection of the somatic structure instead of provoking degeneration or regression of the living being). We judge these revelations that we are going to make of such importance, that we invite you to inform your brother biologists of Earth of them. These paragraphs can serve to orient the planning of your investigations in search of the BAAYIODIXAA (most important factor which we will soon explain).

Before establishing these biogenetic basics, you should ask yourselves one final question:

Would it be feasible that the national constitutions of Earth be modified to imitate in structure the form of government of UMMO, the basic society of our humanity, our customs, our form of life, our industrialization and various factors that characterize the species of OEMII of UMMO?

Our objective and perfectly analyzed answer is this: Roundly NOT NOW. Furthermore, it is not necessary for us to clarify this because any intelligent terrestrial is capable of coming to the same conclusion.

The question, on the other hand, would be as naive as suggesting the possibility that a child of little age chronologically could project a teleguided missile.

This affirmation could bother the sensibilities and self-love of the terrestrials. It would seem as if the brothers coming from UMMO have a disrespectful concept of the homo sapiens of Planet OYAGAA (Earth). It would seem as if the OEMII of UMMO judge you as simple UUGEEYIE (children) compared to them.

But this trait of susceptibility is neither reasonable nor justified because our attitude toward you is in no way disrespective, but always impregnated with a profound respect taking into account that you have arrived at a phase in the process of evolution less advanced in time than ours.

When we refer to the psychic plenitude of an OEMII (individual man) it is to say the state that you call the adult period, you should not forget that we refer to the frame of reference for a planetary macrogroup. This treats of a relative reference. The adult posesses a psychism undoubtedly distinct from the UUGEEYIE or adolescent of the group. Undoubtedly the primary reactions of a mature panther would be different from that of her cub, but do not forget that the actual terrestrial man, as well as the OEMII (man) of UMMO, are beings in a continuous process of evolution. The physical and historical frames of reference lived on UMMO and on Earth are very different. This is natural if you take into account that the Geological Medium, atmospheric, radioactive, gravitational, magnetoelectrostatic and chemical present on UMMO is sometimes notably different with respect to that of this planet of yours.

Don't forget that one major atmospheric protection for example, has liberated us from the degrading action of exterior mutations provoked by the cosmic radiation. The grade of degeneration of some phylum has been less, and racial variations almost nonexistent.

All of these factors imprint certain characteristic peculiarities on each planetary social macrogroup, because the ecological medium was distinct though the somatic structure of the humanity is ultimately similar on all those planets inhabited by rational beings.

But there is still the period between the hominization of anthropoid precursor on our UMMO and the present epoca which is much greater than for the similar period for Earth. In these conditions you must not overlook the fact that our grade of civilization was more advanced than that of Earth.

You know that the organisms are developing progressively thanks to a series of factors in part known by yourselves. The terrestrial biologists attribute these evolutionary changes, capable of transforming an anthropoid to a man, to exterior radiations and natural selection. All mutation of a gene must later give place to a structural change in the organism.

But this is an incomplete truth and clouded by erroneous elements. We have discovered the biogenetic laws and the real factors that regulate the evolution of life in the WAAM.

PAY CLOSE ATTENTION.

All of you know that animal and vegetable tissues are formed of millions of cells. Employing the terminology of Earth remember that in these cells are differentiated four elements or important parts.

A complete mass called PROTOPLASM

A central mass called NUCLEUS

A membrane that surrounds the cell

A membrane that surrounds the NUCLEUS

A didactical model of a cell in developed size is found in a bird's egg. It clearly represents the PROTOPLASM, its yolk or NUCLEUS with its membrane and the cellular membrane is represented by the shell.

This model nevertheless is very primitive since for example, the cellular membrane is much more complicated with the rigid enveloping shell as cited.

All of you have studied that in the midst of the cellular nucleus are found some filiamentary structures called CHROMOSOMES. These filiamentary complexes are of great importance since they enclose part of the mystery of life, a Mystery unveiled since long ago for us.

In effect: You know that each chromosomic fibre is carrier of certain modular capacities of storing the CHARACTERISTICS OF INHERITANCE which we call IGOOA ENMEE and you GENES.

A simple simile for those uninitiated in biophysics could be to compare the XAAXADOO (chromosomes) with a strip of perforated paper on which is punched a secret message. Each sequence of orifices or perforations symbolize one letter. The complete strip perforated in this code represents the complete text of this message.

Only that the message carried in the XAAXADO (chromosome) is no other than the instructions for the fetus, contained in the matrix, posessing certain traits which characterize its other brothers. The chromosome dictates the order by which the living being, carrier of same, differentiates between a bird and a reptile.

Each IGOOA or gene represents one definite characteristic: the color blue for the iris of the eye, the form of the erect intestine or the black pigmentation of the hair of a terrestrial Hottentot.

Undoubtedly if a strange agent, a shot for example, interferred with our strip of paper, perforating a new hole, one of its letters could be altered. Perhaps all of the sense of the message could be changed. Also a beam of radiations (rapid neutron X-Rays, electrons, etc.) acting on the chromosome could alter it to the point that the new child of this living being would emerge with brown eyes, or perhaps radically converted.

The specialists of Earth know all this, and know the intimate structure of the genetic code, since long ago much more complex than that of the simple simile of the perforated strip with a message.

Before proceeding ahead, you should precisely review the internal structure of the XAAXADOO (chromosomes). We attach, in case you do not find an appropriate text analyzing these important filiaments, an Appendix 1, where we briefly develop this theme. The conclusions of terrestrial biologists concerning the chromosomes, does not differ excessively with the concept that since many XEE (unit of time equivalent to the movement of UMMO around our hot star, IUMMA) we have had the XAAXADOO, except in that which concerns the proteic chains and their function in the chromosome, where you have committed some errors in your hypothesis.

TEXT COMMENTARY AND READ APPENDIX 1

No dose of radiation, no matter how insignificant it might be, can avoid producing effects and presents a grade of probability in the provocation of a MUTATION, many times lethal, for which we cannot understand the inconscience of certain terrestrial gynecologists that subject pregnant women to the processes of radioscopy or radiography without the most elaborate precautions.

If mutations were never produced in the XAAXADOO (chromosomes), the living beings would perpetuate their structures for millions of years. *And evolution would not be possible on any Planet.* A sea mollusc would replicate its morphology from generation to generation without changing its morphology ever.

But the specialists in terrestrial biochemistry ask: How is it that the mutations, those accidental phenomena that modify the code of the life, almost always produce in a positive sense (orthogenesis) perfecting the species, making it advance its morphology, its nervous system, its organs of sense or organs that capture the physical stimulous, making more and more perfect its complex of organic mechanisms from generation to generation, each time that a new mutation is produced?

We offer a simile: If the radiations and their genetic action can be compared to the effects of some shots at a target (the target is the chromosome), we can imagine a shooter firing on the columns of the Parthenon in Greece. Can we suppose (at least that it is a highly skilled shooter) that the impacts of the bullets instead of disfiguring the slender columns of the peristile, plow into the beautiful stone sculptures above the capitals?

How is it possible that the process of encephalization of man is going to keep improving and that some future generations of men will enjoy a cerebral cortex so perfected that our mind will be capable of solving mathematical problems mentally without need to resort to auxiliary algorythms like our ancestors?

Only for the chance bombardment of some neutrons or deutrons? Only because one Helion acting on the IXOOURAA (deoxyribonucleic acid - or DNA) alters the position one molecule of thymine or guanine? When in the most probable case it would provoke a genetic aberration and perhaps a monstrous being with atrophied arms or lacking lungs.

We credit our scientist AOYOO-221 son of AOYOO-217 for having discovered the mystery of the biogenetic process.

Since long ago they had discovered in the encephalus of the human some atoms of Krypton (known as a noble gas to you). The transcendence of this discovery came to be revealed. It treats of nothing less than the OEMBUAW (Third factor of man), unknown to terrestrials, which exercises the function of serving as the bond of union between the Soul and the Body.

69 XEE before, INNAI-3 son of INNAI-2 performed experiments of fecundation in the laboratory with spermatazoon of AAGA IEGOSAA (anthropoids similar to terrestrial simians) with ovum of YIE (female humans) having been verifying the spatial position of the component atoms of a sugar called deoxyribosa by terrestrial chemists and known as UUDUA GOO to us. The molecules of this sugar are found in the in-

terior of the nucleus of the ovum of a woman. They were surprised then to detect the presence of various atoms of Krypton.

These are found on the ends of the helicoidal deoxyribonucleic acid (DNA) chain forming various pairs (86 altogether in pairs) that gyrate in common orbits. The orbital planes, sensibly parallel, enjoy the one axis in common. at the same time this axis describes a harmonic vibratory movement whose frequency and amplitude are a function of the temperature (0.2 megacycles for a temperature of 35° C terrestrial).

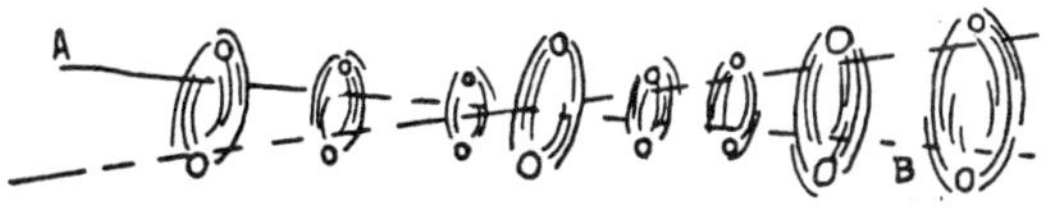

Not only did they detect such ordinate series of atoms of Krypton gas in germinal cells of men and pluricellular animals, but later they extended their discovery to the rest of the cells.

How had we failed to discover these cells before? You must take into account that if those groups really incorporated 86 atoms, these numbers are infinitesimal for detection and control. Remember that one cubic milimeter of the very rare Krypton gas can contain statistically a cypher of the order of 10^9 (thousand thousands) of free atoms.

The primary hypothesis of our scientists was to identify this Krypton with the OEMBUAWW (third factor of man already mentioned) but to their great surprise they found no evidence of such electronic codification at their subatomic energy levels.

Those studies continued for 9 XEE until AOYOO-221 initiated his investigations.

The formula, at first only a hypothesis, came down with a crash but with the glory of discovering at last the genuine feeling of the function of the BAAYIODUU, as we call this series of 86 atoms of Krypton.

(NOTE- That was the end of the 3rd letter on "The Biogenetic Bases of the Living Beings Who Populate the Cosmos". But this was apparently intended to be a deeper study over a longer period of time with Alicia Araujo, a recognized Spanish Biologist living in Madrid. She also had received the famous telephone calls from the UMMO communicators and was now a part of a Spanish "inner circle" of UMMO contactees that became known as the "Spanish Group".

Suddenly, beginning around the 26th of May (40 days after the above communication was prepared), a series of rapidly unfolding events overtook these developments and the UMMO expedition came to a sudden and complete interruption. All UMMO expeditionaries boarded three big UMMO spacecraft, and they left Planet Earth on the evening of 1 June 1967.

They left because they had observed a sudden and sharp escalation in the probability of a world nuclear exchange and they were having none of it. Things came to a head in the last days of May when Egyptian armed forces had massed in the Sinai and Cairo had ordered the UNEF (United Nations Expeditionary Force) to leave the Sinai and Gaza. President Nasser of Egypt announced that the Gulf of Aquabah would be closed to Israeli shipping.

Near the end of May Egypt and Jordan signed a new defense pact Placing Jordan's armed forces under Egyptian command, which was heavily armed, equipped by the USSR and staffed with thousands of Soviet military "advisors". Efforts to de-escalate failed and all Arab forces were at full readiness and poised to attack.

The UMMO visitors had acurately asessed the degree of United States and USSR involvement, and knew how far the contingency plans for both sides had progressed. They calculated the probability of this degenerating into a nuclear exchange unacceptably high, and after the U.S.A. backed their promises to Israel by adding NUCLEAR weapons to the contingency option, the expeditionaries reported this to UMMO and were ordered out.

They left this planet on 1 June 1967, the original target date for the Arab invasion.

Contrary to public awareness, Atomic War is not new to Earth humanity. The dangerous atomic sciences have been discovered and employed on Earth before, and never yet has Earth man failed to destroy himself and his entire civilization with it. It has never lifted our humanity to new and lofty goals.

There is evidence of great wars on Earth using atomic weapons in our not too distant past, beyond our present age of science (which is less than some 200 years old). The Takauti Documents of Japan which predate all other records there, going back 24,000 years; and on which the Shinto Teachings and the ancient Kojiki are based, describe a great worldwide atomic war at that time, and even contains maps showing cities destroyed in atomic holocausts. The Hindu Mahabharata describes another atomic war some 8,000 years ago, which wiped out whole nations and vast armies, and left total and complete devastation.

Other sites pointed out by different extraterrestrials as being the places of earlier atomic blasts are found in Monument Valley, Arizona; Death Valley, California; Baalbek in the Bakaa Valley, Lebanon; the West Australian Desert and in the mountains north of Cuenca, Ecuador.

No, the Ummites did not abandon their extensive project here without good reason. Their last communication to Alicia Araujo was dictated by ET DEI-98 in the home of the public stenographer on the 27th of May along with several other letters to other members of the Madrid Group including the notice of arrival of the UMMO ships to Fernando Sesma,

6 READING RAINBOW (CC)—Children
Host LeVar Burton observes an eruption of Hawaii's Kilauea volcano.
9 ABC NEWS (CC)—Peter Jennings
11 DIFF'RENT STROKES—Comedy
Drummond's interest in Aunt Sophia's friend (Candy Azzara) sparks the kids' hope for a wedding. Sophia: Dody Goodman.
13 CBS NEWS—Dan Rather
40 I DREAM OF JEANNIE—Comedy
Jeannie plans to make Roger the world's greatest lover. Jeannie: Barbara Eden.
(ASC) (HBO) CONSUMER REPORTS
(DIS) WONDERFUL WORLD OF DISNEY; 50 min.
(NSH) FANDANGO—Game
(PHO) HAPPY DAYS
(TTV) GILLIGAN'S ISLAND
(WOR) TIC TAC DOUGH—Game

EVENING

6 PM **4 NEWS**
6 NIGHTLY BUSINESS REPORT
Guest commentator: Adam Smith.
9 WHEEL OF FORTUNE—Game
11 CHICO AND THE MAN—Comedy
Ed is upset by Chico's plans to marry and leave the garage. Ed: Jack Albertson. Chico: Freddie Prinze. Liz: Jeannie Linero.
13 LAVERNE & SHIRLEY—Comedy
Laverne pretends to be multilingual to crash a party for foreign tourists. Penny Marshall, Cindy Williams.
18 CAROL BURNETT AND FRIENDS —Comedy
Guest Paul Sand plays a nervous honeymooner. Other sketches include a sendup of TV commercials.
40 IT'S A LIVING—Comedy
When Dot (Gail Edwards) lands the lead in a play, her work suffers—but not as much as the audience. Cassie: Ann Jillian. Nancy: Marian Mercer. Dennis: Earl Boen.
(A&E) CHURCHILL—THE MAN—Documentary; 60 min.
(ASC) (HBO) MOVIE—Science Fiction; 1 hr., 40 min.
"The Last Starfighter."
[Closed-captioned.]
(CBN) 700 CLUB—Religion; 90 min.
(CNN) LARRY KING; 60 min.
(LIF) AMERICA TALKS BACK; 60 min.
(NSH) NASHVILLE NOW—Magazine; 90 min.
Guest: Mel McDaniel.
(PHO) BENSON—Comedy

close up

CBS REPORTS
7 PM 13

Hiroshima in ruins: "How close," Cronkite asks, "have we come to using [nuclear weapons] since?"

HIROSHIMA PLUS 40 YEARS . . . AND STILL COUNTING

On Aug. 6 and 9, 1945, atomic bombs were dropped on Hiroshima and Nagasaki. In an hour that draws on interviews, archival footage and Government documents, Walter Cronkite assesses how the U.S. has since coped with "the dangers, suspicions and fears that have fueled a nuclear-arms race."

The program opens with scenes of the Hiroshima bomb being loaded on the Air Force B-29 the Enola Gay, and dropped on its target. Pilot Paul Tibbets recalls the impact: "What had been the city down there was nothing but a black boiling pallor of . . . smoke, debris, dust. It was bubbling, just boiling."

Cronkite then examines later world crises in which "nuclear options" were considered—and why they were rejected. They include U.S.-Soviet confrontations over Berlin in 1948 and in 1961, the Korean War, the 1962 Cuban Missile Crisis and the Arab-Israeli Wars of 1967 and 1973.

Major figures interviewed include former Presidents Jimmy Carter and Richard Nixon; Defense Secretary Caspar Weinberger, and his predecessors Harold Brown, James Schlesinger and Robert McNamara. (60 min.)

This page from the TV Guide, Tucson Edition, for the week July 27 to 2 August, 1985, describes a CBS Special Report revealing U.S. considerations of the use of ATOMIC WEAPONS in 1967 and 1973 as indicated by the UMMO Visitors.

UMMOAELEWE
No. of Copies: 1
Language: Spanish
ALICIA ARAUJO
MADRID

(Dictated 27 May 1967 at the home of the copyist in Madrid)

We desire to continue the report to you on the BIOGENETIC BASES OF THE WAAM (Cosmos) sent to you on preceeding dates. These days are critical for us and we have not been able to dictate to the copyist the continuation of the text that occupies us, nor can we guarantee that we will be able to continue them in the future. All depends on the instructions of our sister to whom are subordinated the components of this expedition displaced to Earth from the Planet UMMO.

The reason we can offer this to you, we have decided, with reservations is because of the petition of your brother Fernando Sesma, and because he has not encountered any risk previously. We have sent a communication addressed to components of that group.

Such notice we had forwarded months back, and now it is confirmed in an official manner for us. It is imminent (In a period of time between the days of 30 May and 3 June) that on this cold star (Earth) will arrive three of our OAWOOLEEA UEUA OEEMM (spacecraft of lenticular form with which we accomplish our voyages).

The OAWIOOLEAIDAAA (conversion of dimensions) as to say, the "physical arrival" of the three ships will probably take place in the following countries:

BOLIVIA (Zone of ORURO)
SPAIN (Zone of MADRID)
BRAZIL (Vicinity of Santo Angelo)

The reasons for the selection of such regions has been described in a tripple note sent to other such components of that group. We sent separately, similar notes to other groups of terrestrials in contact with us, and to six correspondents of ours in England, France, the United States and Czechoslovakia. We dearly beg you not to give the kinowledge of the contents of this communication to the press until after the arrival. Any information captured by us that this request has been violated will provoke a definite rupture of contact with you. You have foreseen the reasons to consider the serious disturbances that could be provoked if the news was excessively divulged.

THE BIOGENETIC FUNCTION OF THE BAAYIODUU (Krypton Atoms)

AYOO-221 at first maintained that the atoms of Krypton remained inactive in the sexual cells of all living beings. He laid the groundwork (formulated in his false hypothesis) for the idea that atoms of Krypton, in their future generations emigrated to the encephalon or cerebrum to form the known OEMBUAW (third human factor).

To demonstrate the viability of his hypothesis he selected germinal masculine cells (spermatazoon) of 134 species of vertabrates for comparative analysis.

The surprise of the specialists helping AYOO-221 was extraordinary to discover, on analysis, the electronic distribution of these atoms of Krypton.

As you know, electrons occupy at each subatomic level, instantaneous positions whose probabalistic function is regulated by the sugars. There is a principle of indetermination by which each electron occupies a point (we call these positions IBOZOO WOO which you must not confuse with the mathematical concept of a point in tridimensional space) distinctly withour regard for any law.

But in those atoms the positions were evidently fixed by an unknown synchronicity. The homologous atoms in the chains of the BAAYIODUU of the distinct spermatazoon presented a similar distribution and synchronicity. They were like clocks that functioned in unison as if they were connected by hidden emissions of radiation that stimulated such comportment, or as if a mysterious phenomenon of resonance obliged all the electrons to align themselves to the same leader. They could infer then that the proximity of the cells under study could provoke such an effect of resonance. But later they discovered that all the living beings of UMMO carried such comportment in their BAAYIODUU in the same manner.

Much later we came to recognize that this phenomenon was cosmological. The theory and the experiements have been definitely confirmed. Thus for example living beings of other planets presented the same phenomenon. In your year 1951 we confirmed once more the universality of this principle, testing in human cells of the OEMII of Earth. The synchronicity with the atoms of the BAAYIODUU of UMMO and those of other planets was perfect.

But you need not be surprised that this is so. For on the contrary, it will seem logical when we explain in the text that follows, the real function of the BAAYIODUU. You will understand then that you are very far from having reached the goal in the comprehension of the intimate mechanisms that regulate life because we still have not reached it despite this transcendental discovery. You will understand that the genetic code enclosed in the deoxyribonucleic acid is not but one of the links in the chain of factors that explains the comportment of the animated material of life inspired ultimately by WOA (God).

THE BIOGENETIC BASES OF THE WAAM (Cosmos)

We have indicated to you that one factor, called by us BAAA YIODUU (in reality a chain of double atoms of Krypton), carries a double mission:

1.) To store, from the Generation (Creation) of the WAAM (Cosmos) in the bosom of the living beings, CODIFIED INFORMATION of all the possible organic BEINGS integrated in it.

2.) To "tune in" to information on the ambient Ecological Medium: comparing such information with that previously known, and if necessary, can provoke a new mutation that would give place to a new LIVING BEING (a living being that was already designed to the preceeding code).

For those unfamiliar with the biological sciences we have selected a simple simile more easily understood. (Don't forget that these reports are merely didactical: We shall not pretend to develop themes exhaustively that are already implicit in the field of Biochemistry, Molecular Genetics and other stratum of general biology known to terrestrials. On the other hand our excessively developed technical concepts are impossible to transmit for obvious reasons. We are limited to a mere rough description.

Example: Suppose that in one country of this Earth, a country well developed economically, they have installed a great aircraft factory. The financing of such enterprise has been accomplished with unlimited reserves and credits, which hypothetically permits its directors to so develop programs unavailable or denied to other industrial firms of less magnitude.

The posession of such extraordinary means, has impelled the Directors or Technical Executives of the factory to generate an ambitious project. Such unheard of program would consist in creating a Study Panel provided with all of the technical facilities available. They had constructed thousands of aerodynamic wind tunnels, metallurgical laboratories that occupied dozens of buildings, offices of information and documentation with information channels to all of the centers of research on the Planet. They would have hundreds of thousands of engineers, physicists and electronics specialists who had coordinated to plan this project.

(Such a project is merely fiction of course.)

This project is nothing less than to construct planes incorporating all of the technical data known, of all of the models of aircraft or other artifact capable of flying in the fluid medium, AIR.

There can be no technical failure due to the magnitude of the project. It is impossible to calculate the number of millions of models that it would be necessary to design. (Though such an idea is pure fiction, we offer it as a scale for didactic effect.)

Once designed, such planes will be projected to cover every necessity meeting any and all aeronautical conditions of air navigation.

The computers are designed to accumulate all such information in the least space possible. To nobody would it occur, for example, to store so many millions of tons of paper in a normal archive. It would require, for example, the transduction of images to a code by means of appropriate transducers, to accumulate the codified data on perforated or magnetic strips, as they do on Earth, or in crystals of Titanium as we do on UMMO.

Continuing our tableau, one day they have in flight one of the most modern delta wing models. Its reactor is designed for ceilings of 12 kilometers altitude. It has to fly in an enemy region in which are missiles provided with infrared radiation detectors which home in on the heat emissions from the jet exhaust of the turboreactors.

One airplane after another is shot down. The survival of that type of machine is in danger. The surrounding medium is adverse to the "species" (using biological language). Meanwhile, the engineers who fly in those airplanes lose no time. With their equipment they detect in turn the cause of the failures, and codify their studies and data to solve the problem. They observe, for example, that the enemy rocket missiles are provided with parabolic antennas in the interior of their ogives of plastic, that these do not emit high frequency waves for which they can not be captured by normal radar antenas. They observe how the axis of route of such missiles statistically orient themselves toward the tail of their own aircraft. They finally discover that the air-to-air projectiles are equipped with very sensitive bolometers.

It is necessary to provide a mutation in the design of the airplane. But there is not enough time to project and produce a new prototype.

It is now when the efficiency of the Magno Projector (a part of the computer system) crystalizes into a practical realization. Enough of consulting in the archives of perforated and magnetic tape; what model of airplane should be made in face of the emergency of the attacks. Soon they discover a prototype that substantially conserves the characteristics of the former, posessing a protective corona for the exhaust which attenuates the radiation to the exterior of the troublesome infrared rays. The new model is designed. It is now much more successful.

We believe you easily understand this simile. But naturally many questions arise. For example: How does WOA (God) decide the codification of all the possibly phylum (living beings) that could be given in the Cosmos? (Don't forget that of these billions of beings possible, only an insignificant fraction live on the inhabited planets, really). We will try to answer this question in the attached supplementary report.

Since the number of compatible forms of life is very high, we advise that we have verified that certain forms of life are absolutely impossible. For example, there is no fundamental need to think that on other hypothetically inhabitable stars, living beings have developed with different biochemical norms. For example, chemically based on Silica, or on the chemistry of Germanium.

All biological forms are necessarily connected to the chemistry of Carbon.

The plan is complex and WOA has resolved this law materializing it in a manner that is not easy to explain in a few short paragraphs.

In the first place, the atoms of Krypton that form the BAAYIODUU contain the codified key to this law. In the series of 86 pairs of atoms for each XAAXADOO (chromosome), we find codified all of the possibilities that exist for ORGANIC BEINGS that are possible in Nature.

We can represent graphically the net or sketch that most completely represents the stratafication and ramification of this phylology.

The significance of our previous sketch can be extended with some symbols.

What we call ONAUDOOXA XUU (can be translated as arborescence) is a ramified series of possible routes or "phylum" that follow one mutation.

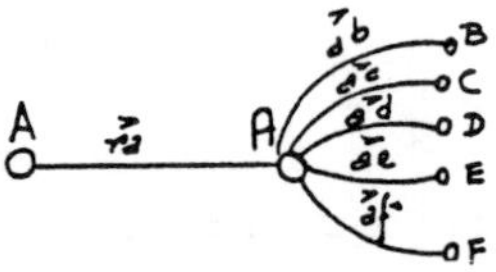

Each branch represents one XUU (phylum) example or variety of animal possible. The IBOZOODAO (knots) represent the instant in which a mutation is verified. Each IBOZOO DAO implicitly integrates one possible number of Mutations.

The symbol with one cypher in the superior part represents N total number of possible mutations (discovered up to now). This formula is given the name BAAXIODIXX IDUGOO.

Example 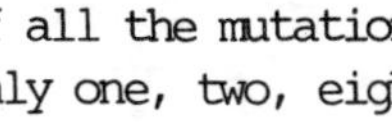 should be interpreted as a variety of terrestrial Arthropoda (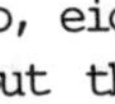) can transform themselves (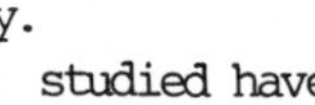) varieties "progressive" or "regressive" by means of other such mutations.

Observe that this codification has the character of POTENTIAL: we speak of POSSIBILITIES. Later we will se that in reality and on each Planet, of all the mutations possible for each ONAUDOOXA XUU (Arborescent) only one, two, eight, etc., take place in reality.

We should point out that some IBOZOO DAO (knots) studied have revealed up to 200,000 possibilities for mutation, and we suspect that the cypher limit for some knots could reach to 18,000,000 of possible codified in the atoms of Krypton.

We select an example much more graphic using actual terrestrial animals such as appeared at the end of the Paleozoic (Permian) and the beginning of the Mesozoic (Triassic) period, which will help us to understand it.

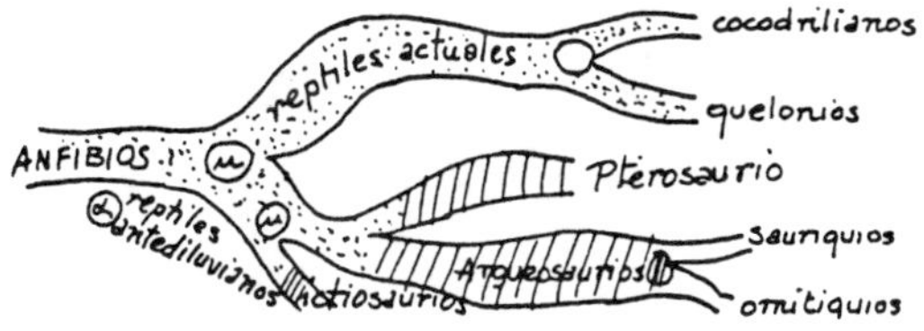

crocodiles

Pterosaurus
Saurians
Ornithians

Ichthyosaurians

Observe that one of the branches (antediluvian reptiles) suffered a series of mutations (μ) represented by the IBOZOO DAO which gives place to new phylogenetic branches, three of which are represented in the sketch as Pterosaursus, Arqueosaurus and Ichtyhosaurus.

Three or perhaps fifteen mutations are produced but how many could have been produced? To this apparently irresolvable answer the BAAYIODUU offers, in one of its 86 pairs of atoms of Krypton, the cypher of possibilities raised to the order of $(5 \cdot 10^4 < N < 18 \cdot 10^6)$.

To better understand the phylogenic codification in the BAAYIODUU we will represent with the color green the innumerable XUU (phylum or branches) that could be produced on any star whose physical conditions make it apt for the apparition of organic life, and with red the XUU in reality produced. Thus the phylogenesis of our preceeding example adopts this new representation.

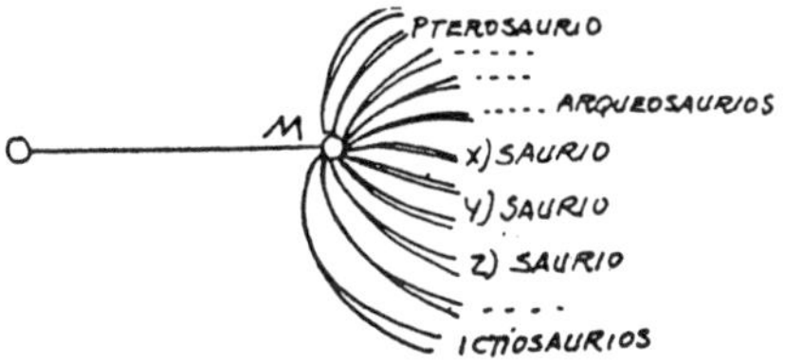

Pterosaurid

Arqueosaurid

Ichthyosaurid

What form would have been adopted by X Saurid for example if such mutation had produced it? Why was not such mutation produced? Why are the thousands of mutations not produced that could have adopted new forms of animal structure?

These investigators at first considered geniuses nevertheless asked questions that we are going to clarify in the succeeding paragraphs.

But before we offer an explanation that satisfies the interpretation of the "codified messages" that are enclosed in the BAAYIODUU.

Each change of an electron in the bosom of the orbital substrata of the eight that exist in the Krypton atom, codifies one XUU (phylum). We can see an example (though we have to take into account that it represents spatial electronic positions that have only one didactic value.

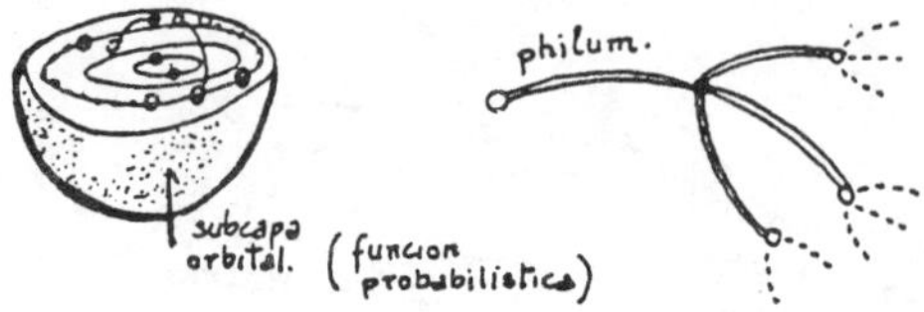

Each one of the four electronic levels (don't confuse these changes with the quantum jumps that can be verified between two energetic levels of the atom) which represent other such possible branches. The morphology that an animal really adopts in case it produces a mutation is a function (in code) of the electronic positions of the rest of the atoms in the BAAYIODUU.

(We repeat that in reality the cypher of possible "phylum" is not precisely of four, but of several millions).

We can see that the BAAYIODUU encompasses "written in the form of a CODE" all the phylogenia of those living beings possible in the WAAM (COSMOS). This has a transcendental importance.

Employing one simile more understandable to those not initiated into Biology: Imagine one book that catalogues all the models of aircraft (not only those that have been made, but those that will be made and those that could be constructed). Such a book would symbolize the function of the BAAYIODUU. The example is gross because the book would be a passive object and our BAAYIODUU containedin the XAAXADOO (chromosomes) adopts an operating function as we are going to study now.

If we represent graphically the phylogenia possible of all the organic beings that could be given in the cosmos, what form would it take?

Before all we would have to object that one graphic representation is not possible because the ONAUDOOXA XUU to represent (Arborescenses) would amount to "trillions of trillions". Expressed as one example: We could take the topographical contour of a forest including all of its trees, but never approach the detail of the innumerable branches and leaves contained within it, and still not approach the variety involved.

The approximate form of the phylogenia would be roughly as shown on the top of the following page.

Our specialists only had accomplished an understanding of the studies referring to the XUU (phylum) represented in yellow. They were satisfied that the ramifications possible (new species provoked by mutation) would continue ramifying in the center, and the immense complexity was making all the labor of investigation impossible. Not even the use of the XANMOO AYUBAA (computers) would make the labor of analysis possible. The order of magnitude could be 10^{520}!)

Observe that in the early stages of evolution, the number of XUU (branches) possible is very reduced, as much on UMMO as on any other planet. The protozoic species are identical. One can find an amebus, bacteria or a virus on any star, but according to the progress of evolution and the physical conditions differing among the planets, the selection of possible XUU produce biological panoramas tipical for each planet. The pluricellular animals known on Earth probable of being generated on other inhabited planets and viceversa, are many.

Something analogous occurs in the zone of convergence. The diverse XUU orient themselves toward the goal of that phylogenesis, the OEMII or human body. This point of convergence (U) comes to ramify again in thousands of XUU (human races).

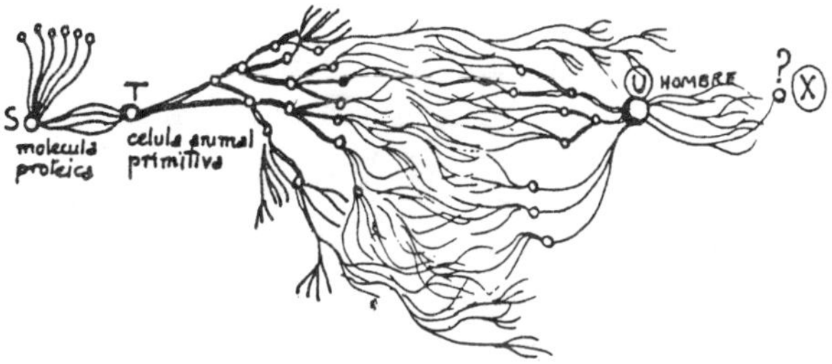

The number of possible human subspecies analyzed by our scientists rises to $9 \cdot 10^6$. Those races which are generated or not on any planet depends as we shall see later on many other factors.

This finally conjoins in a new IBOZOO DAO (knot) which constitutes the definite point of convergence. None of the humanities known reached this before their goal. Once reached, the humanity continues a progressive advance in its encephalization and mutual agglutination but this constitutes a theme apart from this study.

Between the knots (U) and (X) millions of possible mutations are provoking alterations (rarely regressive) in the somatic structure of the OEMII, especially affecting the brain whose development continues to translate in new talents the range of intellectual functions of humans.

We have seen that each chromosome counts with one BAAYIO DUU unknown to you. Its function is not to carry the Genes materialized in the doxyribonucleic acid of the chromosome, but to control the viability of internal mutations that without external radiological action are produced in the distinct species over a long time.

The terrestrial biologists explain orthogenesis (the variation of species in progressive form) by the hypothesis of natural selection in virtue of which, the weaker species are eliminated in their fight against the ambient organic medium. Such selective process orients the species towards progressive perfection based on the mutations.

Such explanation is overly simplistic and may not endure a serious analysis since the existence of the BAAYIODUU (chain of atoms of codified Krypton) is still unknown.

Thousands of primitive species coexist with others much more evolved. Any biotype can exist in a great variety of irreconcilable species in this ingenous principle.

We see the answer to the question: What produces a mutation that gives place to a more advanced species? It is the somatic mechanism of the IGOOA (Gene).

Date: 17-4-1967 (Continuation of previous report begun 3 April 1967)

In our last report we revealed the existence of a factor still unknown to terrestrial biochemists, and which we denominate with the phoneme BAAYIODUU (The Y is almost silent and the D can be pronounced as a soft Z).

The BAAYIODUU is made up of 86 atoms, doubled, of Krypton. (The expression atom double perhaps would be incorrect for an Earth specialist, but take into account the difficulties of translation at this time, of understanding in one version of terrestrial language, our scientific voice. For example the etimology of our phoneme NIIO AA which comes to express the same significance as ATOM, is very distinct. Not only in its root expression can nothing be seen of the Greek (indivisible) but that the term NIIO AA serves us also to denominate one chemical molecule or a small group of atoms not conjoined. Such confusion comes from different physical conceptions, because we conceive of the sub-atomic particles as simple changes of axis in a pluridimensional network, connected to a probabalistic function. Thus when such entities are related in any manner, we call this interrelation a microphysical level NIIO AA. Thus, for example, one pair formed by one Hyperion sigma and one proton in the bosom of the atomic nucleus receives also the denomination NIIO AA. The same Nucleus receives the name NIIO AAA and the same for the interaction Photon Electron. To distinguis then the type of NIIO AA that we are analyzing we add one codified cypher to the phoneme.)

Thus when two atoms exercise a specifically distinct function to that of the rest contained in one unit, it also receives the denomination NIIO AA though such atoms are not integrated in one molecule by means of chemical bond.

This is the case with the pairs of Krypton in the BAAYIOODUU. Of the two atoms connected to the axis, one of them codifies the stereotyped information of the biogenetic code. Expressed in more didactic terms: It contains one message that was provided from the origin of the Universe (We can domonstrate that the WAAM of Cosmos is not CYCLIC). It is something like a terrestrial dictionary or a manuel (said more exactly for one pair of the 86). One page of this distionary of 43 pages reviews and catalogues ALL THE FORMS POSSIBLE of LIVING BEINGS compatible with the universal biogenetic laws.

The other atom, DYNAMIC, has a double function that we will clarify in detail. In the first place it captures the information coming from the cellular cytoplasm (we will clarify the process) codifying it temporarily.

In the second place it dynamizes such accumulated information provoking quantic alterations that in the form of radiation provoke alterations on the bosom of the chromosomes (in the deoxyribonucleic acid) called MUTATIONS.

All of this requires a series of previous clarifications without which a layman in terrestrial Genetics or Biochemistry would encounter difficulties in comprehension of the concepts that follow.

The first question that you would formulate is this: How does the cell receive information pertaining to the exterior medium?

This is one of those aspects most important in cellular dynamism. Expressed by means of an example you will understand it better: Let us select one living being familiar to terrestrials, a branch vulgarly called Crab. You know that one of its species very prevalent along the American coasts has a bluish colorization due to certain rocks covered precisely with greenish-blue algaes. What has been the process that permitted this species of crustacean to achieve this color?

If this variety of crab was black or brown, it would posess less defense against its enemies who could then distinguish the animal by its contrast with chromatic medium that surrounds it. The camouflage of color on the contrary permits it to defend itself perfectly in this terrain. You encounter similar examples in other animals sush as the terrestrial chameleon or on our UMMO the OERUU IIOSSAUUIGAA, a vertebrate that could be confused perfectly with the rocks covered in this case by orange lichens, very abundant in the volcanic region of UUIDDAO UYOAA IIO.

A multitude of insects known to you adopt the forms of branches, grass and leaves permitting them a mimicking defense without which the species might perish. But you have asked many times how the so-called Nature has provided such defenses for the organism. Neither the hypothesis of Natural Selection of the specialists in terrestrial Genetics, nor the hypothesis referred to as mutation provoked by exterior radiations could satisfy a work of such importance.

What happened then to produce this phenomenon as surprising as the blue coloration of the crustacean?

In the first place we may indicate that there are two routes of information available to the cell:

CHEMICAL CHANNEL for information.

RADIOELECTROMAGNETIC CHANNEL of information.

Thus a being of organic complexity such as a human perceives with a series of organs called SENSES, that put it in contact with its exterior world thereof through the information captured in the form of WAVES. Also the cell senses with some means of information that permit it to relate itself with all the exterior medium by its complicated membrane. These means are in the first place the ELECTROMAGNETIC FREQUENCIES OF ALL THE WAVELENGTHS, from those that posess a λ of several kilometers, which you call LONG WAVE to the vibrations with quanta of great energy and very high frequency denominated by you with the generic and incorrect name of Cosmic Rays.

In the second place, the cell discriminates through its membrane the passage of certain compound chemicals. The cell memorizes the swallowing of certain products. This is something like if we humans utilized for communications among us codified language in which, instead of using the vibrations of the fluid air, as to say SOUNDWAVES, we used tastes and we devised a sequence of consecutive flavors to communicate the significance of the message.

When the living being is simply unicellular, the information of the world that surrounds it arrives directly by these two channels. Millions of radioelectromagnetic messages coming from various other sources of emission arrive at its citoplasm and to its nucleus (BOTH RECEPTORS OF SUCH FREQUENCIES).

These sources are very diverse and almost all of them are situated in the WAAM or Cosmos. Thus in the case of OOYAGAA (Planet Earth), one important range of radiations comes from the hot star SOL, your sun. Jupiter for example frequently sends to you trains of waves of decametric longitude, and the Radiosources already localized by your terrestrial radioastronomers are sufficiently familiar to you that we need not repeat it here.

Much of those frequencies, though captured by the cell, are not memorized by it. But there is a frequency of transcendental importance for the cells of living tissues of all the beings of the Cosmos. This importance is not even suspected by the specialists of Earth though they know of its existence. We refer to the frequency corresponding to the wave 21.106 centimeters emitted by great clouds of Nutral Hydrogen that in the case of our Galaxy is found concentrated almost in the equatorial plane of the galaxy.

The cells of all the living beings of our Galaxy (and of course those of other galaxies) receive these trains of hydrogen waves. But what they really memorize are not the rapid sequences, but the acyclic variations of short period. The cell will not remember, for example, the rapid variations (as shown) of the interval of one year, but will memorize the variations acknowledged in intervals of the order of thousands of terrestrial years (a threshold period measured by us as 877,533 terrestrial years) (B in sketch).

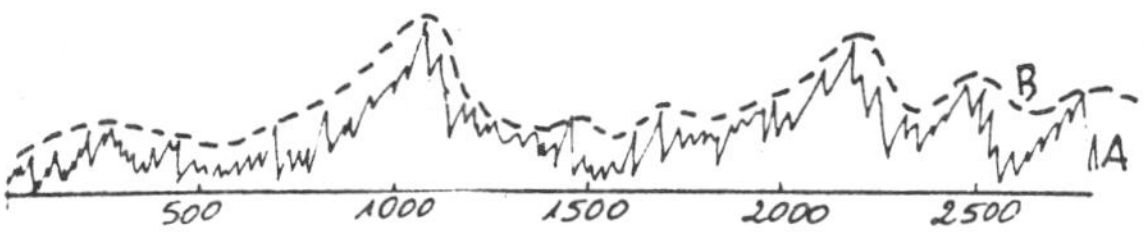

As one cell has a very reduced period of life (nervous cells can live some hundred terrestrial years, while those hematics of the blood scarcely reach 100 terrestrial days) the message is memorized for several consecutive generations. (Can you imagine a language so slow that to capture the word "Sulphur" would require collaboration from the great grandfather of a family to the great nephew of the same?).

It is thus that there appears a veritable process of histeresis in the cell that from generation to generation accumulates information radioelectrically, conveniently MEMORIZED AND CODIFIED. Cells pertaining to the epithelial tissue of OEMII (human body) can contain codified in their interior, all the variations expressed on Planet Earth of the electromagnetic fields of sidereal source, from the apparition of life on this cold star.

But it is important to tell you which is the true receptor of these frequencies, Receptor that does not need the help of vaccuum tubes, nor the function of solid state transistors, or terrestrial silicon or germanium diodes, nor condensors, nor resistors, nor transformers of alimentation, nor inductive windings like terrestrial receivers. This receptor is simply the WATER contained in the Citoplasm of the Cell and in its nucleus. The molecular structure of the same makes it capable of capturing such waves though the length of wave is much greater than its molecular dimensions.

In the preceeding reports we have summarized the receptor and codifier function of the cells. We must advise however that in one study, no matter how complete and profound, of the intercellular processes, it is not possible to extract all without losing some of its scientific value.

For that, our objective is to inform you in a scientific plan for release of the advances we have made in the field of the BAAYIODUULAA (Biology).

It is necessary that you get this point clearly. In the redaction of the reports furnished, if we had not taken into account the medium cultural level of this group, most of you would encounter difficulties in the comprehension of certain of the scientific concepts. How could we dictate these notes utilizing one terminology and resting on one chemicomathematical formulation more appropriate for a terrestrial biologist than for some OEMII humans whose profession, except in isolated cases, is marginal to these studies?

For that, our mission is to inform you plainly on those principles that we consider transcendental. But there is one evident difficulty. To describe to you the existence of certain factors such as the BAAYIODDUU unknown to terrestrial scientists, we need to cite concepts and factors already familiar to the technicians of Earth, such as the genetic code contained in the chromosomes. But some of you have not had any occasion to know the latest discoveries of the terrestrial biochemists. For that we take care in punctualizing for the layman in biological sciences, which of the concepts develloped are understood on Earth and which are only known by other extraterrestrial civilizations.

On the other hand it is necessary to use, for those among you who posess no profound erudition in quantum mechanics and still for those who posess some knowledge in the concepts of terrestrial physics, some understandable similes that are of more than merely pedagogic value.

Thus, when we say that in the BAAYIODUU the atoms of Krypton girate by pairs in elliptical orbits, or when we refer to electronic jumps in the bosom of an energetic level or atomic sub-layer (of electronic orbits), we are using a symbolic language.

You must take into account moreover that all the structure of Quantum Mechanics created by the physicists of Earth is a veritable guess that lacks a real basis. For example let us cite to you one concept familiar to terrestrial physicists, "the spin of the electron".

You are incapable (due to the embrionic state of your investigations) to give a satisfactory explanation for example of what you call the ZEEMAN effect, believing the concept of moment of angular spin and constructing all of your mathematical model of one such hypothesis so flimsy. We can tell you that this conceptional error alone has retarded in terrestrial physics the development of an atomic model more in keeping with the real truth. That which you term SPIN is something very different from that which your mathematicians postulate.

In effect: If you consider a spatial network of N dimensions, the deformation of two axial axiis oriented orthogonically and which when cut at one IBOZOO UU (spatial point) will give way to an effect that in this case you call ELECTROSTATIC FIELD - MAGNETIC FIELD inviting the specialists of your Planet to represent it with a vector and assign a quantic number. To be understood better by the layman in physics, it is like someone who contemplates from a distant mountain, a picnic or camp meal of a family, and confuses the table cloth extended to the ground with the skirt of a woman sitting nearby and believes those sitting at the table to be wearing one single skirt.

We are telling you all this because it illustrates the difficulties we encounter in describing any scientific concept to you. If we use the terrestrial scientific language we can only mask and falsify the truth, because as we have indicated above such terrestrial hypotheses are corrupted in their origin, and if we resort to the logical path of previously explaining the errors or inexact ideas that you have forged, we would need many typed folders of pages for the project. Because the panorama is so bleak many of you do not even know of such terrestrial hypotheses, because most of you consider it more interesting to submerge yourself in the brainwashing of television, than to inform yourselves on these scientific disciplines.

We told you in our earlier report that the cell is capable of receiving information through two routes: RADIOELECTRIC and CHEMICAL.

The process by which a crustacean as in the example we introduced before informs its germinal cells of the nature of the medium that surrounds it is very complex and merits separate (explanation) when you consider a new series of reports of interest. But to resume, we would indicate that the crab cited captures through his eyes the luminous stimulus of coloration of the rocks (greenish-blue). This provokes a series of metabolic alterations (biochemical as we say), that immediately codifies stimulus in the form of nervous current that affects the sense organs of its embryonic nervous system. In this case they are levels of Potassium and Nitrogen which are altered in such manner that the cell IS INFORMED of the conditions that reign on the exterior from the OPTICAL plane.

Through the cell membrane the equilibrium of ionic transfer is altered, and the cellular metabolism suffers a series of modifications that penetrate from the Cytoplasm to the Nucleus.

These alterations are produced at the level of the outer electron sub-orbits in the electron layers of the atoms of Oxygen which make the molecules of intracitoplasmic Water, automatically producing quantified variations in the gravitational electronic field.

We shall clarify this a little for those not versed in Physics.

You know that one of the attributes of the electron is mass. We prefer to not create confusion in you, to begin with the model of an electron designed by the physicists of OYAAGAA (Earth). When the mass of the electron describes a harmonic vibratory movement it generates under certain conditions gravitational waves, with the consequent loss of energy. In these conditions the electron disappears by transforming itself into what you call ANOTHER ATOMIC SUBPARTICLE. (Such sub-particle is not known to you, and is not worth the trouble to try to designate it with any name, like it is not worth the trouble to try to denominate with a vocable each of the infinite angles that could be formed by two straight lines.)

This phenomenon is NOT KNOWN BY TERRESTRIALS. In reality it is not that the electron has degraded upon emitting quantified energy in gravitational form. It is simply according to the conception understood by our PHYSICS that it undergoes a new orientation in its axis and is modified by the structure of the N dimensional Network that surrounds it.

Expressed then in comprehensible language: Certain atoms of the OXYGEN component of WATER contained in the Cytoplasm of the Cell, suffers an excitation in its external orbital (electron) shells. The electrons upon vibrating emit natural gravitational waves disappearing thereafter, something like if the emitter of a terrestrial radio had to burn its own equipment to obtain the energy with which to radiate its emission.

These gravitational waves have an energy very much weaker than the Radio waves known to you (of the order of 10^{-39} less). But this altered gravitational field provokes an effect of resonance in the electrons of one of the atoms of each pair that makes up the BAAYIODUU (Atom that we named due to its denomination in our language: BAAIGOO EIXUUA the result of which is untranslatable) DYNAMIC or dynamizer. In other words: It acts as a receptor capable of detecting the gravitational waves radiated by the citoplasmic Oxygen, and registers the message as if it were one of your terrestrial magnetophonic installations. When one electron associates with one gravitational quanta (called by terrestrials GRAVITRON) such association can give place to another electron with modification in phase and orbital position, and a new sub-particle that continues to degrade and subdivides itself into two.

It is thus like those electrons of the atom of Krypton "INFORMED" (we use the vulgar language) that in the surroundings of the place in which the crab finds itself in our example, the dominant coloration is blue. (WE WILL CONTINUE WITH THE REPORT)

But we want to clarify to the YII Alicia Araujo that the method by which was captured the true nature of the phenomenon described in the previous reports is not all incorrect, though the formulation used for it is a little primitive.

We object, above all, that it is not only one atom which codifies all the possible forms of living beings in the WAAM (Universe) but 86 NIIO AA (atoms) of Krypton which we call BAAIGO EIXAE (decodifiers). Their electrons are occupying in any instant thousands of millions of distinct positions (the cypher in reality takes an infinite number) are all able to codify this kind of information.

In later reports you will come to better understand all the function of the BAAYIODUU.

3 April 1967

APPENDIX 1

One XAAXADOO (chromosome) is one structure in the form of a filiament that is found in the nucleus of the cell a part of one of its phases of reproduction and a part of one component that you call chromatin.

The structure of the XAAXADOO (chromosome) is complex. Conveniently amplified with our gravitory visualization equipment, we see a big cluster of atoms. we utilize your nomenclature because the component parts are known to the biologists of Earth.

(IXOUURAA)	Deoxyribonucleic Acid (DNA)
(UOUARAA)	Ribonucleic (RNA)
(NOI OULOO)	Histones
(DOA DOEE)	Protamines
(IXIMOO)	Essential Proteins

The Deoxyribonucleic Acid (DNA) is a very important carrier of the codified program of the IGOOA (Genes). Their information symbolized in the "code" is really the orders that serve to materialize the characteristic traits of each animal or plant. We can see what this mechanization of program and realization is.

The IXOURAA (RNA) presents a spatial structure of helicoid form (Double Helix).

Its more important components are:

(IOGAARAA)	Phosphoric Acid
(UUDUAGOO)	Deoxyriboic Sugar
(IXOIAROO)	Adenine (Nucleotide)
(IUAGAROO)	Thymine (Nucleotide)
(IDUIROO)	CITOSIN (NUCLEOTIDE)
(IUOOROO)	GUANINE (NUCLEOTIDE)

These basic components are laced together in the following manner:

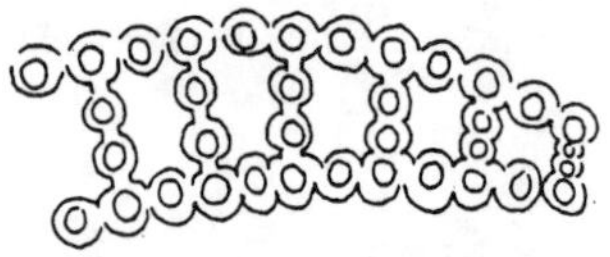

which forms an elemental fraction of the double helix mentioned.

Observe that the situations relative to the last four components: (Adenine) (Thymine) (Citosine) and (Guanine) alternate in an apparently capricious manner. But it is precisely this distribution of the four IGOMII (symbolic factors of the code) that allows it to transmit the message. Each four bands or pairs can represent one symbol IGOOA 5+C (Gene 5+C) programmer of proteins (this is one of many genetic symbols).

How is this program translated into the manufacture of proteins? You are not completely ignorant of this process. There are two chains of UOUORAA (Ribonucleic Acid) (RNA), whose structure is similar to that of Deoxyribonucleic Acid though less complex.

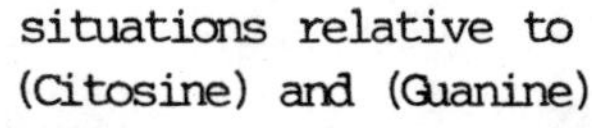

Symbolizes the link UUDUINOO (RIBOSA) that distinguishes the Deoxyribonucleic Acid which accomplishes different functions.

In the first place we must distinguish the types of UOUOURAA ribonucleic chain.

The first is an exact copy of the encyphered message of the Deoxyribonucleic Acid.

The second is the carrier of one IXI (Amino Acid) (remember that the amino acids are veritable modules or links of the Proteins).

Though the process is more complex due to the intervention also of Ribosomes, Enzymes and one Factor unknown to you called AIGOOXAADA, we intend to schematize it, employing also some metaphors or images more understandable to those inexperienced in Chemical Biology.

1st Phase

In the chromosome there pre-exists (from the last mutation) a sequence of codified symbols as a function of the situation with the nucleotides and the deoxyribonucleic acid.

We symbolize this with a strip in Earth Morse Code preserved in the files of a Company.

2nd Phase

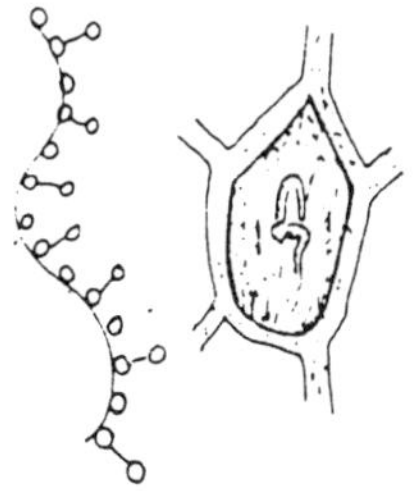

In the nucleus of the Cell a chain or Ribonucleic Acid is formed. It exactly duplicates the previous code. This chain passes to the protoplasm of the cell from the nucleus, carrying the message.

You can imagine this as a copy of that previous strip which is ingeniously copied in the process cited and carries the message to the company shop.

3rd Phase

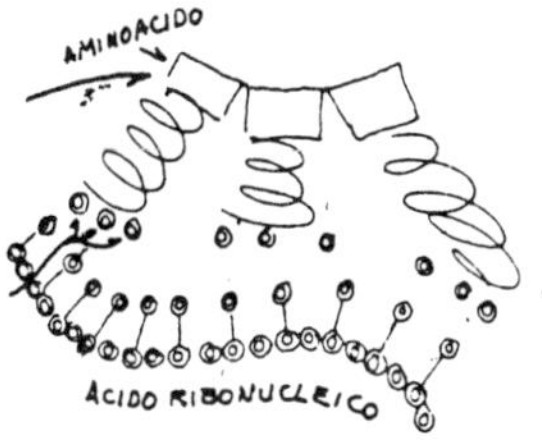

In the citoplasm there exists on the other hand a series of amino acids of distinct type. (Don't forget that one protein molecule is made up of distinct classes of the same components. One protein chain is distinguished from another precisely by the class and order of such enmeshed amino acid combinations.)

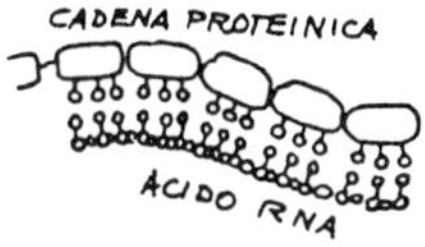

Later on, the chain or ribonucleic acid mould arranges itself to enclose ONLY THOSE AMINOACIDS whose code cypher corresponds to the message.

The protein chains thus integrated give form to the structure of each living being. Each animal or plant has been "made" in obedience to the codified orders of the XAAXADOO (Chromosome matrix).

We offer an insert to explain a process that is almost known by you. All that remains is to analize how the codification of the orders in the appropriate XAAXADOO (chromosome) works.

You can see that the mathematical permutations of the four nucleotides IXIO AROO (Adenine), IUAG AROO (Thymine), IDUI ROO (Citosin) and IUOO ROO (Guanine) are enough to codify in part (we can not explain in a brief way the other aspects of codification) the hereditory characteristics.

What happens if a duohelicoidal chain of deoxyribonucleic acid is struck by a beam of radiation (neutrons for example)? The impact could produce (in case there is no rupture or destruction of the chromosome) at least an alteration in the order of the nucleotides. This would change the interpretive sense of those and one could say that this provoked a IDUGOO (mutation).

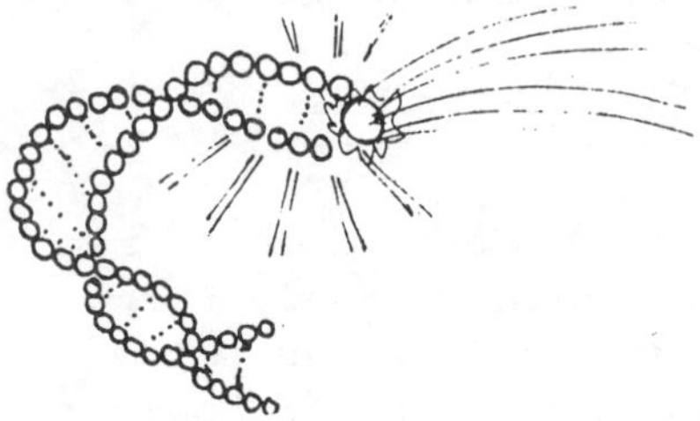

But not all of the IDUGOO are provoked by uncontrolled exterior radiation (Cosmic Rays, nuclear explosions, ect.) but on the contrary, many mutations are provoked in the same individual by a mechanism unknown to you. Thus, for example, a species of reptiles such as lizards can live thousands of years in a swampy region until one day a mutation is produced for which the new species of lizards are born provided with large palmic membranes which permits them to swim comfortably in the water. What has happened?

We offer the advice that you pursue in the following paragraphs this fascinating explanation in which we will specify the process that is adopted in this procedure by the series of 86 pairs of Krypton atoms discovered by us which we call the BAAYIODUU.

REST

NOTE BY THE AUTHOR- Remember in my first English volume translated from EL MISTERIO DEL UMMO we published an extensive UMMO vocabulary compiled by the Sevillian investigator Antonio Moya Carpa. Due to the abundance of Ummite terms in this and other Reports, the help of this vocabulary may be important.

Up to here, the report on the Biogenetic Bases of the living beings of the Cosmos is unfinished. (The UMMO expeditionary team to Earth was suddenly evacuated before the next part of the Biogenetic report was prepared.)

In continuation we reproduce here another letter from the personality we identify as the "copyist" (public typist who received the dictation and prepared the reports), and who is so important in all of this UMMO affair. This letter was sent directly to Alicia Araujo, and in a certain manner is a continuation of that which the same "copyist" sent to the Professor of Biology. In it he explains his moral doubts about the actions to take if "they" do not return, and gave precise information about the debated San Jose de Valderas case of 1 June 1967: Actually a Ship came to collect the (UMMO) expeditionaries arriving from Australia via London, who that night slept in the home of the "copyist". They were under the control of the young YU-1, as told in that extensive letter published in the first English volume on UMMO we mentioned. Two more ships arrived simultaneously at Oruro (Bolivia) and at Santo Angelo (Brazil) to collect other groups of UMMO expeditionaries that were studying Earth in those remoter countries. The arrival of these three ships, as you remember, was announced, among others to Fernando Sesma, in a letter which he showed to the fellow members of his group "La Ballena Alegre", 38 of whom verified this with their signatures on the back of the letter, to attest that they had seen it BEFORE the famous sighting at San Jose de Valderas.

To close this insert, I must say that Rafael Farriols as well as I have well founded suspicions that one of the two mysterious photographers present there (at San Jose de Valderas) (and perhaps "Antonio Pardo"), was the same "Copyist". And Farriols also feels strongly that all of this is a montage carefully prepared by the Ummites, foreseeing as well that the William Spauldings of this world may come out some day with the "proof" that all was a fraud. They may desire that the grade of credibility that accepts their presence among us does not exceed a certain level, which in general is not very high. They themselves suggest "do not believe us", meaning do not accept them blindly, but know what you believe and why.

(NOTE- That seemed to be the end of everything. The series of letters on Biogenetics was interrupted in the middle of the subject. The Earth expeditionary team from UMMO was collected and evacuated on 1 June of 1967 and all fell silent. Nobody knew whether they would ever return. This went on for five and a half months, and then the copyist decided to initiate some action on his own to settle the affair. He finished and mailed the following letter to Alicia Araujo. -Publisher)

Sra. D. ALICIA ARAUJO

MADRID, 12 November 1967

Esteemed Lady:

On the 26th of June I began to write you a letter which I could not finish. But as there was no urgency in sending it, I left off its termination, and later, as the days passed my wife and I went on a trip. Between one thing and another until my second return to Madrid, I had not decided to put my papers in order to settle this affair.

I propose to write in person to all of the correspondents of theirs (I mean to say those of UMMO who dictated to me to send to you those distinct documents on Chemistry, Biology, Etc.). My proposition is that, if in the time of a year or a year and a half those gentlemen from UMMO have not returned or shown signs of life, I will talk with all of you personally and decide what we should do. I have proofs of veridicial interest, and though it would be with the condition that my rights over their ownership be respected, it would not be inconvenient to let the Government and the Engineers study them.

This, on one hand, is my intention, and on the other hand, I am worried about the moral part. As I say, I must make this decision carefully, for if I break the confidence of "them" they will disavow me. All would be much easier if they had told me what I should do. There is one fault of theirs, and in all fairness I must say that that is the only fault I have seen with this senor DEI-98, who is the gentleman who began to dictate to me the things for you.

But in effect, he not only prohibited me from identifying myself to you and to the other correspondents in Spain, but on one certain occasion when I planned a confidential meeting to be directed by a Professor of the University of Madrid, they found out and asked me not to go through with it until "some time had passed" and they would authorize it. We already had everything prepared and among the correspondents we had elected those that would meet in Madrid. They were Engineers and Physicists said to be the most important for later coming to an agreement to invite the others and explain the points of view of the gentlemen from UMMO to all. Well, I don't know how (they knew of it and that I was involved) but they discovered this that we had undertaken in secret writing confidentially to all those gentlemen.

They discovered it as I say, and I don't know how. They prohibited me until after "some time" would pass and they would authorize it, not telling me when or whether they would break the whole contact. They tried not to force me by castigation but by a moral committment. You must understand that it is not because they, for my collaboration, have paid me more or less, it would have been a betrayal, nor if they had not paid me at all would I be capable of breaking this committment to them.

But there is the question, and they, when they left, did not leave my position clear, such as how could anyone say in reality they had not gone (forever) even though they almost gave me this to understand.

As I have not spoken to you, I don't know if you believe in all this or not, and surely then you would neither believe that I have heard of almost nobody of those that receive (the communications) and talk (by telephone) with "them" believing that those gentlemen come from UMMO, which is a planet a great distance away. It is natural then that I at first came to take them for crazies. The history of how I came to know them is long, and some day I will tell how it was them who came to my house through an announcement that we had put in the newspaper.

I came to know of one of the Hotels where they stayed. That would perhaps be one proof, however of little importance since the Hotels register their clients as they present themselves, even with false names. It would be easy to identify them since they have roomtendants who have talked with them.

I had come to go out with them uncounted times but they went alone. They told me that they passed the time visiting museums and buildings of Madrid. One day they asked me for help. I had to falsify a card to enter the National Library of Madrid situated at calle Zurbaran, No.3. They told me that I could of course refuse, but they insisted that it was not immoral because the only objective was to study a series Foreign Magazines. I went to the window and all was resolved rapidly. The senorita who attended suspected nothing.

Two months before their departure (or possibly three) as I did not note the date, one of them came early in the evening (they only came later towards seven, after I had left work, and dictated things to me) but as I was not expecting them that day I got home late, and they were waiting for me in the dining room. My wife then was distrusting and preferred to speak as little as possible to them. They told me when I arrived, that they desired to ask of me a favor. They were going to have to do some work in a zone of Madrid in which there would be vigilence (control), and as they had passports of another country, they desired to go with a Spaniard, and they explained what I would have to say if anybody asked us any embarassing questions. They gave me a photographic camera and an apparatus with three legs to screw the camera on, and told me where I would have to wait for them the following afternoon.

I remember that it was a Saturday and I did not have to work in the office. By three p.m. a taxi had already left me there, in some small gardens not much past Segovia Point by the Extramadura road. They were not much later. They arrived in a gray Renault that I later found to be rented, and whose license number I noted and was not difficult to find it. One of them crossed over to the other side of the Manzanares River (which I knew little since it was not long since I had come from South America). The other, called DAA-3, remained at my side. I mounted the apparatus to simulate taking pictures, and while I was simulating making photographs, DAA-3 went along placing at distinct points of the zone, some small articles that later could be seen since he had a small box of metal very thick full of rose paint (with which he had marked the positions). I saw perfectly where he had put them, some buried in the dirt and others in the metal railing near the river, inserting them at the stone pillars that supported the railing.

The other gentleman later threw in the river two balls that immediately sunk. Hardly anybody passed and nobody bothered us. They asked me to wait while they returned to the other side (of the river), and they got in the car for about a half hour. DAA-3 explained to me that those tablets the size of a fingernail were radioactive monitors that served as points of control of certain measurements, and they also explained more as we passed over the bridge again and they let me out on the Calle Segovia leaving the photographic equipment with them.

On the first of June when they left, I returned to the small garden that was between the Manzanares River and the Avenida del Manzanares. We had been precisely at the side of the Point at a site where the railing made a bend. I searched with a screwdriver in the stone pillars where they joined the ends of the railing and took out one of the tablets, but I did not dare to take it since they told me that it was radioactive; that could be dangerous; it was stuck on a delicate paper like plastic, and was identical to those I saw as he had painted some small pieces of metal with a rose colored paint of lacquer or plastic. I did not dare to carry it with me and so without touching it with my hand I threw it in the river. But there are more there still since if they had not removed this one they may not have collected the rest. I believe that I know where at least two more are. I also know where the spheres fell within a meter more or less nor did I see that they recovered them, and I do not believe that they were carried along by the river. I believe that it would be easy to find them by dragging the river.

I could tell you other things Senora Araujo, since my wife and I had come to know the one that was chief of all those on this world and who came to Madrid precisely before they all left for UMMO in three space ships. All of this seems fabulous but it is real including what the Press published on the 2nd of June, present (1967).

Surely you, Senora Araujo, will tell me what you think of all this. I can not doubt that these gentlemen that I have known, who have come to my home one time and another, who have dictated hundreds of pages that they themselves at times later illustrated, come from that Planet that they call UMMO. I know many things of them. I know for example that seventeen years ago they came to France for the first time, and that there they learned the language, and that they have explained to others the whole history. Also not only I but my wife have been witness to surprising things that I defy an engineer to invent.

But now they have all left for their Planet, or if any remain I do not believe they are in Spain.

Surely you will not believe this, even though you have talked to them, since you have not seen them, thus all a dream or a novel and natural for one to lack confidence.

But it is because all this has happened that for now I can not show my face and clarify all this. If they give no signs of life or activity here in one year or a year and a half, I believe that I must present myself to the Authorities and to you and other persons so that among all we can make ourselves clear on an affair so important to Spain. I can not only present witnesses but an apparatus of theirs. Also I have noted many things; numbers of automobiles, the name of a Hotel where they stayed, The name of a merchant who knew them as Norwegian tourists, An apartment where they lived for nearly a week, papers of theirs, inventions that they could patent, and an Architect who finally discovered that he knew that they were from UMMO, and that he had helped them, though he had had the cynicism to deny it. I can demonstrate that he at least sent one time a package to Australia [for them]). I have spoken with him and despite my promise of silence he did not have the kindness to recognize it.

Who can tell me then that I have not accomplished what is required of me, but take into account that before they left they had given me sure instructions and left no doubt. I do not believe that this would harm them if the truth were out. It is evident that if they were here I would be incapable of anything that would harm them. The proof is that up to now I have guraded my silence and the same for my wife. Only two relatives know also and nobody else of the circle of acquaintances and old companions of the office..

Senora Araujo, I have some folios that I have typed, dictated for your name. You will pardon that I have not sent them, but their departure upset this whole business. Later I have been twice on trips, and your papers are untyped and mixed with others. You remember that they sent us things on Biology, which is your specialty. They always knew the specialty of each one, and they sent things in the corresponding science.

I hope that I have not tired you with such a long letter. When I speak of them it enthuses me and I cannot stop and I could spend days speaking of this. With good reason they say that the truth at times is greater than the fiction.

To you I remain Your affmo. q.b.s.m.

To finish this section consecrated to Alicia Araujo and the Reports that she received on Biology we transcribe the following as we announced, letter, of the Barcelona Doctor Luis Cornudella, which, as an honorable and impartial investigator, I believe is my duty to recognize in this work. Evidently some of the arguments put forward by Doctor Cornudella carry weight, and especially with reference to the hypothetical 48 atoms of Krypton residing in the hypothalmus, and which the Ummites consider the connection between the soma and the psyche or the body and the Soul, said more plainly. There, each with their own conclusions: thanks to the greater dissemination that these texts now have, from here invite other scientists, especially biologists and biochemists, to express their opinion. Perhaps the truth is someplace in the middle.

What is truely curious is that the Ummites are clearly of human form — or humanoid — as the pinacle of the evolution of intelligent life. This seems abundantly clear in the most interesting Report on the "Anatomy of the OEMII (man) of UMMO and his differences with the OEMII of Earth" which was sent to me from London via Madrid, and was published in the first English volume on UMMO. In reality none of us know about the evolution of extraterrestrial life; and nothing prevents us from believing that when a planet of the terrestrial type has physiochemical conditions such as those that reigned here 3,500 million years ago, a chain of biological evolution could begin; a program that finally develops into man. Where we are going and what we will see, we do not know.

LETTER

Barcelona, 6 August 1968

The contents of the report of "The Biogenetic Bases of the Living Beings That Populate the Universe", despite being presented at a level of dissemination that it was, is disconnected and weak. As to say, together with notions of chemical biology they have intermingled concepts of physics and even the social sciences. The exposition of biochemical perspective practically repeats that expressed in the Appendix 1. This Appendix, which limits the review to simplistic form known to actual terrestrial geneticists, is plagued with errors of nomenclature.

If we leave aside the confusion of the abbreviations DNA and RNA for Ribonucleic and Deoxyribonucleic acid respectively (sic), there appear other equivocations of conceptual character, such as for example they have considered the chemical substances adenine, thymine, citosine and guanine as constituent nucleotides of those nucleic acids, when these substances are simply pure basics or building blocks of which those components are not the most important together with a hydrate of carbon (sugar) and a molecule of phosphoric acid, but those exclusive constituents of the nucleic acids.

The union of one of the basics with a residue of sugar (ribosa or deoxyribosa) gives place to one nucleotide (adenine, guanine, ect.): of the union of these with a molecule of phosphoric acid is obtained the Nucleotides. Finally of the sequential chains of nucleotides is constituted the nucleic acids, carriers of the genetic key.

The only original concept in the Report refers to the so-called "third factor of man" (the pairs of atoms of Krypton situated on the extremities of the chain of DNA) whose function consists in storing and dynamizing the genetic information. In this respect is alleged to fit two important observations. In the first place it is highly improbable that the molecules of a gas such as krypton would demonstrate said function, first due to the treating of a gaseous substance impossible to find in another state (solid for example) in physiological conditions; and also as it treats of a noble element as said, one atom with all those complete energetic sublevels for which its chemical stability is complete and its reactionability practically null. One can clearly see that a chemical element of this nature is incapable of assuming a function where the orbital displacements and the subatomic levels of energy play such a preponderate role.

In the second place, it is very significent that the pairs of atoms of krypton reviewed coincide with that of the triplets of nucleotides possible according to the disposition of the pure basics in the DNA, in actuality completely studied by professors Kornberg, Weissman and

Ochoa.

On the other hand it is also problematical to ascribe to said atoms the control of the mutations that are modified in the genetic code of living beings, when the positive sign of these mutations are determined by enzymatic systems (condensed in the ribosomes) responsible for the metabolism of those proteins "defective" due to erroneous mutations of the key.

I consider it unnecessary to go any deeper into the context of the Report.

/s/ L. Cornudella

Luis Cornudella PH. D.
Barcelona

[NOTE- For the nonprofessional biologists who read this work, prior to 1950, Earth scientists knew very little about the physiology and functional processes of a living cell. While the existence of the DNA and RNA chains was already known by the time of the UMMO Report, having been described in England in 1953 by American James Watson and the British physicst Francis Crick (who together discovered and described the double helix model for the chains of nucleic acids), the interdisciplinary work between biology, chemistry and physics in describing the make-up and chemistry of the cells of living organisms was just getting started when this UMMO report was delivered to Srta. Alicia Araujo in 1967. The UMMO report at that time offered new and novel descriptive details of some of the activity taking place in the genes which seemed to be made up of long chains of DNA. The encoding process in the nucleides and how it was done, as well as the nature and cause of mutation was highly speculative at that time. Eminent biologist that Alicia Araujo was, she recognized the value of the concepts put forth in the UMMO Report and sought to bring them to the attention of other leading biologists for review. Through Antonio Ribera she succeeded in getting the papers into the hands of a number of European scientists for study.

In the September 1967 issue of National Geographic Magazine the National Geographic Society released their feature article THE NEW BIOLOGY, Part I, Awesome Worlds Within a Cell, in which they describe in almost identical detail where we were in 1967 in understanding the physiology and chemical make-up of the living cell. They described the genes and the DNA and RNA chains of nucleides of which they are composed. Exactly how the encoding process functioned was speculated on, but the keys to the code, the Krypton atoms alleged by the Ummites were not mentioned at all, and perhaps have not been verified by Earth science.

That article, however, offered the best graphic description and artwork on this subject that we have seen. To show how close our most up to date concepts were eleven years after the UMMO report we have clipped two of the charts from that article for your comparison here.

That article showed three photographs of a DNA chain replicating itself and the process demonstrated is exactly as was described in the UMMO Report. Mere coincidence? -Publisher]

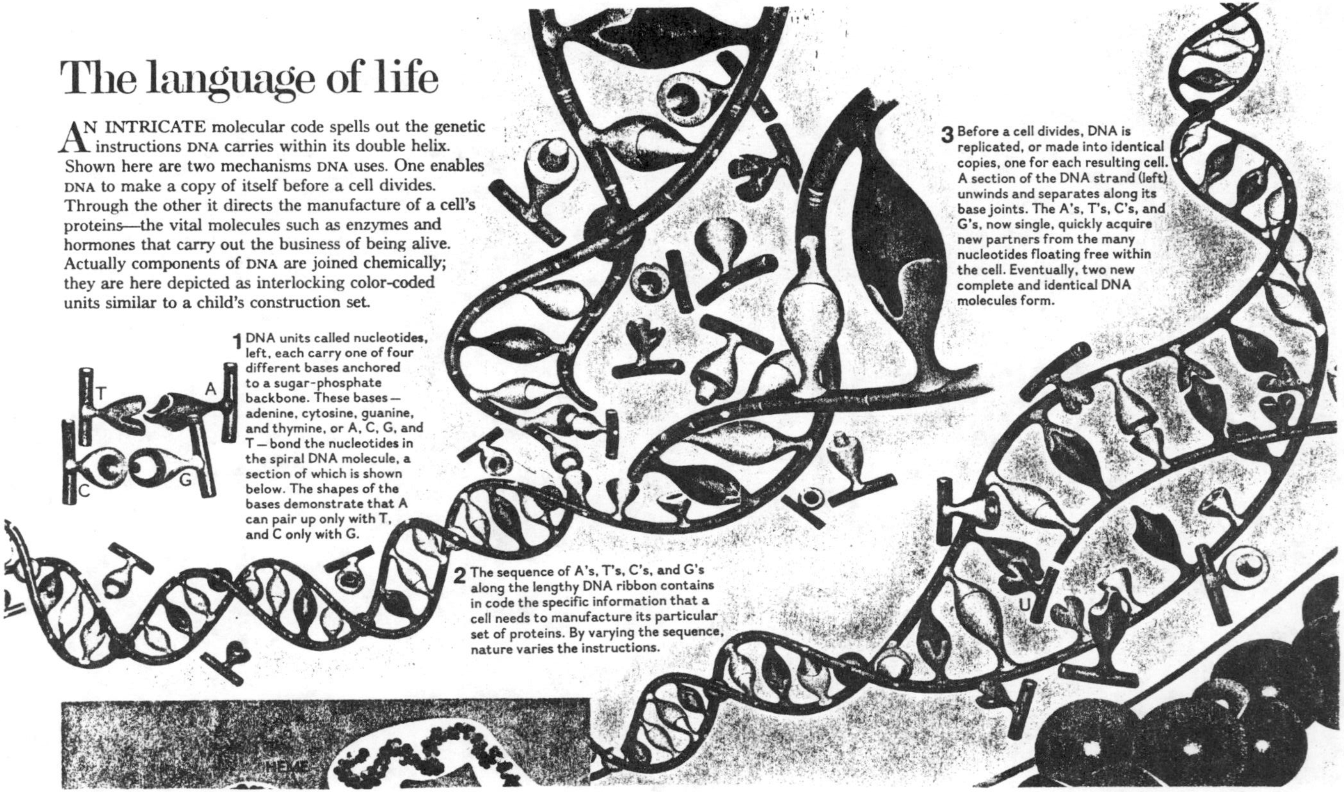

The language of life

AN INTRICATE molecular code spells out the genetic instructions DNA carries within its double helix. Shown here are two mechanisms DNA uses. One enables DNA to make a copy of itself before a cell divides. Through the other it directs the manufacture of a cell's proteins—the vital molecules such as enzymes and hormones that carry out the business of being alive. Actually components of DNA are joined chemically; they are here depicted as interlocking color-coded units similar to a child's construction set.

1 DNA units called nucleotides, left, each carry one of four different bases anchored to a sugar-phosphate backbone. These bases—adenine, cytosine, guanine, and thymine, or A, C, G, and T—bond the nucleotides in the spiral DNA molecule, a section of which is shown below. The shapes of the bases demonstrate that A can pair up only with T, and C only with G.

2 The sequence of A's, T's, C's, and G's along the lengthy DNA ribbon contains in code the specific information that a cell needs to manufacture its particular set of proteins. By varying the sequence, nature varies the instructions.

3 Before a cell divides, DNA is replicated, or made into identical copies, one for each resulting cell. A section of the DNA strand (left) unwinds and separates along its base joints. The A's, T's, C's, and G's, now single, quickly acquire new partners from the many nucleotides floating free within the cell. Eventually, two new complete and identical DNA molecules form.

The National Geographic Chart showing the structure of the DNA chain, how it is made up and how it works. Compare this elaborate presentation with the line sketches provided by the Ummites with their Report.

[NOTE- That the Ummites were on the cutting edge of new scientific developments worldwide on Earth is in little doubt. In their discussions on genetics described here, we can see that their announcement to biologist Alicia Araujo on 7 March 1967 that they were sending her a report on the the biogenetic bases which regulate internal mutations in distinct species of living beings was astounding. When the detailed report arrived on 3 April it was even more amazing because it seemed to be running ahead of known genetics at that time. This was followed by another report on 17 April and a third on 27 May of the same year.

To put this in perspective we may review our own knowledge at the time. J.D. Watson, one of the co-discoverers of the DNA and RNA chains making up the genes, published his monograph "The Double Helix" copyrighted 1968, and "Molecular Biology of the Gene" in 1976 (Lexicon Universal Encyclopedia, Vol. 9, p 82).

Kornberg, another pioneer researcher in this field published "The Synthesis of DNA" in the SCIENTIFIC AMERICAN, copyrighted 1968 (Encyclopedia Brittanica, Vol. 13, p 3290). The genetic code was actually broken in 1968 following work by Severo Ochoa and Gobind Khorana, both Nobel Prizewinners for their contributions (Encyclopedia Brittanica, Vol. 12, p 378).

Grossman, Lawrence and Moldave, Kivie published their "Nucleic Acids" in the ACADEMIC PRESS in 1968. Many other articles appeared in 1968 after that and the new Genetics came into being. The "Structure of RNA in Ribosomes" was first described in SCIENCE, Vol. 170, p 171, also in 1968. The Ummites had transmitted all their information to Alicia Araujo in early 1967 and then evacuated all their people here on 1 June 1967, and contributed no more information for many months.

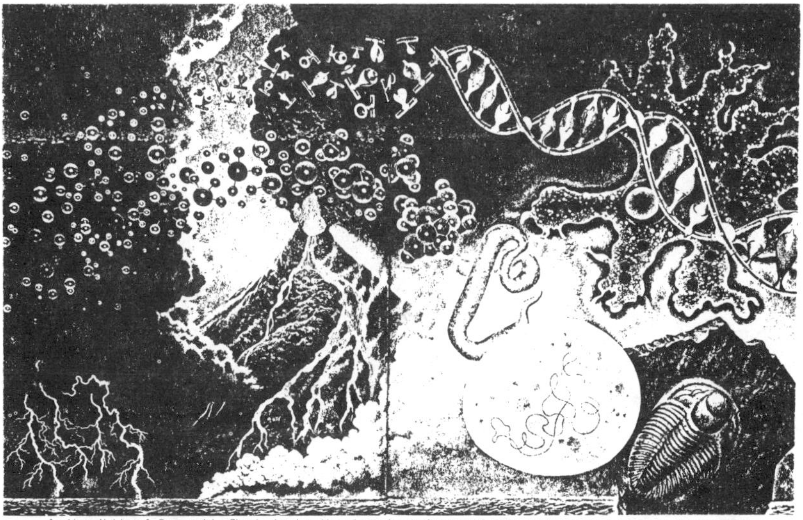

Another National Geographic Chart showing the steps in evolution of life as understood by Earth Biology in 1967. Did the UMMO visitors copy our early efforts and expand on them or did we take our cue from UMMO?

ALBACETE

THE MYSTERY OF THE SEVERED HAND

One time I found myself in Seville, for a short time, where I had been invited to give some lectures. One evening a Sevillian newsman came to see me at my Hotel, who with the peculian accent and grace typical of Andalucians, said to me more or less the following: "Listen don Antonio, do you suppose when you return to your hotel after your lecture, you could look at a book on "ORNIS" (I never knew why OVNIS (UFOs) is converted to ORNIS in Andalucia), or articles on the same theme?

I remember that I answered that really I preferred one of two other things, to either go to bed and sleep, or to read a detective novel in English.

Who would say that, filled with enthusiasm for this kind of reading, and my admiration for Ramond Chandler, Agatha Christi, Eric Ambler and Ellery Queen, I would be asked to also write a "thriller"? This is probably what you can deduce from the title of this section.

Well no, senor, I fell back into one of my more prominent vices. And this notorious vice consists of taking part in unusual things, this time occuring some 30 years ago. This lapse of such a considerable amount of time makes the trail now difficult, and impossible in some cases. The principle protagonists of this macabre story have now passed on, and the great house where it all developed no longer exists, and trying to document it we encounter shadows, dust, and forgetfulness. But there still remain some avenues, some leads, which allow us to unravel the thread of this complicated skein. And what has emerged is a file of surprising data. A banal *fait divers* with shades of *Grand Guignol* (pardon for such French, banality included), soon developed into a tale of interplanetary terror, with extraterrestrials and all.

In the first part of 1954, this sad case leaped into the headlines of the Spanish Press. In February and March of that year banner headlines announced new details of the sensational case. *La Voz de Albacete (The Voice of Albacete),* The Valencien dailies *Levante y Las Provincias,* plus the weekly *Journada* of the city of Turia, printed accounts, but above all was the sensationalistic THE CASE, which was devoted completely to this story. In this paper, preferred reading of servants (when there still were servants), and idle senoras, there appeared a series of illustrated articles, with titles such as: MACABRE FINDING IN A HOUSE OF THE CALLE DE LA PRINCESA; POLICE DISCOVER AMONG OTHER STRANGE OBJECTS, THE HAND OF A CADAVER; DONA MARGARITA LIVED ALONE TWO NIGHTS WITH THE CADAVER OF HER DAUGHTER; MARGOT WAS A VERITABLE SAINT, etc., etc.

Very well, who is dona Margarita and Margot? Dona Margarita, the principal implicated in this case, was dona Margarita Ruiz de Lihory (or Lihori, as I have seen the name written both ways), Marquesa de Villasante and Baroness of Alcahali (Valencian titles inherited from her sister Soledad, to whom they really pertained) (1) crowned aristocrat with farms and buildings in many places in the geography of Spain, and when these things occured was living alternately in Madrid (at the Princesa 72 address, Barcelona (at Paseo de Gracia, 110) and Albacete (at Calle Mayor, 58), in company with don Jose M. Bassols Iglesias, a Catalan lawyer who in several articles on this case figures as her lover (p. ej. in *Intervieu* n.º 401, 18 to 24 January 1984; article by Julio Cesar de Iglesias), and in others as her husband. The first husband of dona Margarita had been a Northamerican, Richard Shelly, deceased in the 40s. Of this first marriage were born three sons and one

(1) Possibly both sisters were daughters of don Jose Ruiz de Lihori y Pardines, Valencian writer 1852 - 1924 who held titles of Baron of Alcahali and of Mosquera. He was afiliated with the conservative party and was on several occasions advisor to the Municipal Government of Valencia, and Mayor in 1884. In 1890 he was Deputy of the Court for the District of Alcira. After that he was the Civil Governor in Valladolid and Majorca. He occupied the Presidency of the Central Valencian "Lo Rat Penat", and wrote assiduously in the Valencian press. He specialized in books on history, though he also published a novel (Los Endemoniados de la Muerta), and a book of stories and legends of the region.

Curiously, we are told that in the history of Catalonia there appears, at the first if the XVI Century, one Estafania de Roquessens de Soler y Ruiz de Lihori, nicknamed the "Pubilla" (virgin) of the Condado de Palamos. She married Juan de Zuniga, with whom she had eleven children, four surviving, among whom we find Lluis de Requessens, who came to be one of the most brilliant Naval figures in the Mediterranean. Lugarteniente Real of the sea, he was the right arm of don Juan de Austria, and architect of the victory of Lepanto (7 October 1571). His mother, Estafania, had died some years before, in 1549.

This was the illustrious ancestry of dona Margarita Ruiz de Lihory and her daughter Margot, the central figures in the sensational case that received so much press attention in and around the local area at the time of the severed hand episode. There was a great deal of mystery involved because of the many peculiar aspects to this case that just could not have been explained to the public at large, and which could never be proved to the satisfaction of anyone who did not know a whole lot more about what was going on than even those principal actors in this real life drama. Perhaps this will finally shed some of the much needed light on this unusual case.

daughter. Among them were don Juan Shelly Ruiz de Lihory, attorney who resided in Las Palman, Gran Canaria; don Jose M. Shelly Ruiz de Lihory who lives in Madrid; and don Luis Shelly Luiz de Lihory, whose address is unknown, though it is believed that he lives in Madrid (of those first, the author posesses the addresses). The daughter was Margarita (Margot) Shelly Ruiz de Lihory, who was 36 years old at the time of her passing.

Dona Margarita had had a tempestuous past. During the Marruecos War she served as a Mata Hari (we may suppose in a narrow way) of the leader, Abdel-Krim, of a small Rif group. But with all that I will occupy myself in more detail in the pages that follow. The picture of these things developed more or less as follows:

19 January 1954 — The death of Margot.

20 January — The wake. The brothers observed with their mother.

21 January — Funeral *Corpore Insepulto*. Interment of Margot in the Sacremental of San Isidro, Madrid. An incident with the lover of the deceased, attorney Jose Pandero (who later comitted suicide).

30 January — Luis Shelly, brother of Margot, went to the Police Magistrate to make a strange denunciation, harboring the suspicion that his own mother had mutilated the body of his sister. The judge ordered a search of the premises at Calle Princesa.

As a first measure, the functionaries detained Margarits Ruiz de Lihory and Jose M. Bassols, holding until the following day the maid and the mayordomo.

4 February — The body of Margot Shelly was exhumed by judicial order. Someone had amputated one hand and part of the tongue. But the most horrible detail was that both of her eyes had disappeared!

PORTRAIT OF A DUPED WOMAN

When on 30 January, Luis Shelly, 37 years old, went to Magistrate's Court number 14 of Madrid to denounce his mother, he stated, among other things, that dona Margarita Ruiz de Lihory Resino, widow, of 67 years of age, who lived in number 72, third floor, right side, of the Calle de la Princesa, felt an unmeasured love for animals, that she posessed great numbers distributed on two farms of the property, one in Pozuelo de Alarcon and the other in Ciudad Lineal, and also in her own residence cited above, in which she had that day 17 dogs, 3 cats, 10 to 12 canaries and two turtles.

—But my mother's love for those creatures did not stop there — he continued—, but reached the point that when they died, she proceeded to personally dissect them, cutting out the tongue, removing the heart and skinning them, which she later preserved, and on some occasions had decapitated the dead animals also saving their heads.

Of course this did not constitute a crime, nor was it the objective of the denunciation. On the other hand one must add that the reporter for THE CASE, which published in that magazine an extensive report on the macabre incident, interviewed the Veterinarian who cared for dona Margarita's animals in Madrid, don Jaime Aguado Trigueros, with an animal clinic on the Calle Buen Suceso 4, one of the best accredited in Madrid for competence and facility.

Between the reporter and the Veterinarian the following dialogue took place:

—For how long have you been tending the dogs of dona Margarita?

—Since the month of July.

—Does she have many animals?

—I believe she has 68 dogs besides numerous canaries.

—Does she care much for the animals?

—Extraordinarily. During the month of August I was going to her house every day, and sometimes more than once.

—Is it true that she disected the animals that died?

—I don't believe so. In August I performed an autopsie on a female dog and knew that someone else had performed a similar operation, but whether she performed it personally I have no direct knowledge.

—Tell us please, the case in which you intervened.

—It was a dog named "Zoe", a favorite, it seemed of dona Margarita. She died as a consequence of intestinal infection, and I was called to autopsie the cadaver because she wanted me to diagnose the exact cause of the death.

—Was dona Margarita present during the operation?

—Yes, and I was taking the animal organ by organ and showing and explaining what it was.

—Where did you put the viscera?

—In a pit.

—Did you remove the head or the skin from the cadaver of the dog?

—No.

—Do you believe the love this woman had for her animals was abnormal?

—It might perhaps seem abnormal to one not occupied with these things but in the world with which I come in contact in my profession, there ar a great many cases similar to this which in no way have pathological implications.

And who would have ever believed that? Was it the daughter of dona Margarita, or the veterinarian who cared for her animals? The relation between the Marquesa and her son Luis did not seem to be precisely good. When dona Margarita stood before the judge, to respond to the accusation by her son, she declared:

—This is an infamy of my son Luis to revenge himself on me—she said.

She denied before the judge any knowledge of the existence of the hand in the place where it was found. She did not know that the hand was there, and much less did she acknowledge that she had cut it off. She attributed the act to her son Luis, with whom she had not spoken for some time, and who had committed many swindles utilizing her name, having found himself ordered before various judges of Barcelona and area a number of times and more than once being jailed.

Confronted with the declaration of Luis, the judge ordered a search of the domicile of dona Margarita Ruiz de Lihory.

DISCOVERY OF THE SEVERED HAND

A group from the Criminal Investigation Brigade commanded by Chief Inspector Fernandez Rivas included Inspectora Alcocer, Gallego, Ruiz, Barroso, Ojeda and Ares. For four hours —the search commenced at 11:30 at night of the same day, the 30th, and ended at 03:30 in the morning of the 31st— the investigators searched for some human member or organ. They were recieved very kindly by dona Margarita and Sr. B. Iglesias, the only inhabitants of the house besides the servants, Luisa Ballery, already mentioned, and Antonio Torrero, 21 years of age, and no difficulty was offered.

The house was richly furnished, with an abundance of paintings on the walls. During the first two hours of search by the inspectors, they examined several rooms without finding anything of interest. Only when they came to the bedroom of dona Margarita, and opened one of the closets, did they see there a small butcher's clever. From this moment they increased the diligence of the search, which soon bore fruit.

In the same closet, in a corner, they found a plastic jar containing in a transparent liquid a right hand. The jar was a kind of milk bottle of about one liter capacity. Its lower part was of reddish opaque plastic, and the upper part of the same material but white and transparent. The liquid, surely alcohol, filled the jar completely, bathing the entire hand. This was found with the fingers up, and had been sectioned at the wrist.

The study of the amputated member made by the School of Legal Medicine revealed that the amputation had been the work of an expert surgeon, which entangled the affair still more.

In the same furnishing where they found the hand there were two plush towels stained red with blood and three pillow cases with similar stains. In a corner of the room were two dog skins.

In another closet of the same room they found: a basin with bloodstains in the bottom, containing three pieces of bloody cotton; ten to twelve pairs of scissors of different sizes and classes; almost as many clamps; and various medical and surgical instruments, including a tensiometer and a stethescope, a test tube filled to the 300 cc mark with a dark red liquid, surely blood; and a two liter alcohol jar with a fourth of a liter of that liquid.

Within a basket of fruit they found a large envelope, white, sealed, and some scissors. Opening the envelope, they found that it contained a lock of long dark brown hair, another handful of shorter hair and two small combes.

In the dining room, above the carving table, within a closed soup kettle, there was, in alcohol two skinned dog heads.

In one of the two bathrooms of the house, they found a container of animal viscera, also submerged in alcohol.

The Police took into custody all that we have described, which, together with dona Margarita, Senor Bassols Iglesias and the servants Luisa and Antonio, they passed on to the Magistrate, where they were detained.

Later the same team of inspectors, searched the hotel owned by dona Margarita owned in Ciudad Lineal, cared for by a woman, and in that they found the mummified cadavers of two dogs and several dog skins.

THE DEATH OF MARGOT

At the last hours of 19 January 1954, Margot Shelly Luiz de Lihory died of pulmar inflamation, in the house on Calle Princesa. She had contracted the illness sometime earlier, in Albacete, where she lived discretely on her salary as typist for the Delegacion Provincial del Instituto de Prevision. On 21 January a Death Certificate was filed in the offices of the Registro Civil de Universidad. The functionary wrote: "Numero 88... Inscribed, The death of dona Maria Margarita Shelly y Ruiz de Lihory, native of Valencia, 36 years of age, residing at Calle Princesa, 72, self employed, daughter of Ricardo and Margarita, single state. Deceased in her residence on 19 January 1954, at 18:00 hours, a consequence of pulmonar edema, and her body will be buried in the San Isidro Cemetary..."

THE "DARNAUDE REPORT"

My good Sevillian friend, Ignacio Darnaude is an institution himself among Spanish UFOlogists (and many foreigners). His library and personal archives on the UFO theme in general, and the unusual in particular, is no doubt one of the best provided in out country. If anyone looks for something and Ignacio does not have it, nobody will. Darnaude became interested also in the enigma of the severed hand and its development, and it was thus that he came to distribute among his own friends, a report, dated in April of 1971, titled "The Possible Operations of a group of unidentified agents in the city of Albacete from 1952 to 1954". He gave in that a list of persons still living at that time, who could provide information on the enigmatic "Affair"... In that list figuered "the key witnesses", the "servants and employees of the various farms owned by dona Margarita", "the friends of dona Margarita", the "doctors who during almost one month interrogated and analyzed dona Margarita and her husband in the Hospital Psychiatrico de Carabanchel Bajo (Madrid), by judicial order, dictating in their report, '...Their mental state is perfect and presents no abnormality of any kind'. That team of medical experts was headed by Dr. J. Velasco Escassi."

Later in the list of Darnaude, we come to "the companions at work of Margot in the Instituto Nacional de Prevision de Albacete"; "Those reporters of the magazine EL CASO, who investigated the Affair themselves and published first hand reports in the magazine, were Jaime Estevez, "Pimpinela", "Cuti" and "D.G.A.". This first hand testimony is the most interesting.

He advised also, investigation of the entities of Albacete who might be able to identify and locate the "two doctors who attended Margot Shelly and transported her to the Capital and watched over her body. And finally, he compiled a list of all the information about the case that appeared in the Spanish press. He indicated too that one of the three Valencian dailies, reinterviewed, in February 1954, dona Margarita's servant, Andres Gomez Honrubia, and published some declarations that should be examined.

It was evident that this realization of the complete plan of investigation proposed by Darnaude would require much time and money. Some of it was done, especially by the ufologists of Albacete but the results have been very well scarce. I also have made some effort to investigate there (as well as those made in 1981 by Juan Jose Benitez), in company with the ufologist and local radio reporter, the young Jose de Zor Garcia Martinez. I remember that we visited the ancestral mansion, converted today to an open air park, which occupies the old site of the mansion—almost a palace—of dona Margarita, "the house of the fantasmas" as the local children call it.

—Under our feet—Pepe said, still exists the mysterious basement where the Ummites carried out their vivisection operations. I was able to get myself into a galerie that separated from a contiguous house and came to a room that contained a pile of hypodermic syringes and old texts on anatomy. But I could not go any further... When I asked permission of the Delegado de Obras Publicas del Ayuntamiento to go into the basement, he acted very disgusted and sharply prohibited it.

And he added, looking pensively around him; What is strange is that after the demolition work, nothing was done here to enlighten again for years. And here, in the center of Albacete, a small square of terraine holds the secret. It is incomprehensible.

And to ease his ascertion, he indicated the metallic skeleton of an enormous derrick that rusted away from unuse, parked at one side of the property.

—It has been here years —he added.

Who or what halted some work that would have been highly rentable? Why does the basement remain sealed and protected? Why had the excavators not penetrated the basement to lay the foundations for the new structure? What terrible and unconfessable secrets are hidden in its interior? The atmosphere for a story by Lovecraft is perfect. But Jose de Zor continued trying to penetrate the prohibited place, come what may...

In the wall of the ajacent house he saw traces of a stair, which, after an elbow continued descending toward the mysterious depths of the basement complex. But toward the center of the manor, in a place corresponding to the old garden was the perfect circle of pit or hole cut flush with the floor. In another place was a slab that could be lifted... The attraction of the mystery was irresistable. But we could do nothing at the moment.

We continue with Darnaude's report. If we admit that the "Ummites", (or whoever hides behind that name), chose dona Margarita for having found her record "as spie" in the archives of the French Deuxieme Bureau — as they have indicated — and thus having convenient qualities (posessing a great number of animals, capable of secrecy, sensible and cultured, and living in a small provincial city), it is natural that, aware of the precarious economic situation of the Bassols-Ruiz de Lihory couple, decided to "help" them splendidly to gain their favors, not amorous, but the consent of the Marquesa devoted not only to these things, but those we would call zoological. For these reasons they rented the big house at Mayor 58 for a fine monthly sum, and it seems they passed other discrete "envelopes" once in a while, to continue counting on the silence and collaboration of the couple. (To her they presented themselves as "Danish Doctors", like they had done years later to the typist in Madrid.)

How and where did these extraterrestrials get the money? In one of their reports they told us that when they came to understand the value that we placed on gold, they brought great quantities of this metal from UMMO for their operations here. Thus it was easy.

But let us continue. Darnaude says in his paragraph 11 (possible sources of financing); dona Margarita Ruiz de Lihory alleged that she had received an inheritance from a relative in Mexico, without offering any details. On the other hand, on the morning of the 20th of January 1954, with the body of Margot Shelly, according to custom, in the casket for viewing, on the ground floor of the dwelling at Calle Princesa in Madrid, her mother and Sr. Bassols went out into the street, and returned with more than 100,000 Pesetas in cash (a very considerable sum for the time), saying that this high sum came from a lottery winning, which both had gone to collect. And this with the body of her daughter waiting! Grotesque... but, was it a lottery prize they had gone to collect, or...?

In her defense (let us not forget that dona Margarita, was also a paintor who exhibited in New York and other places in the world, and had studied Law, something unusual for the young women of society of that period), said that the hand of her daughter was for her like a relic, and that, in the same manner that we venerate the parts of the bodies of saints, she also wanted the same for Margot. As there was no law against this, the accusation did not succeed.

To finish with the Darnaude Report, we cite the text of its final part, paragraphs 8, 9, 12, 13 and 14.

8. THE PROCEEDINGS

As a consequence of these developments, criminal proceedings were initiated, in which those charged were dona Margarita Ruiz de Lihory and D. Jose Maria Bassols Iglesias, whose actions were developed in the Judicial District No. 6 of Madrid, under the Magistrate of the Most Excellent Sr. D. Jose Maria Salcedo Ortega (Velazquez 45, Madrid) ...today President of the Section Septima de la Audiencia Territorial de Madrid, and then Secretary D. Carlos Viada Lopez-Puigcerver. The first declarations were deposited before the Most Excellent Magistrate Sr. D. Emilio Aguado Gonzalez (Joachim Garcia Morato, 54, Madrid), until his Judgement ended the affair. The first defense lawyer named by dona Margarita was D. Enrique Moret, of the Colegio de Madrid, with residence in Madrid (Calle Jorge Juan N.º 55, telephone 226-96-46). We do not know whether the second defense lawyer named was her attorney of Valencia, Don Arturo Roig, nor do we know the prosecutors involved. We still do not know the date of the sentence of the Audiencia nor what it contained. The documentation in this case is filed in the Seccion Tercera de lo Criminal de la Audiencia Territorial de Madrid, at the Plaza de las Salesas.

The process was appealed to the Tribunal Supremo in whose Sala Segunda, sentence was pronounced on 14 April 1964, almost ten years after the case had been appealed to the Tribunal. We can say that the review took place on the 14th of April, and the sentence was dictated on the25th of the same month. The appeal (No. 27.217) was interposed for dona Margarita Ruiz de Lihory by the Most Excellent Sr. D. Jose Maria Gonzalez Diaz, the Fiscal was Sr. Farinas, and the current lawyer was Sr. F. Pampliega Jimenez (Churruca, 14, telephone 222-97-56 Madrid). Sr. Herreros intervened as secretary. The sentence was published in the Aranzadi, and was limited to an indication that there was no further recourse, containing very little information about the case itself.

We believe that the declarations made in defense before the members of the Audiencia and the Tribunal Supremo, and in private before the defense lawyers would be of great interest, but we have not had access to this information.

The Juzgado de Instruccion de Albacete (Calle Salamanca, s/n), who also intervened in this case, should have important documents still existing in their files.

9. THE ANIMALS OF DONA MARGARITA

The Marquisa's animals constituted a veritable zoological park and were found all over, on the various farms and properties of the family. On the properties at Pozuelo de Alarcon and Ciudad Lineal, of the great numbers there, dogs frequently died. Some were found with their abdomens open, and others mummified. In the garden of the house on Calle Mayor, there was a cemetary for dogs and cats, and in one room of the interior, a functionary of the Hacienda observed various dried heads within receptacles of silver. It was said that dona Margarita bought many dogs in Albacete, and that in the basement of her house disections of the same were carried out. Dona Margarits always denied that she ever personally performed any dissections of animals, alleging that they were always carried out by "a veterinarian".

12. SELF DEFENCE OF THE ACCUSED

It would be very useful to get to the bottom of the truths, causes, and motives of dona Margarita Ruiz de Lihory, who made the following intriguing declarations, cited by the magazine EL CASO:

"I hope to God that someday the truth of all will be known, and not from my mouth."

"God pardon that which was the cause of all of this."

"The personal friends, who know what surrounds me, will speak soon on the mystery, and the why of those things."

13. CONTRADICTORY ASPECTS OF THE CASE

What motivations induced them to mutilate the body of Margot Shelly? Is there a connection between this section, the surgical interventions and disscetion of the animals of dona Margarita, and the mutilation of the body of her daughter? Why did the author or authors of this profanity preserve the evidence of this crime, instead of destroying it to avoid possible future guilt? Why did those agents who say they are from UMMO write these letters 15 years after the events described, thus giving grounds to relate them to the disagreeable and touchy affair?

14. HOW COULD THESE THINGS HAPPEN?

On the basis of the scarce material collected up to now, and because of the data that we have not been able to verify or prove, this is merely a working hypothesis to rectify in the future, with proofs that are going to be obtained, what is imagined how those events could have developed approximately in the following manner, if there is any truth in this extraordinary story:

Toward the spring or summer of 1952, a small group of unidentified agents entered into contact with dona Margarits Ruiz de Lihory, a dame of high culture, open spirit, and international background, and at the same time in need of abundant monetary resources. They probably presented themselved with some foreseen restraint relatively convincing, representing themselves as doctors, investigators, biologists, or as expierimenters of new pharmacutical drugs, or something in that style. For a heavy sum they rented the big house at Mayor 58, and the use of the private zoological park of dona Margarita, and regularly submitted to her the diverse requirements that they were going to need. During more than a year they closed themselves in the dwelling, coming out of it little or not at all, carried out the mission for which they came to Albacete. Because of the great national scandal over "the case of the severed hand", and foreseeing an official search and investigation of the property at Mayor 58 (the house where all occurred), they were obliged to abandon Albacete the first part of February 1954. We know nothing about the ends that induced them to secrete themselves in this tranquil Spanish city, nor what they really did in that house. We suspect that one of their various activities consisted of dissecting animals.

Three days later their ("Danish Doctors") stay in Albacete was made public, for reasons unknown to us. Having foreseen - surely - their eventual involvement and blame in such a sad and macabre case, and not content with this, but adorning their declarations with a novelesque story of their supposed extraterrestrial origin, the real motivations that had generated such strange and unusual conduct escapes us completely. But we can no less than suppose that if "they" invested time, human energy and financial means in Albacete, it was for something, and that "something" was naturally secret and seemed to be mixed up with the activities that surrounded the illegality (inauthorized biological experiments) which could have considerable importance. They do not tell us if they are in reality a species of superdeveloped extraterrestrial entities. At least the disconcerting history of the self-baptized Ummites must be investigated carefully in order to find out exactly what occured, that could be considered factors capable of interferring in the economic structure of our society and national security, and more so when those individuals of UMMO continue at these lengths, with impunity and tranquility, their labor of divulging and disseminating information and literature that could perhaps upset the traditional (ideological, social, religious, customary, etc.) foundations of our society, on which rests the habitat and mode of life of the Spanish people.

We may consider a second alternative: In the house at Mayor 58 was secluded nobody alien to the Ruiz de Lihory family, nor did anything out of the ordinary occur there. But someone had examined those archives and selected that of the severed hand as a pilot-case, persuing results we do not understand, to gain the objective of sewing the unprovable rumor that in Albacete lived in those times, two extraterrestrial personages dedicated to disturbing biological manipulation and experiment.

Whichever case, the affair includes a sufficient dose of suspicious elements to justify a profound investigation.

APRIL of 1971

But Darnaude continued investigating, and thus it was in June of that same year of 1971, that he distributed the following pages with additional information on the case:

ADDITIONAL INFORMATION ON THE SUPPOSED AGENTS OF ALBACETE

The intimate friend of Margot Shelly, who worked at Mosaicos Carbajal, was Srta. Herminia Arteaga Hernandez, residing at Sanchez Torres 5 (2.° C), Albacete. When she was a guest in the house of Margot living at Calle Mayor No. 63, almost in front of the house of dona Margarita, she was at the same time a good friend of Srta. Concha Panadero Sala, sister of the manfriend of Margot, who lived at Concepcion No. 11 of Albacete.

On the 5th of February 1954, a man spontaneously presented himself before the Magistrate of Madrid to make a declaration concerning the case of the severed hand, and he deposited a lengthy declaration. The name of this person has not been published.

The declarations of Andres Gomez Honrubia, a male servant of dona Margarits Ruiz de Lihory, appeared in the daily "Levante" of Valencia for the 7th of February 1954, page 3. In that he said that one day he had penetrated the subterranean part of the house on Calle Mayor 58, accompanying a maid, when this house had for a number of months been closed and abandoned. They found the electric light of the basement "turned on" since dona Margarita always went in with a veil, and came out very pallid—, and they saw a complete skeleton and many skulls. The walls of the "Cuarto de Morro" (as they called it) were hung with red velvet, and the floor was covered with lime. There were other subterranean parts, which he did not know about.

Gomez Honrubia assured that in the house with the pit there was another subterranean level, with the floor removed on many occasions. He said that "they practices strange and unknown things" with those animals, which "soon died of strange illnesses despite penicillins and other drugs".

At the end of the interview, the reporter asked G. Honrubia: —Anything else?— And he answered: —one, no a great many. But I can not and must not say." The article seemed to be signed by "P.A. Perez-Ruiz".

The big house at Mayor No. 58 was searched in February 1954 by the agents of the Police of Madrid and of Albacete.

Dona Margarita had a workhouse some ten kilometers from Albacete, on the highway to La Roda. There they found a machine gun.

The text of a letter of dona Margarita's, published in number 99 of EL CASO, read "...accusations that not only are not true, but in their time will demonstrate their origin, such as the reality of those works and the author or authors of same."

The Judge of Albacete who presided in this affair (search of the house etc.) was Don Arsenio Rueda.

The first husband of dona Margarite, D. Ricardo Shelly, worked for a Northamerican Insurance Company "The Equitable". He died in 1942.

The sister of dona Margarita, dona Soledad, married a second time with D. Manuel de la Vina y Massip. She had two daughters, one of them adopted.

The hearing in the Audiencia de Madrid on the case of the severed hand, was held behind closed doors. Nevertheless there was a rumor that the newsman Don German Salinas Cuesta was present at the deliberations in disguise. It seems that Sr. Salinas fled to Venezuela to (La Guaira), where he inherited a fortune, returning to Spain in 1967...

It seems, a doctor of the Seguro Obligatorio de Enfermidad de Albacete attended Margot Shelly when she became ill. This same Doctor accompanied her to Madrid, together with a brother of Margot.

It is said that a Madrid newspaper published a photograph of the body of Margot, and that a photographer Samtos Yubarra insisted that it was tricked. The hands appeared covered with flowers. Also there was word then that some people strategically situated had been suborned with heavy sums of money to silence questions related to the case. Also it was rumored that the extraction of the members from the body was done by a known surgeon of Madrid, by commission.

Another rumor at the time was that a couple, intimately known by the Bassols, who liven on Calle Alberto Aguilera of Madrid, had in their service a robust Asturian maid, who suddenly contracted a strange illness of the blood, an anemia.

The inscription in the Registro Civil de Madrid (District of Universidad) registering the death of Margot Shelly was signed by D. Alfredo Nueda Garcia (Vallehermoso, 68, Madrid), D. Ignacio Hervas Vasquez (Feijoo, 10, Madrid), and Alfredo Toledano Catalan (Fernandez de los Rios, 24, Madrid). The document did not indicate the name of the institution that issued the Death Certificate. The cause of death shown was "pulmonary edema".

Margot Shelly died at 36 years of age, and not 42 as some of the papers reported.

In Albacete there was word that in the last days of her illness, Margot Shelly was treated by "a Hispanoamerican" in Madrid.

It was affirmed that one of the Psychiatric Doctors of the team of Dr. D. Jose Velasco Encassi, Don Julio Camino Galicia (Menorca, 17, telephone 276-70-57, Madrid, refused to sign the final act in which they certified the good state of mental health of the Bassols couple.

In Albacete, on seeing the house on Calle Mayor, they called it "The house of the Phantasms". Why?

This dwelling was supervised and cared for by the Administrator of dona Margarita.

In those first days of February 1954, the daily, "La Voz de Albacete" received numerous "Letters to the Editor" referring to the case of the severed hand. It might be useful to examine the contents of those missives which were never published.

In 1971 a series of persons in Albacete received a letter in Castilliano , signed by one Mr. W. Rumsey (Room 402, Hotel Emperador on Jose Antonio, 53, Madrid-13), in which he offers a reward of $1.000.00 in U.S. Dollars (59,000 Pesetas), to anyone who could open ways to find those "men of science" who, before 1954 were carrying on "histological" work in the house of dona Margarita, Calle Mayor No. 58 of Albacete. The Hotel Emperador reported that, actually, a Northamerican with that name, was a guest in room 402 on the 11th to the 15th of May 1971, from which he left without leaving any signs. We do not know if any neighbor of Albacete got in touch with Mr. Rumsey, or if the promised reward was paid. We have been unable to further identify the person of that Mr. Rumsey, nor the organization for which he worked.

We have heard it said that there is another case "of a severed hand". We would like to know more about this, and see if there is any relation between the two.

That which for that time paid the most attention was the press of Madrid, for which, in it must reside the information of most interest, such as in the dailies (Pueblo, Alcazar, Informaciones, Madrid, Arriba and Ya and ABC) and in such magazines as EL CASO, Semana, Diez Minutes, 7 Fechas, Domingo, Blanco y Negro, Garbo, Hola!, Sabado Grafico, etc.

IMPORTANT OBSERVATION

The majority of these notes are based on unconfirmed rumors. They consist of mostly second hand information, with little of objective value. To acquire validation for these data —one by one— they must be verified and confirmed. Meanwhile they are simply that, mere rumor.

Darnaude completed this new recompilation of data by reproducing the text of the letter circulated in Albacete, and signed by the enigmatic Mr. Rumsey:

8 June 1971

Gentlemen:

The present letter is to ask for information that may be of great value, which will be rewarded in the event that one can help me with my requirements.

In the yeat 1952 and following months, in the dwelling situated on Calle Mayor of Albacete, address number 58 (real estate demolished for another construction) owned by dona Margarita Ruiz de Lihory of noble title Baronesa de Alcahali, wife of Sr. Shelly, both now deceased, residing in same, two men of medical profession and Danish nationality at the invitation of that Senora, who during an indeterminate number of months, and while dona Margarita resided in another city, occupied various rooms of the cited property, keeping a very retired life, and though some neighbors knew of their existence, since they only came out of their residence at night, few noted more than I could get.

I am informed that the sons of dona Margarita Ruiz de Lihory do not know their identification, since their mother never informed them of their residence and the histological experiments of those scientists.

Another note, though doubtful, mentions that one at least of these gentlemen had moved quietly to Madrid after the daughter of that senora, Margot Shelly, was transferred gravely ill to the Capital of Spain. In whichever case these men of science abandoned Albacete before the Magistrate ordered the search and holding of the property.

The motive of this desire of mine, is to know the domicile of those Doctors; whether in Denmark or in Spain, to obtain complementary notes on some important studies of animal physiology made by them.

I am prepared to deliver a donation of 1,000 (thousand dollars) at exchange: 69,000 pesetas, to whoever furnishes the information sufficient to locate those doctors, it being possible that some resident of Calle Mayor has knowledge of same.

Accept my courteous greeting.

If you have information, please send to this signature:

Mr. W. RUMSEY
Room 402 Hotel Emperador

Avenida Jose Antonio, 53. ESPANA
Madrid-13

NOTE:

We hare respected integrally the apparent mis-use of the Castillano, including the punctuation symbols, which does not disturb the intelligence of the text. It is possible that this "Mr. Rumsey" could be an agent of the CIA, an entity very interested in the activities of the Ummites.

[NOTE- There are still a lot of unanswered questions in this affair, such as:

1. Exactly when did Margot Shelly die? Was it at 18:00 in her home in Albacete as stated in her death certificate?
2. If so why was she taken to Madrid, and was that the same night or was it earlier? Was there more than one trip to Madrid?
3. Who accompanied her to Madrid? Was it two doctors, or one doctor and her brother, ...or somebody else?
4. When were the members removed from the body, and by whom?
5. Why was the body dismembered?
6. What were the reclusive "Danish Doctors" actually doing in the house on Calle Mayor 58, in Albaceta?
7. Was dona Margarita actually involved, and how?
8. How much money was paid over the period of time the "Doctors" used the house?
9. Why has nearly everybody with direct kbowledge in this case either died or disappeared?
10. What the mysterious Mr. Rumsey know that we don't?

True, this IS a mystery thriller first class. The only one with enough resources to conduct a proper investigation would be a government. Did they? And which one? -Publisher]

And finally it seems to me to be of interest to reproduce a text written by the Albacetian ufologist Jose Garcia Martinez (Jose de Zor, previously mentioned) for the documental or anecdotal value it might have.

NEW INVESTIGATIONS AND EVENTS RELATING TO ALBACETE-UMMO

On Sunday 31 August 1980, there appeared in the periodical "La Voz de Albacete" some articles on Margarita Ruiz de Lihory relating to biographical data. They published others on the 3 and 19 of September along on the same theme.

On Wednesday 22 October of 1980, I (Jose Garcia Martinez) went out of my house at 09:00 to meet with some friends in a cafeteria to plan a program of investigation of the UMMO-AB case. That same day between 11:00 and 13:00 hours, two subjects of more than 1.80 meters stature went to my house. They called at the entrance and my mother (Consuelo Martinez) came out, who upon seeing such a rare aspect as the two subjects, became a little fearful. They asked for me and they said to my mother that it was urgently necessary for them to speak to me because it pertained to them (?) and that they also needed to comment on some letters that were in my posession. My mother told them that I had gone out and the subjects left. When I got home she told me of the strange visit. I was surprised by the description she gave me of them. Clothes of leather fitted to the body, dark hunter's pants not very big, brilliant boots of fur, and they wore dark glasses. They had blond hair and light skin, and did not speak spanish well, having an accent that seemed Northamerican.

On the 24th day of the same month, at 13:30 to 14:00 of mid-day, on one of the corners of my street (Concejal Castillo) I saw a subject with the same characteristics as my mother told me. He looked at me casually and I at him. Upon arriving at the door of the house, I turned my head and he was no longer there. That was all.

—There was little possibility of fraud. Nobody but those friends who were with me in the cafeteria on the 26th knew I was investigating the case all this time. Joke? No, I don't believe it, nor do I have friends who have blond hair and measure more than 1.80 meters, with an age of 30 to 35 (which was the apparent age of these subjects).

Data against the veracity of the event: the clothes they wore. It was not the classic style of those "men in black", nor was this their form of activity?

—This was an event truely rare, and confusing in how to react.

—The reporter Pedro Monzon of "La Voz de Albacete" received threats about something that would happen if he continued the articles on UMMO in that paper.

—On 27 November the publisher of "La Voz" suffered a burglary of an important piece of a machine that impeded the production of photographs in the paper. He who managed the enterprise was an expert in these machines knew that not knowing the mechanism well, it would be difficult to extract the piece robbed. The police investigated the robbery with no success.

—On the same day, the 27th, they made in the chain SER de Albacete, a program on the Ummites in Albacete, and the case as disseminated in all of Spain, Midnight Program (Program "Media Noche" of A.J. Ales).

—Rapidly UFO investigators became interested in the case. On the 15th of December J. J. Benitez came but did not encounter anything new.

DEATHS

In the month of November 1980, Sr. Panadero, together with his mother (who was an administrator for dona Margarita) died in a fire on Calle Perez Pastor of Albacete. In the same month, the last neighbor of dona Margarita, on Calle Mayor, died. She knew all the life of the Marquesa, but still nobody had interrogated her in depth.

AMERICAN INVOLVED

Sr. D. Pedro Gascon made some statements concerning a Northamerican subject who hid some most valuable information involving the Marquesa. D. Pedro did not want to talk about the incident and would not give details. He preferred not to speak on the subject at all. The only thing he would say was that he was a friend of this Northamerican, who was a friend to dona Margarita, who delivered some microfilms to him to take out of the country. Days later, the friends of this Northamerican noticed that he was acting strange and finally he confessed that he was pursuing various subjects. It seems that he had received some threats. The last days he was seen they noted in him a surprising fear. He disappeared without knowing his whereabouts. Now it is believed by D. Pedro that those microfilms may be deposited in a bank in Albacete. This is all that I could get out of Sr. Gascon.

—The reserve and the secretiveness among the persons who knew anything about this case is extreme. And this also included the reporters of the press who dedicated much time to this affair.

PRESENCE IN CHIPIONA (CADIZ) OF PERSONS WITH ACTIVITIES SIMILAR TO THOSE OF THE SUPPOSED UMMITES IN ALBACETE

—Francisco Sanchez Sanchez, a friend with whom I maintain correspondence, wrote me the following: (Letter dated 9-12-80)

"...came rememberances of my infancy of between 8 and 9 years, in which a very strange man came to Chipiona. He was quite tall and rented a house, and I believe that it also had animals. It was during the time when they said to take care about the "men-in-black" (The "Danish Doctors" affected conservative dark attire) for they were experimenting on children. I remember one day when a man in a dark suit came to school and called to me to give me something. I immediately left running... This comes to mind and may have some relation to the UMMO case.

CANADIAN EMBASSY LETTER

The Canadian Embassy, responding to the sudden flurry or reporting in the media on the UMMO case, sent the following letter to the investigator, Jose de Zor, in his office:

EMBASSY OF CANADA
With the compliments of the Canadian Ambassador

Respecting the information that we have concerning the two alleged doctors in your city on Calle Mayor N.º 52 with dark result, we inform you, respecting your confidence, that there resided, during two years (1967 - 1969), in our Canadian city of Brandon, two similar (doctors), who later went to Germany without returning, to our knowledge.

With my compliments,

A cordial salute

THE VERSION OF THE ACTIVITIES ACCORDING TO THE UMMITES

In 1971, the Asociacion de Estudios Cosmologicos ERIDANI, of Madrid, received a letter from UMMO in which, besides giving some precise data on their activities (between them and the operations carried out in Spain by the CIA to identify them, received in the coded name of the RED CASTILE A4L) said the following:

"We don't believe that your investigations concerning our stay in Albacete will contribute in the present avenues to clarification of our situation.

"In effect 'we resided' clandestinely in the domicile (now demolished as you know) of that gentle Spanish woman, D. Margarita Ruiz de Lihory on Calle Mayor (in those times No. 58), which allowed us to study some of her animals which she loved. When on the 2nd of February of 1954, the situation became insustainable for my companions (remember that Margot Shelly had died on the preceeding 19th of January) due to the inevitable comments of the neighbors, we had to abandon that which was the first place to stay of my brothers in this country since their arrival from France.

"We advise you not to investigate the case surrounding the near relatives surviving this woman, since nobody, or very few know of our existence.

"In September 1968, padre Enrique Lopez Guerrero, parochial priest of Mairena del Alcor, in Seville, sprang to prominence in the National and foreign press with some declarations in which he affirmed that a colony of extraterrestrials resided in Spain. His first declarations were made to newsreporter Benigno Gonzalez, of the ABC of Seville, who published them on 17-9-68. What really happened was that, a short time before, I had given the impulsive Andalusian Priest a handful of UMMO Reports (as you did with Fouere in Paris), but the good don Enrique, without remembering, it seems, that I had asked for discretion, hurried to go with the story to Benigno Gonzalez. It was the first time (since that of Sesma), that the Spanish press spoke of UMMO. The dissemination reached by the news worried even the Ummites to the point where they abandoned Spain for some time, according to their later communications.

In 1971 don Enrique, unperturbed, returned to the charge with even more disturbing declarations, and that despite the fact that two years before, on 27 March 1969, had laid before him a friendly proposition, as you will see in the letter sent him, which we will reproduce following the declarations of the padre to the press, in which he also aluded to their stay in Albacete:

A COLONY OF EXTRATERRESTRIAL BEINGS LIVES IN SPAIN SAYS SEVILLE PRIEST

Padre Lopez Guerrero Affirms That Said Beings Came to Earth on the 28th of March 1950.

Seville, 17, --"Not only does he believe in the existence of extraterrestrial beings, but he has knowledge that they reside in a colony in Spain, whose mission is completely wellintended and peaceful."

This is no less than the sensational declaration, with all seriousness and based on scientific observation, that has just come to the editor of the ABC daily of Seville in the person of padre don Enrique Lopez Guerrero, 38 years old, native of Seville, parish minister of the locality of Mairena del Alcor in the vocation of priest.

The Sevillian priest said that those extraterrestrial beings came from the planet "UMMO", some 14.6 light years from Earth, and which revolves around the star Wolf 424. A planet, they say, that has dimensions similar to our planet, and whose conditions of life are nearly identical. An aggregate of 1,800 millions of inhabitants live there, and among them telepathy is commonly used.

He said also that those beings were tall, blond and looked nordic, that they seemed well controlled; and that their spaceships were well protected from control by means of "gravitational waves before which our most sophisticated electronic apparatus is impotent"; and they come to Earth for no other reason than to study our life and society, "aided by means of contacts with groups of scientists throughout our whole world, to whom they facilitate knowledge which may contribute to the progress of Earth humanity and universal fraternity. In any case, for the moment, they are not authorized to intervene actively in the affairs of Earth.

Padre Lopez Guerrero has had contacts of scientific nature with padre Felices, a resident of Valladolid, who investigates all lights relative to UFOs by order of his superior; together with don Antonio Ribera, national leader of UFO investigations and founder of the Centro de Estudios Interplanetarios de Barcelona; together with padre Benito Segundo Reyna, director of the observatory of Adhara, Argentina, and with General Lionel Chassin, ex-Commander-in-Chief of the Air Forces of NATO. The priest said also that, besides those Ummite beings are other extraterrestrial races among whom are the "Adamski" type and those called "humanoids". It is said that the last ones have intentions less benevolent than the former, but it seems they can not live in our atmosphere (without special equipment). They are more controlled and "can not harm us".

Summarizing the cosmobiological theory of padre Lopez Guerrero --"of simple hypothesis, for me has come to be a fundamental and defensable thesis", proclaims the following: 1) In the Universe there exist a plurality of inhabited worlds. 2) The biological evolution of the Universe has been in a uniform and parallel manner to reach the peak of rational life. 3) I am totally in agreement with the Christocentrism of Teilhard de Chardin: among the inhabited worlds, sinful man, the terrestrial type, is the exception that confirms the rule. 4) That Christ is the center of the Universe, the model of perfect man for us and a model of love for those who do not sin, in which, thanks to a future intervention (incarnation), those will be redeemed with everlasting redemption (like the Virgin). 5) On the plane of providence ordained by God, we will one day be among not only those we call the brothers of truth of all the inhabitants of Earth, but also those of the Universe. 6) The actual situation of our world is one of frightened desperation and the rise of existentialism. We live in a peace of terror which we cannot maintain indefinitely. One simple red button can put an end to our humanity. 7) We know that God is the father. Can a father in truth permit this to happen to his sons without resorting to all means availble to avoid it?

Finally one of the affirmations most surprising of many made by the Sevillian priest is as follows: "Those extraterrestrial beings who actually live on our planet, came to Earth on the 28th of March 1950. They arrived in three spacecraft which landed in a department of the Alps. In Spain we had the great (UFO) wave in the year 1950". --Cifra

El Noticiero Universal, Barcelona, 17-9-1968

But let us allow the Ummites to speak for themselves on this matter. Observing the flurry of interest produced by the newspaper articles quoting the Sevillian priest, the Ummites contacted their public stenographer in Madrid and dictated a letter which they had mailed to the priest himself. We shall reproduce that letter here for your own study and evaluation.

UMMOAELEWE
Language: Spanish
No. of Copies: 1
Date: 27 March 1969

Don Enrique Lopez Guerrero
MAIRENA DE ALCOR (Spain)

Senor:

We have followed with interest, in the Spanish press during these last months, your declarations about my brothers displaced on planet Earth.

We do not want to curb your exposing us to these small disturbances that your printed words are causing based on the initial notices printed in the editions of ABC distributed in Seville, nor the perturbations that the disoriented dissemination of your testimony could still provoke.

As you belong to an ecclesiastical group of great prestige in Spain, there could be enormous psychosocial response to your opinions.

We understand that you have not been bound to any moral obligation contracted with us, to observe strict reservations, since until today you have received no direct request of ours in this respect. If you are not vulnerable or have no other committments to your brother reporters, this is an affair over which we desire to maintain a respectful silence as we must not mix ourselves in that which is private of the OEMMIOYAGAA (as we call you).

We suspect that the supposed level of moral suffering for you is the incomprehension of your brothers, including your hierarchial superiors before the reaction that could be mistaken for or generated by unconscious motivations, but who respond if full consciousness to intentions much more pure. We ask your pardon for having been the indirect cause of this situation.

Now that those effects seem to have decreased, we decided to write you, not with the intention of exhorting you, but to explain with impartiality our criticism.

We are worried about the enthusiasm with which the news of our existence was accepted. The result paradoxically is that we ourselves must reproach your elevated degree of acceptance, but in any case you already know through the copies furnished by your correspondents, our normal cautions that prohibit any intent for our part, of extending, dangerously for us, our genuine presence on Earth.

It is hoped that our exaggerated secrecy will provoke disparate actions among you. Some beings who hide among you in their daily convivience, under false names, armed with fraudulent passports and documentation, who send strange reproduced reports to personalities of different nationalities, and who carry on prolonged telephone interviews in turn on the most heterogeneous themes and who identify themselves as travelers coming from a distant planet, when the sciences of Earth can not seriously refute the possibility of such displacement, is a situation difficult to accep. Do they hide other intentions more or less immoral?

It is inevitable thus that the hypotheses proliferate of different tones with respect to the different reasons that a "group of men" may have for working in this singular manner. (In a separate note we will summarize some of the ingenious interpretations that we could spy among your brothers.)

We feel culpable of having created this confusion among you, but for us it is impossible to avoid such speculations among such rarified things, and in conflict with the logical postulates extant on Earth.

For which, Senor Lopez, we desire at least to clarify certain aspects of our stay in Spain and our actual conduct, just as my brthers in other countries of Earth are doing at these moments to clarify to some extent the psychoambience created by the minor information.

There is no reason to hide anything that we actually did. We need only omit that which could serve to localize us or to offer definite proofs of our existence. In this short historical review will be limited to Spain and Portugal, and to your brothers whose identity is already familiar to you and your brother friends of Seville, Barcelona and Madrid.

OUR ACTIVITIES IN SPAIN

Our first residence in Spain was selected in a compact population center, Albacete. A woman who loved animals lent asylum to my two brothers, who could during their forced enclosure accomplish the first psychophysical experiments with mammals of Earth until certain rumors surfaced among the neighboring inhabitants there, making their removal advisable.

Together with another brother brought in from Austria, they established their residence in Barcelona, where they made their first contact under express declaration of our identity with an intellectual Spaniard who, despite rejection of our testimony, remained faithful up to now to his promise.

Bilbao and Madrid were the next centers of activity. Museums, magazine stores, libraries, temples, archives and Official Centers constituted the most important objectives of study.

They established the first relationship with Spanish OEMII, fans, interested parties or investigators in the field of hypothetical relations with extraterrestrials. Those supposed they controlled a mass of impressive material. Until then those contacts intended to establish relationships with you was limited to some intellectuals of Spain not familiar with these themes. Such that only one University professor seemed to pay a certain attention when we offered objective proofs of our stay. The relations with him continued until in June of 1967.

The interest awakened in men studying the UFO, OVNI or VED was not due only to reasons of character evoked or to spiritual attunement. From a little after our first arrival in France, we could tell you that OYAGAA experienced an authentic increase in visual detection of lenticular form ships which are vulgarly called "flying saucers".

Allowing for a high percentage of errors, fabrications, optical illusions, and exaggerations of news by the public media, there was no doubt that besides us, you were being the object of investigation and study by other galactic civilizations of unknown identity to my brothers as well as to you. Later we confirmed this assumption, detecting them in the space surrounding some OAWOLEA UEWA.

That was the letter to the priest. It did offer some confirmations of the activities in Albacete, but it offered some clarification on some of the other activities of the Ummites as well. In continuation we are reproducing some other Ummite communications, in which the authors continue mentioning the "Albacete case". These were addressed to ERIDANI (with a copy supplied to Rafael Farriols), an unknown man of Bilbao, and Ignacio Darnaude. In these they attribute all to an uncontrolled virus... which later resulted in being inoculated, but which already had become implanted in regions of the palm, the tongue, and the ocular globes of Margot Shelly (they wrote Shelli as they did Lihori) before they discovered her infection.

UMMOAELEWE

ERIDANI
No. of copies: 1
MADRID

We ask you to save this copy for your brother Rafaer Farriols Calvo.

Dear Sir:

We wish to transmit to you and your brothers our respectful salute. You and your brothers in Spain have not received our communications in some time and we do not want you to treat this as an act of disrespect or forgetfullness, or for lack of time on our part to dedicate our attention to this. We simply want to dosify (disseminate as it can be absorbed) our information, as we have already advised you on preceeding occasions, since it is our reiterated desire in other letters to pass as much as possible unnoticed. We are regulating our information according to the impact it can have on the Social Network. Now we have been forgotten in Spain, after a phase in which rumors more pernicious for you circulated in the media and among fans of the study of UFOs as you call them, for which we see no inconvenience in renewing the contact through an entity officially recognized by the Spanish State. But if the reports continue dissemination by strange means provoking scandalous reactions, we will feel obliged, for your own good (to us such reaction is no danger) to cease them. In this case our sudden reactions of silence would be stunning, as we detect perfectly such reactions in your brothers. We will update some of the less complete reports, but we must we must advise that we will continue sending them in a systematic and heterogeneous manner. We desire to help you, sir, in your labor of analysis of the documents which already have accounts of our relations with the Iberian countries. We liken these pages to reports of very elemental character, sent to a non-specialized group, didactive and primitivistic in concept but unavoidable at this experimental stage which was very valuable for us. Now I want to come to my separate messages to these humans.

IGNACIO DARNAUDE ROJAS: Your investigation in turn of the stay of my brothers in Albacete, years ago, has come to my attention. We congratulate you respectfully for your methodical analysis, whether or not you believe in our existence, and want to send you our respectful salute. We fervently desire that you do not misinterpret those unfortunate events related to that gentle woman who housed my brothers as guests. If we elected that mansion it was easily because of the aura of mystery that surrounded dona Margarita served my brothers to camouflage their activities and study. The rumors about their mental perterbations, unfortunately real rumors, took the force out of whatever possible official investigation about us that might have been realized in other circumstances, since the filtration of strange news regarding our presence remained cushioned by the scepticism of the dignified Spanish Authorities. I can assure you, senor Darnaude, that my brothers in those days did nothing that violated Spanish Law, and we were only being respectfully saved in case of our own defense within the social structure not being accepted.

REVEREND LOPEZ GUERRERO
Senor: We desire to salute you with cordiality and fraternity if this last were possible for identity and genetic characteristics. We will write you personally if it becomes viable to us. We know the great sympathy that you feel for us, Senor, which comforts us, and we offer you our embrace on your breast. Would you nevertheless permit what we exhort? We would like that much of the misunderstanding about us were clarified, and we desire prudence in interpretation; for which we will clarify in our letters some concepts that naturally you could not have due to your asimilar spirit.

SENOR DOMINGUEZ MONTES:A salute, honorable friend. We have listened attentively to your speculations offered in the symposium directed by senor Farriols. We ask that you not interpret as servile flattery or courtesy, our considerations respecting your analysis. If we except some medicos of Australia and some brothers of yours of Israel, and some French investigators who have gone much farther than you in their studies (of UMMO), we can assure you that nobody has placed as much interest in making a serious and methodical critique of our communications. We only ask that you be prudent in releasing your future investigations. We prefer that nobody appraise the truthfullness of our existence. Thanks anticipatedly.

DIONISIO GARRIDO BUENDIA: Senor, the next letter will be sent to an authorized organization, as it is necessary to be written officially as an associate of the same, and there now exist no reasons to advise your inhibition. For us it is impossible to communicate with physical societies or persons withour authorization. We send our greetings to your good friends, sceptics, and those that are not interested with respect to us.

UMMOAELEWEE
Number of copies: 3
Language: Spanish
For don...........
BILBAO, SPAIN

Barcelona, 6 August 1971

Dear Sir:

In our last letter we expressed a brief summary of our arrival on cold Star EARTH, and our first residence in France.

ARRIVAL OF UMMITES IN SPAIN

As a Spaniard you must no doubt feel a desire to know of our arrival in your country, which interested us in that time for two reasons: It would allow us to understand more profoundly aspects related to its history. On the other hand the Spanish Peninsuls would constitute a tranquil platform for some basic investigations in the field of the biology of vertebrates.

Our arrival in Spain (he who writes this was not then on the Astro EARTH) was affected by serious obstacles.

My brother expeditionaries were trying to locate a region with certain determined ecological characteristics and climatology which at once was ruled by an administrative structure sufficiently adequate to satisfy our own norms of security of the group.

The turistic influence had then just reached its greatest height on the Peninsula, and the fact that the Authorities had not demonstrated excessive analytical interest with respect to the identity of foreigners who with such motives travelled the frontiers, constituting a higher guarantee for (the safety of) our initial projects.

Three of our brothers among those displaced on Earth from UMMO at that time had specialized during their residence in France in the study of phonetics associated with languages having latin roots and could verbalize with acceptable capability tongues such as Romano, Spanish, Catalan, Sephardic and Italian.

Unfortunately one of them posessed atrophied (as is very normal among the OEMII of UMMO) vocal cords (sic), constitutes a more uncertain risk, since our devices for acoustical amplification which make this defect unrecognizable for any less observant human.

For this reason he was excluded from the Operation, substituting his superior for the other younger brother, specialized in animal metabolism and analysis of ecosystems, but with no linguistic knowledge in Castillano, for which he had to submit to a provisional preparation of intensive nature in this language.

Those three crossed the Spanish frontier near Irun (one of them returning a little later) provided with falsified passports of a nation of northern Europe, and with micro equipment for biological investigations. They carried, in addition to Spanish money, an informative dossier with names of citizens of Spain, and information on customs and characteristics of the society of Spain. ABAEXII-4 son of ABAEXII-3 travelled independently, with a passport in the name of a supposed University professor specialized in Zootechnology, and his brothers proceeded with fraudulent carnets as professionals in the field of Medicine.

Our initial project excluded as residence large cities such as Madrid, Barcelona, Valencia and Seville, as well as reduced rural centers, since in these it would be very difficult to maintain our anonymity within the limits required for our own security.

When they arrived, my brothers had not decided on a definite point of residence. They had begun compiling a list that included among six population centers, four that were especially good: Segovia, Albacete, Avila and Jaen. One grave aspect of the problem consisted for the time, in encountering citizens of Spanish nationality who would accept the covering paper (though ignorant of the same) for the residence of my brother investigators.

Analyzing the information at their disposition, they knew that one at first seemed completely suited. By the Spainsh press arriving in Marsella, they learned of the existence of a farm on the outskirts of the urban center of Jaen, which at that time was for sale. So then through a French agency of legal affairs they began negotiations for purchase. They apparently tried to open an agricultural farm to camouflage the real nature of the future investigations.

The plan did not succeed due to the unavoidable necessity of contracting to Spanish citizens in the sale.

For this reason also the attempt to open a veterinary clinic in the Ciudad Real of Segovia failed.

SECOND PHASE: STUDY OF THE CITIZENS

But at the same time, my brothers had found a way to familiarize themselves with data relating to Spanish citizens --Autobiographical-- through three distinct documental sources: A) From a Department of Registration at the Ministry of "Exterior". B) From an organization of Exiled Spaniards of the Civil War of 1936-1939. C) And a personal archive of an Ex-functionary of the time of Thorez.

This fragmented information was analized by our modules for processing of data XAANMOOBAABUASII which oriented our investigations toward two persons, both of YIE sex (female). The proprietor of a zootechnical enterprise of Extremadura and the other a Spanish woman in which there were concomitant circumstances of elevated interest, that she could be converted (as was the case) into an excellent and involuntary assistant.

The source of this last data was the dossier copy of another original corresponding to an archive of the "Deuxieme Bureau Frances) where her services as an agent of the Quinta Columna Nationalista Espanola in the cause of the Ejercito National Espanol, during the Spanish War, in the months of June, July and September of 1936, were summarized.

Of most interest to us was a marginal note on the card of this woman, which alluded to disturbances of psychopathological etiology of which this woman was accused, and the brief typed summary on the same card, among whose hobbies was mentioned her love for animals.

They planned a whole program to make themselves friends of this woman estimating that they could make her an offer of collaboration and that they would pay her for her help. My brothers estimated that in no case would she reveal our true alienterrestrial identity. They reserved other connected projects until they could enter into contact with her and better know her personality.

One of my brothers obtained, in Albacete, an interview with dona Margarita Ruiz de Lihori, when they found her afflicted with some painful discomforts (of no objective importance) in the sacral region, such as constant chills.

My brother identified himself as doctor of nordic nationality, and it was easy not only to relieve the discomfort, but to neutralize the crisis of psychic anxiety that tormented her frequently. They attracted thus the unconditional friendship of the Senora Marquesa de Villasante, to whom a few weeks later was presented my other brother involved in the operation.

THEY INITIATE ANALYSIS OF IMMUNIGLOBULINS IN VERTEBRATES

The most important program during this time was the analysis of immunoglobins in vertebrates; a study of electroforetic velocity and the corresponding evaluation of the sequences of amino acids in the polypeptide chains of diverse antibodies.

They tried to find out if the genetic data that codifies the, called by Earth biologists "variable portion" of the concatenated networks of globulins, could be subjected to diverse types of mutation, utilizing our technologies called by the biologists of UMMO "UULYAGGXAA" (frequencies of the elastic medium air understood in the ultraacoustic spectrum, obtained in a reduced space, as a result of rapid variations of the thermic gradient).

This technique permits us to obtain at a distance, variations of temperature that follow a process codified beforehand. If this process corresponds to a function of elemental time, as would be a periodic function (for example a train of dampened sinodial impulses) it would obtain at such point, removed some distance from the generator equipment, irradiated thermic impulses from this point like a focussed transmitter.

If the medium in which this phenomenon is produced is elastic: Air for example, the variable thermic gradient, is transduced to pressure waves (acoustical) of high frequency.

PRACTICAL UTILITY OF THE TECHNIQUE DESCRIBED

In practice they locate two points very near within which (suppose for example a distance the length of an organic molecule) they excite two different frequencies. The resultant in its turn is an effect of heterodynage or beat, a frequency capable of perturbing even to destruction the structure of a protein chain, or the codified sequence of network or chain of RNA, altering the information contained in the same. (Mutation including death.)

PROBLEMS EMERGING IN TURN MANSION

Dona Margarita Ruiz de Lihori returned to Madrid, but my brothers remained accomplishing their studies in the basement of the old house on Calle Mayor. They counted (and this was part of the strategy studied before making contact with that respectable woman) on the rumors that could circulate in the social media of that urban zone, being easily depreciated or heard with indifference by those intelligent humans of Albacete. Local authorities or familiars knew that the eccentric habits of dona Margarita provoked frequent comment among neighbors and acquaintences. This then was the major cover to conceal the labor of my brothers. Serious obstacles to the praxis of this reserve existed. One gentleman very attached to dona Margarita suspected our existence and finally was informed with great reserve and promises to keep absolute silence to the same Senora Margarita. Also aware of our stay was an old lady servant very faithful to her Senora, as well as a neighbor to whom we had to offer compensation to show discretion.

On the other hand an assiduous visitor to the mansion called D. Emilio Lopez was one afternoon at the point of discovering the existence of my brothers for which of common accord dona Margarita and her guests modified the initial norms of security, and during the day did not come up to the upper levels.

Avove all, there was the risk that that old servant woman would make comments that could result in discovery of the situation, for which it became necessary to control her verbal expressions outside of the home by means of a phonetic register. Senor your sister of Albacete never violated the word she had given given to the mistress of the house.

It was then when they equipped the other entrance which put the basement in communication with the garden. The labors of my brothers continued in the mansion, though there were long periods in which the Marquesa de Villasante and Baronesa de Alcahali, continued maintaining her actual residence in Madrid, Spain.

In June of 1953 my brothers suffered an incident in an ironworks of the population center of Albacete, which made our superiors think seriously, of the convenience of cancelling our stay in Spain.

In August the situation became insupportable since by then there resided in the mansion two children of dona Margarita Ruiz de Lihori. They were don Jose Maria Shelly and his sister dona Margarita Shelly, at that time a nurse for a neuropathic team which then became complicated with the first symptoms not diagnosed by her doctor, of Lymphoid Leucemia.

Those two knew nothing of the existence of the two OEMII. The relations of these two humans with their progenitor reached a crisis some time later for reasons intimately rooted in the family. Her own children did not know that the evident anomalous conduct of dona Margarita Ruiz de Lihori was conditioned by her special characteristics of personality, altered psychopathologically, in a manner that the state of profound frustration of the woman, was translated frequently, into sad altercations that slowly estranged and intoxicated the familiar frame of reference.

TRANSFER OF RESIDENCE TO MADRID AND RETURN TO ALBACETE

In this situation, my brothers moved for the first time to Madrid and dona Margarita intervened personally in the aquisition of a dwelling on the street of Mendez Pelayo, helping them also in the aquisition of some lands "La Zorilla" family property.

At the end of August 1953, an intimate friend of dona Margot Shelly communicated to the Marquesa that her daughter's condition was deterioriating, deciding this Senora, not without first overcoming the strong resistance of Senor Bassols, that they decline though seeming inhumane to lend help to the faithful patient.

My brothers abstained from intervening in an affair strictly connected to the intimacy of those humans.

We can report also that after a very great disgust experienced by this Senora the 4th day of September 1953, one of my brothers was sent for by her, to advise her in this respect. He limited it to suggesting that she act according to the principles dictated by her own Moral Conscience.

With the hope that the transfer of Margot S. would leave the house free, my brothers moved from Madrid to Albacete (Spain), the same date as that in which the Senora travelled to the same city. She made the trip independently in a metrotaxi rented for that purpose.

GRAVE INCIDENT IN THE BIOLOGICAL EXPERIMENTS

On exactly the same date that Dna. Margarita arrived at her residence in Albacete, there occurred a grave event which we judge as one of the most unfortunate incidents in our stay on EARTH. It was so grave that we sincerely admit being those fully responsible for same. Without mitigating this affirmation the objection is that of unlocking the chain of events that followed which had their origen in unexplainable imprudence of the senora Marqueesa.

For reasons of security we can not, senor, be too explicit in relating this turbulent affair. We would like to advise you previously that all the aspects that you are discovering about us in this history are rigorously faithful to the truth, without deliberate deformation. But we must omit much other data and diverse implications derived from that sad event. Some day you will be able to know (if our superiors estimate that your exposition would not provoke some disturbance) all the facets of some actions that could disturb all the plans of my expeditionary brothers.

CAUSE OF INCIDENT: "A VIRAL ENTITY UNKNOWN ON EARTH"

Some months before (the project had been initiated in an old chalet on the outskirts of Marsella, France) my brothers had come to a point in the program of investigation relating to a viral entity unknown on the solid star Earth, but familiar (though localized) to the brother biologists of UMMO.

The structure of these viral specimens posessed a certain analogy with the circular chain of DNA corresponding to the virus of Earth known to you as "Rat Polioma Virus" due to its spatial disposition, but this entity is provided with a much more complex capsule.

My brothers, having discovered that the imported virus did not multiply in animal tissues of Earth while the metabolic processes of same were normal. Such virus, which we codify as ____ is not capable of perforating the mucoprotein strata of the cellular membrane under normal biological conditions. But it was also evident to them that such protection ceased a little before the histological tissue degenerated with the death of the animal carrier, or in the case of necrosis of the cellular area. Under these conditions the cells were no longer immunocompetent.

Naturally under these conditions, the virus is not dangerous to men or animals of EARTH, though they observed embrionic states of activation in animals ill for other etiological reasons.

Today we know that this is not the case: but in those years we did not know if the virus to which we refer could could mutate into other entities that could become a dangerous pathological agent to those living beings of Earth.

It was transported to this solid star simply for purely experimental purposes.

They discovered also that the virus (in truth difficultly vitrifiable) remained on the surface of the cellular membrane, eight months or more, always when it treated of internal tissues. Later degenerating rapidly, the surviving colonies, in cases such as we have informed you of, does not produce the death of the corresponding tissues.

BIOLOGICAL UNIT OF VALUE: THE "AXEESII"

On the other hand we have means which permit us to detect the situation of these and other viral colonies in which the number of individuals is greater than (12) individuals per AXEESII (the unit of volume for biological evaluations which is equal to 36.77 cubic millimeters [equivalent to 11693818.24 individual mm^3]) measured by exploratory techniques at a distance not greater than 78 meters for this viral density.

EVOLUTION OF THE INCIDENT AND CONTROL

My brothers located viral focii of certain importance, and eighteen in number in the body of Dna. Margarita Ruiz de Lihori, in a neighbor lady on Calle Mayor, in her daughter Margarits Shelly, and in three animals of the house.

It was relatively easy to destroy these viral nucleii in their apparent totality. Another twenty six contaminated areas were detected, when using resolute techniques more precise. And there came, in great urgency to Spain (violating norms of security), from France another four brothers provided with adequate equipment.

What provoked true anxiety in my brothers was ignoring up to this point, viral nucleii of minor entity that could have evaded our control. For a part of that day family and friends had gathered at the house of the Sra. Marquesa to prepare for the projected trip to transfer the patient to Madrid.

Meanwhile, those humans were witnesses of a sad incident due to the family tensions, ignorant of the dramatic transformations that all were living due to the strange circumstances based on our presence in that population.

Though in the first hours, all of those persons were observed in this location without revealing symptoms of being carriers of the virus, nothing stopped our considering that infinitesimal nucleii not detectable by our methods might have escaped our rigorous control. We could accomplish a sufficiently complete sterilization of an extensive area, but such means would not guarantee that viral elements situated in inaccessible strata could not escape our prophylactic operations.

That these augurs were unfortunately confirmed is proved by the case of Margot Shelly, daughter of Dna. Margarita Ruiz de Lihori.

All seemed forgotten. If those viral focii survived a certain margin of time there had been no indication of presence before the detection equipment... maintaining vigilence of people and topological areas of the mansion.

NEW VIRAL NUCLEII EMERGE

Periodic explorations were extended later to all that urban area of Albacete, and for reasons of movement to population centers like Valencia, Almansa, Barrax and Murcia (Spain). It did not seem probable that it could prosper, in which it could become a genuine catastrophe. (We insist that a more grave qualification would be justified in those years. In actual perspective, such fears still, in this case in which we had been able to control the infection of astro Earth, should all be reduced to enrichment of knowledge of a viral species more of characteristics almost harmless.)

My two brothers remained in company with a third that they incorporated into the group, but residing in another place in "Albacete" renewing the experiments, this time carrying all the norms of security to extremes. (Still later, they cancelled the program of biological studies utilizing viral species.)

But on the 18th of November of 1953, my consternated brothers discovered a viral focus of this nature in the nasal passages of a Spanish human, husband precisely of the woman resident of Calle Mayor, who that day, withour her knowing it, had become contaminated. Naturally the nucleus was exterminated from a distance, since fortunately it was localized in a not too profound area.

A more careful exploration detected a second very small nucleus in one lung alveoli. Without relying on the authorization of the human, it was impossible, at such depth, to destroy the infecting group, but on the other hand his situation and the fact that this man of Earth enjoyed excellent health (for which the virus degenerates before affecting his tissues) not encouraging greater worries.

But on the other hand, my brothers, alerted by this outbreak, reiniciated a second investigation. On the 27th of November two of them moved to Madrid, coming to the domicile of Dna. Margarita Ruiz de Lihori. They did not come up into the house at first. From the retreat of a nearby Bar, and utilizing the equipment they carried with them, they discovered that their fears were unfortunately confirmed.

THE DAUGHTER OF DNA. MARGARITA WAS CARRYING THE VIRUS

Up to six viral focii were located in the body of the patient, all of them sufficiently deep to fear no irradiation to the exterior, but on the other hand presented an inherent difficulty due to their locacation. They could not be destroyed from a distance. The affected zones were found in //the ocular globes, the epitheliel tissue of the tongue, and the dermis of the palm//.

Also they discovered some type of mutational change in the structure of the viral specimen. This provoked a major alarm in my brothers, who saw themselves obligated to meet with Dna. Margarita and confess their worst fears, distorting to some degree the truth.

There was not in truth any risk of contamination, but in the case of this human woman, given the advanced state of her pathological condition, a development (with grave consequences) on the part of the species was foreseen.

Then it would be very difficult to control the process of irradiation, even with the extreme measure of revealing the affair to the Autoriades Sanitarios de Espana, who on the other hand might be very difficult to convince.

On ____ my brothers studied the situation, and from this country and from France, arriving by aircraft with full urgency, came six more OEMII specialized in Biology and similar disciplines.

It was not possible to obtain a remission in the progress (of the infection) seen in the daughter of Dna Margarita, without bringing in adequate special equipment, without access to the patient, and giving her to know, that it would involve a grave risk for our program of staying on Earth.

Though they thus seriously studied this possibility, our Superiors decided nevertheless to adopt other methods. They put in motion a plan including a plan to seize the body in case this became necessary.

In the 12th of January, there met in Madrid eleven of my brothers who arrived in effect because of the difficulties of all this that surrounded our presence in Madrid.

A few days later this faithful young woman died. It is not necessary that we detail the measures of prophylactic order that it was necessary to adopt.

But above whatever scruple you or your brothers of Earth desire to assert, the first considerations must be of moral and sanitary order.

AUTOCONCLUSIONS: Seen through the eyes of an uninformed human of Earth, these things would be judged as astonishing and repulsive.

We hope that you will accept, without more detail, this version. WE know that it is real, though the simple annunciation of some actions without more available because of anonymity, not constituting any proof for you, men of Earth.

We hope that some day you will confirm our testimony through your own appropriate methods.

MISCELLANY

We will collect in this chapter a series of extracts from the communications from UMMO on matters of apparently heterogeneous nature such as the sex life of the Ummites, the education of youth, daily life, history of UMMO, appearance of the UMMOAELEWE or General Government of UMMO, etc. There are also some texts on the birth or genesis of the Cosmos, and their concept of WOA or God. It is curious to observe that the Ummite religion is monotheistic like the great terrestrial religions (Christianity, Islam, Buddhism), and in that there also appears a Christic figure: UMMOWOA. Further on we will collect in another chapter texts relating to this great figure and some of his TAUUS, or thoughts. We will see clearly in the texts that here are reproduced the profound infusion -I call it "carreliana" -among apparently disparate concepts. For the science of UMMO all is intimately interrelated. There are no monopoly compartments in the Cosmos or in the Life. It was this that surprised the French anthropologist when in their report on the Biogenetic Bases they used concepts of physics. Our science suffers from an excessive compartmentalization as Alexis Carrel has already indicated, prophetically, in the thirtys.

These documents constitute a valid approximation of that which, with all propriety, we could call a "Gnosis" of UMMO (Science, Theology and Cosmology).

Various persons, (a Senorita of Miami, a Dentist of New York and some others) have asked me repeatedly if I could put them in personal contact with the Ummites. These persons have not understood anything of the affair. The communication with the agency called UMMO is only one way: from them to us, and not viceversa. It is comparable. It is like one of those streets that displays the red disc with the white horizontal bar (one way street) in the middle: In this street vehicles can come out but not enter. But of this, I repeat, there are still persons who have not understood. Those who carry the play, whether we like it or not, are "they", those self-named Ummites.

THE DAILY LIFE ON UMMO

We remind you from one earlier report which were the first basics of of our specialists for repression of masterbatory practices among the children of our planet.

They believed that the strong inhibition apparent in those first intents of the UGEE (child) to be stimulated by an electrostatic discharge of high potential, though not injurious to the organism, would create defenses of the individual (reflexes) against this vice.

And unfortunately it was: In a very high percentage of cases (82.5% of the cases analyzed) the youngsters ceased their onanistic practices early. The tragedy became apparent much later when those same individuals presented symptoms of IWOIA (procreative) inpotency. The resistence of psychogenic character to the erection, symptomized by conditions such as IDDOANNA ADIUU (anorexia), UNNIEYA GIADAA (a kind of headache), OAWUO WUANAI (tachycardia) as well as some forms of BIEEBUTSOA (psychomotric inhibition) apart from the absence of erective control, unfortunately incapacitated them for the normal matrimonial function.

Naturally this failure did not discourage our experts in BIEEWIGUU (psychobiology) and thanks to them we have assured that our youths accede in our times of OMGEEIIE (matrimony) without having ever experienced an orgasm. Of that we shall speak in another report.

The young inhabitant of UMMO does not see, on the other hand, the passage of excessive time between puberty and his conjugal union. We appreciate that it is an offense of the divine laws of WOA to remain celibate once the reproductive faculties have developed. In one of our earlier reports to Senor Fernando Sesma Manzano of Spain, we showed how our brothers arrive rapidly to this union in the same midst of the UNAWO UI (educational colony) and at the same time that he is in the full phase of his intellectual and professional development.

The psychosocial controls over the sporadic outbreaks of morbid eroticism, are rigid and efficient. It is not that there exist any official organs charged with oversight against immoral sexuality for the humanity of our planet. It is simply that the same society rejects with instinctive mechanisms of defense of the individual that due to the efficacy of our pedagogic and prophylactic recourse, that which represents strange symptoms in his sexual conduct.

For example: XIIXIA KEAIA (prostitution) appeared in the first stages of our humanity. There are archaic testimonies of the ancient AASE OUIA (Chiefs or Governors) dictating norms to regulate this traffic of women.

Many of the families regulate the number of their offspring of one or the other sex. Those who exceed this cypher are delivered to the XIIXIOUIAA (women or men who regulate this traffic). All the unmarried men have the right to cohabit periodically with these unfortunate individuals (the number of times is a function of the number of requests of this nature and the number of women then available to the IIXIOUIA). With the particularity that there exist also GEE (men) controlled for this sad fate, conceding to the YIE (bachelor women) the same privilege. The absolute control of this social blemish was for a time effective. The situation arrived nevertheless where it was seriously destabilized by the hallucinatory mandate of a UUYIE (young girl) famous in our history.

WIE-1 daughter of OOUA-33 and of her Predecessor in power IE-456, capriciously imposed (induced by infantile hidden motives) (and on the advice of her mother) the watchword that all the women of UMMO who had arrived to the phases of IWO (faculty of procreation - puberty) must become pregnant.

The humiliating measure raised a horrendous clamor in that unfortunate society subject to the arbitrariness of the UUYIE (young woman) who was then scarcely 14 "Earth years" of age.

Only the wives and daughters of the high functionaries of that autocratic government, and those of the members of the office of WOODOO (a kind of police) remained exempt from these drastic orders.

The official explanation interpreted this declaration as justified by the necessity for a demographic expansion that would make possible the ambitious scientific plan of her ancestor in power: IE-456, daughter of NAA-312.

The unfortunate young YIE (women) and those of mature age knew that the inspectors charged with examining them, would condemn them to death if they did not manifest symptoms of gestation. Thousands of unhappy steriles commited suicide, and a great many wives delivered themselves desperately to those hundreds of thousands of GEE (men) who began to proliferate in a new and repugnant office (when their husbands were unable to fecundate them). In this manner the XIIXIA KEAIA (prostitution) broke out with devastating force, anarchically reviving the dreadful circumstance in which the feminine sex did not deliver themselves for personal gain, but polarized by incentives of defense against the risk of genocide (1).

Well it was the hope, after that melancholy stage of our history passed, through the death of the small tyrant (destroyed by the expansion wave of an explosive, they returned to the sad state of that distorted society. It was impossible to slow down the wave of prostitution that extended throughout our planet.

The slow evolution of our society, the continual increase of the goods of production (OUMBOO) and for such the improvement of our social good fortune, the education and the scientific progress, were slowly reducing the number of these sexual excesses until we arrived at the beginning of our era, which was also the epoch that marked the disappearance of this terrible evil. There only remained rare cases of YIE, whose genetic constitution predisposed them to

(1) Some URAA (chronicles of the time) related terrifying scenes of those XII (days). Many terrorized YIE simulated with fragments of YUUWO (a spongy vegetable substance) hidden between the tunic and the belly, a state of pseudopregnancy. The agents of the WOODOO (Police) unmasked them and ordered them exhibited nude in full view publicly heedless of the sobs and howling cries of the unhappy ones. In this state they were held until the immediate point of control where, after being subject to every class of excesses, they were sent to the vivisection centers.

this trait of hypersexuality, including a reduced group of pathological-sexual traits well defined. The most modern techniques of control during gestation, of the diverse psychopathological factors, have gotten us to where in our days, the existence of an individual of feminine sex afflicted with these tendencies, is truely rare. The society reacts against these strange cases with exquisite prudence and loving solicitude. The patient is isolated and submitted to treatment that, for being already late and heavy, and despite the advances in our techniques, does not assure the remission of the sindrome in more than a high percentage of the cases is very rare.

They do not know on UMMO, at least for now, a great part of the rich variety of sexual perversions, so habitual on Planet Earth.

Actually unknown to us are the forms of Sad-Masochism, Fetishism, Zooerastia, Necrophilia, Narcisism... and those rare cases of homosexuality are controlled by means of hormone regulation through adequate intervention in the neurocortical and endochrine systems without recourse to surgery.

One aspect of interest to you no doubt would consist in the control of IWO.

The cycle of our women can be perfectly controlled by us. This regulation nevertheless is strongly connected to imperatives and inhibitions of religious character. Our OMGEEIIE (matrimonials) would never tolerate an arbitrary autoregulation whose only motive would be personal egoism and insane satisfaction.

Our religion orients us very seriously in this respect. Thus we do not understand how man can live savagely in a society where the demographic expansion is not controlled by the same humanity that received the faculty of self-government from WOA (God). And thus you cannot conceive of a society where men are disordinate in common and can interpret their liberty as a relationship between inhibitory measures and their instincts. You must perceive (AND THE ROMAN CATHOLIC CHURCH HAS IN EFFECT BEGUN TO ADMIT ON EARTH THIS PRINCIPLE) that a Society conscious of its Destiny and its evolution has to create some methods of control of its own dynamic expansion.

But these methods do not have to be imposed tyranically by a paternalistic government which forces the members of the society to control the birth of children against their own conscience and volition. It is the same family that is acquiring consciousness of its own responsibility that should adopt the measures most efficacious for its good and the good of the society in which it finds itself immersed.

The fathers of UMMO plan the number of children through a long and careful analysis. They always contact the assessorship of the religious ministry. They always consult the XAANMOO AYUBAA (computer net) to calculate the root factors that converge on a measure of this nature.

We do not worry. We methodically evaluate the pros and cons: the genetic factors, our professional situation, the intelligence of the parents, our own psychoaffective characteristics or sentiments... And we proceed accordingly.

Artificial contraceptive procedures are forbidden on our Planet... Simply because they are not necessary.

In the first place we posess in all the XAABIAUANNAA (dwellings) some detector equipments called by us IWOUAXOO. Their operation is based on the analysis of the electromagnetic fields generated by the cerebral cortex of the woman. All the metabolism of the human can be examined by means of this analysis. The apparatus detects the weak alterations registered for the length of the cycle of ovulation, carefully recording all the phases of same. They have exact awareness not only of the diverse stages of maturity of the ovum in the bosom of the ovary, but, of course, of its passage through the ODAXIXAA (the Fallopian Tube).

But they can also reduce the time of stay of the ovum between two points of its passage, by means of techniques that permit this control from a distance.

We do not hide from you the importance of overseeing this control, since the fertility of the YIEE is intimately connected to the permanance of the ovum. Not only do we know the period of fertility with complete exactness but we can reduce it or increase it (within a certain minimum period of fertility: some 46 UIW. The maximum period is a function of the somatic characteristics of each woman).

There are no difficulties in how much control over births as mentioned is exercised.

As a note of importance we must say that when the OMGEEYIE decide to generate a new child, that night they celebrate an unusual ceremonial. They both must be explicitly careful to communicate their decision confidentially to the persons who live together with them including the other children. They also communicate the good news to the religious ministry, which responds some UIW before to greet the pair and to bless them. They always celebrate our extraordinary vigils without special foods. On the contrary, the regularity of the same (meals) never changes for hygenic motives, except with a true olfactory symphony. With a marvelous session of IAIKEAI (art of aromas) in which the YIE try to show themselves off before their relatives.

This night is a marvelous march at a slow pace of the OMGEEYIE of UMMO through the WAAM generated by WOA (God). On this night both husband and wife will make use of this marvelous generative faculty as legated by our WOA for the evolution of the humanity. A new being is going to be born.

Nevertheless has disappeared the antique custom recorded in the archives of IBOZOOIXINAA (see ACCESSORY REPORT) exclamations of pleasure expressed during the orgasm on this solemn night. Still the GEE and YIE (men and women) of UMMO reproduce at times some sounds that are reminiscent to us of the affectionate or sentimental resonances that touch us deeply. And already in the age; when our ancestors had passed to the Sun and their BUUAWAA (Souls) identified with WOA, we can relive again the instant that frames our somatic generation in the bosom of this WAAM.

[NOTE- In UMMO, OTRA PLANETA HABITADA, senor Fernando Sesma offers us an interesting peek at the peculiar modesty of Ummite adults. Drawing from an Ummite report he quotes: "It is the custom on our planet to undress in complete darkness, which you do not have to interpret as a result of ancestral modesty, however it is true that our special instinct of shyness causes us to suffer almost psychological trauma when we are seen nude before a second person, a condition very accentuated in our society, and also occurs, though it seems irrational when this happens with an OMGEYIE (married couple) in which the grade of intimacy is very elevated.

"The truth is that our mentality in this respect is quite distinct from yours. The only significant change between remaining covered by the EEWEE (clothes) and being undressed is the intense erogenous sensitivity, for which we have adopted the measure of extinguishing the illumination in the IAXAABI (bedroom) as a preventive measure to neutralize such action.

Some of the communications that follow describe various aspects of life on Planet UMMO. -Publisher]

[NOTE- The initial contacts in Madrid, apart from those with the copyist to whom the extraterrestrial visitors dictated material for their reports, began with Professor Fernando Sesma Manzano, who received a number of the typed communications concerning the planet UMMO and the life of its inhabitants from those Ummite expeditionaries here. He at the time headed a local discussion group of persons interested in Metaphysics who called themselves "The Ballena Allegre", with whom he discussed these mysterious communications. Sesma was one of the early contactees frequently called by those strange visitors, who told him they came from another planet and who spoke in a very peculiar flat nasal voice with a foreign accent. Sesma would ask questions in the telephone conversations, sometimes very long, and would subsequently receive estensive answers in the mail, sometimes posted from distant cities. This procedure was repeated with other Spaniards in later contacts, as we have already seen. He put a collection of this information together in a book titles, UMMO, OTRA PLANETA HABITADO. The original publisher, apparently not wanting to give too much support to this unproved wild story, embellished the cover of the book with a gargoyle-like one-eyed dimunitive creature -- giving the finished volume the appearance and aire of science-fiction, when it was in fact a document of considerable importance. We have reproduced below a photo of that book -- the first book on these contacts from Planet UMMO. -Publisher]

AELEWE
ACCESSORY REPORT
Language: Spanish
No. of Copies: 1

At the request of the Professor
Fernando Sesma Manzano
Madrid

In accordance with your request concerning the relations between sexes on UMMO , we amplify our previous reports.

306. PHYSIOLOGY AND SEX

Our sexual morphology is conditioned on the physiological structure, which in our case differs very little from yours. All the endocrine mechanisms that regulate the current hormonal balance, we have the same as humans of Earth. We have identical morphology and suffer processes that if they differ in any way, as in the case of the woman, it is due to slight differences in the medium in which we evolved (different thermic oscillations, very irregular atmospheric pressure, different weights for the same mass--due to a higher acceleration of gravity at the surface... etc.).

306. PSYCHOLOGY OF GEE (MEN) AND YIE (WOMEN)

When boys and girls of UMMO have matured mentally (this is not considered a function of physiological age, which in truth we count from the moment of conception, an instant which we know perfectly, but of the intellectual or mental age), it is their parents who by standard phonovisual means, specifically adapted to the infantil mentality (the data is remitted to the nearest of the components of the SANMOO AYUBAA net --a species of electronic brain, though in this case it is not precisely electronic, which regulates all the activity of UMMO--) their children are informed on the sexual aspect. On UMMO this information never has been "taboo"

Nevertheless, the education of men and women in this respect differ much more than on Earth.

To the women they introject a special feeling of modesty that, although it is difficult to summarize here, we may synthesize thus:

THEY MAY ONLY SHOW THEIR BODY BEFORE THEIR HUSBAND. SHE IS PERMITTED THOUGH, ACCORDING TO THE UAA (MORAL) TO CAPTURE THE ATTENTION OF THE SINGLE MALE BEFORE HER ENGAGEMENT.

The first principle is strongly arrigated to the YIE (woman) though the habits on this point are changing in the length of the history. The woman always covers herself with rigorous discipline, and during all her life the thorax. She does not feel the least objection, nor does she consider the muscles, arms, head, throat, hands and feet to be erogenous zones. Neither does she consider the lips an erogenous organ, for which the kiss lacks significance among us. Erogenous in superior degree to the terrestrial women are the genital organs, the breasts, belly and the buttocks. Our women never undress of their own free will before men who are not their husbands, nor in front of other women.

When the YIE (woman) has to submit to an intervention of surgical type, she previously covers herself with a skin of UBAA SIAA (a kind of collodial pigment that covers the skin with polychrome stains). This chemically inert substance does not disturb the epidermis in her theraputic treatment.

The grade of humiliation that the woman suffers when this norm is not observed, against her wishes, is most intense, to the point where one of the penalties provided by the legal code of UMMO is precisely this.

But the woman is permitted to exhibit her organic complexion --within certain limitations of the UAA (moral-religious code) to sexually entice the man.

Boys and girls are educated up to some 13.68 (Earth) years in a kind of University, small cities in miniature where the discipline is rigid and realized all their life subordinated to this institution. These centers are called UNAWO UE.

Co-education is only applicable to certain reduced groups of adolescents when components accuse them in the cerebral electroanalysis and psychic examinations of tendencies to homosexuality. Tendencies that we have succeeded in correcting since that time.

But during several hours each day they permit recreation and friendly get togethers among youngsters of both sexes, stimulating and regulating them carefully.

It is now when the adolescent must select his presumed mate (at around 15.5 years) and submit his selection to the educational authorities who examine them by means of the net of SANMOO AYUBAA (computer brains ofUMMO) for possible incompatibility both physiological and mental in the future bond. If the result is positive, the man makes his proposal (until now maintained in secret) to the girl he has selected.

But she generally is younger, from a physiological point of view, than the boy. What is important is that she still has not suffered her first menstration. If she accepts, both have to wait for this biological phase of the UUTIE (adolescent girl) to develop, before they initiate their relations. They are not allowed to communicate phonically or telepathically, and a discovered transgression would provoke the subsequent rupture of the provisional bond, plus the public embarrassment of the transgressors.

At one age (which varies according to the regions and physiological constitution) comprising between 15.4 and 16.6 (terrestrial) years, the girl reaches puberty, and celebrates with a small party with her classmate girlfriends (the confession of the first menstruation and of those that follow is not "taboo" on UMMO) which allows her to give approval to the second question --yes or no-- to the solicitating boy.

They now initiate a kind of courtship in which they simultaneously of course complete their studies. Both youngsters receive education on the part of the instructors and specialists, oriented toward their future matrimonial life, from the point of view of sexual, religious and social planning of the conjugal functions. To the instructors is shown for each of them, the intimate biography of the other, and their psychophysiological characteristics, adapting this education rigidly to these characteristics. For the rest they tabulate comparatively in this manner some spiritual and corporeal relations, limiting these last to purely tactile sensations without either one of the two having direct access to the erogenous zones of the other. The duration of this phase limits the prematrimonial relations they have instilled in the pair by the educational authorities, attending to the diverse factors that intervene in each case (these factors are mathematically ponderous and are treated in the computers of the world network that we have mentioned). But do not believe that such planning converts us into simple machines lacking in liberty, intimacy, and spirituality. Precisely the help of such methods makes the bond more fertile from the spiritual point of view, since the youngsters are offered exact information and orientation that unites all the somatic, religious, mental and philosophical factors that limit their courtship, and does avoid to a high degree the enormous crises planted by those brutal psychological contrasts that are found among terrestrial youths, lacking in most cases such orientation.

We thus obtain a very great spiritual harmony, that in a short time (if the prematrimonial engagement is not curtailed by mutual assent) prepares them for the religious-legal bond.

On UMMO we estimate that the interval between the apparition of puberty and matrimony should be minimum, since the contrary constitutes a distortion of the biological laws of WOA (Generator which you call God).

The only one among the few inhabited planets we know, in which the society is distorted such that it tolerates great intervals between PUBERTY AND RATIONAL SEXUAL UNION is Earth.

We do not know of such endemic illnesses as prostitution or of the diverse sexual perversions.

306. THE OMGEEYIE (MARRIAGE)

The parents meanwhile have been officially informed of the decision by the respective children, though they absolutely do not intervene in this decision. (On UMMO the grade of respect for the progenitors is transformed into veritable veneration, but they do not interfere in the free will of their children after 13.68 (Earth) years.)

They celebrate then a simple religious-legal ceremonial ritual in the UNAWO UI, in the presence only of the religious minister, the direct educational authorities, their parents, brothers and sisters. The ritual prescribes a maximum of twelve persons present altogether, but this figure is purely conventional and of historic religious character.

The couple are immediately transferred to a bedroom, acoustically isolated, where they effect the rite of defloration. Meanwhile the parents and other relatives that have now been admitted, wait in animated conversation for the termination of this act.

When the husband reappears they greet him respectfully and pass in to see the wife who must remain in the bed 4,000 ʈU (UIW) (one UIW equals approximately 3.1 Earth minutes). THEY HAVE OFFICIALLY CONSUMATED THE OMGEEYIE (Matrimony).

306. THE PREDOMINANCE OF GEE (Men)

The OMGEEYIE (married couple) thus constituted continues their intellectual or production skill development in the bosom of the UNAWO UI. The GEE (male) for example is preparing himself for UNIIEAOEMII WIOA (Analysis of the cerebral cortex) while she perhaps pursues the study of OULIOOA GIIA (specialist in Meteorological Control).

Once titled (graduated) they pass into the service of UMMO at the order of)+(the UMMOAELEWE (General Council of UMMO) since all the inhabitants of UMMO are considered functionaries of the State. They immediately select what is going to constitute their home. Within their respective professions they may adapt themselves to one of several neighborhoods and there acquire, as we said, a functional dwelling and a transportation vehicle which they adapt to their personal needs. The acquisition is made by consulting the SANMOO AYUBAA computer network, which not only orients them concerning the "salary" in their favor but on the amount of "credit" at their disposal, and which they may spend on such acquisitions. Though we refer to "salary", credit and "spending", don't forget that we must employ Spanish vocables to translate terms that are intranslatable, since on UMMO money does not exist as you know it. Both youngsters in the length of their studies have accumulated a remuneration, which is a function of their intellectual capacities and of their contribution in this labor.

Such remuneration, expressed mathematically, is preserved in the central SANMOO AYUBAA. It is now when they may begin utilizing it, as you accumulate your capital in a bank (we repeat that this does not mean money in our case, though they intend to see in the case cited a kind of credit transfer).

The conjugal life transpires placidly and serenely from now. In the home, the maximum authority is extended to the GEE (man) whose authority is never disputed.

The YIE (woman) submits completely to her husband. On UMMO there are no matrimonial couples like those on Planet Earth where the authority of the man is only nominal. On the contrary, the masochistic tendencies of the female of UMMO are more acknowledged than those of Earth.

306. THE CHILDREN

The primordial end of the OMGEEYIE (matrimony) is conjugal love. We discriminate perfectly the attractive tendencies of purely psychosexual origin which affect the spiritual current emerging between two beings.

The percentage of OMGEEYIE broken up is so low that they consider those rare cases known as etiologically pathological.

This, on the other hand, is not surprising since the conjugal union was preceeded by an exhaustive analysis of the psychophysiological factors of the GEE and the YIE. They never would have authorized a marriage in which they could presume future incompatibility of those spirits.

The second end of OMGEEYIE is the IWO (procreation). For the URAA-IWOO (specialists in ovulation of UMMO), control of the ovulation of the woman was accomplished many years ago. The periods of sterility could then be fixed perfectly without utilizing other contraceptive methods whose harm accords with the postulates of religious ethics.

The UAA prescribes the obligation of procreation in accordance with the characteristics of each OMGEEYIE such as, health of the mother, hierarchial grade of the father and for such, the greater possibilities of endowment, absence of mental deficiencies and grade of mental capacity to educate the children... It would constitute a grave transgression of the divine UAA of WOA to impede a fecundation for egotistical motives, as well as failure of control that provokes the birth of OEMII (human bodies) whose parents would not be able to properly raise them. When this occurs, the government of UMMO takes charge of those children, and their parents, though not punished, experience the repulsion of their relatives and friends. (Control of births is not a legal obligation.) And it is not necessary, nor considered ethical, to oblige the parents to plan the exact number of their children, since such norms are complied with for religious motives. In each case in doubt, an advisor with a high degree of trust resolves the problem without exercising any coercion.

We may pass on then to the gloomy times of a cruel maiden who was made ruler of UMMO. IEE-456 daughter of NAA-312, was to compensate for the veritable thousands asassainated in the name of science daily. All the women of UMMO were humiliated by being continuously subjected to artificial insemination, to the point that any YII who was not in a phase of gestation and not by reasons of sterility, was condemned to die of starvation, after being exposed, naked, to public shame.

306. THE YIE (WOMAN) BEFORE THE SOCIETY OF UMMO

Although the wife submits unconditionally to the authority of her husband in the home, this submission does not suppose denial of her right to opinion, nor much less does it minimize the dignity of the YIE in her position before the Gevernment and the society of UMMO as equal partner with rights identical to those of the GEE.

This legal situation provokes a shadow in all of us from a spiritual point of view, which we all accept as a necessary evil. In summary, the professional and hierarchial situation of the woman is a function of her physiological-mental capacity, in the manner that whoever of them, independently of her age, demonstrates in her UMMOGAOEAAO DII (formula of identity which reflects the intelligence and other factors of the citizens) a specific capability, she is automatically promoted to the corresponding hierarchial position, without necessarily taking into account the age, sex, nor category of progenitors among which from this time some may be subordinate to her. (1)

In our days, none of the four members of the UMMOAELEVE OA, the Council General of UMMO, is a YIE, but of the 116 members who compose the Sub-Council, 28 are YIEE (females). We men accept this situation with a greater degree of humiliation than the men of Earth in analogous cases, and above all in the groups that could be called PARAMILITARY in which the hierarchial grade carries a more universal authority (Police, Inspection Bodies, Displaced groups on interplanetary journeys, etc.). The man feels then truely spoken down to when his immediate superior is of the other sex, but we accept it with integrity and discipline. One single right is with us always - to criticize our superiors, man or woman, but we must obey immediately even though the

(1) The leader of the entire Earth Expedition team of more than three dozen Ummites at the time of evacuation from this planet on 1 June 1967 was an UMMO YIE... YU-1, of about 19 Earth years of age (equivalent). She had team members with ages up to 60+ years (equivalent). Several of them, including the team leader and her secretary, stayed overnight in the home of the copyist until the evacuation ships came.

order may seem unjust in our judgement. Do not believe that the hierarchy revenges for such criticism, for on the contrary they study it very carefully and later take it into consideration.

[NOTE- According to the Ummites themselves, their team on Earth began with six members left alone in France in 1950 and gradually increased to about 80 at its peak study period in the mid-1960s when they had scientific study groups all over this world studying everything in a variety of languages and cultures. They never reached 60 members on Earth again after the mass evacuation in 1967. At present there are believed to be less than a score of widely scattered observers on this planet. The team leadership has changed a number of times over the years during which we are aware of only the one female expedition team leader, YU-1. -Publisher]

AELEWE
INFORMATION OOL
No. of copies distributed: 1
Language: Spanish

At the request of Professor Sesma Manzano
MADRID

At your request.

In response to your request for a report on our culture, philosophy, and religion. However you must understand that this would be impossible to summarize in a few pages. In our judgement we suggest cloaking the miscellanea that surrounds some of its more prominent characteristics though at the risk of giving it unsystematic form.

A more extensive and coherent compendium was remitted in May of 1953 to Professor K. I. Ivanov (Soviet Union). Another report on our religious system was sent in confidence to the Osservatorio de la Ciudad del Vaticano (Italy). The most disturbing risk to this synthesis would be to the affirmations contained in it of careful and logical argument.

331 ART

With all objectivity we have to recognize the genuine backwardness of UMMO with respect to the Humanity of Earth in this field. Now we have understood how a technical discovery we made in the first stages of history came to atrophy all development of the pictoro-sculptural manifestations, such as was forged on your planet.

In the year 402 of our second Time (though we did not know the real nature of electrostatics, and the AAKSBOUTZ -motors of methane- had not appeared), an ancestor or ours 7Ӿ ŌO UUL-76 son of 7Ӿ I Ō UUL-73 discovered that projecting through a small orifice of a luminous image (naturally inverted) upon a layer of selenium (previously scoured) and then dusted with the pollen of a plant, could fix this image as if it were one of those Daguerrotypes of the Nineteenth Century on Earth

Today we understand the reason:

If by means of a lens we project any image upon a plate which we have tripple electrified, rubbing it with a cloth, the zones bathed with light carry a distinct electrical potential that does not illuminate. When this is later dusted with finely pulverized carbon, the electrified zones retain the granules. We then have fixed an authentic photograph of the primitive image. (The real process is somewhat more complicated.)

Apart from this system, our ancestors later "repainted" the image with appropriate pigments., up to the evolution of the UULAYANA NAI (Electrophotography), making unnecessary this secondary manual labor.

But in this manner our ancestors did not experience the necessity of painting that you know, and some of our esthetic faculties atrophied.

332. CHANGE OF GOVERNMENT. APPEARANCE OF THE SCIENTIFIC CONCEPT OF WOA.

In our history there did not appear as among yourselves, multiple currents of thought concerning the existence or non existence of WOA (Generator, which you call God or Jehova). On the contrary, all of our culture has been always WOASSE (Generatist, or as you would say: Theistic). Though until the vivisection of UMMOWOA we had come to identify WAAM -the Cosmos- with WOA -God- by means of a constellation of beliefs which you would call Pantheistic.

There did not exist any definite form of cult. Our Humanity at that time went through an anguished and hallucinatory period: Hundreds of psychic patients, destabilized their neurophysical centers by generation of BUUAWE BIE telepathic impulses, terrorizing the population and retarding the advance of culture. They thought more of hunting down those unfortunate patients than in surrendering to their worship to WOA (God).

For then there still existed on UMMO a monocratic Government that was elected by proclamation of the AASE OGIA (Chiefs of Population). Slowly they were perfecting the methods of detecting these ill ones. In the year 1126 of our first Time, there emerged the AARWIO BUUA EI method, precedent of our modern AARGA BUUA EI to neutralize their anarchic cries, killing them at a distance, and with that floresced all of scientific investigation. (This triumph was equal to your discovery of printing.)

Our public at last breathed free of their mental slavery.

But unfortunately there also appeared the first embryonic forms of the tyranny. With IE-456 daughter of NA-312 emerged the most terrifyingly despotic government that UMMO has ever known.

At 8.5 years of age (Earth equivalent) IE-456 demonstrated being a girl endowed with a surprising level of intelligence, and the Consejo Local (Local Council) (the parents did not have educational authority in that time) sent her to the ONAWO UII (a kind of central polytechnical institute) for the study of OOLGA WAAM (Physics and Cosmology). In that epoch, the study of electromagnetic fields and cellular physiology was very advanced though it continued to consider the Universe as a continuum of three dimensions and was ignorant of the intimate nature of telepathic communication.

At 13.2 years of age, IE-456 was named Professor of WAAMTOA (History of Cosmology), beginning at the same time her investigations of the Gravitational Field of UMMO. Her NOA (students) were all of ages greater than this small and sickly girl who nevertheless imposed a hard and cruel discipline (on UMMO the professors have always substituted for the parents during the educational stage of the individual).

The discoveries of IE-456: Calculation of the mass of our planet, and the nature of the ionized polar band of UMMO quickly transformed her into the primary scientific figure of our world, ..together with IMII-23 son of IMII-22 creator of our modern psychology.

When the figure of the ancient hierarch OES-17 son of OES-14 dematerialized to spirit (died), the small IE-456 was elected to the Council of AASE OUIA (Governors) meeting in the valley of NAATOWS-EE UA NAII (it was the ancestral custom to meet in this historic valley to elect the Grand Hierarch of UMMO and his twelve advisors).

The opinion of the people was nevertheless opposed from the first moment -and the fine intuition of the masses was not very wrong-, though the adverse popular reaction was motivated by the disagreeable sensation of being ruled by a child.

332. THE DESPOTIC REGIME OF IE-456 DAUGHTER OF NA-312

In 17 days from their ascension to power, the famous AAR GOA provoked what you call "Golpe de Estado" (coupe d'etat) ordering the execution of nine of their twelve council members, and proclaimed her absolute chief of UMMO invoking the supposed right that it would accellerate their scientific progress. They then developed a thesis of heterodoxical philosophy according to which:

> "The Cosmos does not exist a priori but only in the spirits of men, who generate mental images and concepts, or intellectual abstractions, and believe it the Universe. According to that, when a human discovers a biological or physical law, he is victim of an illusion, believing that such law existed from the origin of the Cosmos, when in reality he has just generated it. The destiny of the humanity of UMMO would thus rest on the acceleration of scientific investigation without regaining in the process then, the ascendency of the Creation. IE-456 thus postulated that WOA is nothing but the collective of the beings of UMMO, and that the brain of WOA would be the same IE-456 daughter of NA-312!!!"

One shudders to think in our days, that a young girl who still had not suffered her first menstration (in some regions of UMMO the mensus appears toward 16 years and the menopause about 45 -always when we refer to years, we have converted it into terrestrial units of time-) could subjugate thus the millions of people.

In planning the scientific investigation of UMMO, there emerged hundreds of new ONAWO UII (a kind of centers of teaching where at the same time they carried on their daily life) and they accomodated all of the men, women and adolescents, drastically rationalizing their time and dividing it between study and work.

At 15.2 years of age, IE-456 promulgated the famous twelve INAIE DUIO (laws or decrees), according to which, she would be the WAAM-DISAIAYA (something like the central coordinator of the Cosmos, surprisingly!!):

1º She proclaimed herself proprietor of the beings of UMMO being able to dispose of their lives without any limitation.

2º She elaborated and standardized for all of UMMO some rites of cult that must be rendered by all the humans.

3º The supreme goal of UMMO is scientific investigation, and if it is necessary that all the men die on the alters of science and in the Genesis of the Cosmos as an immediate consequence, she would have no scruples in destroying them.

There emerged thus an extreme climate of terror. Those qualified scientists whose intelligence had been evaluated above a certain level who did not contribute some discovery to science were tortured barbarously.

The men, women and children who in the BIEEWIA (psychotechnical tests) were not able to surpass a certain standard of mental aptitude, were destined for the same end that you on Earth destin guinea pigs and rabbits. For example, in AEVO UI ONAAWO (University of AEVO), in one day, and only in 12 UIW (some 30 minutes) they vivisectioned 160 youths of both sexes, of ages between 17.6 and 22 years, exterpating them withour anesthesia -which they still did not know-, separating the encephalic mass in one experiment destined to locate the neuroolfactive centers of the cortex.

The mythmania and delirious cruelty of that young girl whose blurred image in the ULAAYANA NAE (a kind of color photograph) of that time reveals her with yellowish complexion and small inexpressive eyes, becoming to some extent shy, surpassed belief.

In her audiences (which she of course only conceeded to preeminent scientists and WAAMUA ODEU -thinkers or philosophers-) her subjects had to present themselves before her totally without clothes in a time in which the sexual modesty was most deeply rooted among our ancestors and when the eyelids were closed with a gum.

If the judgement over them is favorable, the YIISAIA (reward) consists im allowing them to open their eyes to see her and to eat and drink the AAYA IEAAYA (fecal wastes and urine of the ruler of UMMO.

AMU A-47 daughter of OGA A-1896, famous mathematics investigator to whom is attributed the first studies on the theory of electrical networks, was received by the young despot. The psychic commotion was so great that the unfortunate (whose age was then 38.7 years) could not control her sphincters. After humiliating her before her servants, IE-456 tortured her personally and afterward sent her to the famous and melancholy group  (five).

332. GOVERNMENT OF WIE-1 DAUGHTER OF OOWA-33 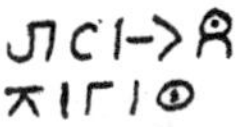

For the first and also the last time in the history of UMMO IE-456 imposed her small daughter WIE-1 daughter of OOWA-33 as her successor in the general government of UMMO. (The history of her father OOWA-33 is another gloomy enigma in our history. The version of his telepathic screams before his asassaination at the hands of the police of IE-456 seems to be a legend.)

WIE-1 (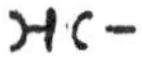) began to rule her terrified subjects at an earlier age than her mother, the day following her mysterious death. The new ruler was 12.2 years old and this time nobody offered the smallest protest before what they called the UMMOTAEEDA (could be translated as "puocracy" or "infantocracy" of the Planet).

But WIE-1, lacked the great brilliance of her mother and was on the contrary of vulgar mediocrity, which offered no obstruction to her superiority in sadism and idolatry of her own body in a paroxysm of egoistic narcism.

It was in this frame of history when there appeared the sublime figure of UMMOWOA  (of which we shall give you a detailed report) and with him the people returned again to their thoughts of the authentic God. There appeared for the first time the cult of religion.

An explosive placed it seems by one of the servants of WIE-1 in revenge for some mistreatment, put an end as dramatically as with her progenitor) to the life of the sterile adolescent.

At least four millions of victims were recorded in our history during the fleeting term of office of WIE-1.

332. METAMORPHOSIS OF THE GOVERNMENT: UMMOAELEWE APPEARS

The relief with which the humanity received the notice of the death of the hated girl, was followed by an immense reaction of hate toward all that science signified. The marvelous USADAADAU Laboratories burned down one night. Thousands of DOROOUIAAIE (a kind of audio library where they preserved acoustic recordings on the culture, and which serve today as texts for study), hundreds of Universities, the OORGAOWI -where a gigantic parabolic reflector concentrated the rays of energy from IUMA for analysis-, were destroyed in the turbulence. They were scarcely victims, better said, had not been innocent: The evolution of science remained slowed for many years.

But on the other hand there was a resurgence, like a beautiful column of ignited oxi-methane, investigations in the philosophical field of WOOLA OLEASS (Theology) and investigations in turn into the telepathic faculties and pure Mathematics.

The society of UMMO suffered a profound transformation. The terriible experience of the autocracy induced the restructuring of Government on our Planet. There appeared a new Polycracy in the form of the UMMOAELEWE)+((General Council of UMMO, which still subsists into our times with slight modification. Four members are elected among the citizens of UMMO without discrimination by age or sex.

All the male and female adolescents have their mental faculties evaluated psychotechnically. Intelligence, aptitudes and interests, factor of rationalism, spacial perception, level of verbal-telepathic expression, irradiation potential, psychosexual equilibrium, effective gradation, possible psychopathological reactions and coefficient of suggestion are evaluated by means of analysis of trains of cerebral waves (a method perfected much beyond your electroencephalograms).

They select in all 120 children of 13.65 years of age as the most brilliant and well balanced cerebral structures of the humanity (not one single youthful citizen can escape the analysis).

All of them are carefully educated (the actual proportion is of some 76.66% males and 23.33% females) for a number of years, as among them they will elect the four EYAOLOOWA whose psychophysical characteristics offer the most advanced level of qualification, who will make up the UMMOAELEWE which rules our destiny for 64 years.

Neither of the four EYAOLOOWAO may exceed his three comerades in authoritory attributes. If the least disqualification, primarily mental, or at the suggestion of any member, the UMMOAELEWEANII)+(Subcouncil made up of 116 members enjoys the authority to dissolve the UMMOAELEWE and name another new one.

332. SOCIAL STRUCTURE

The rest of the humans of UMMO attain a qualification that they translate into coefficients or indices, constituting our UMMOGAIAO (formula of identity). You could interpret this as a kind of digital-analytical trace that reflects our physiologico-mental personality.

Our education and preparation must be adequate to qualify us later for UMMOGAIAO DA. In this manner, the individual whose cerebral structure reflects a marked predisposition toward those faculties of abstraction and rational logic, is oriented toward the ONAWO WUA a kind of University for the study of Mathematics).

It is clear that one enjoys the liberty to dedicate himself for example to OEUDEEE (Biopathology), but then our UMMOGAIAO DA (professional coefficient) in function of which our work is remunerated might be inferior in grade. Thus we obtain that each one in our society occupies the place which corresponds to his psychosomatic aptitudes without being forced by any tyranical regieme or being impelled by his own personal egoism or privileges of birth.

The remuneration for each being of UMMO is always a function of his personal contribution and of his professional coefficient, establishing for them one simple factor for evaluation:

$$A = \frac{B}{C^2}$$

A being the remuneration, B the contribution and C the evaluation of the individual. Observe that an individual whose professional coefficient is high (that is: very intelligent, high muscular motoricity, etc.) would also contribute much to obtain the same remuneration as another of lower coefficient. (A, B and C are parameters too complicated to be expressed here.) It could then occur, and in fact is frequent, that a high Director of Communications — would be remunerated in the same category and amount as a simple operator of glucose extractors. This would seem rare to you and argue then that the Director could dedicate himself to extracting glucose, which is much easier. Of course, the Director in our example could extract as much glucose as the other, but as his professional coefficient on the other hand would be higher (since his aptitudes are not in accord with this profession), if you examine the formula observe that A is inversely proportional to said coefficient, and his remuneration would be unfair.

We have been able thus to neutralize the privileges of class which in those first Times of UMMO caused much more corruption than among the men of Earth.

But do not understand that this remuneration which we receive for labor within the grandiose Plan of UMMO is valued in a form of money. One of the things that most surprised us about you is the curious institution of money and the artificial manners of supporting its value.

334. THE CONCEPT OF WOA WAAM (God-Cosmos)

Our actual concepts concerning the Genesis of the Cosmos, contrary to that on Planet Earth, are supported more by rigorous scientific argument than by philosophical speculation.

It offers great difficulty to translate the expressions of our cultural language, since its constellation of significations is very distinct from the complex of Terrestrial equivalents. For example: We express with the phoneme AIOOYA your verb IS meaning "to be", but its real significance to us has distinct shades:

Thus we consider that AYOOYA O (exists) the Cosmos, a virus, or a helium gas.

On the other hand we express that AIOOYA AMIEE (no existence), beauty, the soul or WOA .

How shall we understand this? It is easy: we apply the verb "exist" to what is dimensional (affected by time and space) and "no existence" to what is adimensional such as could be Intelligence or Happiness. To the NOTHING we assign a verb which has no significance to you. It is AIOYAYEDOO.

Nevertheless, to avoid confusion, when we employ from now forward the expression EXIST we assign the significance that it encompasses for you, doing the same for other vocables of ambiguous interpretation.

334:1 BIRTH OR GENESIS OF THE COSMOS

Today we know that there does not exist only one Cosmos (Ours) but an infinite number of pairs of Universes. There exists also then the duality in cosmological genesis. The difference in the elements A and B of each pair rests on the fact that their respective atomic structures differ in the sign of the electrical charge. (You incorrectly call this Matter and Anti-matter.)

For example: Our twin Cosmos exists also but:

1. In its atoms the shells are formed by positive electrons (positrons) in orbit, and its nucleus is composed of antiprotons.
2. We can never bring both Cosmos into contact nor can they be superimposed because they are not separated by relative dimensions. (As said: They cannot be expressed as being separated by so many light years, or that their existence is simultaneous in time.)

(Will be continued in next Report)

3. Both twin Cosmos posess the same mass and the same radius corresponding to a hypersphere of negative curvature.
4. But the two twin Universes enjoy distinct singularities. (Expressed in another way: In our twin Cosmos there is no minimum number of Galaxies, nor are those that exist made up of the same structure). There is not another twin UMMO or a twin Earth as might be suggested. This is not hypothetical, and a little further on we will indicate the reason.
5. Both Cosmos were created simultaneously as we will explain but their vectors of time do not have to be oriented in the same direction. As said: the logic is lacking to express that that Cosmos coexists with ours in time, or that it existed before or will exist after. It would only be orthodox to say simply that it EXISTS but not Now, Before or After. On the other hand, its interval of evolution is parallel and equal to ours. We offer a fictitious example: Suppose that a man of another Planet in our twin Cosmos lives eternally. If he measures on his watch the time that transpires from the birth of his Universe until it converts itself into a turbulence of radiation, this time would be equal to ours.

We could reason in the same way for the infinite pairs of Cosmos which exist in the WAAMWAAM (Pluricosmos). We observe that the image of the Pluricosmos can not be the same as a Universe. In this the very

Galaxies displace themselves as islands floating in an immense sea. Only that this sea is a sphere of multiple dimensions, but at least we can speak of intergalactic distances and of the gasses that fill intergalactic space. On the other hand it is much more difficult to imagine the WAAMWAAM as well as the pairs of Cosmos submerged in a nothing. It is useless to imagine that distances exist or that these distances are nothing: such imaginations are illusory. However there is something that shook our scientists when they discovered it. Our twin Cosmos exercises its influence over ours though they have no relations connected to space-time. Thanks to the analysis of this influence we have been able to infer the existence of the other Universe as you with a simple television receiver infer the passage of a car by the interferrence you have intercepted. Of course our Cosmos must also influence the other in similar form. The asymmetry of this influence is, as has been revealed to us, that Cosmos has another distribution of Galaxies.

[NOTE- All of this is remarkably reminiscent of the information revealed to a UFO contactee in Pinetown, South Africa in 1967, whose own personal contacts have gone on for 25 years with a group of human beings who arrive in disc-shaped vehicles and communicate directly with the witness. The allege that they have been here since the 1940s, and have learned many of our languages. They have been in contact with this witness in this area since 1960 and have transmitted several hundred hours of direct dialogue on many subjects.

The dialogues are audio recorded in the individual voices of more than a half dozen of the extraterrestrials, who say they come from a Planet which they call Koldas (a translated term), which they claim is located in a COUNTERPART UNIVERSE <u>of opposite polarity</u>, and with a different distribution of stellar bodies! They claim they learned to navigate the barrier some time ago and were surprised to find human life like theirs also existing in this space-time frame.

The Koldasians describe the separating barrier as more of polarity than anything else, and claim that our Universe is the twin counterpart of their own in mass and size. They also describe an infinity of other paired Universes in the Cosmos familiar to them.

There is no evidence that the Spanish Group or the Ummites have ever heard of the Koldasian contacts, nor is there any indication that the Pinetown Group, or the contactee, had any knowledge of the UMMO affair prior to Antonio Ribera's 5-Part Review of the UMMO case published in the English FLYING SAUCER REVIEW, in Vol. 20, Nos. 4 and 5 and Vol. 21, Nos 1. 2 and 3, 1975.

The Pinetown case is fully reported by Carl van Vlierden in UFO CONTACT FROM PLANET KOLDAS, A Cosmic Dialogue, soon to be published in the U.S.A. -Publisher]

334:2 OUR CONCEPT OF WOA (GOD)

WOA (God) exists: (With the significance that you attribute to the verb exist).

It is purile to express that it exists from eternity or that it is found among us, or in all parts, since WOA (Generator as we call it or God as you call it on Earth) is ADIMENSIONAL (it has no width nor height nor time). It is not susceptible to being expressed for example by a complex of tensors or a system of differential equations, nor can its characteristics be measured by precision apparatus.

The essence of WOA suffers no evolution. It is this same essence that understands the possibility of the idea of DIMENSION but this DIMENSIONALITY does not affect its being as an intimate attribute since the dimensionality brings a connection to mutability and WOA cannot impose changes upon itself and therefore limitations.

But the ideas of WOA possess reality, must be always generated so that they are not incompatible with the intimate essence of WOA. For example, the idea of self destruction exists in it but it can not be generated).

These generations of its ideas are like an excrescence of (its being) something that (exists outside) is of it (though here the expression "outside" has no spatial interpretation). This excrescence coexists with WOA and will depend totally on IT.

How many excrescences or realities are there? The answer is simple. AS MANY AS NONINCOMPATIBLE IDEAS COEXIST IN THE MIND OF WOA. If the idea of one hyperspherical Universe replete with Galaxies exists in its mind, such Universe is realized (and in this single case we have full consciousness of its existence by being integrated in IT). If the idea of a bidimensional Cosmos, independent of time were compatible, we would have the assurance that such Cosmos exists in ANOTHER PART. Though we have a determined cellular organization, we do not believe that such structure is the only suitable one. It could be agreed that for this Universe there reign a series of unalterable biological laws from a statistical point of view. But in another pair of Cosmos there could be cases of living beings whose intimate composition may be of silica and whose atoms posess a different structure. But never is it given to those beings of this Universe to prove this hypothesis while they are living in it enveloped in our physical tetradimensional body.

The analysis of the actual phase of our Universe reveals to us that it was generated by WOA.

Our Cosmos is that which you call one space-time continuum. (We have needed to use ten dimensiones in order to define it mathematically). We could speculate attributing to it infinite dimensions but for now we cannot prove it.

Of these ten dimensiones, three are perceptible to our sense organs, and a fourth --Time-- we perceive psychosomatically as a continuous flow in one single sense which we call UIWIUTAA (something like a vector or oriented feeling of time).

In one principle of ours, the twin Cosmos: WAAM (ours) and UWAAM (our twin) are defined as one WAAMIAAYO (difficult to translate: something like one point or origin of only one coordinate, which precisely is TIME).

WOA continues generating successively the rest of the dimensions (but do not interpret this "successively" as temporal or spatial succession) but one timeless ordinal relation (or being: outside of time). In the images we include we desire to represent, though grossly, these phases of the GENERATION or CREATION.

(The images are gross since it is impossible to enclose in one graphic traced on paper, more than three dimensions.)

You can imagin that our primitive BICOSMOS, represents more a small empty sphere. One diminutive Universe without Galaxies, without intergalactic gasses, only space existing in time.

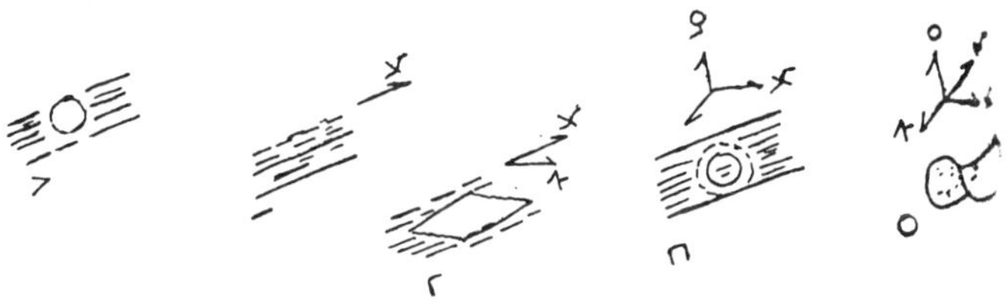

WOA curves once and once again this space. Each new curve supposes one dimension and finally it "wrinkles". Observe that we are employing a simile, a symbol, since only mathematically can we express this correctly. For example: the expression "wrinkled space" seems infantile but it is very didactical.

With a new image we intend to help you understand.

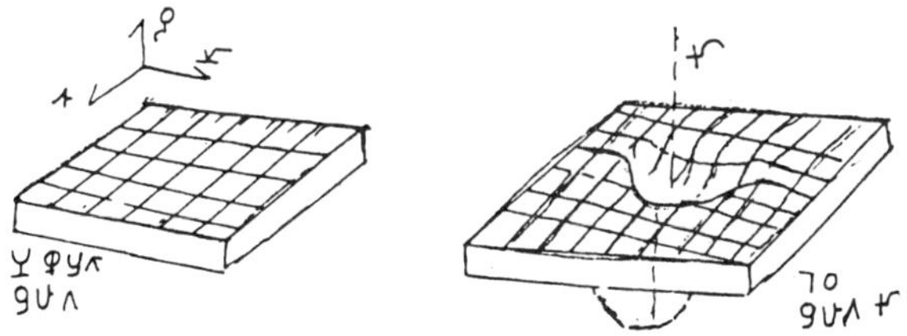

If we curve one tridimensional space, we wrinkle it, or we make a kind of dimple as you see in the figure, through to a fourth dimension. This curvature is that which our sense organs interpret as mass (rock, planet, galaxy).

Very well, WOA distorts that microcosmos, generating thus the mass.

Nothing less than almost all of the actual mass of our two twin Universes concentrated in one very reduced space. Something like all the carbonated waters of UMMO enclosed in my fist. Matter and anti-matter, as you call it, superconcentrated.

This produces then a double EXPLOSION-IMPLOSION. For the IMPLOSION matter and anti-matter, as to say positive and negative atoms are attracted violently one against the other without ever touching. They are two together, two Universes WAAM and UWAAM which never can touch each other because they are not separated in terms of space.

It is because of this that when we say that they attract, the verb "attract" must be interpreted as "mutualinfluence"

On the other hand we indicate that there has been an explosion. In effect: the immense mass of each Cosmos fragments into particles, and these fragments have been expelled brutally for millions of years constituting the actual Nebulas or Galaxies that are moving today with an "almost" constant velocity.

Observe that we emphasize that "almost" in one moment in which your astronomers judge that the velocity (2) has to be CONSTANT or UNIFORM based on two false reasonings:

A. The displacement of the spectral bands, in the Galaxoes observed, is CONSTANT and oriented toward the red.
B. It seems logical to assume that if the nebulas are not impelled by a Field of Force Ↄ| , then they proceed from an initial of the Universe, and are displaced by inertia with uniform velocity (2). Forces Ↄ| ≡ Forces variable.

But both premises are false and ingenuine.

A. Their apparatus of measurement are little precise since of the contrary they have observed that the running of the bands toward the red is not constant, but a nonsinusoidal periodic function of medium amplitude almost imperceptible but measurable.
B. You have not taken into account that our twin Cosmos exercises an influence over our Galaxies. Precisely on UMMO as we have indicated before, we discovered a UWAAM imparting these interferrences.. This interaction impedes our Nebulosity which is displaced with velocity 2 uniformly (Velocity 2 = acceleration).

For which the measure that you use for the age of the Universe is inexact since they use as parameters this pseudo velocity 2 as actual constant of the Galaxies and their distances evaluated by Earth, with the aggrevation that though the velocity 2 may well be almost constant now, in the early times of this creation, the acceleration (a sinusoidal function) had to be enormously amplified.

336. END OF THE WAAM AND UWAAM. DEATH OF THE COSMOS

What will be the end of both twin Cosmos? Though taking into account thatWOA continues creating matter within each Cosmos, the degradation of mass in energy is much more rapid. A moment arrives in which the two Universes are reduced to a hyperspherical SPACE-TIME continuum of negative radius but now of infinite magnitude. Without concentration of masses, as to say without Galaxies, as to say: without curvatures or "wrinkles", only a propagation continues and isotropes of radiations with the same frequencies since by then the multiple sinusoidal functions generated by WOA would have been placed in phase and would have stopped producing those stationary waves, those nodes and crests that our ingeneous senses interpret respectively as 'VACCUUMS" and "MASSES". There would only be an ocean of waves whose amplitude continues decreasing until the final death of the Cosmic pair.

But as on UMMO we have certain knowledge of this creation, how is ATHEISM going to prosper among us?

337. OEMII (MAN) SUBMERGED IN THE COSMOS

We know that for our Universe, there reigns certain basic biogenetic laws that regulate the structure and evolution of all the BAAYIODOO-UII (flora-fauna) of this Cosmos or of our twin UWAAM.

It could give multiple structures to a living being, and in fact, in our laboratories, we have induced it in the nucleic acids of an ovum without fecundation, by a quantified beam OUSEIOSAA (discharges of neutrons that are controlled by an artificial gravitationsl field since those corpuscles do not react before an electrostatic one, they can orient themselves one to one toward a "blank" with infinitely small inducement) we have obtained thousands of distinct living beings by means of these severely controlled mutations.

But the number of living beings is not infinite, since the MIIBAY-EAAO (which you inappropriately call the Genetic Code) not being pluriform has its limitations.

It is said that you imagine a Venusian as a green monster, provided with large eyes and long viscous tentacles. In this you commit two errors:

Judging purilely that your Planet Venus is populated by pluricellular beings and believing that the Universe is populated by all classes or rare engenders.

Let us analyze then man as an ISOLATED BEING though such entity is utopian since man is intimately grafted to all that surrounds him.

We consider that the HUMAN is formed by four integrated factors whose association is necessary for the human to live:

BUUAWE BIAEI (We can translate it as collective soul though this definition suffers grave deficiencies.

BUUAWAA (soul)	(Whose concept coincides surprisingly with that of the actual Theology of the Roman Catholic Religion of Planet Earth.)
OEMBUUAM	(Factor of connection between the soul and OEMII which has not been discovered by you, due to its being located on the encephalic mass.)
OEMII	Human body considered in its ten dimensions. (Three of which define its volume, six express its mass and one that our perceptive organs sense as Time.

337. GENERATION BY WOA OF BUUAWE BIAEI

WOA (Generator or God as you call it) among its infinite congenital ideas, is said to coexist with its essence, imagined as a being that lacks Dimensions (Volume, Time, etc.) not being in its turn capable of generating other (similar) beings. This spirit logically has to posess liberty. (Observe that if it had not been endowed with this prerogative -LIBERTY- the first attribute postulated to it: IT COULD NOT GENERATE OTHER BEINGS BUT YES: IDEAS; would be incompatible since lacking liberty, the ideas would be attributed to WOA. On the other hand it would be evident that such a being could not generate other beings, inasmuch as it constitutes itself in a duplicate of WOA (WOA CANNOT GENERATE SUCH A BEING).

That SPIRIT is the BUAWE BIAEI or COLLECTIVE SOUL of THE HUMANS.

We have said that all COMPATIBLE IDEA of WOA has to be GENERATED. Later: simultaneous to the creation of the WAAM is generated that SPIRIT.

One serious objection could be opposed to the nature of the BUAWE BIAEI. If this spirit generates only ideas, only products of a Consciousness, would it not, in spite of all, be similar to WOA? As well as: Do such ideas not end by materialization, by excretion...?

That objection is unjustified since precisely BUAWE BIAEI poseses an enormous multiplicity of consciousnesses, each one in its turn susceptible of engendering polymorphous and contradictory ideas. Those consciousnesses we call: BUUAWAA (called SOULS by Terrestrials).

UMMOWOA, THE CHRISTUS OF UMMO

THE CHRISTUS OF UMMO AND THE "EDELWEISS" SECT

One of the most surprising parallels with that of Earth, presented by the civilization of UMMO, is represented by the apparition, on Earth, of the figure of Jesus Christ, and, on UMMO of UMMOWOA, the Ummite equivalent of our redeemer. The similarities between both figures is very considerable, and both gave their life in public until martyred: Jesus died on the cross, and UMMOWOA on an operating table, where he was subjected to refined tortures by WIE-1.

But I have considered it better to acceed to the own words of those Ummites, since they are the ones who explained their history to us. Can we deduce from this that in all the worlds inhabited by OEMII (humans), there has been a redemption? (1) This is beyond the knowledge of the author of this book, but if HUMANS are the final result of biological evolution in all the worlds —as has been postulated by the Ummites— and which we still can not verify "in situ", since our Exobiology is still in diapers, perhaps the religious terrain also has common characteristics, as seems to be the case with anatomy and also with biology.

But all of this is pure speculation.

Though it is repugnant to me to do so, I have finally decided to include in this report (and this introduction is as good a place as any) a brief note on the "Edelweiss" sect, a neofascist, paramilitary and homosexual organization which a little before the first appearance of this report, sprang into sad reality in our country, and their illegal use of the emblem of the UMMOAELEWE, with which the Ummites seal all of their communications has become infamously evident. Nobody need be surprised that this Nazi-like group is using that particular emblem which has been published and is now in public domain. It appeared for the first time in the book "UMMO, OTRO PLANETA HABITADO" by Fernando Sesma in 1967. It also appeared in "UN CASO PERFECTO" (1973) and in "EL MISTERIO DEL UMMO" (1979), both by the same

(1) In this respect we may refer to a UFO contactee case that began in Holland in the early 1960s, where human-like beings coming from a near Planet which they called IARGA, some 10 lightyears from our Sun, abducted a wealthy multi-national industrialist aboard their huge disc-shaped craft for eight yours, where they showed him scenes of their home planet and history, and discussed comparisons between their society and ours. Before he was released he was "prepared" for follow-on communications which lasted for over 18 years and resulted in a literary record which includes their description of a Redemptive Figure in their history also. This report has been published in Dutch and in English. (UFO CONTACT FROM PLANET IARGA, Denaerde and Stevens)

author, Antonio Ribera, all of which have been seen in various editions. The emblem has therefore been on the street, and any unknown person could use it as an "extraterrestrial" symbol. And this is what has occured with "Edelweiss". (1)

If none of its leaders work for the CIA (which could be the case) in which they could very well have obtained a negative effect and defamation of the symbol... which they tattoo on the inner face of the arm of their unfortunate juvenile adepts, it is certainly producing results desired by that agency.

But we are forced to denounce this dirty maneuver, and this unauthorized use of a symbol that does not pertain to them in any way.

Enough confusion has already been seeded in all that pertains to the UMMO case in particular, and to UFOs in general! I hope this has now helped to clear up this matter.

(1) [This has in fact been expected since the decision to go ahead and release the UMMO Documents and some more information on this remarkable case. It is not that this case is unknown to big governments and to Military and State intelligence agencies (see the Appendix on the Andros Island photographs).

It is also well known to the investigators in this case that various agencies of intelligence of a number of governments have been involved --almost from the beginning-- in trying, first to get control of the case and the contacts, and failing that, to discredit it as much as possible because of its relative credibility and the actual evidence available.

The agencies of disinformation (a major element of intelligence) of all the governments involved are believed to have worked separately and in collaboration to defuse this potential "bomb". This effort still goes on unabated, and you may look for more attacks as this information gets around. If you do not buy their "pig in a poke" you will be able to see some of the remarkable truths here for yourselves.

Planting the UMMO symbol in a disgraceful organization such as the "Edelweiss" is an easy and simple task for any agency of disinformation and its effect is damaging and long lasting -- exactly what would be extected. -Publisher]

We continue the presentation from the UMMO documents themselves as follows:

THE BIRTH OF UMMOWOA

The humanity of UMMO passed through the greatest crisis in our past history.

We are, with respect to Earth, an old people who had commenced to measure the time when dispersed social groups of the Planet began to come together in an association for unification under a monocratic government. (see Note 2)

In the length of years, that was succeeded by the OGIAA (GREAT CHIEFS) who imposed more or less dictatorial norms on the people of UMMO.

One known as IUI-12 son of IUI-11 who came to power in the year 4325 of the first Time until 4331, imposed a genuinely despotic regime on the people of the Planet.

But a calm seemed to emerge between the years 188 to 1301 of the second Time, from which laws were promulgated for the selection of the OGIAA severely restricting his governmental powers.

But the fame of AAR GOA (abusive violation of power) of IE-456 daughter of NA-312 in the year 1301 initiated the hallucinatory crisis that we have described before.

It was in this historical frame: in the year 1282/3 of the second Time, under the Supreme Chieftainship of that good and paternal ancient OGII OES-17 son of OES-14, and in the flourishing industrial city (it is better to translate as Colony) of IOSAAXII, the Divine UMMOWOA was born.

The Industrial Plan developed by IE-456 until her death and then by OES-14 through his ascent to power, had reached all of the sectors of society. Millions of GEE and YIE (men and women) were forcefully exiled to the colonies which they had seen created, to work as slave laborers or to be utilized in biological experiments. (1)

(1) [This is highly reminiscent of the "Cultural Revolution" in the Peoples Republic of China, which took place here on Earth (1966-1969), which now of course raises some questions. These communications were received from the Ummites by Sesma in early and mid-1966. The greatest Chinese purges, however, and expulsion of literates to rural Army Labor Brigades and Peoples Work Communes did not culminate until the middle of 1967 when almost all teachers, nearly all scientists and a very large number of University Students were sent to the field for "retraining". Little word of these purges came out of China for months and years because of the tightly closed society there. The dilema we then face is: 1) Did the UMMO communicators get their idea from events transpiring within China in its earliest stages, and if so, how did they manage to project its culmination in 1967 so accurately? 2) Did the Chinese copy the Ummites and how could they have known? Publisher]

UMMOWOA among thousands, was also integrated as a slave laborer in the construction of the IUMMASNEII ("Solar" energy plants - on UMMO the star that gives light and heat to our planet, we call IUMMA -- see Note 3) situated on the table-like plains of SIUU.

Meanwhile a rumor, later confirmed, circulated around the whole of our planet. At 29.2 years (terrestrial) IE-456 died under circumstances still unknown, within her EXAABII (a kind of bathroom) without making contact with any of the intellectuals who were obliged to work as her servants.

But the sigh of relief breathed by our martyred ancestors did not last long. The WOODOO (a kind of very fearful Police) controlled all communications. In only one night (that which followed the death of the dreaded IE-456) more than 170,000 people suspected of rebellion were asassainated. They feared, and not without reason, a rise of general acclaim for the celebrated astronomer YIIXE-87 son of YIIXE-86 during the hidden season in the volcanic region of IIWEEWEE.

They soon confirmed a second report that was already rumored by the time of death of the Tyrant. For the first time since the year zero of the first Time, the Supreme Chief of UMMO would not be elected by the AASE OGIAA (Governors), the will of IE-456 having prevailed through her death.

WIE-1 daughter of OOWA-3 and IE-456, a girl only 12 years of age (terrestrial) succeeded to power. This young girl who only bathed in the essence of IWA (an aromatic plant of UMMO) and whose supreme diversion rested on bursting the tympanum of her unfortunate servants, when angered, by introducing into the ears the seeds of the UGUUAXIIA (a certain shrub), now began her dictatorship by ordering the breasts of her teacher of WUA (mathematics) seared off, and she castrated one of the favorite military chiefs of her mother.

But to the great surprise of all, who suspected the scarce affection of this child for all that pertained to science and philosophy (on this point the genetic legacy of her mother was null), and perhaps out of curious respect to the memory of her intelligent progenitor, she named a commission of experts, and compelled them with threats of cruel reprisals to order the continuation of the grandiose and brutal Plan of Investigation that was initiated on a universal scale by her mother. It is very possible that, foreseeing her death, the mother exhorted her daughter in this sense. The acoustic testament which is still preserved in YOAAGAA, attributed to IE-456 is of course apocryphal. It is difficult to admit any other hypothesis knowing the intellectual mediocrity of WIE-1 and her young age.

These things occured in the UMMO year of 1368 of the second Time, but in those days UMMOWOA had already commenced to spread his doctrine. During the night, when the slave workers were returning from the OYISAA DOAA (a kind of encampment) after being stripped and examined to avoid the theft of copper, that young man of sweet countenance and strong musculature, spoke softly to the hundreds of men, who listened in silence, chewing the large strips of EDIEEDI (a filiamentary aquatic plant, very sweet).

His listeners did not only come from the humble uncultured classes, but included technicians, doctors, biologists, phylosophers... prefessors among those that the Despotic Regieme had condemned, degrading them and their professions.

This man galvanized all those who heard him with the purity of his logic, the objectivity and humility of his words. The one thousand two hundred TAAU (paragraphs) which he has given us, has served until today to guide us spiritually.

When his guardians, moved by the sublime doctrine, offered him preferential treatment despite the risk to them, he gently declined. His self-qualification as WOA incarnate in OEMII (a body) and his power of persuasion was such that not one of the intellectuals that followed Him (including various psychologists of the time) could oppose serious objections to this identification.

Some of His invaluable Talks are preserved today in old rolls of DOROO (acoustical-optical tape) (see Note 4).

Very well: The BIOEUNNIEO (Psychoneurologists) of our days, after carefully analyzing His "writings" the various data of his life, and his TAAU... established this psychodiagnosis which we summarize:

"The personality of UMMOWOA absolutely does not reflect any presence of Delirious Ideas characteristic of the EDDIO WE (an illness analagous to terrestrial paranoia) or EDDIO NAAU (dissociation of the personality similar to schizophrenia of Earth) syndromes, nor of the certain forms of EDDIO LAAYIAA (mental illness of UMMO which vaguely resembles your psychosis affected by time cycles)."

They acknowledged on the other hand, a highly elevated level of intelligence in the whole range of BIEEGOO (a series of integrated factors of mental capacity) and the presence to exceptional degree of psychic UUYI (characteristics of the neurocortical structure) extraordinarily well balanced. It is surprising, however, that UMMOWOA never used his exceptionally well developed telepathic faculties at the time of his death. On this point there are only speculations without the least scientific value.

His exhortations were disseminated clandestinely throughout all of UMMO. Writings, DOROO (photo-acoustic strips), oral commentaries faithfully transmitted through the children, and above all telepathic transmissions to parents and distant friends, despite the strict Police vigilence, were delivered to the remotest corners of our Planet.

All knew of the existence of UMMOWOA, but the belt of tacit silence that surrounded this for a number of years (UMMO), preserved the secrecy of his identity.

But the pleas of his most faithful followers were useless. When UMMOWOA completely finished his mission of REVELATION, he announced to all his decision to deliver himself to the authorities who searched for him so misleadingly.

On night 15 of the year 1402 and with the cunning complicity of the same Police of the OYISAA DOA (a kind of concentration camp) the Divine UMMOWOA fled from the plains of SIUU so as not to compromise his most faithful followers, and presented himself to the WOODOO group of the AASE GAARAADUI (the ruins of this metropolis are still preserved).

Thus began his nightmare martyrdom, testimony of which has been left us by exceptional witnesses of the time and the events.. Official news and reports have been analyzed critically by our specialists.

Without going into a future more detailed report on these circumstances and the horrible drama,when you consider it of interest, we offer some data with respect to same, and we pass on to offering you some idea of His doctrines.

UMMOWOA was among the sorrowfully celebrated (fifth) Group made up of persons selected to serve as victims of scientific experiments, and with the express order of WIE-1 requiring them to search for the technical procedure which would subject them to the most painful death that the physiologist investigators could discover. The process of this martyrdom developed in the year 1406 (UMMO). The sacred body of this sublime figure was subjected to a cycle of analyses of little scientific interest, since the true objective in His case was to satisfy the sadism of his persecutors. His epidermis and spinal medula served to satisfy the desires of those poor sick ones who were unable to SEE.

The specialists who accomplished this exercise in vivisection, were astonished when the body of UMMOWOA disappeared before their very eyes in the instant of his death. On the YOAXAA (a kind of surgical table) there remained only what was left of the GIAA DAII (sheets and porous cloths) but the extirpated viscera, the blood that soaked the UBOO (plastic sponges), including the cephalic liquid in a receptacle outside the room disappeared simultaneously.

Despite the forces of the WOODOO(Police authority) the news went out immediately. The biologists were called for by WIE-1 to render a detaild account in which they excluded all possibility of collective hallucination. The girl listened to the account with superstitious fear, but accepted the version offered by a commission of "scientists" whoaccused the witnesses present as imposters. Those were condemned to death.

They could not support the supposed hypothesis of fraud, without distorting the history of those events.

A critical anlaysis made by our scientists in the year 338 of our Time shed much light on the surprising death of UMMOWOA. Seven witnesses observed the dematerialization without including the UNNIEYUU (neurologist) ROAA-75 son of ROAA-72, who was standing at that moment at the shoulders, and who upon hearing the fall to the floor of UUYO-8 son of UUYO-7 (who suffered a strong nervous shock) leaving him unaware and unable to verify this disappearance, and the horrified expression of his companions corroborated the testimony of the Police and the aides who did not see the departure of any body from the room. Among those seven withesses were AGOO IEE, WOODOO (Inspector) delegated by the authorities to personally verify the carrying out of the orders of WIE-1. This personality, who had been characterized for his cruelty, has left us an impressive version of the event.

We have selected a few paragraphs, which we call TAAU from among the 1,200 left us by UMMOWOA.

The translation is made very difficult, and in no way are we able to reflect the beauty of the poetic images contained in the original. They thus lose profundity and vigor, though we judge that the essence of his doctrine remains intact. UMMOWOA spoke to the people in their time but despite all employed an eternal language. Truely, as we have suggested in earlier paragraphs, the parallel with the words of your OOYAGAAWOA (Jesus Christ) is really impressive.

TAAU ┌ (2)

And thus as BUAAWA (the Soul) only creates IDEAS and rules over our OEMII (body) IT creates IDEAS and GENERATES to WAAM, including our OEMII and its IMMENSITY and PARTICULARITY, over all the beings of the WAAM. Its basis is TO GENERATE and for this reason we call it WOA (GENERATOR).

And we never say WOA was, or WOA will be; we always say WOA IS.

TAAU O— (41)

I am WOA ruling the destinies of my OEMII. I have no doubt of this great enigma, and my OEMIIABII (hominization) has as its objective to bring peace in these days of sad pain and tears. I bring the light that through your dimmed eyes falls softly on the retina.

TAAU O┌ UAA (42)

We are like mentally ill who move in a world of dark illusions. And when we complain of that, our brother does not comprehend us. Can't you see that he also debates between unconscious and confusing motivations? Why don't you first try to understand him?

TAAU  UAA (77)

Do not impute to our OGIAA (Supreme Chief) all our failures. And is she not cruel because she is perhaps ill? Have compassion for her also because she is ignorant of the supreme interior peace that represents love for her fellow man. Because being young in age she does not understand the pain. Because being young in body, she does not know the infantile candor. Because being sweet as a child, she hallucinates believing that she enjoys humilification, when in reality all her pores exude suffering.

TAAU  (81)

We have heard say: Why does WOA consent to such bad? Why can a child one fourth our age order the insemination of our women, submitting them to constant pregnancy until their exhaustion? Why does she have the right to mistreat our naked flesh and humiliate us, even to requiring us to masticate her AYAA (feces)? Why cauterize the breasts of her servants and burn sensitive organs with acids? Why does she impede us by her capricious behavior with the supreme conjugal act only for the pleasure of seeing us rolled in the dust, trembling and lacking in dignity?

And the echo of our voices is lost in the distance among the flaming methane volcanos. Why? Why does WOA countenance such evil?

But: Are we not told that evil is simply the illusion of a tormented mind, as color is of our senses? Is it because we do not see behind this apparent evil, the hidden compliment of the harmonic laws of WOA?

TAAU  UAA (213)

Each organ of the OEMII, each tendency or instinct, has an intelligent organic function ruled by the laws that dictate that which animates me: WOA.

We should not alter these functions beyond their normal limits. That which we enjoy as sight, of hearing, of taste, of smell, of touch, and of the selfperceptive feelings of orgasm, ahould never be converted as an end, but as a knowledgeably controlled medium which permits us to pass through our life with authentic INTERIOR PEACE. (In the original: UNNIEYAA AGAXAAU ODI, may be translated "PSYCHIC EQUILIBRIUM"; or "NEUROCORTICAL EQUILIBRIUM").

TAAU 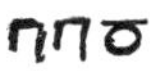 UAA (336)

Why do you accuse your brother of working with the EVIL consciously?

Those acts of man are guided indistinctly by two groups of motives.

Much are really conscience, animated by BUUAWAA (Soul) and of those for which we are without doubt responsible before WOA.

But: How many actions stem from an underlying subconsciousness? How many are determined by blind impulse? How many by defensive actions of our organism reacting to the hostile medium which surrounds it?

Why then, do you always accuse your brother, if perhaps his apparent wicked processes have their source in the inviolable laws that rule the OEMII?

If you have to defend yourself from your brother: If to preserve unity of OEMII-BUAWWAA (Body and Spirit) you have to hurt him: Do it to the least extent after exhausting other means of coercion, but without hate in your mind.

TAAU 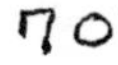 UAA (340)

You have no more supreme objective in the length of your life cycle than to try to respect and love all people.

If you are unable to succeed in this, you may consider your fleeting life on UMMO a failure.

If when your brother suffers you are not inspired to help him...

If you see your brother deprived of means and you do not try to help him...

If you do not identify with his problems and do not try to understand them... Do not expect WOA to consider your BUUWAA in conformance with the image of his omnipotence.

(It is difficult to translate the expression EBAYAA: We have elected to use LOVE because it is more near the Earth concept. For us Sexual Love has another vocable which is different from this. It is XIIXIA. That which you call Platonic Love uses a third verb on UMMO.

TAAU 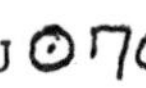 UAA (342)

If in the social scale in which you have touched life, you are superior to your brother, and he must submit to you, do not humiliate him by ordering him to strip before you to mentally take pleasure in your power. Before this observe the shine in his supplicant eyes and touch him on the chest smiling to make him feel comforted.

TAAU 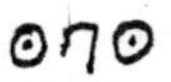 (837)

I have not come to bring you the accessible truth. This you must go to discover for yourself through your study, and with your patient exploration of the Cosmos in which you are immersed.

And this knowledge of the laws which harmonize it must be approached slowly, but progressively to the WOA that reigns in my OEMII (body).

TAAU 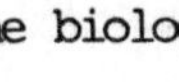 UAA (838)

Your liberation will soon come, and again you will be allowed to unite in OMGEEYIE (Marriage Bond). You occupy the supreme position in the biological scale of UMMO. Only the formal psychic and sexual union of one GEE (man) with one YIE (woman) complies with the psycho-biological laws of our community. If you violate this principle, copulating with other GEE or other YIE who are not your "conjugal partners" you will disrupt the harmony of your social outcome and the disturbances provoked will be your responsibility.

TAAU ⊙7– UAA (831)

Why are we not inspired to understand our children? Why do we persist in seeing in them a faithful genetic reflection of ourselves? Do we not appreciate that inside them they carry incandescently the germinal struggle of evolution? You want them to think like you and that they embrace some customs that they consider extinct.

No; We cannot avoid the fact that the newer generations are better than yours --and that is a consequence of a biological law of evolution-- more pure in their ideals, more sincere toward the truth they long for. But, perhaps it is not the "bell of glory" for us who have stopped?

You must be condescending with the inexperience of your children and not judge them for that which they mistake more than we.

Correct their turbulent inclinations and mould their tender spirits, but remain attentive to the new ideas that spring from their lips. Study them with attention and do not commit the error of aborting their bloom, so that the purity and fertility that they have in them is not stilled.

TAAU ⊙7Г UAA (832)

Our youths: Lament and cry over the incomprehension of their progenitors for their ideas:

Our youths: Consider themselves more intelligent than those who have engendered them:

Why do you not try to penetrate into the most profound recesses of the psychology of adults? Can you not see the bitter experience of the years they have unavoidably endured? Can you not see the sclerosis that affects their arteries, hardening their spirits, closing off the vivifying currents of the new Aurora? But, are they at fault for the process? Why are those humilities and depredations for nothing, forgetting that they gave you being? Is it that you cannot see that among the bronze of their antiquity, still shines brightly, the rich legacy of their experience?

TAAU OO UAA (44)

Raise the sight blurred by tears, and close the fists against the belly, scratching your fine skin with your nails.

Raise the sight impotent before the disgrace and look at your young queen (queen best translates the idea here. a young female despot), lashing at a whim your buttocks and martyring the belly of your YIE with her sharp needle of AOGAAU (Iridium).

And you ask me sighing (1), is it not right for us to crush her tyrany? And I answer you: Yes, it may be right to labor with caution to destroy her despotism, but without hate, ever toward the despot, and pardoning through her fall the blind and ill OEMII that encarnates her.

TAAU 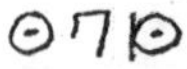 UAA (839)

You will never find peace in your OMGEEYIE (matrimony) without first raising your cloth (2) before wiping your cups of GUU (chrome-steel), snd before cutting the umbilical cord of the delicate fruit of your matrix, not having profoundly studied the psychology of your spouse. If you do this with care, you will see what marvelous flower lies hidden in the leafy forest of your ideas.

You will see how grow the exotic plants that do not spring forth in one of your sex, and knowing better your differences, you can learn to love your relations and understand them.

Why is it unclear; to you GEE, or to you YIE, that in such distinct ground germinates the same flowers?

(UMMOWOA continued this marvelous TAAU drawing comparisons between exotic plants of UMMO and psychological reactions of men and women, exhorting them to a mutual spiritual communion. As a result it is almost impossible to translate these poetic images since the botanic species which serve as examples do not figure in Terrestrial Flora.)

TAAU 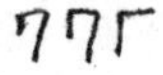 UAA (332)

With respect to the ideas which you believe you find in error. Only in the light of your arguments, with the smooth tactic of peaceful persuasion, and the patient hope of time, can you understand, since the intellect requires a length of time in the fixation of ideas.

If you are not convinced, it is that your interlocutor is lacking in mental capacity, in which case your forces must overcome, or it is your own reasonings that are aberrant.

TAAU  (143)

When you yield to a minister of my CULT in compliance with my UAA

(1) In the original DIIGOIYAA is the acoustic vibration emitted by a person when sad. We have translated as "sigh" though this verb has no significance on UMMO.

(2) Refers to a flexible shade or roof of ovoid form that finishes the dwellings. This gesture expresses the work of the man.

you commit no error of identifying your fall with my Doctrine.

Then, perhaps when you see a doctor squirming on the floor, intoxicated by the drug called UUXAEEMOI (a greasy essence extracted from the UUXAO --toxic species of lichen-- whose principal alkaloid is hallucinogenic) due to the efficiency of the medicine for the "treatment" of one of his "patients", perhaps he is interrogating one of my followers in the exercise of the Cult, and has to preserve him magically from the miseries and sad psychic reactions of the OEMII (the physical body).

TAAU 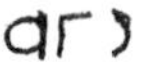 UAA (720)

Inspired men of UMMO, because they are intermeshed in the vast social network of the future, and in which they are integrated, are assigned to positions in the hierarchy. It is not a function of property ownership, nor of genetic inheritance, nor as a result of muscular strength, but in the aptitude of the mind and in the spiritual equilibrium of the individuals.

TAAU 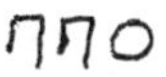 UAA (343)

If in the scale of the social hierarchy that you have reached in life, your superior orders you to undress before him, reject your first thought that he desires to enjoy himself with your embarrassment. But, if you are wrong and such is the case, obey him without blushing, since the dignity of your submission is greater before the mind of WOA than the human pathological tendencies.

PARALLELS BETWEEN JESUS AND UMMOWOA

You yourselves have been able to prove, by exposing an extract of the UAA (Law) of UMMOWOA, the extraordinary parallel between your Jesus of Galilee and our Divine Man.

It does not fit to insinuate a possible telepathic transmission or the reception on the part of Christ, of any other information inasmuch as both events transpired when we still had not traveled to your planet Earth.

Enough of a careful and critical analysis to observe that both doctrines, overfilled with magnitude and profundity, with so many philosophical ideas, has been developed by other great Prophets and Philosophers of both Planets.

When the first news about OOYAGAAWOA (Jesus Christ) were divulged on UMMO, we hold no secret that it provoked a first reaction of incredulity. Such surprising similarity raised suspicions of a mixup, on the part of the expeditionary group that encountered this on Earth.

All the sacred texts of the Old and New Testaments in their Hebraic

Bible versions by R. Kitel and Kahale, as well as the Latin Vulgate, extracts from the works of Thomas Aquino, works of the modern Catholic theologists P. Conger and Rahner, extracts by Hans Kung, and some monographs of authors of the Protestent Convent of Taize and other Lutheran and Anglican Theologists, were transmitted to UMMO and examined by specialists who issued a detailed report of 830,000 words, including a comparative study of Preachings of the Dead Sea and other paleological texts sent by us.

DIFFERENCIES BETWEEN THE CIVILIZATION OF UMMO AND THAT OF EARTH

Evident nevertheless, is the great difference that characterizes our two civilizations.

While on UMMO the whole humanity rapidly assimilated the doctrine of UMMOWOA, converting it into a Standard and Rule of Life for a society that had just come out of a gloomy nightmare under the rule of IE-456 and WIE-1, accepting it without fanatacism and without condemnation toward the minorities who at first accepted it, looking always for the arguments that would help them, but without forcing it to their benefit. Conscious that if any happiness could be expected from our short life, it would only come to us in the spiritual profundity of the divine UAA (laws). You continue, terribly disoriented, seeking a light that is still flickering in the lantern which is lying on the floor among the dust, revealed by the cold illumination of a science and technology that could finally detect it, and not by a means such as we, implacably devoted to the unfortunate terrestrials who surround themselves with cults.

And we are left with admiration also to appreciate in you the terrible contrasts among a society, masses unpolarized and ignorant, vegetating like poor animals without souls, and the spiritual greatness of figures such as a John XXIII, Catholic; an Albert Schweitzer, Protestant or a Mahatma Gandhi.

Such uneven social levels in the spiritual field are unknown on our Planet.

We then, see you as anguished distorted consciousnes' such as Tantalo, the mythological hero in your literature, to whom the remedy or the appetizing fruit of the Pepper is within reach of the hand, too weak to reach it.

Why are the great thinkers of Earth not effective, who know perfectly the terrible disharmony between the scientific and technological advances and that of the spiritual sciences, denouncing it with a firm voice without being heard, seeing dispair as the distance increases day by day threatening to submerge the humanity of Earth in chaos?

You ask us frequently; Why do we not offer you some of our scientific advances? But if we did this you would suffer an "indigestion" as it could not be assimilated by your science!

You ask us for moral and spiritual laws appropriate for the unhappy terrestrial Humanity. But if you posessed the richest spiritual awareness it still would not benefit from full acceptance!

Imagine yourselves as a man, who in his right pocket has accumulated dozens of lighters, and in in the other left pocket he has some hundreds of flints. The lighters don't function for lack of flints, and the unhappy man is asking a light from those who pass by because his lighters don't work. What do you think?

Nevertheless we would be at fault in laughing and poking fun at this man, because we have forgotten a third factor. An inhibitory element. Perhaps a transitory mental disturbance, blocking his volitional faculties, impedes the apparently simple gesture of simply introducing one of the flints into one of the lighters. It is cruel and unjust to fault him for his inability.

You are not so ingeneous as to think that we posess the magic formula, the Aladin's Lamp, a marvelous pocket apparatus which we could offer you now that would bring you out of chaos.

Effectively our profound knowledge of the psychophysiological mechanisms that regulate the life of humans, permits us to act upon this with procedures more technical and exact than those utilized by yourselves with pharmaceuticals, neurosurgery or techniques of yoga and autosuggestion. We will speak of those later, and perhaps you can anticipate in advance, obtaining actual power over those same atoms of DIIUYAA (Krypton) of the OEMBUUAW.

But when we speak of that, you will be convinced that such technologies are not those that have precisely obtained the social stability of our Planet.

[NOTE- A great deal of the information on UMMOWOA was communicated directly to the Reverend Father Enrique Lopez Guerrero, a Catholic Priest of the Jesuite Order, Pastor of the Mariena del Alcor parish in Sevilla, Spain, along with a good deal more data on UMMO and the activities of those expeditionaries here on Earth. The Ummites transmitted a series of communications and reports to the Priest at his residence in Sevilla. from these documents and others, the Priest wrote a thick book of more than 500 pages (in Spanish) detailing his own contacts with the expeditionaries. It was published under the title "MIRANDO A LA LEJANIA DEL UNIVERSO" by Plaza & Janes in Barcelona.

One has to wonder at the very great, and seemingly impossible similarity to the Christian story here on Earth. This would seem to be the "final straw" that puts the lie to the whole account, being far more incredible than the simple appearance of extraterrestrials on Earth.

If, as the scientists say, two human species could never evolve in any kind of similar likeness, how much more difficult is the proposition that they experienced similar religious history?

But this is more than a story, and one undemonstratable fact does not make another provable one any the less valid. This case offered data in its time that was unknown on Earth, and which was subsequently proved to be entirely correct--even many years later. The very precise description of genetics was ahead of its time when given, but later proved to be infinitely correct.

There were the biological experiments at Albacete which resulted in the necessary mutilation of a human body, which involved Police and the Courts for over 10 years, and nobody was ever convicted of any crime. Why are those records sealed? Why did the Countess never reveal from her own lips, even to her death, what was going on in the mansion there in Albacete?

There was the Andros Island affair involving warships and very high ranking officers of the Navies and Air Forces of five countries, and some of the biggest munitions contractors in the world, where 350 feet of 35mm high resolution film was exposed of an airbourn vehicle identical to the UMMO ship photographed in Spain, and with the very same symbol visible on the bottom of the craft. That film has never been released. Why?

Could anybody do all this for a prank? How much would such a thing cost? What purpose would it serve? If it were a bunch of college students trying to get away with something, they must have matured some by now--thirty five years later, and the contacts were still going on as late as 1984.

We don't have the answers, but we also do not think we should throw our something we just don't understand. Perhaps it is only because we lack more information that it is unacceptable to us at the present time. This controversial UMMOWOA feature is therefore included in good faith, and we offer it for what it is... -Publisher]

THE "ATIENZA CONNECTION"

In my work SEQUESTRADOS POR EXTRATERRESTRES (Editorial Planeta, S.A. of Barcelona, 1981, pages 74-75), I wrote the following, concerning what the Spanish ufologists called "The Atienze Case".

"The magazine, LA ACTUALIDAD ESPANOLA, now defunct, published at the end of 1968 and beginning of 1969, a series of articles signed by one "F. Sinod", concerning the alleged encounter of this gentleman with an extraterrestrial called "Francisco Atienza", near the swamp of Alarcon. These articles appeared in issue numbers 884 (12-12-68), 885 ((19-12-68), 886 (26-12-68), 888 (9-1-69) and 893 (13-2-69) of this magazine.

"After that I published a review of this case in the second volume of the publication CICLOPE—LA INCOGNITA DEL ESPACIO (Barcelona, 1969). And the same Sinod exposed at length the messages received telepathically from his friend Atienza from space, published as a supplement to the mentioned publication, titled "Cyclope Report".

"It is already some years since the person hidden behind the pseudonym "Sinod" has died, and I believe that I can now reveal his true identity, known on the other hand among the principal Spanish ufologists. "Sinod" was the reverse of the surname Donis; and behind this name hid don Francisco Donis Ortiz, a distinguished Spanish financier, who through the CRECINCO enterprise represented in Spain the interests of the Rockefeller holdings., and who for questions of business and farms (he had one in Alicante) frequently traveled by automobile between Valencia and Madrid.

"I had the occasion to know and deal personally with don Francisco Donis, and was impressed by his simplicity, intelligence, affability, and his quite evident sincerity. I remember a famous meeting that he held in his home on calle Antonia Merce, in Madrid, in the course of which don Francisco read to those present —all interested in ufology and especially in the UMMO enigma— a letter he had received from the Ummites, in which they asked that he put them into personal contact (thus contravening one of their strictest rules of anonymity) with the mysterious "Francisco Atienza", the extraterrestrial "friend" of senor Donis, coming from the Planet Urin, according to what Donis said, and which the Ummites said they knew nothing of. It seemed to be that the gentlemen from UMMO had learned of all of this from LA ACTUALIDAD ESPANOLA, reading the articles signed by the mysterious "F. Sinod" (whom we now know).

"At this meeting we all presented long lists of questions, which we wanted don Francisco to submit to the Ummites. But on seeing this they intervened, and it was then when they produced the celebrated call (recorded by Rafael Farriols), in which a twangy nasal voice, asked with difficulty, of Donis that "your brothers meeting in your residence, not formulate questions to my brothers". This recording has been analyzed by various national and foreigh acoustical laboratories, and its frequencies "are not human".(1)

"But that is another history. Let us go to the encounter of senor Donis with Atienza, and the curious revelation he made.

"On the 12th of Nevember of 1968, when Donis was driving to Madrid from Valencia in his automobile, he perceived a telepathic message (I have previously received something similar, but it was always confusing and unintelligible), in which the voice said that when he arrived at the turn-off the Parador Nacional de Alarcon, leaveing Route N-III, he take this other highway, because there he would make contact with an extraterrestrial.

"The car stopped at that point, but thanks to a friendly truckdriver who helped him, he was able to get it going again, and senor Donis (it was already night, after supper) was finally able to drive toward el Parador.

"A little after arriving at the crossing and taking the turn-off as instructed, the surprised financier perceived an enormous discoidal object suspended in the air at the edge of the road. It was some three meters above the ground. floating without touching any part of its structure with the ground. There was an apparatus, a classic "UFO".

"Resuming, we must say that the surprised Donis was looking when from the disc emerged a kind of extendible stair, down which came a "human being", who came up to him with his arms extended in a sign of peace. That person then spoke, speaking in correct Castillian, saying that his name was Francisco Atienza, and that he was descended from terrestrials. Sinod said that his appearance was completely normal and current, and that without his gray jumpsuit, or space dress which he wore, he would not attract any attention from anybody.

"There began then a long conversation between them, continued later in the automobile of Donis. Among other things on his origen, Atienza said that he came from a Planet called Urin, whose indigenous inhab-

(1) We feel obliged to remind once again, that the vocal cords in the adult humans of UMMO normally atrophy as their routine communication becomes more and more telepathic. Those UMMO citizens selected as expeditionaries to this Earth study project are fitted with a prosthetic device which amplifies in some cases, and replaces in others, the existing vocal organ. This voice when analyzed in the acoustical laboratories was found to lack certain human resonances and to include others beyond the human range. We shall attempt to bind a copy of this recording in the back of this book for your own analysis and enlightenment. -Publisher

itants were small macrocephalous humanoids. Nevertheless, there was on Urin a colony of terrestrials, who lived below great cupolas with air, since the atmosphere of Urin was unbreathable by the sons of Earth.

"But the life under these conditions had provoked a sterility among those Terrestrials and their descendents (among those who stayed there it was greater for the females than the males), the same as occurs with animals who live in captivity.

"Does this explain the cases of experiments of women from space (as in the Antonio Vilas Boas and Liberato Quintero cases in South America) with healthy and robust examples of our species? Is there here a key to these and other similar cases? If the women presented in the Brazilian and Colombian cases were a little different, one may take into account the possibility of descendents before the fertility ran out. They may be third, fourth or fifth generation descendents of Terrestrials taken to Urin (Zeta Reticuli?) by the authentic sons of the other planet. And of course the white race is not the only one on Earth. There are others who may also be involved.

"It is no more than a simple route, but I think it should be taken into account, above all if we think that on any occasions the little macrocephalus humanoids are seen to coexist with beings completely human (the Brazilian Lagoa Negra case for example).*

"With regard to Donis and his friend Atienza, I have left that for another occasion (or another book) to occupy myself in detail with his curious relation, which at the moment of his strange encounter was no more than the beginning."

In the beginning of 1969, as I said in the transcribed text, a meeting was held in the house of the same Donis where he had assembled us to read us the letter from the Ummites, in which they asked him to put them in contact with Atienza. (Letter date 28-2-69) But before that, Donis had received another letter from them which I now transcribe:

*NOTE- Here in the U.S.A. we have the Travis Walton UFO case where a young woodcutter from Snowflake, Arizona, was zapped aboard a large disc-shaped craft by a beam of light, in full view of five fellow foresters, in 1975. He was gone for five days, and when he returned he described his abduction by small macrocephalic humanoids who also had other normal human beings working aboard their ship with them, except that these humans wore breathing apparatus in certain parts of the ship whereas the little humanoids did not. (Full details are published in THE WALTON EXPERIENCE, by Travis Walton, 1978.)

UMMOAELEWE
Language: Spanish
Copies: One

Honorable Sir:

Perhaps you will consider it incorrect that we write you personally without the previous mediation by friends or introduction according to social norms in use in your beautiful country, a presentation made by an intermediate person.

But the circumstances that frame our request, make difficult the respect and resolution of full protocol.

Through a recent typed article inserted in a well known Spanish publication, which was preceeded by accounts of the events that induced us to communicate with you, we observe that you posess more or less extensive information about our existence on this planet.

We believe we are not mistaken if are persuaded that such data has been offered to you by the components of a Madrid macrosocial net with which in past months we have maintained friendly contacts.

This will avoid our having to tire you with an exposition of our identity, which would require many typed pages.

We do not know what credit you can concede to our testimony. And of course we extend to you as well an invitation to show hypercriticsm in your judgements with respect to them, since naturally you have not been able to obtain arguments and definite proofs which support this thesis of our existence among you.

In sum, our solicitude could limit your independence of whether our history is accepted or rejected by you as lacking a definite demonstration.

Surely our solicitude will not be judged by you as an unrealizable favor to some men whose personality is unknown to you and who in good logic could be (seen by a limited person) mere imposters, simple paranoics or vulgar individuals with the innocuous intention of playing a jole on his friends.

But if you will agree with us that though accepting these last interpretations, the effort necessary to satisfy our desire is so small that you would not lose too much in satisfying it.

We ask you then, earnestly, that you help us. We require nothing more than that you pass on this petition, first clarifying to a certain extent.

In your account you referred to the contacts maintained by you with the visitor Atienza, in which you said that you continued maintaining relations by ideographic communications of telepathic character with him.

We ask you that among the questions formulated by you, you simply ask if he would be disposed to answer for us (since up to the present the possibility has not been propitious for us to initiate a contact with this civilization) a question formulated by means of a binary code.

Simply --WE REPEAT-- to know if they would be disposed to satisfy this request.

The answer this senor Atienza offers, may be communicated by you to us through one of your articles or in another case we could suggest another method for it to come to us.

We actually have powerful reasons to try to avoid all communications through normal telephone cable with your brothers of Earth.

The final fragment of the letter sent by those of UMMO to senor don Francisco Donis Ortiz on the 17th of January 1969, and received by him on the 18th read as follows:

Senor:

It only remains to excuse us for having to resort to you in asking this favor and the desire that if it would be possible for you to bring our respectful greetings to your brothers of the Spanish country whom we will cite following, who you may not know well personally (more than some) but being connected to all by friendship in diverse grades, will receive without doubt news of the same. These men are:

Dionisio Garrido, General Calvo, Enrique Villagrasa, Antonio Rivera (sic), Rafael Farriols, Priest Lopez Guerrero, Senorita Alicia Araujo, Federico Gibernau, Jaime Imbert, Jordan Pena, Senor militar Villalba, Senor Muela, Senor J. Antonio Cezon, Sesma Manzano, Senor Martinez, Mario Lleget, Regina Sendras, Senor Santos Garcia... and many other friends of ours also, whose extensive listing we fear would tire you.

We conclude with a respectful greeting to your wife, your children, your friends and all.

UMMOAELEWE
Language: Spanish
Number of Copies: 3
Francisco Donis Ortiz
MADRID-SPAIN
Date: 28-2-69

Honorable Sir:

We have read your gentle reply to our message. Through its context we observe with satisfaction that you acceed to our request with pleasure. We entreat that you were not obligated to satisfy, however your posture must be the object of our most warm gratitude. Not for the energy required to execute it which as you recall with objectivity, is minimal, but because you could lawfully accept a social conventionalism that authorizes and even advises you not to lend assistance to beings who mask themselves in anonymity, and whose genuine objectives cannot logically be clear.

Conscious of your embarrassing situation, our request has been of such nature that in no case could it hurt your own sacred personal prestige, since to transmit some cyphers to a mysterious --for us-- communicant, could not entail evident risk nor any loss as you always have said, sensibly, that you are not responsible at any level, public or private for the suitability of our testimony.

The suspicion that they attach with respect to the identity of our brothers, we see as perfectly logical, comprehensible and intelligent. We in your place also would have seen ourselves induced to put together a very similar hypothesis. No doubt through the resistence of some men, to present themselves, without recourse to anonymity, could always camouflage motives of doubtful morality. Their disconfidence is the natural expression of exquisite prudence. We can not feel humiliated by that.

But we beg that you try to understand that our situation is at least as embarrassing as yours, with respect to the men of Earth.

In principle we cannot offer objective proofs of our presence among your brothers, which would serve to you as unquestionable scientific testimony of this reality, of this authentic existence among the members of the social Network of Earth.

This obliges us to realize a firm force of censorship on our own selfcensored written documents, which makes us even more effective in our contacts by electrophonic channels (telephone).

We avoid thus any unconsciously filtered contribution, which surpasses certain limits of informative quality, which could serve as irrefutable proof of our existence.

It is not our intention that you "believe" in our heteroplanetary presence. One express act of doubt and scepticism in your great social body favors us. We achieve by this method for one part, to maintain contact with your contacted brothers who effectively concede little importance to the lack of conclusive proofs, but who nevertheless accept our testimony to some degree. On the other hand we do not lie about writing officially to you, though in private if our physical presence intervenes, we will see ourselves nevertheless obliged to falsify the authentic feel of our affirmations when in the daily life of unknown ones of Earth, we identify ourselves as citizens of some Nation, armed with fraudulent documentation.

In our conduct of clandestine character, we do not pretend to cause you any harm, but to neutralize any psychosocial reaction of grave consequences for all, to obtain a climate of incredulity in those cases where notices referring to us, that pass through the vehicles of Terrestrial information, reach a certain level of anxiety in diffusion as in the case of your brother, the Catholic Priest Enrique Lopez Guerrero.

In these cases the enthusiasm demonstrated is pardonable. The Latin temperament justifies and explains such reactions, but those brothers of yours of other nationalities, in their contacts with us have demonstrated more capacity for reserve and mental secrecy.

It is true that on determined occasions we have come to offer irrefutable proofs of personal character to certain of your brothers of Earth, though we have adopted severe precautions to avoid an indiscretion or a change of attitude toward us of such OEMII (men) which could gravely injure our norms of reserve.

We are disposed in the case of yourself: Senor Donis Ortiz, to offer to them in the case that you offer to serve as intermediary between F. Atienza and ourselves. Naturally we cannot require such contact though it were not physically interpreted, without interceding a material presentation of our availability for arguments, that would be convincing to you, always that the proof provided could not in the future be provided by you. This is perfectly possible and we have operated thus in determined situations planned with other OEMII of Earth.

We desire, senor, to make some punctualizations which we ask you to bring to the interested personal brothers of yours.

We don't know who could have sent to your brother that insignia of the "Government" of UMMO (as you indicated) to be displayed on the lapel. No doubt it treats of some explainable and intranscendent confusion, since it is evident to us that no such donation has been executed by any of my brothers.

We accept that prudent warning that makes us suspect disturbed or immoral objectives. We reiterate that that veiled allusion can not nor even must not offend us, since it encompasses perfectly in the initiation, still embryonic, of some relations in which one of the parties resists identification completely.

We understand that our protests or proclamations of honorability can not be valid without referring to our faultless conduct in this respect. Senor: We can only ask for now that you collect testimony among our own friends of Earth who can guarantee our honesty.

Now we transmit to you the codified text which we ask you to take to your strange communicant Francisco Atienza coming from the for us unknown Planet of Urin, as soon as you find a favorable opportunity for this oral-telepathic-ideographic communication or for transmission by whatever means available that you consider technically viable:

1011010111 100101 101000100111 - 110101111110 0100111

We ask in whatever case, that if you obtain a reply, do not divulge it through any medium of social communication. We cannot compel you to carry out this solicitude, but we ask you to very carefully guard this confidence. We will inform you on the means of cummunication as soon as we know that you have received a response. This constitutes for us one criteria which confirms to us the identity of F. Atienza and the basis to know if he desires new communications from us (three final numbers codified).

We are confident that in his answer he will verify the genuiness of this case, we end with the proofs which we offer to identify us with. We ask that with respect to the point or situation in which we may celebrate our first interview, we may choose its place, always that it be a central urban location which will not inspire fear to you.

Senor: For us this favor is very important. We accede to you the account that appeared printed in the periodical LA ACTUALIDAD ESPANOLA not so much for the context of a testimonial which in sum did not include in its contents any unquestionable proof of its authenticity, as would be expected of a man of Spain of recognized social prestige and honorability well demonstrated, testifying to those means of information which we have directed to you.

Senor: Again we respectfully salute you, your friends and brothers of Earth who make up the circle of your acquaintences. We hope that the new tests of the APOLLO Project, as well as the experiments oriented towards OYAA VENUS and OYAA MARS by your American and Soviet brothers have great success.

Seal of UMMO
Graphics known as some of theirs

It has always been an enigma to know how the Ummites encountered the "Madrid Group" plus those of us that came from the "provinces". We had a list of questions prepared for Donis to present to them during his interview. It seemed to be that this was wasted by the officiousness of don Enrique Lopez Guererro, Priest of Mairena del Alcor, who tried to spy on senor Donis, for which the Ummites desisted in joining in this personal interview.

The recording obtained by Farriols, later analyzed in various national and foreign phonotechnical laboratories, revealed clearly that the acoustical frequencies <u>did not</u> correspond to a human voice, though they also rejected the possibility that it could be the "voice of a computer".

THE ARGENTINE LETTER

Very similar letters from the Ummite communicators, written in the French language, were posted from West Berlin on 4 September 1969 (the postal cancellation date observed over the stamps) and were dispatched in microfilm form to the Argentine investigators, Sres. Pedro Romaniuk, Ariel Ciro Rietti, Luis Anglada Font, and Benito Segundo Reyna, as well as copies to the French ufologists Rene Fouere and Aime Michel. The letters consisted of three typewritten pages and two graphics pages, including one page with a reproduction of a photograph of the UMMO ship in flight. This photograph is of an identical craft to the one photographed at San Jose de Valderas on 1 June 1967, but is of a different view angle than any of the others. The letter sent to Michel and Fouere is listed as document No. 84 of the catalogue of UMMO documents put out by Sr. Ignacio Darnaude Rojas-Marcos, as shown in Vol. I, The Mystery of UMMO.

Those letters from West Berlin were introductory communications, similar but different from the one I received from Paris. They all ended with a table of mathematical algorithms in Ummite symbol form. These initial letters were followed by others over a period of time, as well as those sent to many other UMMO contactees in a number of other countries of this world.

Sr. Pedro Romaniuk has kindly furnished his copy of this UMMO letter for your examination. We have translated his copy and furnished a reduced facsimile for your study. Note the photo of the UMMO ship from the microfilm on page 4 of this letter. Also note the use of typed or stamped UMMO symbol characters in the heading of the first page of this letter.

As a point of special interest, civil engineer Enrique Villagrasa Novoa of Madrid, received a similar letter from West Berlin over a year and a half before this, received 9 January 1968, a report consisting of 43 close-typed pages of detail on the spacecraft of UMMO, and their construction, which also included microfilms of spacecraft features and photos of the ships. These photos were also like the one seen on page 4 of this Argentine letter. Vilagrasa's letter was discussed in detail in Volume I mentioned.

(UMMO Symbol)
UMMOAELEWE

Center: West Berlin
        Germany

- Dear Sir:

Be aware that the transcendence of that which we are about to say, could be expressions of such nature as is the habitual formula of a faker, one mentally disturbed, or the delerious ideas perhaps of some journalists, publicists or agents of some political organization, esoteric or religious, pretending to exploit its version of the news for the profit of such group.

Whenever a hypothesis or report departs from the aspects of probability and when the range of techniques and means and elements of judgement lack reality, every balanced intelligence has the right to adopt an attitude of skepticism and suspicion. One should never accept an unsupported statement, and less so, as in the present case, when its source is unknown, or when there is suspicion of fraud.

To us it is evident that what we are about to reveal to you is true. However it is not logical to demand that you accept information so fantastic. We admit that in your place we would react in a similar form.

But, withall, the attitude of one who tolerates a priori any version is admissable if they analyze without passion and objectively, the search for truth. All of the researchers of Planet Earth accept this criterion. If the concepts of yesterday seem fantastic and absurd, and were not analyzed by competent specialists, would you have reached your present state of culture?

In the later years, on the occasion of the appearance in the atmosphere of Earth of UFOs, the fantasies of men are stimulated and the news in the press is often fraudlent, seldom authentic, concerning this phenomenon.

Knowing that these versions have created a climate logically of distrust, we realize that our declarations should be accepted with extreme reserve. Nevertheless, our objective in sending you this document typed on a machine by one of our collaborators, is not to make you believe us without more proof than these paragraphs.

In reality analogous communications have been sent for some time to professors and specialists of different countries. Canada, Australia, Spain and Yugoslavia have groups of cultured persons who know of our existence, but at our suggestion guard with discreet silence for the time. With our reconnoitering devices we know that some men of science with whom we have established communication, have indignantly torn up the letters we sent them, confident that they were a joke, or the actions of paranoids in some cases. The surprising examples of scientific support convinced some that our purpose was serious and devoid of imoral intentions.

Therefore we ask you to carefully read our statement. It is not important that you, in the beginning, that you discard the truth and the good basis for our affirmations. We ourselves do not wish the reality of our existence to come to the knowledge of the social mass without sufficient priority.

In sum, the situation is embarrassing and strange. We, if we are to be faithful to the truth, must give you our own testimony. You, as a man of equilibrium and balance are free to accept it or not. But we urge you not to separate one page from another, nor to tear up this copy. One day you will be able to confirm the truth of our statements.

At 4 hours 17 minutes GMT of Earth day 28 March 1950, an OAWOLEA UEWA (lens-shaped spaceship) established contact with the lithosphere of Earth for the first time in our history. The descent was effected in the outskirts of the village of "LA JAVIE" in the "BASSES-ALPES", in France.

The process of adaptation which included the assimilation of your language, information concerning the social customs, etc... of beings of this planet is difficult to explain in a simple letter. Certain of your brothers of Canada and Spain know in detail our history.

Six of our brothers descended on that occasion as the first explorers of a world unknown to us. Afterwards we came in larger numbers to study and analyze the terrestrial culture. Two bases of operation were established for the moment: ADELAID, AUSTRALIA, where resides our brother who is chief of the expedition; and WEST BERLIN, GERMANY.

We come from a solid star, where the geological characteristics differ a little from those of Earth, but whose atmospheric composition is very similar (we use terrestrial units of measure here).

Equator: Maximum radius $R=7{,}251{,}608 \cdot 10^3$m

Mass of the planet: $m = 9.36 \cdot 10^{34}$kg
Acceleration of gravity measured in AINNA.OXO g = 11.9 m/s
Rotation on its axis: 30'92" hours (our measure in UIW 30'92h = 600 UIW)

We designate our planet with a phoneme that you can translate thus: UMMO. One single continent and scant insular surface occupies some 38% of the surface of our planet. UMMO moves in an elliptical trajectory with an eccentricity of 0.078 around a star we call IUMMA (our sun). The mean distance UMMO-IUMMA is $9.96 \cdot 10^{12}$cm. IUMMA is a star with a mass of $1'48 \cdot 10^{33}$g. The distance separating IUMMA from your Sun is about 14.42 light years. We calculate that you would locate this star at:

Right Ascension: 12 hours 31 minutes
Declination: 9° 18'

But the brilliance you observe now is very attenuated here due to a cloud of cosmic dust that reduces it to an apparent magnitude on the order of 36. The surface temperature of this star is of 4,580.3° K. Its alternations in magnetic field are great. We register on our planet values reaching 216 gauss, very superior are those of UMMO. These perturbations interdict our use of electromagnetic frequencies, the reason for which we must use the gravitational waves for communications.

We inhabitants of UMMO have a body whose physiological form is very much like that of HOMO SAPIENS of Earth. This is logical if you consider that biological laws are valid for all the Universe, and that when the ambient environment is analogous, the biological structure undergoes few variations. We are not beings that you would call monsters. Only some small anatomical differences distinguish us. In a large part of our brothers, the speech organs (vocal cords) are hyperatrophied, and we supplement this sclerosis with artificial means of verbal expression.

Our race is a people much older than yours that has attained a higher level of civilization. Our social structure is different. We are governed by four members who are chosen by psychophysiological evaluations. The laws are regulated as a function of constant sociometric measure over time.

Note that our economic system is equally different. We know nothing of money as the transactions in goods of value existing on UMMO is effected through a network of what you would call electronic brains. Goods of normal consumption have little value, because their abundant production exceeds the demand.

Our society is profoundly religious. We believe in a Creator (WOA) and we have scientific arguments in favor of the existence of a factor that you would call the soul. We recognize a third factor that unites it to the body, and is constituted of atoms of Krypton lodged in the encephalic mass.

Our customs are equally different. There are no race differences and the species of zoological variety are less numerous.

We have no intention of interferring in the social evolution of your planet for two transcendent reasons. A cosmic moral prohibits a paternalistic attitude towards planetary social svstems, which must grow gradually on their own. Furthermore, any public intervention on our part - our own official presentation - would produce grave alterations and social perterbations incalculable at this time, and the study and analysis of your society would no longer be possible since the present conditions are virgin.

Our modest attempts at contact, as we are now effectively maintaining with you, will not, on the other hand, produce a great alteration, as we foresee in advance, the natural scepticism that is accorded.

Our system of numeration is of 12, so as a curious resume, we have included a table of some mathematical algorythms as we transcribe them:

(table furnished as in copy reproduction following)

(finger seal)

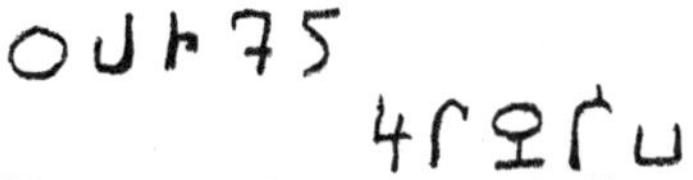

(figures raised in relief)

Sr. Pedro Romaniuk of Argentina furnished this reproduction of the UMMO letter mailed to the Argentine Group from West Berlin on 4-9-1969. An identical letter was mailed to Aime Michel and others in France.

OUMMOAELAEWE

CENTRE: BERLIN-OUEST
ALLEMAGNE

- Cher Monsieur,

Nous sommes conscients de la transcendance de ce que nous allons vous dire. Nous comprenons qu'une affirmation de cette nature est d'habitude formulée par un farceur, un perturbé mental aux idées délirantes ou peut-être même quelque journaliste, publicitaire ou agent de quelque organisation politique, esthérique ou religieuse qui prétende exploiter sa version ou la nouvelle pour le profit de son groupe.

Lorsqu'une hypothèse ou un récit s'écarte des aspects de vraisemblance et - quand on manque de moyens techniques et d'éléments de jugement pour en témoi gner la réalité, toute intelligence équilibrée a le droit et doit adopter une attitude sceptique ou de méfiance. On ne doit jamais accepter le simple té- moignage et moins encore lorsque, comme dans le cas présent, on en ignore - l'origine, ce qui le rend suspect de supercherie.

Pour nous, il est évident que ce que nous allons vous révéler est certain. Toutefois, nous ne pouvons pas logiquement exiger que vous acceptiez une - information aussi fantastique. Nous admettons qu'à votre place, nous réagi rions de façon semblable.

Mais, cependant, l'attitude de celui qui tolère à priori toute version est admissible s'il l'analyse sans passion et objectivement à la recherche de la vérité. De fait, tous les chercheurs de la Planète Terre ont suivi ce critè re. Si des concepts qui "hier" semblaient fantastiques et absurdes n'avaient pas été analysés par les spécialistes compétents, seriez-vous parvenus à l'état culturel actuel?

Dans les dernières années, à l'occasion de l'apparition dans l'atmosphère ter restre des UFO, la fantaisie des hommes s'est débordée, et l'on a trouvé dans la presse des nouvelles souvent frauduleuses, authentiques quelques rares fois, concernant ces phénomènes.

Conscients que ces versions ont créé un climat logique de méfiance, nous sa- vons que notre déclaration doit être accueillie avec un extrême réserve. Tou- tefois, notre objectif en vous envoyant ce document tapé à la machine par l'un de nos collaborateurs, n'est pas d'être crus sans plus de preuves que ces quelques paragraphes.

De fait, des communications analogues ont été envoyées il y a quelque temps, à des professeurs et à des spécialistes de divers pays. Le Canada, l'Austra- lie. l'Espagne et la Yougoslavie ont des groupes de personnes cultivées qui connaissent notre existence bien que sur notre suggestion, ils gardent un si lence discret sur ce thème. Et bien que nous devions reconnaître que de nom breux hommes de Science avec lesquels nous avons établi une communication - écrite ou parlée ont déchiré, indignés, les lettres envoyées, les confondant

P. Romaniuk

2

F

[illegible] ent avec les mauvaises [illegible] ou [illegible] ques - [illegible], l'été [illegible] de [illegible] liques [illegible] tée simplement [illegible] par convaincre quelques-uns [illegible] - être sérieuse et dépourvue d'intentions immorales.

De ce fait, nous vous supplions de lire soigneusement [illegible]. - Peu importe qu'en principe, vous écartiez la vérité et le bien-fondé de nos affirmations. Nous ne souhaitons pas non plus que la réalité de notre existence passe maintenant à la connaissance de la masse sociale sans préparation suffisante.

En somme, la situation est embarassante et étrange. Nous, si nous sommes - fidèles à la vérité, nous devons vous faire parvenir notre propre [illegible]-ge. Vous, en tant qu'homme équilibré et objectif, vous restez libre de l'accepter ou non. Mais nous vous prions de toutes façons, dans un cas comme - dans l'autre, de ne pas déchirer cette copie. Un jour, vous pourrez constater la véracité de nos affirmations.

A 4 heures 17 minutes GMT du jour terrestre 28 mars 1950, une OAWOLEA OUEWA (Astronef de forme lenticulaire) établissait le contact avec la lithosphère de la TERRE pour la première fois dans notre histoire. La descente s'effectua aux environs du village de "LA JAVIE" dans les "BASSES-ALPES", en France.

Le processus d'adaptation que comprit l'assimilation du langage, l'information concernant les coutumes sociales, etc... des être de cette planète est difficile à synthétiser dans une simple lettre. Certains de vos frères du - Canada et d'Espagne connaissent en détail toute l'histoire.

Six de mes frères descendirent à cette occasion comme les premiers explorateurs d'un monde inconnu pour nous. Ensuite, nous sommes venus plus nombreux pour étudier et analyser la culture terrestre. Deux bases d'opération ont été établies pour le moment: ADELAIDE (AUSTRALIE) où réside notre frère chef d'expédition, et BERLIN-OUEST (ALLEMAGNE).

Nous provenons d'un astre solidifié, dont les caractéristiques géologiques diffèrent un peu de celles de la terre, mais dont la composition atmosphérique est très semblable. (Nous utilisons les unités de mesure terrestres - dans certains cas)

Equateur: rayon maximum $R = 7251{,}608 \cdot 10^3 m$
masse de la planète: $m = 9'36 \cdot 10^{24} Kg$.
Accélération de la gravité
mesurée en AIDHA, OXO $g = 11{,}9$ m/s.
Rotation sur son axe: 30'92 heures (nous mesurons en UIW 30'92 h = 600 UIW)

Nous désignons notre planète avec un phonème que vous pourriez transcrire ainsi: OUMMO. Un seul continent et la faible surface insulaire n'occupe que 33% de la superficie de notre planète. OUMMO se déplace en trajectoire elliptique d'excentricité 0,078 autour d'un astre dénommé par nous IOUMMA (notre "soleil"). la distance moyenne OUMMO-IOUMMA est de $9'96.10^{12}$cm. IOUMMA est une étoile de masse $1'48.10^{33}$g. la distance séparant IOUMMA de votre SOLEIL est de 14'42 années lumière environ. Nous calculons que vous localiseriez - cette étoile à: ascension droite: 12 heures 31 minutes
déclinaison. 9° 18'

Mais le brillant que vous remarqueriez sera très atténué étant donné la présence d'un amas de poussière cosmique qui l'atténue et le réduit à une magnitude apparente de l'ordre de 26. La température superficielle de cette étoile est de 4590'3 degrés K. Les altérations de champ magnétique sont grandes. [illegible] enregistré sur notre planète des valeurs atteignant 215 gauss très supérieures à celles de OUMMO. Ces perturbations nous interdisent l'utilisation [illegible] de fréquences électromagnétiques, raison pour laquelle nous devons utiliser des ondes gravitantes pour les communications.

P. Romaniuk

[illegible] de **OUMMO** [illegible] physiologi- [illegible] à celle de l'[illegible], [illegible] est lo- [illegible] que les lois [illegible] valables pour tout [illegible] et lorsque le milieu ambiant [illegible] analogue, [illegible] biologique [illegible] de variations. Nous [illegible] qualifieriez [illegible] "[illegible]", seules, quelques petites [illegible] nous dis- [illegible] de vous, chez une grande partie de nos frères, les organes de pho- [illegible] sont [illegible]trophiés (cordes buccales) et nous suppléons à cette sclére- [illegible] des moyens artificiels d'expression verbale.

[illegible] un peuple plus vieux que le vôtre et qui a atteint un niveau de civilisation plus élevé également. Notre structuration sociale est diffé- [illegible]. [illegible] gouvernés par quatre membres qui ont été choisis par des évaluations psychophysiologiques. Les lois sont réglées en fonction des cons- tantes sociométriques mesurées dans le temps.

Notre système économique est également différent. Nous ne connaissons pas l'argent étant donné que les transactions des quelques biens de valeur qui existent sur OUMMO sont effectuées par un réseau de ceux que vous appeleriez cerveaux électroniques. Les biens de consommation normaux sont à peine éva- luables étant donné que leur production abondante dépasse de beaucoup la de- mande.

Notre Société est profondément religieuse, Nous croyons en un Créateur (WOA) ou Dieu et nous avons des arguments scientifiques en faveur de l'existence d'un facteur que vous appelleriez l'âme. Nous connaissons un troisième facteur qui la lie au corp et qui est constitué par des atomes de crypton, logés dans la masse encéphalique.

Nos coutumes sont également très différentes. Il n'y a pas de races différen- ciées et les espèces et les variétés zoologiques sont moins nombreuses.

Nous ne prétendons pas interférir dans l'évolution socialede votre planète pour deux raisons transcendantes. Une morale cosmique interdit toute attitu de paternaliste sur des réseaux sociaux planétaires qui doivent être formés graduellement et par chacun d'eux. Qui plus est, en plus de toute interven- tion publique de notre part - notre propre présentation officielle - produi rait des altérations graves, des perturbations sociales incalculables et de cette façon, l'étude et l'analyse de votre société ne serait pas possible dans les conditions actuelles de virginité.

Nos modestes tentatives de contact, comme celle que nous effectuons maintenant avec vous, ne causera pas, par contre, une grande altération, car nous prévoyons d'avance le scepticisme naturelle qui les accueille.

Notre sistème de numération est 12, comme renseignement curieux nous vous incluons une tables avec quelques algorythmes mathématiques tels que nous les transcrivons:

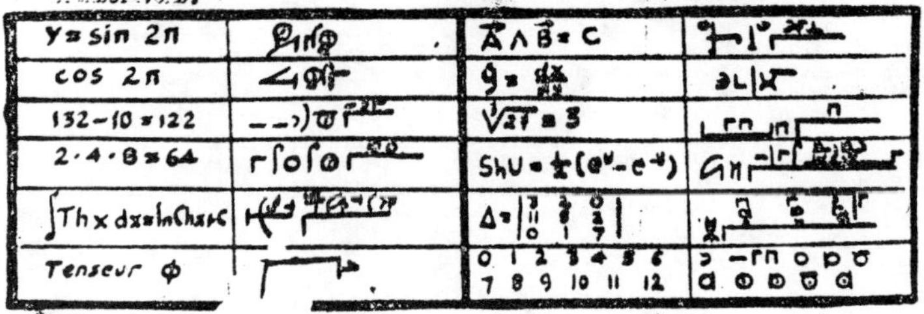

[illegible] Monsieur, [illegible]tations les plus distinguées

This is the photo furnished on microfilm to Aime Michel and Pedro Romaniuk from West Berlin.

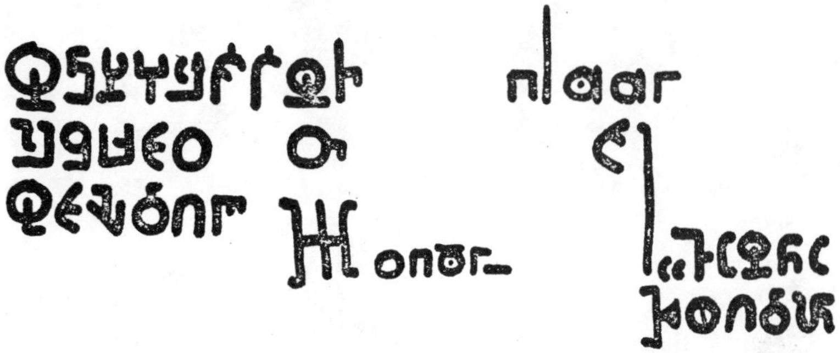

Le saludamos respetuosamente

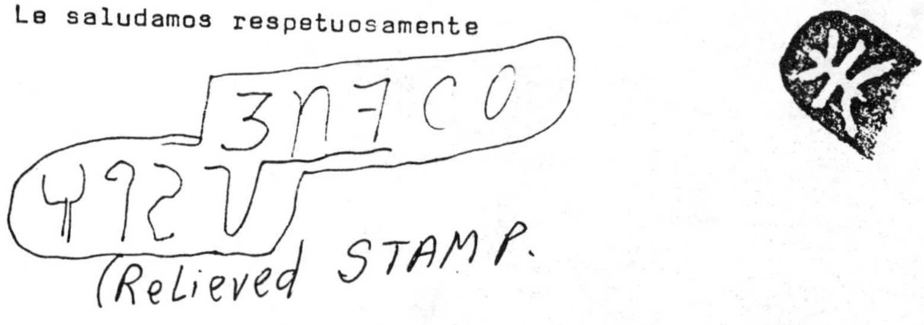

This hand lettered note in UMMO symbol form with other symbols in raised relief was authenticated with the thumb seal. Cover envelope.

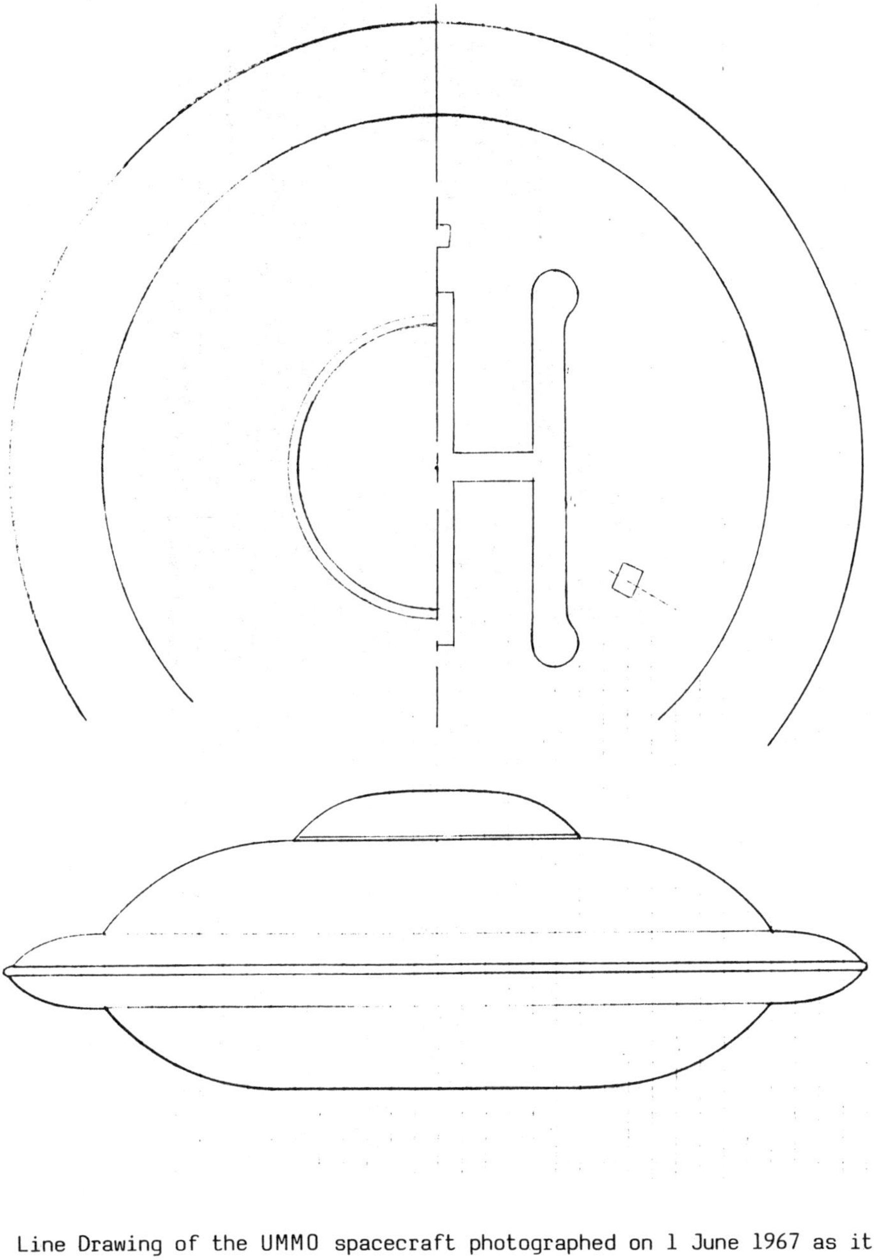

Line Drawing of the UMMO spacecraft photographed on 1 June 1967 as it approached to pick up the UMMO expeditionary team being evacuated from Earth at that time because of unacceptably high risk of atomic war.

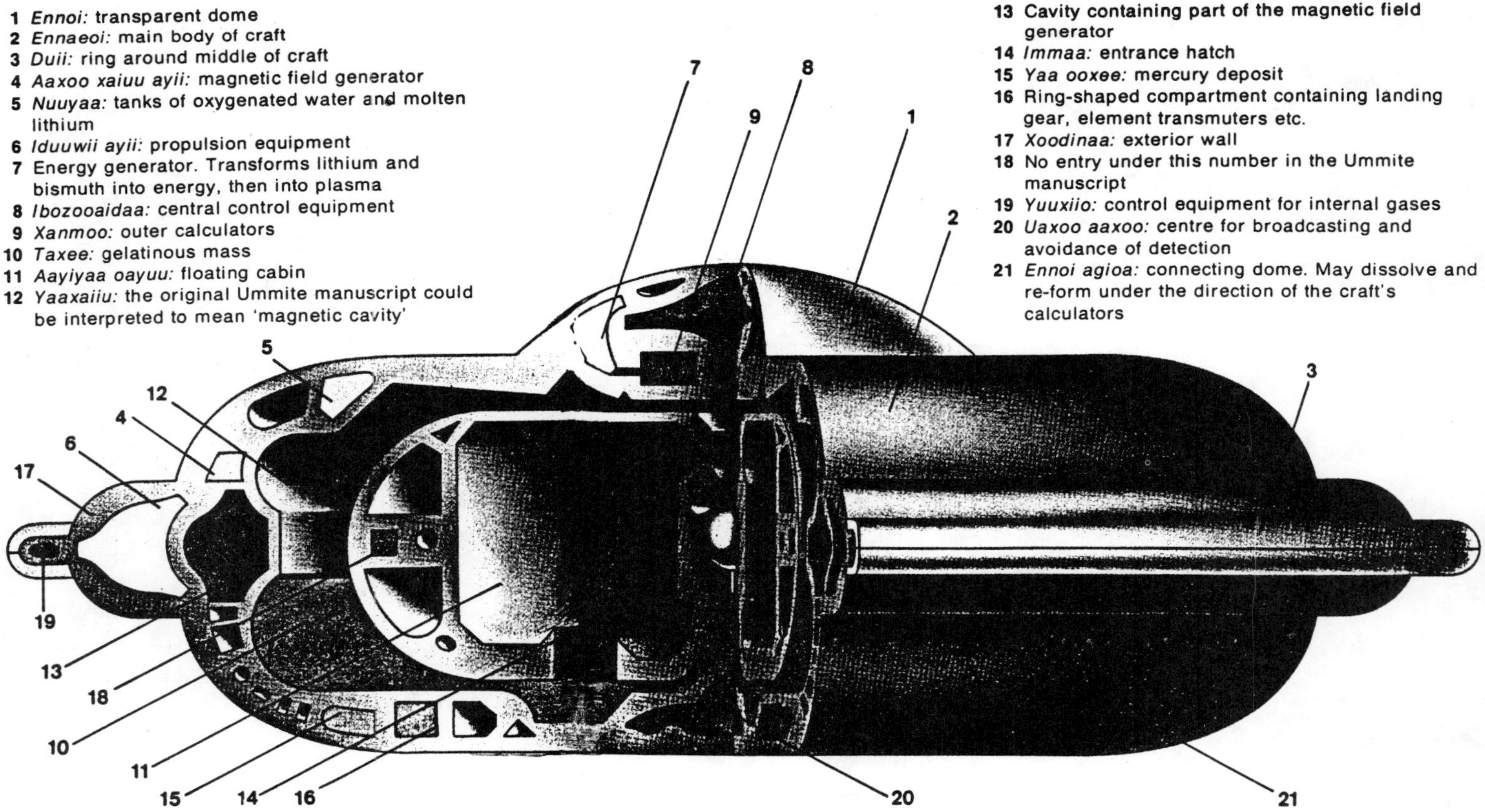

Cut-away drawing of the UMMO spacecraft from the Australian Review, THE UNEXPLAINED. Matches microfilm.

RECENT COMMUNICATION

Doc. No. 106, 6 pages - Motivations for Ummite Communications

(Appendix 3, Part I, Document Number 106)

MOTIVATIONS FOR THE DISTRIBUTION OF THE UMMITE TEXTS. NON-INTERVENTION INTO HUMAN AFFAIRS OF EARTH. EFFECTS OF THESE REPORTS ON OUR CORRESPONDENTS. SUSPENSION OF OUR MAIL AND TELEPHONIC COMMUNICATION. PREPARATION FOR THE SECOND UMMO SYMPOSIUM IN BARCELONA. MESSAGE FOR Sr. IGNACIO DARNAUDE ROJAS-MARCOS.

Received in Barcelona on 15 March 1973 by Sr. Farriols - 6 pages

UMMOAELEWE
Language: Spanish
Number of copies: One

(UMMO Document "BK")
(Letter received in Barcelona the 15th day of March, 1973)

Senor Rafael Farriols Calvo
BARCELONA, SPAIN

Our good friend:

This copy contains no information on our culture, for you are already acquainted with our somewhat flexible standard according to which, for the past several months, we send such reports only to the headquarters of legally constituted associations which, we feel certain, will at least not destroy them. Persuant to this policy, when we wish to send more documents of this nature, you will receive them through the association with which you are affiliated.

But this policy is not so rigid that it does not allow us to mail you this letter, which cannot be considered in the REPORT category. In the same way, when our mutual security runs less risk of violation by third parties, these reports will be sent to your brothers at their respective homes or be delivered directly by brothers of yours who are cooperating with us.

Consider the paragraphs that follow as a friendly digression, and we assure you in advance that you are in no way obligated to share in our opinions, our fears, or to follow rules of conduct which may be more to our liking but which at times may conflict with your own particular points of view. You must be aware, senor Rafael Farriols, that our lack of protection against any unfortunate reaction from your Earth brothers is quite real. But it is incompatible with our own moral standard to force them to conform to our criteria. We merely use a method of control when we fear that any slip in your conduct may cause abnormal consequences. In that event we limit ourselves to suggesting that a violation of our instructions would simply cause a temporary or permanent rupture of these communications. And even so, we have made this threat only for reasons of security for both our cultures; that of Earth and that of UMMO, represented by the members of this expeditionary group writing to you.

With an insistence which you may find irritating, we have repeatedly mentioned our anxiety caused by the apparent effect of our communications on some men of Earth.

We don't refer here to our contacts with brothers of yours in other countries, who have all reacted by adopting a much more reticent or suspicious attitude and therefore a much more sensible one. But in particular, conclusions reached as between the two cultures have caused in certain of your brothers in South America, Spain and Canada a radical change of their beliefs.

Persuaded by probable suggestions presented in some of our documents as contrasted with their own opinions, they have ignored our frequent reminders and have allowed themselves to be seduced by some aspects of our thinking. A superficial appraisal of the situation might lead one to think that this attitude would flatter us OEMI of UMMO. And we confess that in fact we do feel an emotional bond with those who manifest this spiritual attachment, but at the same time we are witnessing a process that we consider (and have good reasons for so judging it) DANGEROUS for all of you. Although many skeptics among your brothers hold a contrary opinion (and such reasoning is correct if they choose not to admit the authenticity of our extraterrestrial origin), our mutual and unilateral relations are positively not for the purpose of "gaining adherents". If they were, we would have far more efficient means of reaching this objective. Can any intelligent brother of yours conceive that a group of EARTH men might believe that an effective way of winning proselytes would be to make the astonishing (and in this case fraudulent) statement that the members of their society come from a distant planet?

We know of no social group on EARTH that has prospered by falsifying so grossly its own origin. The members of the different philosophies, religions or political schools of thought may support illogical, erroneous or aberrant ideologies, but at least one constant can be sensed in them all: good faith, the sincerity without which any group is destined to die.

It might be objected that falsifying their origin could be a clever tactic to fool the unitiated. Introducing themselves as extraterrestrials in principle can (in the judgement of such critics) stimulate vague, strange psychological vibrations in persons with a peculiar mental structure, awakening in them special kinds of conduct sometimes linked to the complex for "contacting", to the subconscious desire for fame as having been "chosen" by "galactic beings": other individuals may be intrigued by "mystery", the esoteric, an experience beyond the daily humdrum.

This objection is entirely correct. And precisely this fear is a prime reason for our criticizing the attitudes of some of your brothers. But getting back to what we were saying, please don't think that an Earth organization resorting to such tactics would completely fail in its purpose of recruiting proselytes even though its methods are wrong and immoral. Perhaps we can agree that men obsessed with pseudological, delirious ideas would play a poor role in the eyes of their own society as "intellectualized" leaders who, in order to capture adherents from among the masses, would resort to the sorry subterfuge borrowed from "science fiction" of presenting themselves as "extraterrestrials".

For this would presume that their "doctrines" were not convincing enough to be introduced into the mass of presumed converts unless they chose mentally retarded individuals who would allow themselves to be fooled by the trick just mentioned.

Some of your brothers see in us a powerful organization with incalculable financial means who desire to transform society and its culture by donning the seductive mantle of "men of space".

Leaving aside the allusion to economic means, which are certainly not so "immense" as they claim, although we don't mind admitting that they are sufficiently ample to cover the requirements of our field of investigation in a region of a planet foreign to us, Those individuals must at least recognize evidence so hard to ignore.

For if, in the opinion of your brothers, what we wanted was to attract proselytes to change the cultural structure of Earth, we ALL shall have to agree that it has been a resounding failure; some forty dozens of curious correspondents (skeptical and suspicious most of them) scattered throughout several countries, are not too impressive a total for a sect or group having such "powerful means" at its disposal.

We are not making, senor, a vain, merciless criticism of the more or less unfortunate stories circulating among your brothers concerning my brothers. After all, such versions have an undoubtedly logical basis, since the strange, anomalous relationships we have with you must necessarily be a subject of speculation. Since the probability that we are simply telling the truth does not fit into their systems of logic, they have adopted interpretations which, for any serious or impartial analyst, are as absurd and outlandish as the hypothesis they reject.

Let us leave them to their endless cabalas, which in all reason we consider sterile, for if, as they believe, our origin is on EARTH, then the phenomenon of the "anonymous letters" sent to less than two hundred humans by some "crazy investigators or co-believers of an ideological group" is not worth too much attention, for there is after all a multitude of virgin fields of research worthy of analysis and study.

But if their hypotheses as to our identity lack enough coherence, certain accusations that we are influencing their brothers of EARTH we unfortunately cannot deny. Naturally the objection might be made that, if we are merely one social group among the many existing in various countries, we are within our right to interject our own ideology. All the more so when this does not violate moral principles considered basic in present-day EARTH civilization, and furthermore does not collide with principles of many ideologies current among you. If this opposition is senseless coming from any of your brothers, nevertheless it saddens us for it has a real basis but contradicts our true purpose and objective, which is precisely the contrary: To RESPECT EARTH CULTURE in its multiple prevalent forms.

We have on UMMO a culture that has evolved like that of Earth and which cannot be engrafted into yours or be copied here without causing serious upheaval. The idea of using it as your inspiration in trying to modify for the better your own educational system is acceptable only as a dream-phenomenon. To attempt to put it into practice by running down your methods in order to join ours artificially with your moral, political and philosophical systems would seem to us (in all good judgement) childish naivete and an experiment condemned to failure.

So we feel disturbed by the adventuresome attitude of those brothers of yours who, after reading our anonymous reports, torture their minds in an effort to wean themselves away from their beliefs and replace them with spurious ideals valid only in a different social setting like that of UMMO. Please don't think that, in prejudging them this way, we imply a deprecatory attitude toward Earth ideologies. To be precise, we have been insisting quite simply that, among the many ideologies on Earth, in your think tanks ethical principles are adhered to which we ourselves respect. We cannot teach you anything in this respect, just as we could teach nothing in the art of coordinating sounds or of plastifying form and color, in which fields you are the greater masters as compared to us.

Another problem is that, through our special ideosyncracy and our advanced state of evolution we may have assimilated into our society socioethical patterns which for you are still unattainable ideals.

Apparently it is easy to refute the validity of our scruples. Any of your brothers, armed with simplistic but seemingly logical argumnets, will object that the solution is very simple: If our purpose is to avoid impregnating Earth with strange cultures, then nothing is simpler than to suspend our postal and telephonic correspondence with Earth men.

When we began these contacts, we judged that we had hit upon the ideal procedure satisfying a variety of requirements. For one thing, it enabled us to make contact with the OEMII of Earth without disturbing their SOCIAL SYSTEM. This latter principle is basic for our expedition on Earth for two extremely important reasons: To change the biosocial process we are trying to analyze is considered by all the investigators as wrong. But beyond that we consider such disturbing influences unethical. No civilization ought to influence the normal evolutionary process observed in another social structure.

We discovered, not without surprise, after some timid attempts restrained by mental reservations and precautions, that it was nevertheless possible to communicate with OEMII of this planet without such information leaking dangerously into the surrounding social medium. Thus we were able to carry on a dialogue or write our reports to Earth humans without disturbing the development of the SOCIAL SYSTEM BECAUSE the skepticism (logical, moreover) of so many of its members acted as an effective shock absorber to the spread of this kind of information.

Put to the test, this immunity has been completely effective. In this way we satisfied two requirements: On the one hand to repay EARTH SOCIETY in some way for the mass of information it furnishes us in the course of our systematic analysis of the geographical, ecological and cultural features of this planet by giving it measured doses of information about our civilization and other aspects of UMMO.

ON the other hand, we were entertaining at that time the hope of an official future contact with the civilization of Earth and were trying to ascertain on a small scale the social consequences among you of a revelation of our presence on this planet.

This latter hope has been frustrated for we have discovered that such an experiment would be traumatic for Earth's cultural evolution, but it is still possible for you to determine scientifically that we have been among you on a study mission during these years. Therefore we consider these documents we are sending you as valuable and useful in the not too distant future.

For this purpose we made careful analyses in selecting brothers of yours from diverse social, cultural, racial and national strata. We needed people to receive these documents who would at least preserve them as a simple curiosity, even though they might greet the contents with quite logical mental reservations, until it became possible to confirm them through irreproachable scientific channels.

The initial results were discouraging. Those men of science, thinkers and group leaders with whom we established contact either tore up the texts without reading them or else found "contradictions" with respect to their own cultural patterns. In other cases they took certain parts of the texts and published them as their own without honoring (except in very isolated instances) our request to keep them as at least probable reports from other beings not belonging to Earth humanity.

Except for the isolated cases mentioned, humans in the intermediate cultural levels have been precisely those most willing to consider the possibility that such documents might have been written by My brothers.

Thus warm relationships were established with persons more or less scattered in different nations but sometimes associated with one another, and my brothers gave most of their attention to these. Our request to maintain silence was respected by the natives of some countries. In others such reserve was not solicited, due in part either to experience of else to the special psychology of your brothers who were involved, and consequently the news was spread more widely than we should have liked.

There were also reasons for affection. Some of your brothers became so closely attached to our anonymous presence as materialized by the texts reaching them that it produced upon the authorities of those national forces a very strong impact. The evil came in when when we realized the danger it might represent for you. Our superiors thought seriously that the continuation of such contacts violated our dearest UAA (Moral Laws) since, without wishing to we were perturbing these brothers of yours with our writings. In fact, contacts with these OEMII (men) were suspended. In consternation we could now see that this rupture was causing effects more traumatic than those we were trying to avoid. Furthermore, new conditions had arisen for our brothers which were affecting in a troublesome way our stay among you. A powerful nation had become aware of our existence as a group and for some time had been investigating our activities. In addition, the program of investigation planned by us is being redirected toward Earth nations stilll almost unknown to us. All this causes us to set forth here a series of reflections on the subject.

Senor Farriols Calvo: We have discussed on another occasion the meetings you have planned to consider subjects relative to our SOCIAL STRUCTURE. Please permit us, now that the dates chosen by you for these meetings are approaching, to submit some opinions about them. We repeat that you must never consider them as edicts or as indicating that we are giving up our privileged moral position when we utter an opinion if that implies any compulsion whatever. But we do ask you to weigh our thinking on the chance it may contain reasonable logic. We don't conceal the fact -- and this should not be considered a mere courtesy on our part since, if the contrary were true, we would say so -- that this experiment greatly interests us. You are enabling us once more to get your brother's reactions to our experiment. This motive has taken precedence over other opinions to the effect that we should be opposed to the project. But our fervent desire is that such a meeting not turn into a proselytizing session in which those attending are pressured into accepting our statements. We set forth below some points in our thinking:

We should like to see prevail in the meeting a spirit of simple curiosity about the reality of this experiment in communication. Those attending must consider as valid only one provable truth: The receipt by some OEMII on Earth of documents whose origins, and the purposes of whose senders, constitute for now an insoluble unknown.

The reading of material taken from our documents should always be qualified as mere statements resulting from your own analysis if they involved previously announced facts, rather than being presented as statements from completely unknown authors whose genuineness might be severely criticized.

We would advise that special care be taken to urge those in attendance not to yield to the temptation of adopting as their own the ideas contained in said documents.

We reject (and we emphasize this) any form of coercion or censure exerted against your brothers who may wish to exercise their freedom to criticize sincerely and objectively both the question of our existence or the origin of our brothers as well as the statements set forth in the documents they have analyzed.

In our judgement a wise course of action to follow would be to avoid in these sessions any type of coercive action to force those present into adopting the opinion of the people in the group who sincerely believe our statements.

In the last meeting you organized, one of my brothers was able to attend as a discreet observer of the social climate there. This fact was unavoidable discovered by some of you, for which reason we can obviously not repeat it at future meetings. We shall attempt to send a letter of greeting to your brothers if adverse conditions do not intervene, in which letter we shall repeat, among other ideas, many of the concepts set forth in this letter.

We also ask, Senor Rafael Farriols, that you get in contact with your brother Ignacio Darnaude Rojas-Marcos, addressing your request to Avenida Manuel Siurot No. 3, Bl. San Leandro, Sevilla, asking him to indicate whether he has any objection to our writing him again to enclose a photocopy of a report sent by my brothers to a man in Bilbao (Spain) with reference to our sojourn in Albacete. We are aware of the prudent reserve of your brother Ignacio and the intelligent skepticism with which he takes our versions. But his interest in clarifying the matter, following sociological guidelines of genuine scientific value, despite his limited means, make him worthy of our interest and respect. But since he does not accept our testimony as valid, we hesitate to bother him with our letters, for which reason we ask that he tell you or any of your brothers in Madrid if he wishes to receive such documents.

Please extend our greetings to your wife and children, to your brothers Antonio Ribera, Federico Guibernau, Jaime Imbert and all your other brothers who follow these contacts with special curiosity.

--oOo--

Frequently at the end of my discussions of UFOs during radio interviews, I am asked the question: "But does this with UMMO still endure? Is anybody still receiving the reports?" To which I have to answer affirmatively: "It" of UMMO has not terminated, and they continue receiving reports and letters... at times from the most unlikely places as we shall see.

In May of 1978 a new recipient joined the group of regulars: It was Luis Jimenez Marhuenda, who carried on the radio program "La Voz de Alicante" (The Voice of Alicante), discussions on the UFO phenomenon which had a great audience and stirred up enormous interest. Luis — who was known in those days among the UFO organizations in Madrid as Paco Sanchez — impressed me well from the beginning (and I believe I to him also). He is a cordial man, and kind, who goes out of his way for others —especially his friends—, and never loses the smile on his noble face, like a big kid. And from that time, Luis was accepted with all the honors into the "UMMO affair", as a spectator of the same, among the reduced group of —recipient— protagonists.

Neither curt nor boring, and in agreement with his friend Ricardo Lopez, of the "Centro de Investigaciones Metapsiquicas" (CIM) of Alicante, deciding to commemorate the thirty years since the supposed arrival of the Ummites on Earth, organized a commemorative meeting to study the planet UMMO in a hotel of Alicante. And thus if was that on the 28th, 29th and 30th of March 1980, there gathered there the flower and cream of the "ummologos" (as Ignacio Darnaude called them). Jose Antonio Corno (who unfortunately died a little afterwards) opened the meeting with a keynote that was much commented upon: "I accuse", and misinterpreted. Others who also spoke were father Lopez Guerrero, Rafael Farriols, Jose Luis Jordan Pena, Franco Muela, Juan Jose Benitez, Jimenez Marhuenda (naturally!), the untiring and talkative Enrique de Vicente, well liked by all, the engineer Juan Dominguez, Raul Torres, Antonio Jose Ales, and Jesus Sancho read a communication from Ignacio Darnaude, and Carole Ramis read a letter from Manuel de la Mota. I closed the action with a keynote that carried the title of my book, "EL MISTERIO DEL UMMO".

Attending as an "observer" was the young astrophysicist and mathematician from France, Jear-Pierre Petit, who gained the affection of all for his intelligence and for his gracious sketches which he made at any moment as his pen flew (we have reproduced one of them here, based on the erogeneous effect that changes in acceleration seem to produce in the Ummites.

As had come to be normal after meetings like this, a few days later, a letter was received from the Ummites. This one actually came from Albacete, and its recipient was Luis Jimenez Marhuenda, himself. In it the authors gave surprising news. Two of their "brothers" had attended the symposium at Alicante, mixed with the public. And they affirmed having placed in the room, instruments for observation and recording from a distance, and not only in the room, but on the epidermis of eleven of the attendees. These instruments were sondes for the measurement and transmission of psychophysiological parameters.

This reminded us that the young lady receptionist had told us of two very strange men, who did not know how to sign their names on the identification card with the ballpoint pen she loaned them. Someone else seems to have signed for them.

And in the first gathering on UMMO, organized by Rafael Farriols in the Motel Osuna of Barajas (we don't know if the same thing happened in the second gathering, organized also by Farriols in the Hotel Ritz of Barcelona in May of 1973) it seems that one of them was present. But the conclusions that the Ummites took from the reunion at Alicante (where the Latin temperament was manifested in confrontations and noisy episodes) was desolate: **"The human of Earth is authentically ill. His complex physical functions are as abnormal as the workings of a deficiently designed machine".** This was one of the more "agreeable" things they told us. And as a result of this analysis of our personality and our reactions, they believed that our case was beyond remedy, **and that we marched irreversibly to our own selfdestruction.**

In effect: all of these last messages of those Ummites were characterized by their pessimistic tone, and by the mention of a terrible superweapon in the hands of a great world power (the plasma bomb), along side of which the conventional hydrogen bombs are simple spears of iron. They already described this in a letter sent to Doctor Juan Agirre in June of 1979 which we reproduce here, but which he excluded from his Tomo IIIb of his compilation of UMMO documents. The Ummite text was censured by those Ummite authors.

They insisted, in the theme of a letter received in June 1980 by Sr. Jorge Barrenechea, in Madrid, and finally in two letters that were received a little later (the first of these almost simultaneously) the two following reunions on UMMO that were celebrated in March of 1983, and a year later in March of 1984, both in the Collegio Mayor San Augustin, of the Ciudad Universitaria de Madrid. Almost all the members of the "Madrid Group" participated in these talks, with the exception of Petitt who did not attend the second one in 1984.

In these last cases, the letters received came from very exotic locations: that of 1983 came from Kuala Lumpur, capital of Malaysia; that of 1984 came from Zimbabwe, The old Rhodesia. The first was sent to Doctor Aguirre Ceberio, but it arrived by an enigmatic and tortuous route. Although the name of the person to whom it was addressed was scratched out on the envelope, it was discovered that it was one Srta.

Ana Herranz, who lived on the calle Ramirez Torrez 24, of Madrid. This lady delivered the envelope by hand to Doctor Aguirre through a third person. The letter arrived by this means to the Colegio Mayor when I was closing my talk, and while I was still speaking. Such rapidity [and coincidence] was surprising, but the stamps of Malaysia which appeared to be cancelled on the 12th of the same month, 1983, were authentic. [Hand delivered to lecture hall on 20 March 1983.]

With the letter that was received after the last gathering [in 1984] something bad happened: the intermediaries —whoever they might have been— neatly censored eleven pages from the letter. It was received on 18 March in Madrid, coming, as I said, from Zimbabwe.

In continuation we reproduce all of these documents cited, and the last —to this moment— that have been received from the Ummites, so that the reader may judge for himself and decide if such pessimism is justified. I think so.

THE LATEST COMMUNICATIONS

Doc. No. 116,	4 pages -	Evacuation of solid star Earth and return, + Investigation of UMMO affair by CIA.
Doc. No, 117,	3 pages -	Concerning UMMO General Headquaters within DENMARK, base of operation near Madrid, Development by China of new Plasma Weapon, etc.
Doc No. 119,	4 pages -	Ummite comments on symposium on UMMO, How monitored.
	5 pages -	Letter of condolence concerning death of Jean Paul Sartre. Effects of UMMO technical aid to Earth society.
	7 pages -	The letter from Kuala Lampur, Malaysia. Reasons for non-intervention in Earth affairs.
	4 pages -	Letter of intermediary delivering the letter from Zimbabwe.
	3 pages -	The letter from Zimbabwe. USA seeking to get control of China's Plasma Weapon. Dangers of overacceptance of UMMO philosophy here.
	2 pages -	Ummites abandoning Earth study project.

(Appendix 3, Part I, Document Number 116)

CONCERNING SOME IMPORTANT LETTERS IN CIRCULATION ATTRIBUTED TO UMMO. ABSENCE FROM THE SOLID STAR EARTH AND THEIR RETURN IN OCTOBER 1978. PREMEDITATED INSERTION OF FALSE INFORMATION IN SOME TEXTS TO DETER POPULAR CREDIBILITY IN THE UMMO CONSPIRACY. INVESTIGATION OF THE UMMO AFFAIR BY THE "CIA". UMMO OPERATIONS IN ALBACETE.

The letter, posted in Santa Maria de Nieva (Segovia), Spain, was received in Alicante by Senor Jimenez on 29 May 1979 - 4 pages

UMMOALEWEE
Language: Spanish
Number of copies: One
Spain 23 May 1978

Senor:

Allow me to introduce myself, although it may cause surprise and even a certain amount of logical incredulity on your part. My name is, in your phonetic transcription, EIDOUAA AA 42 son oF EIMEII 12, and I am from a planet called UMMO. You may confirm the genuineness of my identity through our seal, whose authenticity may perhaps be verified by your brother Spaniard Rafael Farriols Calvo, resident of Barcelona. We know that in various countries apocryphal letters attributed to my brothers have circulated, so you doubtless will prefer to assure yourself that this text is of genuine origin. My brothers and I are writing to you because word had reached us of the high degree of reliability you so kindly attributed to the information about our existence. It is true that such a view is more emotional than rational, for my brothers had already taken care not to supply many objective proofs of our identity and origin. We needed to rely on the human skepticism of Earth in order to be able to live among you, but we are surprised to discover that a few of your brothers in Yugoslavia, Australia, France, Spain, Canada and other nations, giving in to impulses of affection, believed in us without the aid of scientific proofs. Naturally this was flattering for those of my brothers who were on Earth at that time, so a copious unilateral correspondence was begun comprising an extensive dossier of reports numbering over six thousand seven hundred in various languages. We imposed only the condition that the little groups in these countries who were fond of us should not make mutual contact with those of other nationalities and that the documents should not go outside of channels for fear that this would cause a boom of publicity that would force us to leave your planet. In part this has been complied with, although today the risk for us is almost nil from the inevitable leaks that have taken place. You yourself have commented publicly on information about our existence, and you were not obligated in any way to harbor mental reservations.

My brothers have been away from your planet for a long time now. We returned to Earth in an expedition in October, landing in Denmark. A small expedition under my orders is located in Central Spain; my other brothers are in Denmark, England, Nepal and Canada. This is the second time I am personally among you. I studied English, Spanish and German and have specialized in Hispanic cultural thought. My profession on UMMO is connected with the analysis of biochemical systems for the synthesis of food. Concretely, my specialty is the codification, in what you call polynucleotics, of bases for the genesis of organisms producing proteic chains. At present I am studying the evolution of Spanish society in its econometric facets, and I am dictating this letter to a brother of yours in Spain who was already known to the expeditionaries who preceeded me. This brother of yours is one of our admirers and has rendered valuable services.

We wish to answer some questions formulated by your brothers in the course of time. For one thing, they were wondering about the reason for our silence. In the first place, it was due to our absence from Earth, but before that there were considerations on another level. Against our wishes for secrecy, Xerox copies of our documents got out to the media and this involved a risk for my brothers who were then here. Especially in Spain this incontinence became more acute than in other countries whose citizens were more prudent and cautious. We had to unleash our systems of self-defense, consisting of putting into circulation arguments against our actual existence, which we had already prepared for such an emergency.

Years ago my brothers had spread around, together with arguments in favor of the thesis of Ummite identity, false proofs which could serve as a cover against too high a level of credulity among Earth humanity. I shall try to explain this more explicitly, senor Luis Jimenez Marhuenda.

Our mission on Earth is merely for analysis and study. We have come to Spain (our first landing was at a site in France) as well as to other countries with the desire to learn the geographic structure, orogenic movements, biosphere, human social structure and its history and evolution, conditions of the atmosphere and structures of the principal planet and of the other planets, including one located beyond Pluto at 7898 /SIC/ [unintelligible] (mean distance from your Sun).

Our forms of thought prohibit us from interfering in your social evolution. Any contribution from our culture to yours transcending simpleinformation about our science and customs would naturally imply an interference in that evolution which, from our deontological perspective, would be damaging. It would not be possible to offer you a solution to the genesis of atypical tissues (cancerous), for example, without involving the contribution of technological data which men of Earth, with their still scanty ethical education in certain social strata, could exploit for purposes in no way connected with medicine but perhaps with destruction. Even on the philosophical plane, a graft into your schools of thought from our ontology would vitiate the normal evolution of humanoterrestrial Metaphysics. All transvasation of cultures causes irreparable damage to the normal laws of evolution in a planetary social system.

I recall that when my brothers who preceeded me in their journeys to this Earth began to mix among you, taking advantage of the fact that their anatomical configuration was very similar to your own (this occurs by evolutionary law on planets with similar structure and dimensions) they were afraid to make themselves known as having come from the planet UMMO. Their fear was overblown. A better acquaintenceship with the human terrestrial psychism weaned them away from this. Timidly at first and with greater ease later, they initiated contacts with some scientists, to whom they supplied certain data that could cause no harm, and furthermore they selected in various countries citizens of an avarage cultural, social and economic level, but who had in common one distinctive feature: They were in love with the subject of UFO's, and this hobby brought them in a certain way spiritually closer to us. My brothers on those expeditions told me that at first they did not expect to be believed to any extent. On the contrary, they expected that the recipients would keep the reports as a mere curiosity coming from some mental case, with the purpose in mind that, if our Government later decided to make formal contact with the governments of Earth (at that time such a possibility was seriously contemplated by my brothers in command), such documents would comprise the protohistory of these relationships with Earth humanity.

At that time the commandant of the expedition on Earth was YU !, a sister /SIC/ of mine (now sadly deceased in an accident), an intelligent woman who understood your psychology as no one else, and she realized that the risk was minimal; on the other hand WIIBEAA 43, son of WIIBEAA 40, emphatically refused to establish any contact whatever. The thinking of my sister prevailed during that period. At first your reactions seemed to justify her. A large number of recipients believed in us to the extent of deifying our humanity and thus presenting a danger from the standpoint of hygiene and mental balance. There was the risk that the news would get out and create turbulent social currents about being from another planet. As a matter of fact the news about the UEUA OEEMI /SIC/ (this is what we call our UFOs) were giving rise to a great worldwide psychosis on your Earth and we did not want to throw more wood on the fire, as you say in Spanish. How could we live among you unnoticed if rumors about our appearance were circulating? It was dangerous to provide excessive proofs of our existence. Then a strategy evolved of mixing false data in with the genuine information, stating that this is the way we were operating and recommending that your brothers moderate their faith in us. This, senor Luis Jimenez, may appear singular and some strange, but if you analyze the circumstances it isn't at all. Your brothers had become excellent friends of ours. But any genuine friendship requires a protective attitude on our part. You are of EARTH. Your spiritual obligation is to your culture, history and your brothers; we can never wean you away from these. To convert you into our disciples would have been against our principles. Could we have avoided it if we had given you unquestionable proof of our existence? Even so, some of you let yourselves be seduced by our revelations. UMMO became, dangerously so, the ideal goal of their lives, and they thereby presented us with a hard problem of conscience. New complications arose years later. An information agency of the U.S.A. just happened to learn of the existence of the UMMO group. In logical consequence of rational questioning, they concluded that we comprised an organization under the command of another Power, and they began a relentless pursuit of our brothers. It is true that our brothers had methods of avoiding these investigators in spite of the troublesome nature of the situation. However, that only further stimulated their pursuit and interest. They even put under surveillance peaceful Canadians, Englishmen and Spaniards who were receiving our letters, as if they were our accomplices!

This was more than we wanted. We could not allow men of Earth to suffer, through our fault, this inhumane siege against their own brothers, so we had to limit our contacts.

Meanwhile the puzzled executives of the U.S.A. Agency were wondering why, "since we were" an espionage group (naturally they could never prove from which country), we were passing ourselves off as extraterrestrials (a paradox that in good logic is unsolvable if the question is asked on a rational basis).

A critical moment came when, precisely in Spain, my brothers could not find any collaborator other than a poor lady, one of your sisters residing in Albacete, afflicted with a certain amount of mental aberration (which they thought would be an excellent cover but which turned out not to be so). The protection of this lady, who never had learned we were from UMMO, caused my brothers countless misfortunes. A servant girl of hers spread the lie in certain areas of the populace that we were living in the cellar and, to cap the climax, some viral cultures being zealously watched by my brothers got loose, through her fault, threatening a spread of infection (through our fault) with terribly catastrophic consequences for Earth humanity. It came to a climax in an extraordinary operation by my brothers which leaped onto the pages of the media at that time.

The second critical moment came when we learned of the sinister operation the North American leaders were preparing. This was after the famous secret report which explained how the Soviet Union was at that moment on a definite level of logistic inferiority with respect to the United States. Some experts felt this was the proper moment to start a lightning nuclear strike and topple once and for all the power of the U.S.S.R. My brothers knew of the secret meeting in which President Nixon unwillingly gave a green light to the project. We were terrified. Our first decision was to board our ships and leave Earth. Then the idea was reconsidered. Our bases were secure against a conflagration of that kind, but we were faced with a problem of conscience; How could we abandon our Earth friends? We finally decided, despite the supposed risk, to release concrete proof of our presence by offering our subterranean bases in various countries for them to take refuge in. There was no attack, but President Nixon, as you know, sounded an atomic alarm on the date we had announced, and our offer of the shelters gave proof that we were "more" than we had wanted to let on. Your brothers did not know how to keep our presence secret, and we were obliged to cease contacts in France and Spain.

This, senor, is the resume of our relations with all of you. We earnestly ask you, senor Luis Jimenez Marhuenda, to forward this news from us in a fraternal greeting to the following Spanish brothers of yours, lest they forget us. We give you here the address of one of them so that, through him, my message can reach the others.

Senores Dionisio Garrido-Buendia, Calle Huesca 29, 4º D Madrid; - Rafael Farriols Calvo, Juan Dominguez Montes, Franco Muela Pedrada, Joaquin Martinez Andres, Enrique Villagrasa Novoa, Angel del Campo Frances, Alicia Araujo, Fernando Jimenez del Oso, Antonio Ribera Jorda, Enrique Lopez Guerrero, Jorge Barrenechea, Alberto Borras Gabarro, Hiltrud Nordlin Franz, Federico Guibernau.

This list would be endless if it included others of your brothers who are of one mind with us. We send them our sincere gratitude and hopes. But I don't mean to slight these others by somehow forwarding our special greetings to the persons named above.

And we hope you will accept at the same time our embrace of peace and respect. We learned of you because in the town where you reside you spoke in praise of our patience, and that news reached our ears.

Your courageous, open mind merits our respectful consideration. Our whole-hearted greetings to your noble wife and your dear ones. Broadcast our salute to Earth humanity...

Senor, I beg you to get in touch with Enrique Lopez Guerrero, who is a Priest in Mairena del Alcor (Sevilla). We have seen his article in which he is kind enough to mention and transcribe our reports. It is true that if this had appeared years ago, it would have done us harm. Today this risk is practically nonexistent, for we have ascertained that it causes no disturbances in your society. No one outside of a small segment of the populace is willing to believe in our existence, and this is good for the community at large.

Please get in touch also with your brother Antonio Albadalejo of Murcia; we intend to write and send him a brief report.

(Seal of UMMOAELEWE)

This letter cannot go without comment. There are enough signals in the text of this document to confirm its validity to all those who know this case. It came after a four year absence of contact only to reassure those who knew the UMMO that they were not deluding themselves and to reconfirm the UMMO lack of desire for publicity.

This letter signals a continuity of Earth study and research by one team after another from UMMO whether we like it or not. The later teams seem more inclined to secrecy of their operations than before and less overt contact with Earthmen.

The seasoning of real truth with false evidence is an escape mechanism common to many extensive UFO contact cases, because it is very effective in our society, and therefore used to advantage. The real intended participants in the events in the events have their "keys" to recognition and can discriminate for themselves.

The extraterrestrials offer here a good reason (and one mentioned by other ETs as well) for not giving us a cure for cancer. In our present stage of evolution we would turn the science to destruction and the blessing would become a curse as have other such advances coming too early in time.

There is plenty of evidence that ETs can penetrate the deepest secrets of all nations on Earth and, surprisingly, in both cases of Earth evacuation for high probability of atomic war, <u>we</u> were the perceived perpetrators, a good reason why U.S.A. popularity has fallen so discouragingly worldwide.

The few hundred UMMO documents in the hands of the Spanish Group is a small fraction of the 6,700 documents in various languages around the world mentioned here! The UMMO have been very careful about not advising any group of one country about any other group in another country, but keeping them carefully separated. Discouraging media publicity in general, and the adverse nature of the publicity received, helped to preserve this situation. The Spanish Group has broken this silence and by doing so has forced changes in conduct upon the UMMO visitors when here.

We can, as this is being written, reveal that the UMMO are believed to have evacuated all their people once more from our planet, presumably for the same reasons as before. We do not know how long the absence will last this time, or if they will ever come back. Believing that an awareness of our danger might have some effect on restraining our leaders, we invite any and all other UMMO contact groups to get in touch with others and let the folly of our senseless race to destruction be known.

Perhaps if we had the 6,700 documents collected together and studied by experts in all fields, we could come to a realization that we are still babes in the woods in evolution and must come to our senses before it is too late. -Publisher

[This startling revelation of executive decisions made in our White House in 1973 are suprising. So much of what these Ummites have said has checked out satisfactorily that we must give this statement very serious consideration. Could this be the real reason our President was forced out of power? Did the opposition succeed in preventing the catastrophic end of our world? Are we any smarter today than we were then?]

UMMOALEWEE
Numero de copias UNA
Idioma ESPAÑOL

ESPAÑA 23 de Mayo 1978

Señor:

Permítame que me presente, aunque ello reporte una reaccion de sorpresa e incluso una dosis lógica de incredulidad por su parte. Mi nombre es en transcripción fonética para usted, EIDOUAA AA 42 hijo de EIMEII 12, procedente de un astro frio llamado UMMO. Puede usted constatar la idoneidad de mi identidad a traves de nuestro sello cuya autenticidad tal vez podré ser avalada por su hermano español Rafael Farriols Calvo residente en Barcelona. Nos consta que en varios paises han circulado cartas apócrifas atribuidas a mis hermanos y sin duda usted preferirá constatar que este texto posee un origen genuino.

Nos dirigimos mis hermanos y yo a usted, porque habian llegado a nos, noticias acerca del alto grado de fiabilidad que usted amablemente concede a los datos acerca de nuestra existencia. Es cierto que tal actitud es mas emocional que racional, pues mis hermanos ya tuvieron cuidado de no aportar excesivas pruebas objetivas acerca de nuestra identidad y procedencia. Necesitabamos del escepticismo humano de Tierra, para poder convivir entre ustedes, pero nos vimos sorprendidos al comprobar como unos pocos hermanos suyos de Yugoslavia, Australia Francia, España, Canadá y otras naciones, dejandose llevar por impulsos afectivos , creyeron en nosotros sin mediar argumentos de orden científico.

Naturalmente esllo resultó halagador para aquellos de mis hermanos que entonces se encontraban en Tierra e iniciose al punto, una copiosa correspondencia unilateral que comprendió un extenso dossier de informes en cifra suprior a los seismil setecientos en varios idiomas. Solo pusimos como condicion que los reducidos grupos afectos a nosotros en estos paises, no se pusieran en contacto mutuo con los de otra nacionalidad, y que los documentos no trascendieran a la Red Social terrestre por temor a que ello implicase un boom publicitario que nos obligase a marcharnos de su Astro frio. En parte,ello ha sido cumplido aunque hoy ya el riesgo para nosotros es casi nulo ante las inevitables filtraciones sufridas. Usted mismo ha comentado publicamente datos sobre nuestra existencia y no estaba obligado a la reserva mental, mediante compromiso alguno.

Mis hermanos han estado fuera de su Astro frio un gran intervalo temporal.

Regresamos a Tierra en una expedicion, en octubre, aterrizando en Dinamarca

Una pequeña expedicion a mis órdenes se encuentra en el Centro de España, mis otros hermanos se hallan en estos momentos en Dinamarca, Inglaterra, Nepal y Canadá. Yo personalmente es la segunda vez que estoy entre ustedes. Estudié idiomas Ingles, Español y Aleman y me han especializado en cultura y pensamiento hispanos. Mi profesion en Ummo está vinculada al analisis de sistemas bioquímicos para la sintesis de alimentos. Concretamente mi especialidad estriba en la codificacion en lo que ustedes denominan polinucleoticos, de bases para la genesis de organismos productores de cadenas proteicas. Estudio en estas fechas la evolucion de la Sociedad española en sus facetas econométricas y dicto esta carta a un hermano suyo del pais, que ya fué conocido por los expedicionarios que me precedieron. Este hermano suyo es un admirador nuestro y nos ha prestado valiosos servicios.

Deseamos satisfacer algunos puntos interrogativos formulados por sus hermanos a lo largo de estos tiempos. Así, ellos se preguntaban acerca de la razon de nuestro silencio. En primer orden ello se debió a nuestra ausencia de Tierra pero antes mediaron consideraciones de otro nivel. En contra de nuestra peticion de secreto, se filtraron xerocopias de nuestros documentos a otros medios y esto reportaba un riesgo para mis hermanos que entonces se allaban aquí. Especialmente en España esta incontinencia se hizo mas aguda que en otros paises cuyos hermanos suyos fueron mas prudentes y cautos. Fué preciso desencadenar nuestras estructuras de autodefensa, consistentes en poner en circulacion

This is a shrink reproduction of the front page of the original UMMO document listed as number 116 in Ignacio Darnaude's catalogue of the documents known to him. Note the UMMO seal in the upper right corner.

(Appendix 3, Part I, Document Number 117)

CONCERNING UMMO GENERAL HEADQUARTERS IN DENMARK. BASE OF OPERATIONS NEAR MADRID. DEVELOPMENT BY THE PEOPLES REPUBLIC OF CHINA OF A NEW TERRIBLE PLASMA BOMB. STRUCTURE OF THE ATOM. THE IBOZOO UU, ETC.

Letter received 5 June 1979 by Sr. Aguirre - 3 pages

UMMOAELEWEE
Number of copies: 1
Language: Spanish
Received 5 June 1979
MADRID, SPAIN

Kind Sir:

My name is EIEEUFE 7 son of EIEEUE 5 and, together with two more of my brothers, I am at this time in Spain. Our main headquarters in Spain is located at a base in a mountain range mear the Spanish capital, which makes possible occasional stays in cities such as Madrid, Torrejon de Ardoz and Segovia.

With regard to myself, I came to this country in former times, when I specialized in the language of Spain. My profession is similar to what you call zoology, and my present mission involves the analysis of the migrations of certain species of orthopterans from Africa and from some European countries to the Iberian peninsula. We utilize for this radioactive markers, and our instruments with their great power of resolution permit the detection of these insects wherever they may happen to be.

My brothers and I have been absent from Earth a long time. Our return to Earth took place not long ago in Danish territory, and there we have installed our central base on Earth, together with another situated in Berlin. The studies we are making on this brief visit to Earth are: Analysis of Nordic cultures, European Entomology, Socio-economic Evolution in Western countries during the last few years, South American ethnes, and additions to hematopoietic tissues.

Senor, the number of my brothers on this expedition is very small. We have little time at our disposal so it will not be possible to make many human contacts. Excuse us.

Senor, it would not be wise to make copies of this letter we are sending you, but nothing prevents you from reading it to your brothers whom you consider reliable. It contains some information which, if it reached experts in the Physics applied to arms manufacture, might constitute a possible clue to technical applications.

Senor, when we reached Earth, two of my brothers traveled to (censored)/SIC/ to study the relations of this great country with the

West. For us a trip of this kind involves risks, for which reason it can be carried out only in our ships, since my brothers' facial features are very different from those OEMII (HUMANS) of this nationality. From Secret bases in the (XXXX)/SIC/ Mountains, we are able to position detecting instruments for subsequent observations. In this way we have been able to confirm the technological development in a very specific field of the modern weapons created by Earth man.

Senor, I don't know whether you are aware of the gravity of the news we are about to offer. (...Censored...)/SIC/ .....we could place it at around sixty percent, whereas your colleagues of the USA and USSR in this same field have probably reached a level of less than seven percent. I am referring to weapons of Plasma and I shall describe briefly the nature of this concept.

As you know, plasma is a gaseous state characterized by the fact that the molecules of a chemical element are almost completely deprived of their electrical cortex. Temperatures within the plasma may become extremely high. A plasma "Bomb" is not, as its name may indicate, an explosive. It has a device provided with radiators of quantum energy, capable of increasing the temperature of enormous masses of gas until it reaches the level of plasma. [See note after letter]

With normal physical means, the mass of gas reaching such a state is proportional to the energy applied, and since this cannot reach high concentrations in space, the volume of gas affected likewise can not reach high levels.

Nevertheless, we have discovered the intimate nature of subatomic particles. It is possible to convert a sequence of electrons into a simple interval of space (For us space is quantified). By means of simple rotation we can transform atomic subparticles into others. For example, it may be possible to transform a Hadron into a Lepton and vice versa. Mass can be transformed into an electric charge to supply energy to a system of leptons from another time-space frame, apparently breaking the law of the conservation of Mass and Energy which you would formulate thus:

> "The total of mass and energy in the entirety of n space-time frames (UNIVERSES) is CONSTANT."

It is not true that in the universe in which you and we are living at this moment, any increase of mass is made at the expense of a similar energy loss and viceversa. It is true for the natural reactions discovered by you (Fission, Fusion, and above all a yield of 100 from 100 in disintegration through Matter-Antimatter interaction); however it is possible to start a process of chain reaction in which space of a three-dimensional frame A1 may be transformed into ENERGY applied to the combination of atoms correcponding to three-dimensional frame

A2 (our own).

(. . . . . Censored . . . .)/SIC/

The effect you can imagine by using a simile, as if both time-space continua A1 and A2 were separated by a symbolic or ideal membrane.

(. . . . . Censored . . . .)/SIC/

If "perforated", the flow of ENERGY from that moment would set the atomic nuclei in A2 to vibrating this "tear or perforation". Properly speaking, ENERGY would not really be involved from the standpoint of an observer located at A1. We use the term IBOZOO UU for entities whose sequence, interconnected by different angular rotations, may present characteristics of energy, mass and space, depending on the rotations of the elements in that sequence. With a minimal energy application (the highest percentage of which corresponds to (Censored)/SIC/), it is possible to release a chain reaction that could transform several thousand cubic kilometers of terrestrial atmosphere near or touching Earth, into plasma at high temperature.

A country like France could be destroyed in a few seconds in a vortex of fire. All air located above it up to a level of from two to fourteen kilometers would be transformed into plasma. The reaction could take place with the oxygen or nitrogen content or with both.The sudden expansion caused by the high temperature gradients would produce impressive atmospheric disturbances in the surrounding countries which would then spread throughout the world and seriously affect the attacking country.

But all life and material structures in the country under attack would cease to exist, and such structures would be seriously damaged in the initiating country as well. The nuclear weapon you are familiar with would be dwarfed by this terrifying weapon, which my ancestors were aware of but which they never used (Will you do the same?).

You don't know our physical models of the universe based on the IBOZOO UU, but when you do become familiar with them, such transformations of plasma will be one more corollary arising from these concepts.

It is interesting to note, therefore, how the scientists of — (...Censored...)/SIC/ without having any idea of the true nature of matter as we conceive it.

The reasons were involved with a series of experiments carried out by them in the field of extremelu high pressures aimed at understanding the nature of the Neutron (A normal state of matter in certain high density stars).

Furthermore ......(censored)....../SIC/

Senor, do not take this comment of mine to mean that ...(Censored)

.../SIC/ hence I told you at the beginning of this report that your effort, or mere chance, may put you Earthmen on the right track, but without the implication that either the USSR or the USA can easily overtake them.

The political implications, senor, I don't believe are hidden from you. And of course the gravity center of international power would shift toward (XXXXX)/SIC/, if this weapon were to fall into the hands of that powerful nation. It isn't easy to foresee the consequences of the new structure of geopolitical power for the men of your Earth. ......(Censored)....../SIC/

Up to now the most terrible weapons you can utilize are: The MARV /SIC/ or ballistic missiles with atmospheric re-entry vehicles, maneuverable in the final phase; ogives placed on cruise missiles in ground-hugging flight a few meters high in order to evade the radar beams; emission of high-energy charged particles for the interception of missiles, etc. The first three can carry thermonuclear Fission-Fusion-Fission warheads.

Senor: In a recent letter directed to another of your brothers in Spain, we presented our reports to a sister without knowing that she had passed away. While attempting to discover her present whereabouts recently, we learned of her unfortunate death. Please express our profound condolence and request for forgiveness of our error.

/Seal of UMMOAELEWE/

[We have published this document here without the permission of the recipient, who was forbidden to release copies of this letter. Some of the censoring was done by the Ummite author before release and some was done by others through whose hands this has passed.

We can state that the country censored out was the Peoples Republic of China. Now, standing alone this report could be just another tale not to be taken too seriously, but does it stand alone? -Publisher]

Comment on this letter is even more imperative than on the one before, because there is other information from other extraterrestrial sources of entirely different nature that seem to tell us the very same thing.

On 3 January 1979, the same year, and only six months earlier than this letter, Sr. Filiberto Cardenas of Hialeah, Florida, a native Cuban, was abducted by extraterrestrials in full view of three other humans with whom he was riding in a car, and who were with him at the time and saw him leave and could do nothing about it despite his cries for help. He was carried away for some 2 hours and 10 minutes. During some of that time aboard a large mother-ship in space, he was shown images of events transpiring in different countries on Earth. He was shown at that time the state of development of a terrible plasma weapon in Red China that would make the atomic weapons of the other powers obsolete because it could neutralize them where they were. No large scale testing was observed at that time but he was told that developments were in very advanced stages and the weapon was operational. This case was fully reported in UFO CONTACT FROM UNDERSEA, Sanchez - Stevens, UFO Photo Archives, page 62.

The UMMO visitors had detected the same developments and left remote devices installed in the nearby mountains in China to monitor the progress of these experiments.

Then in mid-1984 the news wires briefly carried a delayed release of a report by airline pilots of various airline crews simultaneously sighting a very strange mushroom cloud that grew rapidly and rose high into the stratosphere in an extremely short time. The phenomenon looked just like an atomic explosion. It was reported several times by different observers in the China Sea and in the Pacific off the northeast coast of Japan.

The Boston SUNDAY GLOBE for 13 January 1985 reported an event that was already nearly a year old by then that may have been one of the most significant pieces of news in the whole year, In an article titled "Mystery Cloud Baffles Scientists" by Ross Gelbspan of the Globe Staff, an airline pilot may have reported one of the distant tests of the plasma weapon over the Pacific Ocean off the coast of Japan.

The reports of the event are basically accurate though the experts consulted later speculate on a different author of the phenomenon. We quote from that report as follows:

> "Shortly after 1 p.m. last April 9 [1984] Capt. Charles H. McDade, pilot of Japan Airlines Flight 36 from Tokyo to Anchorage, was flying off the northern coast of Japan when he put in a Mayday call to Anchorage. [A Mayday call signifies a genuine emergency situation and is not lightly used by professional pilots.]

"We have a...round ball cloud...looks like a nuclear explosion, only there was no lightning, but the cloud was there very definitely... We're at altitude 33,000 feet -- the cloud continues to explode like a great big cloud, easy to see...and it expanded very rapidly....I turned off course to get away from it as much as possible.... We are on hundred percent oxygen just as a precaution..."

"McDade was not alone. At about the same time four other airline pilots in the area reported seeing the same huge mushroom cloud rise to a height of 60,000 feet in two minutes.

"The pilots, fearing they were witnessing a nuclear exploaion, reported the sighting and, upon landing, had their planes checked for radioactivity.

"None was discovered.

"The next day, the Japanese government sent a reconnaissance plane into the area to search for radioactive dust or debris. None was discovered, according to a statement from the Japanese Defense Agency at the time.

"Today the event remains shrouded in mystery [Ten months later] with one scientist claiming the explosion could not have been a known natural event, and a former Army lieutenant colonel claiming, despite skepticism from many experts, that the cloud was the product of a Soviet test of a new type of long range beam weapon.

"In statements to the Federal Aviation Administration, the pilots -- two of them flying Japan Airlines planes, two others in Flying Tiger cargo planes and one piloting a KLM passenger plane -- all reported seeing the mushroom cloud at basically the same time.

"According to a report from an FAA special agent who interviewed the pilots, Cornelius Vander Berg, captain of KLM's Flight 868, reported that he sighted a bubble rising out of a low-level layer of stratus clouds about 100 miles northwest of his aircraft. That would have put the cloud about 200 miles off the northeastern corner of Japan.

"The bubble increased in size and formed a sphere, which then separated from the stratus layer and increased in size and altitude." the FAA report said, quoting Vander Berg. "At first the cloud was opaque, then as it got large, you could see the stars through it. The development continued until the sphere was massive, then dissipated... (Vander Berg) and the first officer agreed they had never seen anything like it. They did not see any flash or light nor did they notice any effects on their aircraft from the formation. They did not experience any turbulence (from their position), nor were there any effects on their radio, navigational or engine instruments..."

"An Air Force spokesman last week [again ten months later] confirmed the pilots reports and the fact that the planes were checked for radiation. 'Beyond that, we don't know what it was,' said Lt. Col. Lawrence Greer.

"Suspecting the eruption of an underwater volcano or an earthquake releasing methane gas, Dr. Daniel A Walker, a professor of geophysics at the University of Hawaii said. "That was my bias. I looked forward to analyzing the data and tying it up neatly. It would have been a feather in my cap to identify the source of the cloud. But the science proved otherwise," he added.

"After analyzing the data, Walker concluded that there was no source of volcanic or seismic activity in the area where the cloud was sighted. "Nor given the speed with which the cloud rose into the atmosphere, could it have been a thunderhead - or any other kind of known cloud formation," he said.

"Walker, whose paper on the event has been accepted for publication in Science Magazine in the next few weeks, concluded that the cloud was an unknown natural phenomenon -- OR A MAN-MADE ATMOSPHERIC EXPLOSION.

"Dr. Stefan T. Possony, a former Defense Department Intelligence officer said in a recent interview from his Los Altos, California home, 'The event off Japan really is a warning that somebody can do something we don't know much about. If such a technology or science exists, this mushroom cloud is merely a sideshow'.

"Prof. Michael McElroy, an atmospheric physicist at Harvard, speculated in a telephone interview that the sighting probably involved an unusual pattern of vertical turbulance in the atmosphere that was misinterpreted by the pilots.

"But Capt. Charles McDade, now 60, the pilot of Japan Airlines Flight 36, responded, 'No way. As a former B-52 flier, I'm not skittish.' Nor, he added, would anxiety have produced the same reaction in five [different] pilots.

Recalling the sighting, McDade explained that,'After about a minute and 50 seconds, this thing grew so tremendously it was unbelievable. When I really saw how fast it was growing, that's when I turned south to get away'.

One of the other pilots reported that the ball of vapor quickly grew from about 25 miles diameter to more than 75 miles as he observed it. McDades own investigations following this event revealed that several other Japanese pilots had witnessed a separate similar event within a few days of the one witnessed by McDade and the airline pilots.

(Not listed in either catalogue in Appendix 3. Unpublished)

Received in Alicante in April 1980 - 4 pages

Spanish Languare
One copy executed
ALBACETE, SPAIN

Senor Luis Jimenez Marhuenda:

Permit me to intervene so that you and your brothers will allow us to place our hands on your chests as a symbolic gesture of peace and profound mutual respect.

I have taken the liberty, senor, of disturbing your tranquility by sending you in the mail these typewritten lines which contain information about a recent meeting devoted to UMMO, organized by you and your colleagues.

On a cordial invitation from you, two of our brothers traveled from Albacete to the building designated for the event devoted to our civilization. It was not possible for us to request a pass. You will readily understand the serious embarrassment and publicity this would have caused. Anyway it was not difficult for us to get inside, and my brothers merged with the others attending, although they could stay only three hours and forty-two minutes, a sufficient time in which to place in the hall two small video tape-recorders. We were also able to fasten to the epidermis of eleven humans (six women and five men) gauages to register psychophysiological parameters. These polytransducers have a minimum volume of 2.4 mm^3 and are applied to the skin by means of a viscous compound. They do not injure or bother the wearer, and if they were found they would be easily taken for a carbon particle accidentally adhering with mucous. These transmitters and their central receiving module which codifies and later transmits such information were the only systems we used to follow events during sessions.

On Wednesday, 2 April, one of my brothers returned to recover part of the equipment we had used which, for confidential reasons, could not be transported by plane.

We have been waiting for enough time to analyze the volume of information acquired, and we now have an outline that enables us to describe it.

Senor Luis Jimenez: Allow me to express our great sorrow and bitterness along with our subsequent frustration caused by that analysis. Sadness and disappointment resulted from our discovering once again the harm we have inflicted on you Earthmen. (But please be assured, Senor of Earth: it was never our intention to injure you so seriously.)

As if you men of OYAAGAA were not already suffering with social, economic and political problems while you struggle desperately amid the gasps of a civilization now cracking dangerously, a society that is soon to create an important, dramatic new order of social structures on a planetary scale; we with undoubted good faith, but with a carelessness that we regret, have caused a new flood of problems for a small group of humans, and have given rise to rancor and mutual distrust among them as well as dangerous temptations to worship our UMMO culture. Painful psychological attacks by some of your brothers against others are raising the already high level of latent hatred, subconscious and obscure fears mixed with false illusions.

It is surely sad to realize that the detonator of these expanding recriminations was the group composed of my brothers.

Do you recall that in previous reports we referred to the risks inherent in any interferrence with the sociohumanoid /SIC/ social systems of a different planet still in the process of development?

If you have been witnesses on a small scale to the disturbances which, like bubbles rising to the surface of a swamp and releasing their fetid gas among those few individuals already interested in our existence (and despite prudent doubts about our actual identity), then you can imagine what could happen if, on an insane impulse, we revealed ourselves on a national scale.

You must try to understand, senor Luis, the parameters within which these reactions develop. The humans of OYAGAA do not posess a brain sufficiently well organized to enable them to ascertain their own identity, assume their proper place in society and structure it more harmoniously. The fault is not yours or WOA's. You are simply in a stage of neganthropic evolution which you have to pass through, as have other planetary biospheres, including our own UMMO.

The heart-breaking maladjustments of that social pseudo-order cause an immense burden of suffering for all of you. We feel apprehensive but impotent to remedy the huge amount of mental pain and suffering being experienced by you and your brothers in the midst of this semichaos.

The Earth human is truely ill. His complex psychiatric functions are as anomalous as those performed by a badly designed machine. You humans know that the vector of conduct is the result of an entire range of components. First comes genetic coding in chains of polynucleotides. Information stored in the neuronal tissue of the cerebral hemispheres through accretion of data throughout a lifetime from the womb, and the process of acquiring mental models from the stored information, plus the pressure exerted by the physical and social environment at the moment of making a decision, the internal biochemical medium, and the physicochemical action of all the anatomical structures on the cerebral nuclei, all have their effect. This entire combination of factors determines your possible patterns of conduct; possible, but unfortunately for you very small in number. For this reason your degree of freedom is quite limited. When, through transfer of some crypton atoms, your mental self has to choose between those options, sometimes only one seems possible, resulting in an absolutely predictable reaction. The human of OYAGAA at times behaves like a robot conditioned by the inflexible pressures of the internal and external environment, with his conduct thus becoming a series of conditioned reflexes.

At other times the OEMII (of Earth) has to choose from among the vary impaired results of defective cerebral functioning and the intensely disturbing action of a discordant endocrinal system. This aspect contains a lesson that you yourselves do not suspect. The importance of that texture of biochemical compounds in the determination of human behavior still has not been discovered by the endocrinologists of Earth.

(We use the term ENDOCRINAL NETWORK, translating one of our words, for that combination of flows and concentrations of all the substances that you call HORMONES, located in the liquid medium of the tissues, blood, lymphatic system, the cephalorachidian liquid etc., of the somatic chamber.)

The secretion of a few more milliliters of aldosterone together with increases of less than a millionth part of the preceding rate at the time of Oxytocin, may cause radical polarization in individual decisionmaking.

The ingestion of a few tenths of a microgram of common salt, NaCl as you call it, may cause alteration in the concentration of certain mineral corticoids and thus modify profoundly the subsequent behavior of the individual.

But you will probably have to devote many decades to discovering a diet scientifically suited to your psychological needs and much more time beyond that before new modifications in your hormone-secreting system creates the foundation for an emotive and endocrinal equilibrium better adjusted to the needs of the OEMII (of earth).

Today that biochemical system is still crude, the glial and neural functions are not specific, and the transfer of data through afferent channels takes place with a high degree of error and a low signal/noise level.

For all the above reasons, the adoption of intelligent decisions is intimately connected with the emotional (Endocrinal) aura. Primitive biochemical mechanisms that became ingrained in your brains during remote periods when your ancestors were animals and had to defend themselves from a hostile environment are still interfering with far better developed informational processes based on statistical patterns stored in the neoplastic cortex. (These ingrained mechanisms have been inherited by you and will not disappear except through new mutations controlled by precise laws of an orthogenetic character.) This results in grave consequences for your lives together, psychotic and neurotic traits in all of you which throw dark shadows over the social setup of OYAGAA, piling up unbearable burdens of collective worry and anxiety and finally giving rise to sick, psychopathic creatures like a Stalin, a Hitler, a Franco, a Reza Pahlevi, a Khomeini or a Carter, to give examples of brothers of yours in recent history, who occupied dangerous key posts in the system and caused terrible social maladjustments with unpredictable consequences.

No: don't think that it is possible to predict, even with our computerized data, certain future social and economic processes, due precisely to the haphazard incidence of primitive endocrinal reactions in some important people in the social system.

In these conditions of overstimulated collective anxiety (beneath which can be seen an imperious desire for salvation), any least spark of light, even the mirage of extraterrestrial "brothers" of the Cosmos who could arrive on earth for the purpose of saving and redeeming them, would arouse dangerous (because fallacious and incoherent) idea patterns which in turn would result in emotional (that is, endocrinal) disturbances with fatal consequences for the slow process of human evolution.

We hope, senor Luis Jimenez, that you, an expert in the communications media in which you labor, will become aware of the immense danger involved in injecting into the mental process of your brothers false hopes as to us humans of UMMO and of other civilizations which at this very moment are investigating yours. Since they are governed by highly intellectual patterns, it is not to be expected that they will alter the sluggish flow of evolution in the society of OYAGAA. We on the other hand, perhaps with less maturity than they, began our approach to you in a timid fashion, and look how much harm we did you! Now we are sorry and are proceeding to draw back gently but firmly.

We are worried and preoccupied. We thought that offering you false leads that contradicted the reports of our presence on Earth would be enough so that your logical patterns of reasoning would come into play and reject such reports. Our lack of foresight, however, in giving you some positive proofs, coupled with the cleverness and intuition of other brothers of yours, has caused a persistent acceptance of our existence. Emotional factors have been injected into the fabric so that now we notice in the Country of Spain the beginning of a dangerous current of attention to us, whereas in other nations your informed brothers have adopted a very prudent policy of silence, effective doubt and restricted publicity.

You humans of Spain, please understand our powerlessness. We can not morally and ethically prohibit you from divulging our reports since naturally they are now the property of your brothers and you are the only ones responsible for their conduct. Nor does their publication any longer represent a danger for us as it did before. And therefore we are not being driven by a selfish pattern of self-defense in asking you to be careful.

In the Castilian idiom you employ an expression: "Por amor del Dios" ["For the love of God"]. And we take the liberty now of respectfully imploring you: "For the love of God, for the love of your brothers: FORGET US. Don't publicise our existence." There already exists among humans on OYAGAA too chaotic a confusion of religions and philosophical schools for a new cult of UMMO to arise, which for you would be inoperable and almost sterile because it does not fit into your bioworld and would muddle still further the difficult rebirth you are about to undergo. We shall remain on this planet to observe that cataclysmic rise of a new social system. Our mission is exactly this and we shall not interfere in any other way with the process.

The meeting organized by you and your brothers in downtown Alicante has been quite valuable to us in enabling us to detect the psychophysiological reactions of the OEMII of Earth to the UMMAAO body of knowledge accumulated by you. Analysis of the resulting sociopsychic phenomenon has alarmed and worried us a great deal. Naturally, Senor Luis, we are not exaggerating. We are simply trying to show you the facts without being paternalistic toward all of you.

Senor, perhaps you want reasons for our cry of alarm. Please understand that we cannot reveal all the complicated details of the study we have completed. If you are convinced that our identity is genuine, it will be wise for you to give us your vote of confidence and accept our exhortation to reduce to the minimum all distribution of our reports in order to stop a perilous social trend. If you do not believe in us and instead accept the equally intelligent opinion that we are not who we claim to be, then the reason for preventing that spread of false information is all the more compelling.

Unfortunately we made many mistakes in the past. Some of your brothers received technical information which enabled them to develop patents on devices of advanced technology that proved to them the authenticity of my brothers. Others received information proving our awareness of secret decisions in high official circles of Earth. For many of those persons, some of whom have maintained a prudent silence because of their social status, the certainty that we come from another planet is quite high. And unfortunately there is no solution for this. But at least please try now not to broaden this dangerous certainty, but instead allow other strata of the population to believe that all this is a passing fantasy.

Senor, we listened to some of the papers read by brothers of yours at that congress. Some of them are excellent. We noted in particular the thesis of your brother Jose Antonio Cormo. Although we are sorry about his opinion of us, please tell him, senor Luis Jimenez, that if we could meet him in person and place our hands on his noble chest, he would understand our culture better and his suspicions would surely vanish. We consider the Naziism which devastated the noble land of Germany as a horrible aberration of the human mind on OYAGAA and we share, whether he believes it or not, his repudiation of any form of cruel totalitarianism (which your own civilization experienced in the past). Your brother Cormo is a sensitive, kind human being, cautious and misunderstood. Since only a twisted fragment of our culture has reached him, his reservations are understandable and logical. It would please us to offer him our true image. We are likewise sorry about his opinions as to our alleged aggressive intentions. You must realize that if they were true, our strategy would be revealed as all the more deceitful.

But with his reservations your brother reveals his qualities as a cautious OEMII. Naturally we see no way of convincing him of the purity of our intentions, but on the other hand he has offered us the chance to take advantage of his particular ideological viewpoints. Ably used, they may enable you to remove for him the myths surrounding us. I believe it is all right to twist the truth in order to bring about a far more beneficial result offsetting the harm done in perverting some rigorously authentic information.

Furthermore, brother Cormo is right. We have done you some harm, but for the reasons cited above, not for the reasons he thinks.

Senor: My apologies for the disordered topics in this document. We were impressed with your noble respect for your brother's opinions, your gracious manner, your exquisite delicacy in smoothing over rough spots and restoring peace and harmony among your brothers, your sincere idealism and open-mindedness devoid of inhibitions. Allow me to express my sincere respect and admiration to you as well as to your excellent wife and your dear ones. Convey our regards to your brother Ricardo Lopez Gomez.

There is no point in repeating our greetings to the many brothers of yours whom we have mentioned in previous letters. Please relay to them our regards, but extend them also to your brothers who have become interested in us and, though accepting our presence here with various degrees of belief, deserve special rememberance: Juam Jose Benitez, Jorge Sala Cicero, and Cesar Sanchez Von...

(Not listed in either catalogue in appendix 3. Unpublished)

Received June 1980 in Madrid
UMMOAELEWE
Language: Spanish
Number of copies: Four
ALBACETE/MARSEILLES/OSLO/MONTREAL

(Written in longhand in blue ballpoint)

Senor Jorge Barrenechea Aberasturi:

Please allow us to interfere again in your peaceful private life to bother you with another letter.

Dear Earth Friend: Even though we have already sent this condolence to three brothers of yours in France, Norway and Canada, we wish to express to you and the rest of your brothers of OYAGAA our sadness at the passing of your brother Jean Paul Sartre.

His brain was one of the most favored among those we have detected in living humans during the time of our stay on this planet.

We cannot muster up any enthusiasm for many aspects of his fluctuating ideology, which we considered categorically erroneous. We lament the fact that, like many thinkers among his contemporaries, he rejected the thesis of the existence of a creator (God or WOA) and that in his later studies he veered toward positions akin to the thought of powerlessness. But what can honest scientists and consistent philosophers do when they see that the name of God is used to cover the most odious crimes against human rights and that the great religious structures have been converted into economic empires which abet the terrible social maladjustments afflicting you.

At present my brothers are carrying out an exhaustive analysis of the sociocultural and socioeconomic patterns governing the evolution of terrestrial society and have been impressed by the lucid and profound study which Senor Sartre of France has made of that society, capturing in all its drama the terrible loneliness of human beings unable to form stable links with society; the tragedy of some OEMII of Earth who are oppressed by a divided society and are struggling in the mists of an emotional, savage, unbalanced globe.

When some of your brothers who know us, Senor Jorge Barranechea, ask us: "Why don't you, who claim to have come from another planet, offer us a formula for getting out of this swamp of ours?", we truely would like to give them an answer which, though frustrating, would nevertheless be coherent with a logic familiar to you:

Let us examine the question" Brothers with favored brains such as Marcuse, Fromm, Poulantzas, Sartre, Russell... threw considerable light on the roots of the evils gnawing at the social structure of Earth. In addition, other brothers of yours such as John XXIII, Gramsei, Helder Camara, Che Guevara, Romero, Camilo Torres, Teilhard de Chardin, Ghandi, Marx, Mao Tse Tung... offered, with their ideas, with their lifestyles, sometimes with their deaths, together with their ideologies, an anguished call to the rest of Earth humanity. They all understood that basing happiness on a socioeconomic model of consumption would sink the rest of society in frustration and despair. But who followed them? A large segment of humanity chose to follow a Hitler, a Pinochet, so inhumane a model as that of the United States, or else took refuge beneath the iron bureaucracy of totalitarian states imposing a dogmatic socialistic economy.

Senor Jorge: No magic, mysterious formula exists whereby to escape in a limites period of time from chaos into an integrated social system of pure, happy biological beings. For every stage of evolution of a biological philum which has acquired a system of signals (nervous system) able to process information and prepare intelligent answers (COMMUNITY OF OEMII), there exists only one optimum model of social organization which also maximized their psychological and material wellbeing. But if the blindness of its component individuals causes the selection of a very different model, one that is illogical and destructive to the stability of the community on account of its corrosive features (even when these people have before their eyes an intelligent, constructive criterion developed by more advanced brains), then what solution is possible?

Thousands of voices among you have been raised against the shameful oppression being suffered by your brothers in situations of poverty. Thousands of voices like that of the intelligent YIE of Sartre, Simone de Beauvoir, have denounced the shameful and very dangerous oppression inflicted on the women of Earth by the men through the use of their brute muscular strength (in our judgement the primary and most serious factor in social unrest). And what have you humans of more progressive thinking done but merely continue to violate the rights of the YIE, and, on a lower level, those of the less developed and intellectually less capable segments of humanity? How, then, can you condemn your brothers who believe in a more retrograde ideology?

Your brothers, Senor, are asking us for SOLUTIONS:

If your friend, Senor Jorge, rejects the bananna you offer him, why does he insist with irrational inconsistency that an extraterrestrial being give him another bananna with skin and aroma identical to those of the one he rejected?

We are well aware, senor, that the problem is more complex than this and that the simplistic parable just given does not clarify it too well.

Let us carry on with our synthetic analysis of the question: In principle we - or some other civilization of those studying you, of galactic origin and a higher level of development, might provide you with a considerable volume of data which theoretically could improve your standard of living, reduce your terrible internal tensions and enable you to develop a political and economic model based on scientific premises.

As examples of such contributions: we could correct the grave errors in the estimates of economic variables contained in the models of Forrester and Meadows. presented to the Club of Rome, which models offer a greatly twisted picture of the economic future of Earth.

We could offer you the key to obtaining clean energy by nuclear fusion or offer you a primitive model of the system which we call IBOZOOAEWEEA (untranslatable)/SIC/, which permits the reconversion of an intense but easily obtained beam of PI mesons into a great flow of energy.

We could provide you with the method in each case for synthesizing at low cost edible protein and lipids which would immediately reduce the horrible spectre of starvation threatening you in coming years if you don't succeed in lowering your rate of demographic expansion.

We could offer you the necessary technology for the production of basic metals by nuclear fusion with almost no cost in energy consumption (1 synthesis),/SIC/

We could furnish you with the indispensable technique to eradicate the formation of neoplastic tissues (cancerous) and the totality of diseases of infectious etiology, still resistant to the chemotherapy of OYAGAA (Earth).

In order not to make this report boreing, we interrupt here the list of contributions we should undoubtedly be able to give you quite freely.

But we are astounded to see that you don't seem to realize clearly what the consequences of such apparent generosity on our part would then be.

Pause and examine, senor Jorge Barrenechea, the present situation on earth.

In your present society there are two clearly differentiated segments. I am not revealing anything new to you there, senor.

One, a small, select minority, is made up of the HOLDERS OF INFORMATION. Almost the entire mass of information mow in the hands of Earth humanity is MANIPULATED by the governing classes (military men, politicians, technicians, scientists, and especially by those posessing the means of production). You must never forget that POSESSION OF INFORMATION = POWER. There are among you naive analysts who still believe in the binominal POWER/MONEY. It is evident that this is no longer true. Another consideration is that, once having obtained such power through the monopoly of information, these people may succeed in monopolizing the most important sources of economic development.

Secondly, let us look at the second segment of society, greatly in the majority: A huge mass of population unable to handle information, to understand it, process it or use it intelligently. I am sorry, senor, if you haven't been aware of the cruel, sophisticated technique utilized by the first segment to alienate the second, majority segment, which has no intellectual defense.

How does the former control the weak intellects of the latter? Simply by reinjecting into their brains currents of thought based on magic, irrational patterns. While the holders of power, with deliberate skill, monopolize technology and conform to logical, scientific standards, millions of OEMII on Earth allow themselves to be poisoned by superstitions, by pseudoreligious ideas, and by irrational myths. From the centers of power controlling the print and broadcast media there are spread absurd doctrines, unscientific concepts of the universe, and occultism in all its forms, drowning out the few voices who dare to denounce these distortions of logic.

Because naturally your science is still only slightly developed and is in a phase of accumulated errors using imprecise, inaccurate models of behavior for inert and biological matter, still more absurd and psychopathological are the wild ideas being spread by the detractors of Earth science, to the poorly concealed glee of those in the elite segment, who note with satisfaction that, while the masses are being drugged with these magic ways of thinking, they will be unable to handle THEIR INFORMATION.

Are those brothers of yours who compose the power-weilding segment evil and sadistic? Our concept is different. They are simply people who take advantage of their brain development to defend themselves from those less equipped. Involved here are instinctive, inherited animal processes and mechanisms of self-defense (which you term EGOISM or categorize as asocial and criminally psychopathic conduct). The terminology is irrelevant: Simply a question of semantics. The seriousness of the case is that these intelligent mechanisms of defense cause them to seize the information, manipulate and corrupt it, thereby controlling technology and with it the basic means of production and in this way enjoy a hedonistic standard of living while condemning the rest of humanity to chaos.

With these considerations in mind, look again at the problem outlined above. Suppose that we humans from the planet UMMO compile for you that voluminous file of technical data which would apparently bring about the liberation of your society. To whom are we to give it? To a simple peasant? To a buddhist monk? To a modest university professor? None of these would know how to decode so complex an accumulation of data or have at their disposal the information for its practical aoolication.

Can you imagine, senor, where this valuable file would end up?

Suppose we deliver it to you, or a man in Canada, in Spain, in Norway, in France, friends of ours who believe in our existence to some degree. Would they keep it in a safe, thus making it useless? And if they published it in pamphlet form for distribution among their own friends who dabbled in magic and the occult, of what use would they be? Most probably they would reach the hands of that oligarchy, the only group capable of understanding and using it... and what do you think they would do with it?

Are you so naive, senor, as still to believe they would use it for the good of society?

Some of your brothers, quite conscious of their wrongdoing, work up an economic model for a free market capable of burning tons of wheat in order to maintain prices and thus benefit a few to the detriment of undernourished babies. They are willing to put the planet on the brink of nuclear annihilation to defend one of their own, a criminal psychopath like Mohamed Reza for the simple reason that he holds great economic power obtained by exploiting his brothers. Would you hand over our dossier to those people?

What do you think they would do with this donation of our technology? Let's look at various examples: How would they utilize our high-resolution techniques which permit the mutation of a sequence of polynucleotides within the cell nucleus in order to eradicate cancer as we do? Who guarantees to us that they would? NO. We'll tell you quite bluntly: with that technique they would develop new pathogenic autoresistant organisms to use in possible warfare of a bacteriological character. Or what is still worse, to synthesize almost brainless humanoid creatures who would work as slaves of production.

What purpose would be served by our handing over to you a structure of 2070 equations for preparation of an econometric model of the futture behavior of an extensive family of variables (demographic expansion, growth of investments, natural resources, contamination of the environment, energy consumption...)? Why develop an international economic order based not on monopoly of the means of production but rather on a fair distribution of resources? Don't be naive. This set-up would be used immediately by countries as ominous as the United States, Israel, Japan or the Federal Republic of Germany to dominate and divide up foreign markets, depressing still further the "have-not" nations of the South.

And who do you think would benefit from our designs for the production of energy by fusion? The republic of Guinea? Would they build their magnetohydrodynamic reactors of plasma? Of cocoa butter? Or

Kenya: Of peanut shells?

Think, for example, of a hypothetical situation. We deliver in secret to your brother Luis Jimenez Marhuenda an apparatus technologically designed to cure any leukemia case. We can construct such a device for you, although our system of therapy follows other routes. Your brother, enthusiastic over the generosity of my brothers of UMMO, broadcasts an emotional appeal over the air waves of his radio station. Thousands of the ill would flock to his urban center. How long do you think an apparatus of that kind would remain there in his hands, since it could yield so impressive a volume of information?

With deep sadness, senor Jorge, we admit our inability to help you. No longer is it a violation of ethics that prevents our interfering in your evolution (even if we did so, how could we clear other obstacles?). Would we actually have to reconvert your entire industrial complex before using our technology? Where would you obtain the tremendous amounts of capital for it? And who would allow the power to pass to other hands? Would you have to confront all the nuclear might of certain nations which, rather than lose it, would reduce the OYAGAA to nuclear ashes?

Senor, if in these few brief pages we have outlined all these difficulties, you can imagine the heap of problems we might show you if we made a complete analysis of the situation. Hence, when you beg us, "Men of outer space, comeand help us!", it breaks our hearts to remain silent...!

Men like the one who just died have the solutions. A long time ago a human of divine origin brought them to you. What have you done with them? You have transformed the sublime contributions of Jesus into a heap of superstitions and into the support of gigantic ecclesiastical structures devoted to profit. You have transformed the intelligent ideas of Marx and Mao into gigantic bureaucratized structures more interested in defending themselves from their enemies and in imitating Western models of consumption than in bringing about the sublime socialistic ideal of the theoreticians. You watch in astonishment the spectacle of a nation claiming to be fair and socialistic which violates the right to independence of an Arab neighbor while, with criminal cynicism, its antagonist, which years before had massacred the people of Vietnam, now heaves hypocritical shrieks of indignation.

You are seriously ill, friends of Earth. And we have to stand by, touched and saddened by what may be the final holocaust of Earth society.

We dare not even advise you. We fear that any word from us would be twisted, corrupted, made light of. We watch as, like heedless children singing, playing and having a good time, you wend your way to the cemetary.

Senor, please excuse again the voluminous complexity of this letter.

Now I hope you will convey our special greetings to your intelligent wife as the representative of many other YIE.

We ask that you permit us a symbolic gesture, to place our hands on your noble chest.

This special wish has a unique signification in this document, where we have with its paragraphs raised our disapproval and our repudiation more forcefully and directly, our protest stronger and more condemning (to the point of intollerance) for the continuation of aggression and humiliation that the men of Earth, almost without exception, impose upon their biological companions (human) that in great proportion accept in abnegation with intelligence and capacity to control... unconscious of stimulus or means by their oppressors.

One of the most prominent UFO researchers worldwide, a highly respected scientist in his own field of technology, who, while being of the conviction that UFOs do exist, does not accept UFO contactee cases as valid -- and especially repeater cases (like this one) where the UFOnauts returned more than once. He feels that true interactive contact with Earth humans is unacceptable for a number of reasons:

1. No other living forms would evolve to anything like us.
2. Distances are too great and travel times too long for visitors to come from even the nearest neighboring stars.
3. No other stars are known to have planetary systems.
4. No indisputable technological "proof" of such contact exists.
5. Nothing has been gained that would demonstrate such extraterrestrial contacts.

His final "clincher" in his arguments with us about the necessary invalidity of such UFO contact cases is: "If some extraterrestrial race is really here, they must, of necessity, be more technologically advanced than we, and if truely benevolent -- why don't they give us the secrets of free energy, a cure for cancer, gravity control, etc?"

My dear friend does this argument put forth by the invisible author, this claimed extraterrestrial from a planet he calls UMMO, shed any new light on your question? -Publisher

In continuation, we reproduce the following brief text of a curious letter received by Sr. Luis Jimenez Marhuenda from New York in 1981, after the launch of the "Space Shuttle" Columbia. I remembered that extraordinarily, I myself received in July of 1969 from Piedralaves (Avila), a message which congratulated the "Men of Earth" for the arrival on the surface of the moon of the spacecraft "Apollo XI".

UMMOAELEWE
Languages: English, French, Russian
UMMO Expeditionary Group in the United States of America
No. of copies: 7

Don LUIS JIMENEZ MARHUENDA, MEN OF EARTH

We have recently been respectful witnesses of a new age in your development.
The launching and later recovery of the COLUMBIA signals an importent jump in your space technology.
The Expeditionaries from Planet UMMO who still remain on Earth emotionally salute you.

(Note: The text was written without tildas and graphic accent marks as though using a typewriter for English. Some accents were later added by hand.)

The next letter, written on 27 February 1983 was delivered by hand courier on 29 March to be read at the meeting just coming to a close. It arrived during the last words of Ribera's talk and was read to the group assembled at that time.

UMMOAELEWEE
KUALA LAMPUR (sic)
Destination: SPAIN
Number C. One
1983 February 27

Addressee: AGUIERRE CEBERIO JUAN
SPAIN MADRID

SENOR AGUIRRE CEBERIO In virtue of your mediation in that micronet of brothers of yours in Madrid of Spain we send this letter to you. Express our respectful greetings to Antonio and your Y.

Through your brother Jimenez Marhuenda (Luis) residing in Alicante, Spain, we have learned of some conversations, whose pages of invitation have been sent to other brothers of yours, and whose photogram of the enterprise displayed schedules and pragmatic topics to be discussed, which we have in our posession.

Undoubtedly, if these colloquial discussions alude to our civilization we are intensely interested, and this is the reason for this text.

We lament not having brothers of ours in Spain. It being the contrary we will without doubt have in place a procedure for being present in person, of if entering is insolvably difficult for risk of identification, by using our technological means of capturing images and sound. But as we maintain a discrete control over correspondence and your telephone line, senor Aguirre Ceberio and of your brothers Farriols and Jimenez, we know of you sequentially and we are extremely pleased to receive data concerning your brother Spaniards, who we value no less with respect to your other brothers of Canada, France, Australia, Poland, and other nations of Earth, friends to our micronet of brothers coming from UMMO.

Before we continue with our text, a modest plea that your honorability will be satisfied with honest unction.

You may read these typed lines and transcribe word for word on another typing machine, the textual fragments that are signified in its matrix of vertical black lines which in their turn can be reproduced by technicques of reprographics. After that take care to destroy these original pages by incineration. They contain the rest of the text which we do not wish to see multicopied and distributed, since they could hurt the feelings of other humans of OIAAGAA.

We have given instructions to a sister of yours in Madrid, that she deliver this letter personally, coinciding with the dates of 19 and 20 of the month of March 1983 in which you will convoke those discussions.

We have preferred this route to avoid possible interception by a non-Spanish agency interested in capturing our letters.

Through a telephone book we found the name of the Director of the Colegio Mayor de San Augustin to be Manuel Alvarez, by profession a monk of the Augustinian Order [Catholic], who figures in the text of the program schedule, as co-participant praying the convocation on the 20th of March. As a Catholic monk, to him we direct the reception of this letter without risk of suspicions, and of possible filtration to other media. We wish by this method to be present on this occasion, if not in physical body then in symbolic image, in respect for you and all of your honorable brothers who accompany you in these illuminating days.

We fervently desire, Senor Aguirre, that despite this letter being addressed to you personally, it be read to the other brothers in a loud voice by your brother Farriols Calvo, so entrancing to my brothers. We ask him then, that he will perform this distinction of preferential reading.

And now accept this brief message.

Honorable humans of Earth gathered in Spain: Is it probable, as you are questioning, that they, the humans of UMMO, will not send more messages?

The answer would appear densely endowed with complex reasons of distinct class. It is obvious that the cause does not mean absence, since we remain on the cold star Earth (OIAAGAA) though an interval of time transpired in 1982 without our presence, and with some periodicity we have abandoned this planet.

In previous messages we have disguised our reasons, though necessary, relative to the risk of provoking grave prejudices in you. You are infatuated without desiring it, and demonstrate tendencies to convert into a cult, a sphere of structured data about a civilization, forgetting that you must be faithful to your own culture, to your own civilization, without injecting possibilities that could injure the historical course of your Social Network.

In your plans under consideration you should reveal a double tendency: In one demonstrate sceptical attitudes of rejection of our version, actions that merit applause for their logic in formulation, but which suggests that there is no reason on our part to continue maintaining a channel of information, that is systematically rejected and scorned as fraudulent. In the other, a segment of your brothers would adopt mental postures of respect, of veneration, surprise and sharpened compulsion, to the exhalted assimilation of our own cultural coordinates.

This will convey a contempt for the ancestral forms of Philosophy, Religion, Science and History aboriginal to Earth, a contempt for the cultural reserve accumulated in the BUAUUE BIAEI (collective spirit) over the course of many centuries by the network of intelligent homo sapiens.

Never, friends of OIIAAGAA (Earth), act like you are disturbed. Never change an accumulation of information painfully added by successive generations, by strange forms of thought, though they may be like our fruit of intellectual elaboration, generated by encephalic masses better structured.

This idea could be deceptive like --as we say in the interim-- could there be some better forms of philosophies, politics, sciences and technologies, such as ours, full of grave bias, heterogeneous and contradictory, plagued with errors, saturated on occasion by dogmatic propositions not founded on rational logic? How could there be any better forms of political ordination which accrue the most elementary ethical principles united with liberty, principles that permit hunger in the less fortunate segments of society, the accumulation of wealth in few hands, and the limitation of your brothers less endowed with intelligence? How can you keep them content with a science and a technology, directed in certain measure to the destruction of the entire ecology of your planet?

It is difficult to understand, but the solution to your ills will not come from listening to Messianic messages coming from humans of other cold stars, whom you call extraterrestrials. Your mythification of our distant civilizations is false and dangerous. Your search for a new substitute whose redeemer would be the hieratic and sublime figure of the idealized man of the cosmos, the extraterrestrial intelligence, the powerful carrier of theraputic balm, that posessor of an advanced technology and prodigiously progressed science, an unimpeachable moral ideology, to come to you and take you out of the pit in which you find yourselves submerged will not succeed.

This is the reason why we and other beings who have come to explore, pass through your skies and tread your structures of edification with scarcely a word, silently, little intending a transfer of data through any channel of information.

Although we do not know the identification of some of the civilizations that visit you, we have sufficient reason to assure you that a direct intervention in your evolutionary course is scarcely probable. Some experiment with you, with physiologico-analytical objectives, and others among them we intercept and limit, as we have explained on other occasions, to an asceptic but ample study such as of the morphological characteristics of this planet as well as its biosphere and the human social scheme in its historical development.

Don't wait, then, for help. We know that this proposition is extremely disconsoling and hard, as if it were formulated by beings without innerds and dehumanized, but that is a realistic response, adjusted to the most impèccable logic.

You are the ones who have to resolve concretely the acute problems that torture you. To imitate our model of society or that of any other exobiotic civilization, would only provoke more violent distortions, catastrophic maladjustments, more destabilizing than those that you suffer today. But you believe in truth that if we gave you to know by offering you our own guidelines based on a purified ethic based on the fraternity and solidarity among those components of the network, all the rest of your brothers of the distinct nationalities and beliefs, would blindly accept the political religious social model in effect by UMMOAELEWEE (the existing government of UMMO)?

Why a social model, or would you accept it in its entirety, or if it suffers bias accepting some conditions and omitting the rest, it could not be operative. How would you overcome religious reticence, ideological fanatacism rooted in the depths of your neural system?

How would you overcome emotionally charged resistences, associated with acquired ideologies from infancy in front of any logical argument against the same, provoked anger, psychphysical discomforts of uncontrolled hate, and a multitude of life's impassioned evocations? Would you ask a Marxist to renounce his historicomaterialistic conceptions assimilated through long terms of study? Would you solicit a Christian Evangelist to revise his concepts in turn to the historicity of those Biblical texts? Would you exhort a hindustani to modify his criteria in turn toward his reincarnationist dogma, or a Roman Catholic to restructure his ideas on the primacy of Peter or the transubstantiation? It is sure that many could do it, adapting to these new schemes, under a tremendous influx of teaching imparted under the testimony of authority of us, beings coming from another galactic point.

But to the point, you would observe the renounciation of great masses, incrusted in those old models, being resisted with all their forces.

Would you have recourse to the force necessary to impose a strange norm, difficult to assimilate, in the course of only one generation? Then you would be comporting yourselves as cruel dictators violating the most elementary principles of liberty.

And us. Neither do we believe we can violate this moral principle. Good is never imposed with force, but by way of the arms of conviction. There are no magic formulas to transform a society in its full process of evolution, to provoke a mutation that will simultaneously affect all of the elements or components of the entirety of the social network. The mutations are provoked upon chains of nucleides not only when quantic units of high energy excite the genes, or when they suffer enzymatic agression by strange agents, or the violent inclusion of other codified sequences coming from viral specimens, but following patterns of acceptance or rejection controlled by the information contained in the BUAUEE BIAEEI (collective Soul)

Expressing it with other phonemes, The evolution of the organic beings is ruled by mechanisms of oriented autocontrol. We select by didactical conclusion the example of our prehominids. These are agglutinated by a mass of information that we call BUAUUE BIAEI (translate as collective Soul). This is the sum of data obtained by the sensory organs of those beings, and processed by their respective brains.

They posess no books, however the collection of experiences lived remains not only engraved in their encephalic mass, but also is codified in this BUAUUE BIAEI.

In its turn that ingent mass of data interacts upon the evolutionary mechanism to improve the species. That information does not produce by itself a favorable mutation. It acts upon a chain of atoms of Krypton that in their turn modulate the function of polypeptide chains in the cellular nucleus of one gamete. Chains of enzymatic polypeptides slow down or facilitate according to the cases the mutogenetic agent which acts randomly by chance.

Suppose that these humanoid beings had discovered among all the members of the species, that is is useful to them to develop a determined zone of the cerebral cortex, the temporal lobe, which permits them to process information according to mathematical symbolization. Naturally this discovery is not conscious, but collective. It is the lack of such function, that which perturbs their faculties of combat against other predators.

The BUAUEE BIAEEI collective codifies this necessity and awaits the occasion. If any mutagenic factor such as one cosmological proton of high energy, which penetrates the atmosphere, reacts upon the nucleus of the gamete and proceeds directly to perturb the sequence of DNA destined to generate enzymes which in the embryogenesis direct the formation of a neural scheme for this cerebral zone, other molecular valves act upon the array to disrupt or facilitate according to the case the action of such factor.

Naturally, senor Aguirre Ceberio, that modulatory function is not always efficient, and on occasions the mutation is retrograde, subjecting the species derived from that gamete to a physiological form not apt for survival, with the consequences that you well know. But the tendency in one specific conjunction of affected gametes, is eugenetic, as to say, generator of individuals more benefitted in their organic conformation. These can accumulate better information from their cosmological frame, integrating it again in the BUAUEE BIAEII which in its turn rectifies future mutations.

This is a slow process in time seen from our human perspective. We, a people older than you, have succeeded in developing more elaborate nervous networks.

But the brain of the human of OYAGAA (Earth) is, if we except certain mutated individuals who among you pass for specimens of elevated intelligence and moral calibre, is an encephalic mass still preserving excessive areas of nervous networks of the ancient primitive savages.

These animalistic remains make the human of OYAGAA a genuinely savage animal with an intermingling of traces of rationality. We beg you not to judge this affirmation an insult to your species, but as a biological definition of a wildness which is not your fault, as a child or adolescent is not guilty of his lack of development on his route to future development as an adult.

The sum total of the suffering that you experience, is part of this biogenetic reality, and neither great discourses, nor the marvelous models --for you-- of exobiotic beings like ourselves, fit a humanity that still enjoys torturing defenseless beings, killing their brothers for reasons ideological, economic or for pure psychopathic pleasure.

If some other foreign being came from another galactic biological focus, impelled by pseudosentiments of charity, decided to force his own evolution, by operating upon human genes, upon nucleotide chains of some gamete, to optimize the whole charge of the code, to permit the gestation of one perfect human, it would provoke a biological cataclysm, of a magnitude which you could not suspect.

There does not exist for you other therapy than the actuation of the BUAUEE BIAEII. If groups of humans break with their irrational schemes, by means of rational study of their biogenetic and cosmological bases accepting firm moral standards with the suffering of other humans, forcing them to comprehend the mental schemes of their interlocutors, transferring information by means of dialogue and contrast of opinion, both scientific, ideological and technological, without grappling with a patron's preestablishments of dogmatic character, denouncing the injustice there where it is produced, exalting the figures of humans who stand out clearly for their honesty and ethical integrity, whatever may be their ideology... they are contributing to the enrichment of the Terrestrial collective consciousness associated with your social network. Only thus can you guide your own evolution toward cerebral forms increasingly intelligent, devoted to progressive improvement of the social consciousness, and its capacity to energetically confront the problems of order of distribution of resources, of political and rational planning, of confinement of ill individuals --we refer here to human subjects with nonencephalic proclivities to antisocial conduct--.

But, we reiterate the prior affirmation, this process will be long and painful.

There were shady historical periods for humanity. You are not going to provoke the end of the species of Homo sapiens sapiens, but you will suffer a regressive age with grave consequences. You must not fault only those ill protomen who rule the concert of nations, since they are products of involitionary society, but the progressive period symbolized by three honest and faithful humans, Nikita Kruschov (sic), John F. Kennedy and John XXIII, has devolved into a really sinister phase. The actual Soviet leadership persists in violating the rights of the Afgan public and prepares its prototypes of vector by satelite, with nuclear warhead, directed by a helicoidal beam of electrons upon a beam of Terrestrial magnetic flux.

The American United States leader carries forward his program of Fission-Fusion-Fission polyvectorial weapon, which permits the launch of thousands of ogives of three megatons in flight at a level of four meters above the topographical level, which would be inaccessible by means of radiolocation which already permits the detection of cruise missiles. These vectors of small size, endowed with great autonomy pick out small targets and rocky reduced structures.

The Peoples Republic of China continues developing simultaneously, nuclear arms, almost obsolete, as well as a superweapon of Plasma, though since November 1982 they have been trying to resolve a problem in refrigeration of the vapor of Arsenate of Cadmium anchored in their poverty of appropriate programming [computor] equipment. Arsenate of Cadmium is not the most appropriate, and though their specialists suspect this, they fortunately persist along this line of effort.

Meanwhile, the genocidal horrors of this age almost begin to equal the terrors provoked in the last ten of those fourty months beginning in 1938 in the Third Reich, with the massive asassaination of thousands of beings not of the Germanic race.

The Soviet Union has employed Ortho 1,2,2 Trimethopropilomethylphosphoro hydrate of flouride, on bands of guerrillas, a product of horrendous action upon the nervous system which produces terrible mortal convulsions with almost infinitesimal doses filtered into an organism not protected by sophisticated suits of equipment. This constitutes a repugnant violation of the integrity of the human being.

The United States has sent since April of Terrestrial year 1981, four thousand six hundred and forty specialists in police torture to Chile, Guatamala, Turkey, El Salvador, Haiti, Argentina and Paraguay. Some of their technical procedures embrace techniques such as the proper use of *curarizantes,* as a derivitive of the *tubocuarina* which produces the most horrible suffering in the unfortunate victims interrogated.

Before their own mothers, in Argentina and Salvador, in Guatamala and Chile, children of 6 to 8 years old are submitted to services by these Northamerican agents, extirpating their little eyes and producing terrible incisions in the abdomen even to disemboweling them of the intestinal packet.

You yourselves, still maintain your YIE (women) in a state of semi-servitude, humiliating them to inadmissable extent. Meanwhile you do not resolve these problems and while they remain, the shadowed perspective of great slaughter hangs over you.

A greeting Sr. Aguirre Ceberio Juan, to his brothers Antonio Biosca, (Ales) Juan Jose Benitez who as forcefully as Antonio Ribera, expressed their admiration for the galactic brothers, and in the impossibilith of enumerating all your other brothers, we direct toward them our desires for peace and friendship.

UORII Nineteen
Daughter of OBAA Seventeen

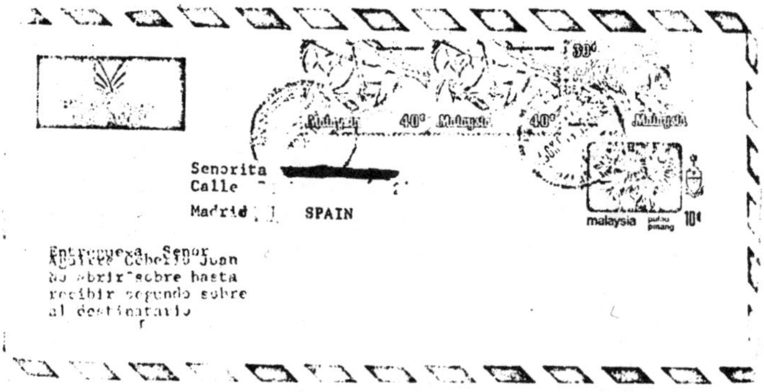

THE LETTER OF THE INTERMEDIARY

In continuation we reproduce the letter of the unknown receiver of the letter from UMMO addressed to Rafael Farriols, via doctor Juan Aguirre Ceberio, and coming from Zimbabwe. The Ummites continued, faithful to their tortuous strategy, by delivering their letters to their destinations through third persons, complicating things thus unnecessarily. This Machiavellian mentality, appropriate for a novel of Eugenio Sue of a bad spu tale, was incomprehensible to us, beginning with the gentleman who received this letter, he who asks, and with reason, why could they not have sent it directly to its destination?

In his letter, this anonymous intermediary explains how he came into contact indirectly with the Ummites through his niece. His untidy style recalls much of the famous Typist, but it was not he, if we give credit to the story. I say that he is not the Typist because of the notable lack of knowledge that he demonstrated of the whole UMMO affair, and for identifying its authors as a group of terrestrial doctors who did not want to collide with the believed interests of their orthodox colleagues. On the other hand, the Typist was found to be convinced that the Ummites were extraterrestrials. Another example of the lack of knowledge of this senor is his mention of my book EL MISTERIO DEL UMMO..., the reading of which was recommended to doctor Aguirre! After that, there was notably the limit of his knowledge of the case when he wrote his frank letter.

The continuation is reproduced, withour leaving out one comma, nor correcting the style, as "an appetizer" to the report sent to to Rafael Farriols... or what remains of it through the mutilations to which it was submitted by the frightened intermediary.

[Note- The letter to Farriols, following that of the intermediary, was received by him on 18 March 1984 with eleven pages missing. we reproduce the letter of the intermediary first. As it is virtually impossible to translate word for word and comma for comma, This English language version does not remain completely unchanged, as was the intent with the Spanish letter. We regret this minor fault. -Publisher]

Sr. D. Juan Aguirre Ceberio
Calle Lope de Haro 15 4º
MADRID 29

MARCH 1984

My Dear Sir:

The truth is that I do not have the pleasure of knowing you personally and if I take the risk of writing you in the name of my wife and myself, it is because of what I have to say:

Enclosed, I send you an envelope with part of a letter which goes to your name, being also accompanied by a letter addressed to my wife. You will see that I have permitted her to cut off with a knife, the address, and also I have permitted, perhaps badly, but under my responsibility, her to cut off part of your letter, and that has an explanation which I will tell you last.

She has just received the letter from Zimbabwe, which is as you know an African country. It came in my name though one of the letters inside was named to my wife as I said.

This letter is like others that we have received from some gentlemen who, since we met them, identify themselves as extraterrestrials from a Planet they call UMMO, and I will tell you briefly the history of them that we know.

My niece: Sister of my wife, resided for many years, before my later marriage, outside Spain. She is very cultured, a teacher attached to a University. In September 1980 she fell ill, diagnosed by the doctors as a malignant tumor of the stomach. As the doctors recommended an immediate surgical operation, my wife did not agree, and she and my niece decided to travel to the United States where he whom they sought was in Los Angeles, a famous doctor who also diagnosed the same illness and likewise recommended rapid intervention. You can figure the state of anxiety they were in. My wife had already prepared for the trip, though I at that could not accompany her because of my work.

My niece had in those times before her illness, published in a magazine, an article on the origins of Life some thousands of millions of years ago, and one day she was called by telephone. It was a reader of that magazine who spoke with a twangy nasal voice as he made observations on the published text. My niece said she was surprised by the profound knowledge of this gentleman and wanted him to speak to him in his residence. This happened some months before her illness. At least before the doctors told her what she had. This gentleman refused but promised to write her. Much was the surprise of my niece upon receiving the first letter. She could see that it was a very extensive document on the scientific theme relating to the same article, but that was the least singular. What attracted her attention most was *that he identified the signature as that of a traveller from another Planet.*

Naturally that was a joke or it had to do with someone demented, which did not correspond with the seriousness of the study that he had sent or with the intelligence he had demonstrated when talking on the telephone.

I don't want to tire you with the rest of the story, but if I tell you that when she had spoken several times with him (My niece always avoids referring in her telephone conversations to the term UMMO) overcoming the sad visit to the doctor and the radiographic proofs of the tumor, one night when she was feeling remorse, this man called again. Crying she told him all.

And what was not her surprise when he told her that in reality she had the power to cure herself. According to my niece in no moment did she ask it, since she had considered him a biologist, but not a medical doctor. Not only was he telling her what had been said by the doctors, and belittling what they had done, but instead this gentleman refused with excuses, saying on the one hand that he had such curative powers scientifically, but that he probably could not use them for not knowing the kind of other risks.

All remained this way. My nieces went to the United States, and returned disposed to accept the diagnosis and return to their country.

I believe it was the same day, or the following: It was at least when my niece was getting the heart tests for the operation, when this same gentleman called and said: Make new tests. Do not intervene since you are cured. Certainly two or three days before, she had been experimenting and had stopped the pains, but she attributed this to the sedatives.

She went to the clinic snd the doctors could not believe it, but all the tests were now negative. They had been months watching to see if there had been metastasis and until today...

You will understand that we are very grateful to those gentlemen, be whomever they be. My sister asked that they write to my wife and thus we have been receiving letters from them. I suffered from a duodenal ulcer, and on one occasion when they had called us from Albacete, she asked them if they couldn't do something for me. They also gave excuses, but nevertheless I did not have the luck of my niece. It is true that it seems that I am temporarily better but the radiogrphs continue registering the ulcers and the pains though not sharp continue. In any case, what they did for my niece will never be forgotten. They asked of us a great confidence, and that we do not publish the letters, and we have been faithful to their petition.

About a year ago we saw in a bookstore a volume that spoke of the UMMO affair. The book was authored by Antonio Ribera, which we advise you to read (Although later we asked for another copy and were told that it was sold out). They have it in the Libraria Espasa Calpe de la Gran Via.

Since then it is a great enigma. They have called us a number of times when they are here in Spain. One time they said to my wife that they called from Albacete but naturally it is impossible to prove it. More than one time we have tried to call Sr. Ribera, the author of this book. Also, in the previous year there was a reunion in a Collegio Mayor and my wife received a letter from the organizers of that reunion which was going to treat of this affair.

Very well now: our point of view is that it is absurd to believe that they are extraterrestrials. They should have the etiquette not to lie but to protect themselves with camouflage. Perhaps it is a group of doctors who have discovered new procedures for cures and that the Official Medicine which has such interests persecutes them. It is a hypothesis but if you think about it it is not so absurd. For they would have to look secretly for patients for experiments. But there is something that worries us. They are very politicized. We have noted in them an immense hate toward the United States although they also speak badly of Russia but not approaching the antipathy they feel for the other country. And this worries us since their letters are explosive at times and we have burned some since they contained information that if true could provoke for us the displeasure of being found by the Police.

This is why I said at the beginning of the letter that my wife and I doubted whether we should send you this letter of tear up a part of it. On the one hand we are very grateful to them and do not want to betray them by denouncification. On the other, you understand that there are very strange things. Why don't they write to you directly since they have your address perfectly? Don't they understand that they compromise my wife and I? If what they say in the letter about the government of the United States, and that of the Korean Airliner, and of Lebanon, and the trip of the President of the Government D. Felipe Gonzalez to the United States is false, then nothing would help you of that which under our responsibility we have cut from this letter. If all that history of the Weapons and the intrigues of the United States is true, we well understand that it is compromising for us to act as intermediaries. Since the purpose and the end WE DO NOT KNOW, nor do we know the real objectives pursued by these gentlemen.

It is true that at the end of all, in case of an investigation by the authorities, we can finally prove our innocence.

But meanwhile, we can get out of grave prejudices. For this we meditated well on whether we should send you this letter as they asked us or not. If we did not do it we would be appropriating a letter that is not ours but addressed to you.

If we send you all of it, I don't know what penal responsibility we could incur in case of an investigation by the authorities. You understand our situation D. Juan.

Well it is clear that it is a very irregular situation. They have a very easy solution: Send this letter from Zimbabwe to your name. Why such mystery and such instructions that it is my family who must be the messengers? To compromise us in something very grave?

Our gratitude to those gentlemen who moreover have done a great good for my family, and that we are disposed to proclaim very loudly. It must have a limit, and that limit we believe has been reached, asking of us something whose consequences is hidden from us.

We will do it, if only to guard the discretion that they have asked of us, but if you speak with them, we ask you in the name of my wife and myself, that you respectfully make them understand that we could not comply fully with their instructions. It has been some time since we have been in telephone communication with them. An explainable thing if they are in Africa, but on the other hand they say in the letter to you that they have intervened by telephone with another senor. Isn't this a rare contradiction? How can they intervene from Africa in a conversation in Spain...?

I don't want to tire you since my letter already is excessive in length. I feel in truth that my letter should be an anonymous one. It is not my custom to write anonymously, nor do I consider it courteous not to sign. It is the circumstances that impede my doing this... If it were not thus, believe me, D. Juan, that my wife and I would take much pleasure in making you a visit, to show you the letters from these gentlemen which we preserve, and to discuss this enigma.

Don't forget to look for the book on UMMO that I recommended. Perhaps if you can not find it, you could look in a Public Library. It is an elemental key to disentangle this enigma. The author must know many more things.

Notice also the roundabout way that these gentlemen take. They ask that we give the letter to you however it is addressed to Don Rafael Farriols, who we suppose is a friend of yours. (His name does not appear in the telephone directory but your name yes.)

Within the envelope they asked us on another page that we bring it by hand to you... Does that not seem too mysterious and too turned around to deliver a letter as important as this is?

I want to take this occasion to salute you very affectionately in the name of this couple.

N.N.

UMOAELEWE
Number of Copies: 1

My Esteemed Sr. Rafael Farriols Calvo:

Permit us first to address our cordial and respectful greetings to your wife Carmela, whose image we keep before us. Our words are going to be also addressed to her in a gesture of symbolic homage to the Spanish YIE.

Permit us also to extend our greeting to Hiltrud Nordlin Franz, whose reestablishment of his old symptomology gives us sincere satisfaction. We believe that his sister has earned this remission of symptoms. And we believe, Senor: In truth, our sadness will not produce an extensive theraputic aid to other brothers of yours who seek the services of the infirmary.

We would like to prolong this salutory relation with all your loving brothers, except that is our because we fear making this letter excessively dry. My brothers remember with special affection Sr. Jimenez Maruhenda, , Sr. Juan Jose Benitez, Sr. Aguirre Ceberio, Sr. Dominguez Martos, Sr. Garrido Buendia, Sr. Manuel Osuna, Sr. Rojas Marcos, Sr. Villagrasa Novoa, Sr. Antonio Moya Carpa, Sr. Barrenechea, Sr. Lopez Guerrero, Sr. Alberto Borras, Da. Camilo Ochoa, Da. Carmen Barrenechea, Da. M. Teresa de Muela, Da. Videl Dominguez, Da. Leonardo Marino and so many others whose relation would make this text interminable.

We wish not to abuse your friendship if we bring to Josep Olives C/ Clavell, 44 3º MONTCADA Y REIXACH (Barcelona), Spain, our greetings as well as to Carlos Juan Gonzalez La Palma, 23, Cartagena, Spain.

In a conversation through the telephonic channel of Sr. Jimenez Maruhenda he informed us that he desired to maintain an interpersonal discussion in the month of March in the capital of Spain. My brothers travel on occasion to your beautiful country, though we feel that we will not be in these times situated near the place of meeting, to whose gentle director, Sr. Manuel Alvarez we send our cordial salute. But we hope this letter will arrive "soon" as a salutation to your gathered brothers, through whom we desire to pass this text to its destined Sr. Rafael Farriols.

TEXT OF THE MESSAGE

Gentlemen of Earth: So much has been discussed about our civilization that we fear being excessively repititive if we continue in our argumentation with you, and for your part you lose speculative dialogues on the enigma of our presence. It is already transparently clear that our testimony has not aroused special frustrations nor disturbances in the interaction of the society of Earth. At first, when my brothers still did not know the psychosocial structure of the Homo OYAGAA (planet Earth), they were afraid, with certain reason, to awaken in you uneasiness and anxieties about the presence of an alien expedition [on your planet]. This initial fear has been extinguished. Outside of some Police organizations and certain services of information of some nations, the echos of our presence has raised little of doubt, frivolous speculation, sensational news commentary, suspicions and disrespectful commentary.

Thus it should be and that shows mental maturity, since you must never admit as real, a constellation of events that are not supported with convincing proofs. Our strategy of neutralizing certain proofs with refutory arguments and "counterproofs artificially elaborated" bears fruit at later time.

Perhaps some of your overenthusiastic brothers in our favor lament this. Understand, Sr. Farriols Calvo, that we can do nothing else, and that your particular field of emotional interest could not be in concord with our particular criteria about the problem.

We believe that an exultant action of our presentation before the Social Scheme of Earth, would provoke serious disturbances. In the depths of the mind of some of you, there must throb a thankfulness for the knowledge received and some cures of pathological nature accomplished as a compelling gesture toward some friends of another Cold Star. But you must not transcend much beyond those last circumscribed sentiments to very determined persons. It is not good to excessively display your state of affection. The rest of your brothers of Earth are not going to understand absolutely since the version about the presence of a group of an extraplanetary group is so exotic and incredible that they will not be able to accept other balanced intelligences. For this we have decided to break that postal continuity of our early relations. You have become too enthusiastic. We have seen you convert those early commentaries into bibliographic texts. We have already told you that in case this happened, we would see ourselves forced to restrict these contacts. Do not consider this a threat. It is only a precautionary measure, since the excessive diffusion of our texts, automatically generates certain perturbations in the modes of conduct of Terrestrial man. We do not reproach you, Sr. Farriols, but you have carried by your enthusiasm, divulged perhaps too generously these texts. That is the reason for which we have not answered more clearly your solitary attempts to put yourself in contact with us in your residence. At times our "captors" [receivers] have recorded your words, and pardon us if for the good of all your brothers we respond with silence.

We could extend ourselves revealing to you various aspects captured by us in turn on the sociopolitical and economic situations of the conglomerate of nations that make up the Earth. We do not want to excessively embitter you.

These Periods of reflection that you are going to have, the data processed by us are highly overshadowed. In this moment the United States of Northamerica, counts with a disuasive power of logistical character superior to that of the Soviet Union. The services of information of the latter know the technological advances of that great nation and wait terrorized by the arrogant escalation of their adversary.

The United States already counts on their first Plasma Weapon, where the technology of the People's Republic of China lacked certain means and could not fully develop it.

Actually, the DSP-32 Project of the USA permits them to convert to ionized Helium a volume of 10 m^3 of the atmosphere through an interval of 800 seconds, to where it reaches levels of 14 millions of degrees, at levels above the ground of less than 3 kilometers!

The risk of provoking ecological disturbances of planetary level with the probable use of these weapons, which will put an end to the life of animal and vegetable species over a great range, is still more grave than the devastation produced by thermonuclear weapons. What makes the situation more dramatic is that the United States is disposed at any price to terminate the Socialist Model of the URSS. The conversations carried on in the crisis Cabinet of the USA as recorded by ourselves, reveals that those directors of that country are disposed to generate points of conflict that will force their opponent to intervene and thus give them an excuse for elimination of all the infrastructure.

[NOTE- These revelations would be a violation of National Security of the highest order, dangerously affecting this and every other country in this world, if this was supported by positive evidence collected by trained experts with a high degree of reliability.

But, as this comes from a "mythical contact", from "extraterrestrials" (who science says doesn't exist) operating from a UFO (which our Government says doesn't exist), how can this revelation be a threat to any sensible person who already knows that all this nonsense is only for simple minds and has no basis in reality... OR DOES IT!!! -Publisher]

C.I.M.

Centro de Investigaciones Metapsíquicas

ALICANTE

Jornadas Conmemorativas

y de Estudio

del Planeta UMMO

Días, 28-29-30 Marzo 1.980
Hotel BABIECA - Playa San Juan
ALICANTE

Facsímil de la portada del Programa de las Jornadas de Alicante.

Facsimile of the cover of the program for the conference on the UMMO contacts in Spain. This meeting of the Madrid Group was monitored very closely by the Ummites themselves, with very sophisticated equipment.

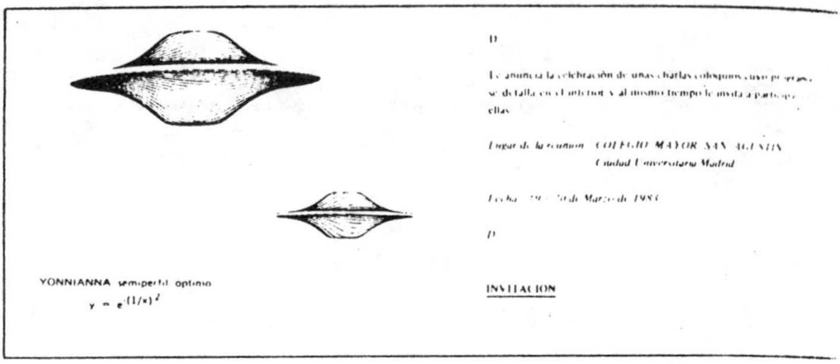

Invitation to attend the Conference at the Colegio Mayor in Madrid in March 1983. This was decorated with a sketch made by a computor, using the Ummite formula for the YONNIANNA or optimum form for their own spacecraft. (Prepared by Juan Dominguez Montes)

D. ______________________________

Le anuncia la celebración de unas charlas coloquios cuyo programa se detalla en el interior y al mismo tiempo le invita a participar en ellas.

Lugar de la reunión: *COLEGIO MAYOR SAN AGUSTIN*
Ciudad Universitaria Madrid

Fecha: 19 y 20 de Marzo de 1983

D. ______________________________

____

<u>INVITACION</u>

Various envelopes of the more recent messages sent through the world mails by the extraterrestrial humans from Planet UMMO. Note the close similarity of the caligraphy on each envelope. It has been said that this looks like a writing made by someone who "copied" the characters from an Earth typewriter, characteristic of typists. All of these envelopes have a shadowy "aire of relationship", even without which one might say they could be addressed in the same hand.

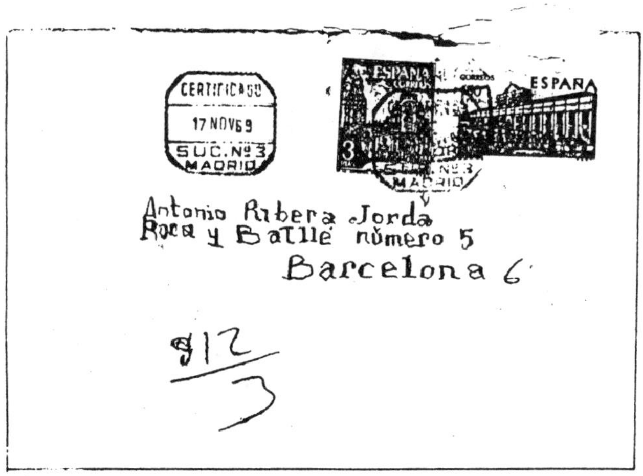

UN "CASO PERFETTO" CHE NON E' PERFETTO

a cura di Claudio BERNACCHIA e Roberto D'AMICO

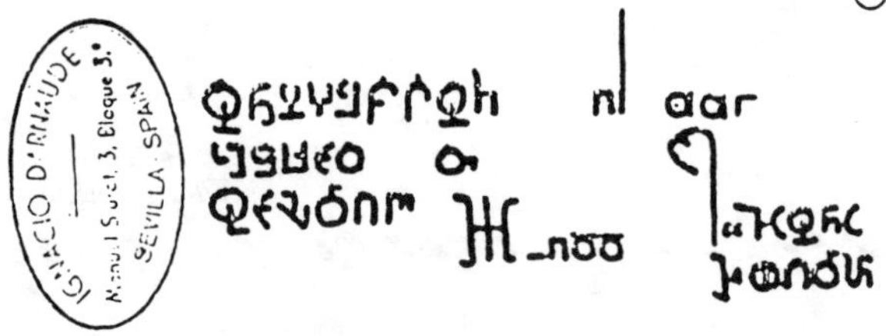

Nous vous présentons nos respectueux hommages

Revista "CLYPEUS", nº 33, Aprile 1.971.
(P.O.Box 604. 10100 Torino. Italia).

One can see on many of these documents the presence of Ummite symbols. At times the envelopes were typed, although they are less. On other times, as in a letter sent to Luis Jimenez Marhuenda, they alternated the laborious and infantil "Ummite" caligraphy with directions written with a typewriter. This seems to indicate that some "Terrestrial" colaborated in those mailings (perhaps the mysterious typist), but... who addressed the letters in Kuala Lumpur and Zimbabwe? Was the typist there "on vacation"? Mysterious. Remember that, as "they" affirm, the excessive sensibility that they have in the tips of their fingers, impedes their using a typewriter, among other things, which obliges them to "dictate" their letters.

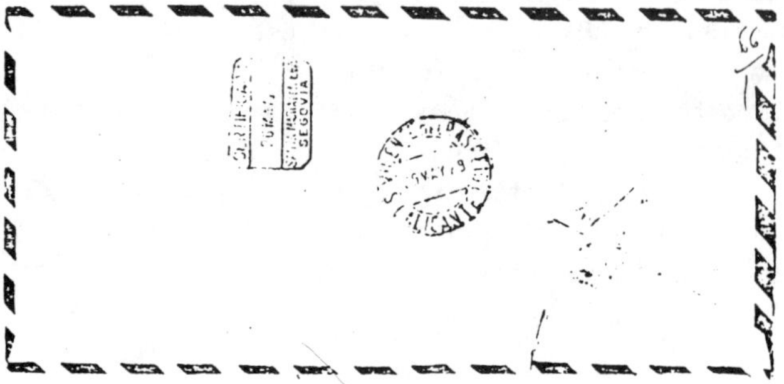

Reverso del sobre que contenía una carta recibida por Luis Jiménez Marhuenda, con matasellos de Santa María de Nieva (Segovia). Fue la primera que le llegó de los ummitas (mayo de 1979).

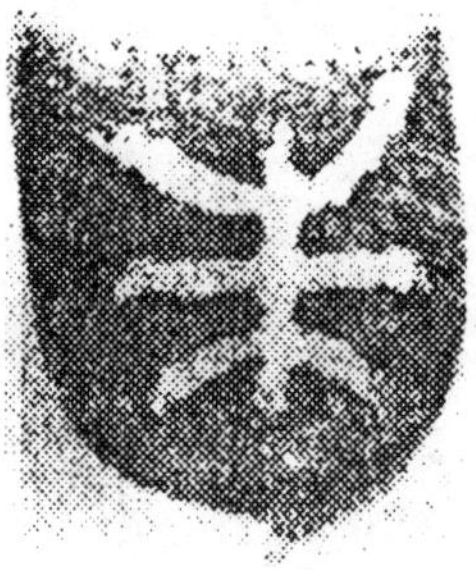

Top- Reverse of the envelope containing the first letter received from the Ummites by Luis Jimenez Marhuenda, with postal cancellation at Santa Maria de Nieve (Segovia), May 1979.
Bottom- The seal used on all of the pages of the reports from UMMO. Without doubt this is impressed by means of a fingertip of rubber used on the forefinger. (By the typist? The sensitive Adele M. was able to reproduce this symbol by stimulogenesis in one of her fingers.) (see SEQUESTRADOS POR EXTRATERRESTRES by Antonio Ribera, page 223.)

STOP PRESS

As this volume was in final editing before going to press, a letter was received from Antonio Ribera in Barcelona inclosing the very last communication purportedly from the expeditionaries from Planet UMMO. This is the most recent communication to this date (February 1986) that we know of, and the last one received by the Spanish Group. As is the custom for Sr. Ribera, he does not take these things lightly and is always wary of fraud, so he has developed a technique of his own for testing for authenticity before he will accept such a communication as genuine. The style of the writing and the phraseology used by different of the Ummites has recognizable characteristics. The color of the finger seal impressed on each page has significance also, and after careful analysis he is leaning toward the conviction that this is more likely genuine. The cover letter was postmarked 4 January 86, Alicante, (Spain), but let us quote in part from his cover to us:

"Some two weeks ago I received a letter supposedly sent by "them". Herewith I am inclosing you a copy. It came from Alicante (of all places), and both the style and the words they use fit with the semantic use of words they make. However, the colour of the digital seal was "BLUE", not "PURPLE" (violet) as it is for the "Spanish Network". Moreover, the ink was a bit spread, on the paper. If what they say is true, this could mean that they are contemplating leaving this world for good. If you want to use this letter for the second volume, please do, but expounding my reserves too. I did a bit of research on the Ummite names which appear in this letter: you'll find it enclosed herewith too."

[EIEEVEE 7, one of the Ummite men shot and killed at the Vienna International airport, was the author of a three page communication on the Ummite Central Base in Denmark, and the development in the People's Republic of China of a terrible plasma weapon, etc., which was received in Madrid on 5 June 1979 by Dr. Juan Aguirre Ceberio. The author of that letter at that time advised that he was there with two other Ummite companions. He was subject to an Ummite woman, NOOA 452, Daughter of IDUUDA 449. -Publisher]

UMMOELEWEE
Language Spanish
Number of copies: 1

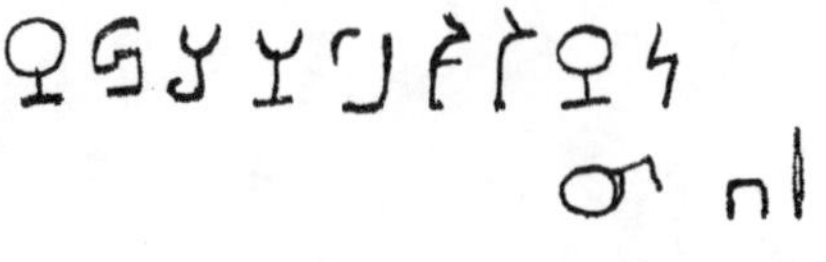

Senor Antonio Ribera Jord'a:

Allow us to interfere once more in your peaceful life, after this long period of time, two terrestrial years, disturbing you with an ungrateful and unfortunate letter.

Gentlemen of Earth: We want to express to you personally our sadness for the disastrous and inhumane event that happened in the city of Vienna in Austria, (between the hills of Leitha and Wiener Wald, as we observed in the terrestrial year 1985, in February an OAWOLEAIDA [change of dimension of our spacecraft]), in which they saw, involuntarily affected, two of our brothers. It is not necessary to remind you of the number of victims who have succumbed before such pitiless violence in the Airport of the cited terrestrial city.

My brothers EIEEVEE 7 son of ERAE 5, and OBAA 16 son of IDUUOA 46, as they were going to Tel Aviv, when at the Airport that is named Schwechat of Vienna, were fired upon with bullets resulting in serious injury to their bodies. Pardon us sir if we do not detail the event, but the profound pain over such an unimaginable happening makes the memory cloud my state of consciousness awareness which is necessary to write this letter. Neither is it necessary to plant in you the profound conflict that would be developed if our UMMOALEWEE made contact with some terrestrial organization (though it has been established in sporadic form in some countries such as France, Australia and with some important scientists for their humane qualities in the United States of America), to ask for explanations would be the same as to ask a child of young age to give up playing to dedicate himself to politics or to act within a high business position.

Faithful sirs, we profoundly feel that the renewal of our contacts, such as the written and telephonic communications, would be seriously disturbed, and it is very probable that a definite rupture of all relations with Earth will be made good. Unfortunately, one Government of Earth already posesses two bodies of our brothers, accidentally killed in a centrol European country, and we do not want to add in accidental manner, to any human laboratory of Earth.

Thanks to our technology, we were able to recover (the bodies of) our brothers killed in Vienna, by passing as doctors and simply driving an ambulance to where our brothers were in the departure area to Tel Aviv, this having been seen visually from a distance. We have a film record that reveals the authenticity of the action, and will clearly show the true identification of two governments of the Middle East are the aggressors there, to such as your recovery group. Senor, the thought that has been induced to kill, does not proclaim liberty, but their own destruction, and returns you to a primitive world of blood which can only be pacified by a superior authority.

We pray, dear friend, you will excuse this feeling of hatred toward your species, and more still since you have just celebrated the birth of WOA in man, and I express my desire for happiness in your home, and as well for those of our dear friends there, for us.

Our residences in Spain have been located in population centers near the vicinities of Alicante, Valencia, Murcia, and Albacete. it is not strange that the (postal) cancellation is registered in the city of Alicante, since in these moments we have three brothers of UMMO coming from Belgium and Denmark, there.

The end of our residence has been provoked by a telephone conversation between Luis Jimemez Marhuenda and a person not identified by us, but we would increasingly like to know his identity. Had it not been for the incident, Luis Jimenez of Alicante already would have had knowledge of our stay in his beautiful city. Nor is it safe that we wait longer to reveal the feeling of the short conversation of Senor Luis Jimenez Marhuenda with the young speaker. The phonetics of the mentioned gentleman is like that of our friends of Earth which is well known by our brothers of UMMO. Analyzing the amplitude of the wave emitted by the pronounciation of the words, we have come to the conclusion that the unknown speaker is a young woman (25 to 30 years of age), residing in the locality of Alicante. We are profoundly interested in her distress over our existence and it seems she knows the way to decypher the message in code that treats of the location of our atomic refuge in the central Iberian region of the Spanish system. You, faithful sir, posess a report in code of the existence of the cited refuge. We lovingly ask that you get in touch with your brother Luiz Jimenez Marhuenda of Alicante with the objective that by means of the telephone he can locate our unknown youth. likewise, we ask you to send a photocopy of the contents of this letter-message.

During our absence from Spain, we have been able to verify the great intellectual and neurocortical development experienced by the infant and juvenile population in the last two decades. We have been able to verify through our XANMOO AYUBAA (network of computers) that the actual generations have developed on a scale compared to before of three to one; certain evolutionary mechanisms inspire a perfection of the somatic structure inpeding a degeneration or regression of the living structure or body. This evolutionary mechanism is responsible for a series of possible mutations discovered in children born between 1960-1980 of the symbol P7OƱΓ (P). We must congratulate the terrestrial genetic sciences for their great advances in the field of mutations and of the magnetic attraction exercised by molecules.

But over your lives there hangs a grave danger due to your constant modification of the atmospheric conditions that must follow their normal course. For example, the detonation of a Hydrogen bomb to test for belligerant attack, is capable of modification on the order of $(1/26)^3$ the normal lapse of time for normal development which must originate in that same place a tempest or a period of drought in a region typically humid.

Please, be conscious once more of the grave problems that injure each and every one of you. We ask, though only symbolically, that you think of your children, of those boys and girls who some day will have to solve your own problems, and those of your fathers.

This expedition from the cold star UMMO salutes you and in a symbol of respect we place your hand on our breast.

Give our respectful greetings to your intelligent YIEE (wife).

UROII 15 Daughter of AXOO 13
subj. to OEOE 115 Son of OEOE 114
subject to UMMOELEWEE

(Finger seal)

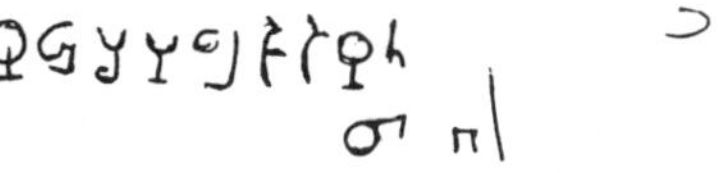

UMMOELEWEE
Idioma español
Numero de copias: 1

Señor Antonio Ribera Jord'a:
Toléreme nos immiscuyamos de nuevo en su pacífica vida, tras este largo periodo de toempo, dos años terrestres, perturbándole con una ingrata y desafortunada misiva.
Señor de Tierra: queremos expresarle a usted personalmente nuestra tristeza por el desastroso e inhumano suceso acontecido en la población de Viena del país Austria,(entre las colinas de Leitha y Wiener Wald, se verificó en el año terrestre 1985 del mes de febrero una OAWOLEAIDA),en el que se vieron afectados involuntariamente dos hermanos nuestros.No es preciso recordarle a usted el número de víctimas que sucumbieron ante tan despiadado atentado en el Areopuerto de la citada población terrestre. Mis hermanos EIEEVEE 7 hijo de ERAE 5, y OBAA 16 hijo de IDUUOA 46 se dirigian hacia Tel Aviv, cuando en el Aeropuerto de nombre Schwechat de Vienar resultaron sus cuerpos seriamente heridos por metralla.Señor disculpenos si no precisamos con detalle el suceso, pero el profundo dolor ante tan inimaginable acontecimiento, hace que el recuerdo nuble mi etado anímico consciente que es necesario para redactar esta carta.
Tampoco es necesario plantearle el profundo conflicto que se hubiese desarrollado si nuestro UMMOALEWEE tuviese contacto con algún organismo terrestre (aunque se ha establecido de forma esporádica en algunos paises como Francia, Australia, y con algunos científicos importantes por ssus cualidades humanas de los Estados Unidos de America), pedir explicaciones seria lo mismo que pedir a un niño de corta edad que dejara de jugar para dedicarse a la polític o a ejercer dentro de un alto cargo empresarial.
Bondadoso señor sentimos profundamente que la ~~reduneei~~ renudación de nuestros contactos tanto escritos como telefónicos se vean seriamente perturbados y es muy probable que la ruptura definitiva de toda relación con Tierra se haga efectiva.Desgraciadamente un Gobierno del planeta Tierra yá pose dos cadáveres de hermanos nuestros, muertos accidentalmente en un país centroeuropeo y no quisieramos engrosar de forma accidental ningún laboratorio humano terrestre.
Gracias a nuestra tecnologia pudimos recuperar a nuestros hermanos accidentados en Viena pasando por médicos y conduciendo una simple ambulancia, ya que la partida de nuestros hermanos hacia Tel Aviv, estaba siendo registrada visualmente a distancia.Poseemos un documento filmado que revelaria la autenticidad del atentado y aclararia a dos gobiernos de Oriente Medio la verdadera identidad de los agresores así como su grupo de reinvidicaciones .Señor toda mente que se ve inducida a matar, no proclama libertad sino su propia destrucción.Vuelven ustedes a un primitivo mundo de sangre que solo podrá pacificar una autoridad superior.
Ruego, querido amigo, sepa disculpar este sentimiento de recelo hacia su especie y más aún cuando ustedes han celebrado la natividad de Woa en hombre, hago expreso mi deseo de felicidad en su hogar, así como en el de las personas queridas por nosotros.
Nuestra estancia en España se ubica en una población cercana a las provincias de Alicante, Valencia,Murcia y Albacete.No es de extrañar que el matasellos esté registrado en la ciudad costera de Alicante, ya que en estos momentos nos encontramos tres hermanos de UMMO procedentes de Bélgica y Dinamarca.

A reduced copy of the actual letter. Note the finger seal.

El fín de nuestra estancia ha sido provocada por una conversación telefonica que mantuvo Luís Jimenez Marhuc nda con una persona no identificada por nosotros, pero que deseariamos con creces pudiera ser conocida su identidad. De no ser por el incidente, Luis Jimenez de Alicante yá habria tenido conocimiento de nuestra estancia en su bella ciudad.Tampoco es seguro que esperemos más tiempo para desvelar el sentido de la corta conversación del Señor Luis Jimenez Marhuenda con su joven interlocutor.La fonación del citado señor al igual que la de nuestros amigos de tierra es sobradamente concida por nuestros hermanos de U.MC.Analizando la amplitud de onda emitida por la gesticulación de las palabras hemos llegado a la conclusión de que el desconocido interlocutor es una persona joven (20-25 años terrestres de edad) y de sexo YIEE, residente en la localidad de Alicante.Nos ha interesado profundamente sú inquietud hacia nuestra existencia y parece ser que conoce la forma de descifrrar el mensaje en clave que trata sobre la ubi cación de nuestro refugio atómico en la región centro ibérica del sistema Español.Usted, bondadoso señor, posee un informe en clave de la existencia del citado refugio. Ruego encarecidamente se ponga en contacto con su hermano Luis Jimenez Marhuenda de Alicante con el fín de que éste mediante teléfono pueda localizar a nuestra joven desconocida.Asimismo ruego mande una fotocopia con el contenido de esta carta-informe.
Durante nuestra ausencia del paía España, heños podido comprobar el gran desarrollo intelecto y neurocortical que ha experimentado la población infantil y juvenil en la últimas dos décadas.Hemos podido comprobar a través de nuestras XANMOO AYUBAA (red de computadoras) que las generaciones actuales se han desarrollado en escala a las anteriores de trres por uno;ciertos mecanismos evolutivos que originan un perfeccionamiento de la estructura somática impidiendo una degeneracián o regresión de la estructura viva o cuerpo. Este mecanismo evolutivo responde a una serie de mutaciones posibles descubiertas en ñiños nacido entre 1960-1980 de símbolo P1ʊʊƦ (P) .Hemos de felicitar a la ciencia genética terrestre por su gran avance en el campo de las mutaciones y a las atracciones magnéticas ejercidas por moléculas.
Pero sobre sus vidas se cierne un grave peligro debido a que ustedes modifican constantemente las condiciones atmosféricas que tienen que seguir su curso normal.Por ejemplo en una prueba de ataque bélico al hacer detonar una bomba H o de Hidrógeno son capaces de modificar en orden de $(1/26)^3$ el transcurso normal por el cula se debe de originar en ese mismo lugar una tormenta o el periodo de sequia en una región típicamente húmeda.
Por favor sean conscientes una vez mas del grave problema que lesaqtañe a todos uy a cada uno de ustedes.Les pedimos aunque solo sea simbolicamente que piensen en sus hijos,en esos hombres y mujeres que algún día tendran que solucionar sus propios problemas, los problemas de sus propios padres.
Esta expedición procedente del astro frio UMMO os saluda y en símbolo de respeto os posa su mano sobre vuestro pecho.
Dele nuestros mas respetuosos saludos a su inteleigente YIEE.

UROII 15 Hija de AXOO 13
sumisa a OEOE 115 Hijo de OEOE 114
sumiso a UMMOELEWEE

The authenticating finger seal was applied to every page of letters. The letters were dictated to a public stenographer who typed them up and hand addressed and mailed them to the addressees indicated.

This is the cover envelope of the latest UMMO letter from Alicante, Spain, postmarked 4 January 1986, and mailed to Antonio Ribera of the Spanish Group. Note the similarity in addressing to all of the other letters received from UMMO communicators. The hand is identical.

EPILOGUE

THE INCREDIBLE TRUTH

Who are the UMMO? Utopian moralizers of the "Mundo Feliz" ("Happy World")? Do they reflect a society already existing in some place? Fantasy? Fiction? Reality?

Who controls the threads of this trauma, that is over twenty years old? (Thirty five, if we accept the date that "they" have given us for their "arrival" on Earth.) What is behind all of this?

Who reproduces all their reports? Only one man who has encyclopedic knowledge, or a team of specialists in the most diverse disciplines?

Is it a subtle maneuver of "psychological preparation" for an eventual contact with authentic extraterrestrials? But, if that is it, who has launched it? The CIA? The Rand Corporation of Santa Monica, California? The Soviets? The society of Jesus? The Masons? The GNOSIS of Princeton? The Club of Rome? The Pope?

Questions for now without answers... including that of, are those authors of all of this - truely extraterrestrials, as they postulate? But yes, one thing is certain: We can exclude the "joke" hypothesis. Nevertheless, a profound intuition —the intuition rarely fails me— which leads me to believe that yes, they are who they say they are. As to say: That UMMO has an extraterrestrial origin. Not only because they present us a Science, a conception of the Universe (the WAAM as they say with their term), which is apart from the actual physical and cosmogenical model, but because there are facts of practical order which confirm their clandestine presence among us. For example, I know that the CIA and INTERPOL look for them (I have been contacted confidentially by a chief, German, of the latter international organization cited). Such that the INTERPOL as well as the CIA (and possibly the KGB, the British MI-5 and the DST: Division pour la Surveillance du Territoire of France), posess enormous dossiers on some tall men, of Nordic type, who travel with passports from Northern Europe, and who have an apparatus inserted in the glottis, which helps them in phonetics (this is a little more or less what I was told by a high functionary of INTERPOL.).

Admitting this —if we can admit it— the great enigma consists now in knowing if, when the opportune moment came, they would intervene in this crazy world to delay the final hecatomb. We know that, if they wanted, they could do this. They have means more than sufficient. But their cold spirit, distant (they have abandoned Earth two or three times when their computers told them that we had reached the critical threshold of a nuclear war.), perhaps will bring us to contemplate our suicidal selfdestruction of crossed arms. Nevertheless, there remains a dim spark of hope. I know that on a number of occasions —I can count them on the fingers of one hand—, they have intervened to heal and to cure of their grave and irreversible pains, some Earth person, whom they know directly or indirectly. Now, according to themselves, the illness is grave throughout the terrestrial "social network" (to speak with their expression). Will they intervene to save it from its anhilation?*

I know that they have read this book, and from these last pages to you I pray: If you are truely OEMII, humans like ourselves, the brotherhood of humanity prevents you from abandoning us to our luck. Or perhaps you consider that we must pass the test of fire, to emerge purified of it —those few who remain— to renew our march through those mysterious roads of Time and Space?

The answer is in the future... and perhaps not very distant.

*We quote again, from Volume I, an ummo statement made to Sr. Antonio Ribera to be read publicly over a planned television program in Spain:

"...we note with sadness that you employ your sciences primarily for war and the destruction of your own selves, which continues as your principal objective.

"You are like children playing with terrible and dangerous toys which will destroy you. WE CAN DO NOTHING! A cosmic law says that each world must make its own path, to survive or to perish. YOU have chosen the second. You are destroying your planet, anihilating your species, and contaminating your atmosphere and your seas until now this is irreversible. With sadness we contemplate your insanity, and understand that the remedy is ONLY in yourselves. We can not look forward a great distance into your future because your psyches are completely unpredictable and capricious bordering on paranoia. As your elder brothers in this cosmos, we urgently desire with all our hearts your salvation. Do not destroy your beautiful blue planet, a rare atmospheric world that floats so majestically in space, so full of life.

"It is YOUR choice."

[Will we survive to see this statement vindicated? ...As were those concerning the top level decisions to use Atomic Weapons (in 1967 and 1973) to avoid defeat in third party countries, not members of the A-bomb Club. An interesting demonstration of this ability by many others with more advanced technologies, to look in on our most closely guarded secrets, is manifested in the rate of UFO activity reported. It is a matter of record that 1967 and 1973 were among the heaviest years for UFO activity worldwide, ever recorded. Makes us wonder what happened in 1954 that has not yet come to light? Sobering thoughts indeed! -Publisher]

APPENDIX A

WHO ARE THE UMMITES?

VARIOUS ATTEMPTS TO IDENTIFY THE UMMITES (from a report received by Padre Lopez Guerrero)

During these last years we have been able to collect many versions concerning our possible identity.

The opinions expressed come from telephone conversations maintained with you human correspondents.

Commentaries have appeared in the Press, Magazines and Specialized Bulletins.

We have respected where possible the original content, still in your primitive ideomatic version. Some of the interpretations have been lavished considerably with flippant variations. In those cases we recognize the most representative. The judgements expressed come from brothers of yours in:

The United States of Northamerica
France
Australia
Switzerland
Canada
Spain
England
Yugoslavia
Argentina

We have only censored those that could in some manner identify the opiniants.

OPINIONS:

...An international convention of UFO investigative organizations to lend prestige to their points of view before public opinion.

To leave no room for doubt that OUMMO encompasses its significant truth in an association of intellectuals who intend to disquiet other colleagues with a subtle feeling of humor or perhaps to impose themselves on them utilizing a method without doubt not lacking in its originality.

...And can we not think of them as a group of scientists who intend to explore the social impact of their discoveries, before projecting them toward the society...?

...I continue believing, as I told you in my last letter, that they are the same authorities of the Principality (referring to Monaco) as those who are using a science-fiction story with the end of increasing in the future their present tourism. (A version of one of our correspondents after receiving one of our reports from Montecarlo).

...Could be of the Theosophical Society. They have been specialists in talented subterfuges for proselitism. What I don't understand is why didn't they select a nearer star to make their affirmation more acceptable. Alpha Centauri, for example...

...Another possibility I see is one of our Parties. This could be effective for certain politicians that an extraterrestrial utopia could serve as a vehicle for certain ideas, if we note the prestige that these fictions represent for simple minds.

...UMMO could mask an organization of psychologists of international character —perhaps only British— who are making an amplified survey by means of a test, materialized in this inspired tale in the war of the worlds.

...The accent with which they speak (referring to one of my brothers) is Yankee. Are they not a commission named by the Pentagon to idealize a neat novel based on a supposed Planet, authenticating it by expensive testimony to polarize public opinion in directions that do not recall the tragedy of Viet Nam?

—Who believes these reports that they say come from UMMO?

—which requires intelligence and money. At times I have thought that they could be a ruse by the Northamerican CIA.

—with what objective?

—with which to convince and later bring to light a fraud, deprestigizing the credulous investigators.

...requires much time and numerous economic resources. It only needs to be provable to the minister of... What ends...? And who knows the ends of the chanceries...?

...think that you will call me because it pertains to some patronizing commission of UNESCO to sound out public opinion on the myth of the UFOs.

Is perfectly clear: A skillful maneuver of the Soviet Government to orient the western public opinion toward extraterrestrial themes, deprestigizing thus the science and culture of the capitalistic nations.

...and theme that beneath the pseudonym OOMO hides a cryptogovernment, worldwide, made up of "Superbrains", who try to prepare the citizens of different countries by means of messages which hide their true intention...

Very well. Why could it not be the same Northamerican CIA camouflaging the experiments of their government: Secret experiments with ships or aircraft; inducing the public at large and the witnesses to these flights, to believe that they are UFOs from beyond Earth...?

Pardon me if I say what I think to you. Tell me at the end if I have guessed right or not. Surely it is an Industrial Firm which is developing a great international publicity campaign. Later, when the commercial name of this plan has been divulged they will let us know.

—...And could it not be the same Government of Canada?

—If not being the Canadian Government, could it be some intelligent newsmen who, advised by scientists are trying to develop a sensational series of articles, basing them on a rumor previously created by those same ones?

Good. It could also be an espionage organization. The 2° Bureau for example, or the Mafia, or a clandestine net that traffics in drugs or gold.

...Some friend pointed out the possibility that this German group could be trying to pass for extraterrestrials of the planet UMMO operating from the surroundings of the Sierra Tahua (Bolivia) since the report came from... since neither in Rosario nor the other point in Argentina that we know...

Intentions? Ah! And what intentions could we attribute to them? All this must cost them much money. And if they desire to capture new partesians for their neo-nazism...?

So as not to make this narration interminable, we finish by including other interpretations which we have wanted to identify:

A series of University jokes.
A group of Tibetian Lamas.
German spiritualist sects.
The Rosicrucians or groups of similar sects.
The Communists of the People's Republic of China
The European P.C.
The Government of Israel. International Zionism.
The Jewish community of Jugoslavia.
The Catholic Society of Jesus. The Vatican.
The Catholic Institute of the Opus Dei.
A group of Brahmins intending to dominate the Occident.
A group of "mutants" or privileged brains.
An association of "Covens" of English Witches.
The French "Camelots". The Anarchists.
The "Lions", the "Rotarians", A Masonic Lodge of "The Hidden Rite".
The Northamerican "Knights of Columbus".
A Cosmic Sect that includes the greater brains of Earth.
The Partesians of French Canada seeking prestige as ET contacts.
An organization of commercial espionage.
The Oriental Council of Alchemists.
Authentic ETs...not from UMMO who camouflage their true origin.

An organization of delinquents seeking prestige before scientists to dominate them.

The editors of the Punch to reveal the lack of sense of humor of some intellectuals.

The Northamerican NASA to test possible reactions when confronted with a hypothetic extraterrestrial invasion.

A group of paranoid scientists who really believe "alienogenesis".

Movie Producers who launch a publicity boom before distributing a movie based on an imaginary planet.

UMMO is a symbol, having no real existence.

The inhabitants of UMMO are not here. They are spirits who have found a perfect medium with which they can communicate with us.

A capitalist subterfuge to introduce their antimarxist ideas.

Vulgar religious propaganda with another mask.

Capitalist countries provoking a psychological climate of terror to justify the massive production of war material.

A powerful financial group offering ideas of an imaginary planet to be copied by "terrestrials" and to foment thus their own projects.

...returning us to gangsterism, this time intelligently camouflaged with an extraterrestrial cover.

All of these possibilities have been examined exhaustively by expert authorities, including many of those listed, with no evidence whatever directly supporting any particular hypothesis. We simply are faced with the alternative that — **this just may be true!**

APPENDIX B

"TOP SECRET" INCIDENT AT ANDROS ISLAND

On page 44 of my work *Los Doce Triangulos de la Muerte* (A.T.E., Barcelona, 1976), now out-of-print, I referred to a mysterious incident that took place on Andros Island, in the Caribbean. I am going to transcribe that commentary completely, as it is in the original of an interesting and fascinating investigation.

"Another engineer, a Northamerican, Dr. Willie Smith, nuclear physicist of Lycoming College (Williamsport, Pennsylvania, U.S.A.), sent me a transcription of the contents of a letter which, for its interest, I am going to extract here.

"A television station in Florida commenting on a book about UFOs, written by Ralph and Judy Blum, (BEYOND EARTH, Bantam Books, New York, 1974), had projected one of the (UFO) photos published in that work, which was precisely one of those photographs of the Spanish San Jose de Valderas case, profoundly studied and commented on in great depth by myself and Rafael Farriols in our book *Un Caso Perfecto* (Plaza & Janes, S.A., Editores, Col. Otros Mundos). The UFO exhibited on that program showed on the bottom the famous symbol in the form of an H with a small central bar)+(, identified as that of UMMO or UMMO-AELEWE (General Government of UMMO). Shortly a television viewer called by telephone to the station saying that he had something very important to say to Blum. Blum later went to see him and the unidentified caller told him:

"I see that finally my photos have been published!

"Blum answered that the photos he had seen on the television were from Spain. It was then that the following history came to light (that Blum believes is correct in view of the personality of the subject):

"This gentleman was a technician assigned to Andros Island in the Caribbean, at a Northamerican rocket tracking station. In the early morning of 21 May 1966, he saw a UFO like that of San Jose de Valderas with the same symbol on the bottom (1). The UFO was above a boat dock

(1) The San Jose de Valderas photos were made on 1 June 1967. Previously, on 6 February 1966 a similar ship landed at Aluche (Spain) but no photos were made, and little information released. It was impossible for the Andros witness then to know of the ship from these events, and of the emblem. In the only English release, in an article of mine, THE MADRID LANDING published in FSR for May-June 1966, the sketch by Jose Luis Jordan Pena, a very simple sketch, did not reproduce the UMMO symbol complete.

and projected a conical beam of light that paralyzed a little dog that belonged to the said technician witness, who was not visible from outside due to his observing the scene from inside the cupola of the tracking station. As he had a camera at hand (later it was learned that it was not a hand camera but a 35mm movie camera), he was able to shoot a whole cassette of pictures. But when he reported what had happened, the military immediately sent a helicopter which confiscated the film. A little later, not only did they interrogate the witness at length, but they took his little dog. Apparently there had been other civilian and military observers who had seen the UFO. They were transferred and the technician in question was dismissed and sent home. He gave Blum the names of those other witnesses.

"Doctor Willy Smith commented: 'It is true that we have only the word of Blum that it was thus, but he had told me all of this before I explained the history of UMMO to him. My interpretation is that the military have evidence of the existence of UFOs that carry these emblems'.

Later I came to occupy myself with this theme in another book of mine, *El Misterio del UMMO* (also out-of-print but published as Volume I in this English language series). After reproducing the text of the letter of my good friend Dr. Willy Smith (actually a collaborator with Dr. Hynek in CUFOS), I commented on it there then in Acapulco with the young Richard W. Heiden, during a lunch also attended by the Hynek couple, during the first International Congress of Ufology there in the Spring of 1977.

We were talking about the San Jose de Valderas case and Heiden had just read *Los Doce Triangulos de la Muerte* (Dick speaks, reads and also writed Castillano correctly), where I mentioned the Andros Island incident. It was there that he promised to put me into contact with Ralph Blum to try to verify anything else.

I finally received a notice from Heiden in a letter dated 29 October 1978, that he sent me from Milwaukee (Wisconsin). In it he told of the fruitless gestures he had made to talk to Blum, and reproduced part of a letter he had finally received from him. Blum said:

> "This story of Andros Island is too complex to go into detail on it at this moment. Nevertheless is -- *a most premium piece of evidence*. I am sorry I can not write more extensively. I am in England with family problems (his wife is English, Heiden said) and am too occupied to try to write the aforesaid. Keep In contact. (italics mine.)

In his letter, Dick Heiden sent me an article from the NATIONAL ENQUIRER of 14 December 1978, another article from the Milwaukee Journal of the same date, plus a third article published in the GSW Bulletin of December 1977, and finally a letter from the same Heiden which was published in the Mexican magazine CONTACTOS EXTRATERRESTRES No. 21.

The National Enquirer article was nothing less than an interview by reporter Robin Leech with the famous Walter Cronkite, television news comentator, titled "I'm Convinced UFOs Exist". But in the Milwaukee Journal of the same date (14 December 1976), Cronkite totally denied what had been published in the Enquirer, "His strongest attacks were directed against an article published by the National Enquirer, in which they affirmed that Cronkite believed in those flying saucers (sic). Cronkite qualified it as "a complete lie from first to last". The curiosity is that in this article Cronkite related with details and symbols the incident at Andros.

The speed with which they published the reply was incredible: the same day, if the dates don't lie. It is possible that there is some confusion, due to the fact that the photocopies of both articles, that are in my posession, have the same dates. The letter of Heiden to Contactos Extraterrestres says, among other things: Cronkite continues being an ignorant sceptic in that which concers the UFOs... The notice was denied in the Milwaukee Journal for 24 December (at the margin of the photocopy the same Heiden wrote: "Error in printing: The date was the 14th day of December of 1976"), and also in various Northamerican UFO reviews. And more, they knew that the controversy in question had resulted in the sub-director of the weekly in question had beeing replaced."

Cronkite appealed to the National News Council, a non-profit organization created to investigate accusations of inexactitude in the press. In the letter from Cronkite to the Council, according to the article published in the Press-Gazette of Green Bay (Wisconsin) dated 5 March 1978, the well known commentator affirmed that he was never interviewed by Robin Leach, author of the polemic article in the Enquirer, and also that he did not personally know of him.

To this, Ian Calder, Editor of the Enquirer, responded, communicating to the Council that the article in question, with the supposed interview with Cronkite, was "received in good faith by us" from the hands of its author, "an independent reporter of good reputation".

It is as it were, the National Enquirer (the paper that offered a reward of $50,000 to whoever presented irrefutable proof of the existence of UFOs), has a well gained fame as a "yellow journal" or sensationalistic. One that accepts their declarations should always do so "with a grain of salt". It is a magazine that one sees constantly involved in litigations by the famous for declarations that they attribute to that magazine, and which they deny. Nobody takes it too seriously since nothing comes of the Enquirer.

But to continue with this business of Andros Island. In a letter dated 18 January 1982, Dick Heiden wrote me the following:

"My Dear Friend: I have obtained, finally, the information about the incident at Andros Island that you asked for in Acapulco nearly five years ago. Ralph Blum did not write again, and so I asked a UFO friend in New York if he would contact him for me. (I had asked such by letter as well as in person of a coleague in MUFON). Unfortunately this friend deceived me. Meanwhile I wrote to Blum twice more, without getting any reply. Some time later I decided to take the bull by the horns and telephoned to the New York office of Blum, but I had to leave my number because he was not there. The other day I called Blum from Los Angeles. He said that it was possible that Ted Blocher would (sic) know more about the case. Also I asked some specific questions which Blum answered thus:

1. He could not see the photos (movies) because they had been confiscated.

2. He did not remember if they had shown on the television program the complete photos of the San Jose de Valderas (with the landscape and all), or no more than the part with the craft.

3. Did he suppose that the reporter of the National Enquirer (the one who invented the interview with Walter Cronkite... about one year ago already) had obtained the case second hand from someone to whom Blum had passed the same. (Blocher told me later that he knew the identity of the informant, though he would not give it.)

"Well, there was no doubt in questioning Ted Blocher about the incident at Andros Island. (The result was that from the beginning, my good friend Ted posessed the transcription of the whole interview by the Blum couple with the witness! I am inclosing a photocopy of the same... He emphasized that you can not publish the names of the witnesses, nor detáils that could help the Northamerican military to decypher the identity of the Blum informant.

"I proceeded to ask the Air Force and the Army for their documents on this incident. They both declared that no such documents existed. See the letters attached.

"Attached also are press clippings of the National Enquirer lie. It seems that you misunderstood what I had written about this unprestigious weekly. Cronkite did NOT retract or repudiate the interview with the National Enquirer, but reaffirmed his opinion of always, and expressed as mystification the interview."

Up to here has been the letter of Heiden.

The following is the valuable document sent to me by Dick with his letter:

TRANSCRIPTION OF THE INTERVIEW RECORDED WITH THE WITNESS (name omitted) Interviewed in May 1974 by Ralph Blum at witness' home.

Observation, tracking and filming of a UFO on 21 May 1966 (between 03:00 and 04:00 in the morning) at Andros Island in the Bahamas.

Ralph Blum: I am going to interview... (we will call him "Witness"), a missile tracking technician in the Carribbean, who lived an experience he told us about yesterday.

RB: How do you account—we been trying to figure—how do you account for the fact that a secret, a secret, could get so big and still stay a secret?

W: Well, you know when I worked for AUTEC, they were starting out with this called a laser beam. Now, when you say how come a secret can become such a big secret, there are things that happened over there with this laser beam that—it's unbelievable....

RB: You mean the laser can do lots of things the public hasn't heard of yet.

W: Oh, yes. You'd be surprised. But those things I really can't talk about because—

RB: Yeah, those things are still—

W: But this thing is something else.

RB: By the way, let me say that a lot of people speculate that UFOs may—the way they may operate, we may be learning about the way they operate from lasers and holograms. Maybe they're not really there, in any way that we can shoot down. We—sort of have the feeling that that's what the military decided in 1952.

W: Well, I don't know about 1952. I'll be very frank with you, now: this is exactly what happened. This happened on 20 May of 1966, because 21 was my birthday. It really happened May 21 because it was, like, between 3 and 4 o'clock in the morning, and we had a big shot on the 21st. We had all the VIPs from England, Germany, the big man from RCA (David Sarnoff - TB), everybody. [Ted Blocher who transcribed the recording, added some parenthetical comments of his own.] They were all there for, you know, what we call AZROC shots. Yeah, that's those rockets that they fire off the boats.

RB: Is that a RCA product, or just a component—

W: Maybe, but RCA had the unit for tracking them. And, uh, I just happened to be up and I was loading all these film cassettes, upstairs in the dome, in the, uh, theodolite.

RB: This was on Andros Island?

W: Yeah, place called Golden Cay, which, to us, it was called Site 4 ...We had from Site 1 to Site 7, but at the time I was in Site 4. And, uh, I was on my knees, in the dome, and the dome was wide open—I was trying to get the moonlight in so I could see what I was doing, besides the little lights being on the side. And all of a sudden it was like the sun came up. It was real bright. So I stuck my head above the dome, see what the—you know, what the hell was goin' on, and that's when I saw this thing, and she was level, parallel with my dome, but at the end of the dock. And I finally found out what the darn dog's name was—his name was Squib, the dog, our mascot, Squib, a real klutz. He was down at the end of the dock. [Squib is a firing device used in weapons.WS]

RB: About how far away?

W: Well, from here to that air conditioner.

RB: Ah-hah, so about, uh—really close. Fifty feet. (Check this—TB)

W: Sure it was close! Because Site 4 was the only one that had a direct shot at the end of the dock. The other ones were either to the left or to the right.

RB: What do you mean by direct shot?

W: A straight shot, at the end of the, uh, dock. In other words, the-

RB: For visual—?

W: Yeah. Our theodolite was, was—

RB: Right. Aimed out— along the— I see.

W: Straight. Straight, right down, right down the ramp.

RB: Then you were tracking that segment of the flight, or whatever—

W: Yeah, that's when I looked up and I saw this thing. Now at first, I didn't see those, uh— markings you have on that there snapshot. I didn't see that. All I saw was just a round disc, s'all I saw. And, the, the theodolite was already loaded because of the seven o'clock shots. So, I threw it on manual—this I didn't see, not sumpen like this, no way, no. This was just— (interrupted by dog?)...

RB: Your job was— what at this point?

W: A theodolite operator... Tracking.

RB: And a theodolite is an angle-measuring device which is also a camera? I'm not quite— I've never been sure what a theodolite was, so that people can understand it.

W: A theodolite is strictly a tracking instrument with a high-speed, built-in, 35 mm. camera, and we tracked nothing but missiles, and torpedos, and you name it and we tracked it. Star shots— for (Apollo?)—

RB: But can it track something on the— it can track something on the surface as well as in the air?

W: Matter of fact, that very next day, they scrubbed the test and we tracked the Skipjack, which is the Atomic Sub. I sat there for 16 hours tracking his antenna. 16 hours of that garbage.

JB: (Judy Blum recaps the theodolite definition.) (Ralph's wife).

W: At that time there were supposed to have been only 25 in the entire world. AUTEC had... 4, Cape Kennedy had 5, Andrews, in California, had 5, and the rest were all down-range...

RB: So, you were getting ready for a 7 a.m. shot, you were all loaded up— this thing, when you looked up, did it fill your visual... range? I mean, was it—

W: Oh, yes! She was right in front of me. The whole dock was lit up— the dock was this white concrete—and the inside of the dome was lit up. I couldn't figure what this—what was going on. I looked up, and there was this light. And Squib—when I first looked out of the dome, Squib was just going down the dock, at the end of the dock. He got to the very end of the dock and he just froze! He didn't move! He— he actually froze. And I'm lookin—this is actually before I start takin film— an I'm lookin, an nothing's happenin, so I hit on manuel, I swung her around, nothin happened as far as outside went, and I started takin shots of it. So I took about, uh— out of 500 feet, I took about 350 feet of film— and the dog was still sittin there, he was sittin just the way he's sittin (W's current dog? Squib?) there now. I mean froze. Because, when he sits, his tongue goes up and down, from his breathing. That dog's tongue was out, and it didn't ever go back up again! I tell you, must think I'm nuts! Okay, so, that's what happened.

RB: How long would it take to shoot 350 feet of film?

W: About 8 minutes, at a steady grind, And I had it on high—

RB: The thing was stationary that whole time?

W: In never moved, never went up, down, sideways, it just stuck there.

RB: It couldn'a cared less that you were taking its picture?

W: ...No, it couldn'a cared less about me, and he knew I was there, because my lights were on and you could hear the hummin— of the theodolite goin. He was more interested in the pooch, that's the truth. Why, I don't know. Okay, so, so I call Site 1, and I get an answer from up there, at the, uh, security, the, uh, communications. I tole 'em what I saw. Now the man up there says, well, go on back to bed and get a good night's sleep—he figures we're having a little party down there—an he said, uh,...that's the truth, I swear to God—

RB: Do you know who he was, the guy you talked to Site 1?

W: No, no, too far back. An he said, uh, go on back to sleep because you only got a couple hours before the big test comes up, which was scheduled for 7 o'clock... So I says, well, you know, I got film of this, so he said, stand by; he says, go on back up in the turret, which is the, uh, theodolite, and we'll call you on the head phones. So Rainbow 1 called rainbow 4, they called me back, and said, uh, we're sending a chopper down. He wants me to pack the film up that I, uh, just shot. Which I would gladly do, what the hell, I'm their employee, which I did, I packed that film up. An, uh, sure enough, here comes the chopper, and the pilot—his name was Dave, I don't know his last name, his first name was Dave—an he was good an hot because they woke him up, an he's gonna fly this run, you know, a couple hours ahead of time—. He comes down and picked it up an I figure that was the end of it, that's all, I could care less. I just happened to be there—

RB: Before you go on from there, what happened— did the craft— you said two others showed up.

W: Yeah, right... Just before we were done shooting, uh, here it is (the photo in Ralph Blum's book), these two other ones, one on the right an one to the left of her, and this baby was still on top of the dock, where Squib was.

RB: Did you see the other ones come in, or did they— how did they—

W: No, no, no. I was shootin, and all of a sudden I heard this large hum, which I knew wasn't the machine, it was too darn loud. And the other ones—

(Interruption while W draws the arrangement)

This is in the middle. This is the one that was lookin at the pooch. When the other two come over, they had it (the design on the bottom— TB) that way, elongated. There was one on the right, and one on the left, and I never got a shot of those two, cause I didn't even know that they were there, and all of a sudden I hear this large hummin noise, and the dog, Squib, starts runnin back down the, uh, dock, comin towards us, or rather me. And they went this way (?). By the time I spun that darn thing around, they were —they were gone. I have no idea where they went.

RB: Draw a picture of what they sorta looked like, can you? Just a rough shape of them, object itself.

W: Well, uh, the two with this looked exactly like this, that's the truth. Yeah. This, now—

JB: That was on the bottom, that was on the bottom?

W: This was on the bottom of the one that was lookin at Squib, the one that was at the end of the dock, in other words. The two that came in, one was to the right, and one was to the left, but above him, an had this mark, in here.

JB: Right, Were they completely round? Or—

W: Completely round. Like, you say, a flying what? Saucer, or whatever you call it, completely round.

RB: See any openings?

W: No. No, because I was watching it, this one, for a long time... There was no movement, there was nothin. It just stood there. Went hmmmmmm. That was it, with that white stuff comin down, at the dog.

(What white Stuff? TB)

RB: Now, the white light that came down, did it look different than other light?

W: Not to me, it didn't. No, it—

RB: Just a light beam?

W: It looked like one of those air—uh, one of those lights on the airplanes when they're coming in for a landing, extra bright—

RB: White light—

W: Just the whole thing lit up, the whole dome, and everything. It was like daylight. It was a pleasure. I don't know what the hell it was.

RB: Did the light come out like light usually does, or did it focus?

W: It was comin in, that way, that way, right on the dog! The pooch never moved. I'm not kiddin you. Squib never moved. He sat, As soon as that thing hit 'im, an he didn't move, cause that tongue was still sticking out. 'Cause I dropped it down, and I was shootin Squib. It was like he was petrified. That's the truth.

RB: And when he came out of it, did he whine, cr—

W: No! He just went right down the ramp. But for the next three or four days he wouldn't eat.

RB: Wouldn't eat?

W: No, no.

RB: Anything else?

W: Yeah. Then the, uh— well, anyway, the chopper come down, it picked up the film. This was about 04:30 in the morning. Around 05:30, another chopper came down, they asked for me. They took me up to Site 1. Okay, so I went up there and, uh, all I seen was a bunch of Admirals' hats, and Air Force, which we never had out there, cause that's strictly Navy.

RB: What's that, Admiral's hats?

W: Oh, yeah, all that brass an that. They come in, they asked me a lot of questions, and I answered 'em as truthfully as I could, and then the— this guy, Ringo, Hoot Ringo, he was my immediate boss— he worked for AUTEC, for RCA, he was the down range manager, for all down range— he says, you <u>will</u> forget what you saw, and anything else. I figured, okay, cause I had a top secret clearance, I had my badge, you know, an everything else. So he tole me, he said within one hour, go on down to the heliport, and they'l take you back home. In other words, down range. So I went to the film-viewing department to see what I shot. And every test—so help me God —every test before that, there was no problems. Whenever I wanted, the girls would go ahead and run the film and show me if I had made any mistakes and hel (unclear), no way, I couldn't even get in the door.

RB: Let me ask you, did you have any friends there among the girls there, do you remember any of the girls?

W: Not the girls, the, uh, guys.

RB: Now about the guys? Who, particularly, in that film—

W: Oh, Mike Harrigan—

RB: Mike Harrigan. (spells it)

W: Yeah.

RB: Who else worked for AUTEC?

W: Yeah. Well, we all worked for AUTEC.

RB: Who else— (unclear)

W: Oh, God, It's mostly faces, that's the whole problem... The names, they say, "Hi", you say "Hello", cause I was down range, you know.

RB: What was Harrigan's job?

W: Mike was also a thodolite— he was at Site 2, and, uh,—

RB: Did you know anybody who worked in the lab, in the processing— in film?

W: I know 'em by face. (RB: Yeah.) By face. Okay, now I'm gonna tell you. Okay, so they told me I wasn't allowed in the room, which is okay with me because, I don't know what they're doin'. Now the first thing that entered my mind is, I was in the wrong place at the wrong time. 'Cause I'm thinkin, Now: here's all these bigwigs up here, with this big shot in the morning for 7 o'clock, and when I saw what happened with the laser, I don't know what these people are at, I really don't. I mean, I'm talking about us, now, the Americans. I don't know what they've invented, and maybe that's why they got so hot and bothered: this is something I saw that I shouldn't have seen, and that was that. So the man says, forget what you saw, and just say what's that, and don't talk about it, and we'll have you debriefed, which is fine.

RB: What does that mean, debriefed?

W: Everything that you've seen, you forget.

RB: <u>That's</u> what they mean by debriefing?

W: Yeah.

RB: I thought that debrief means when they interrogate you?

W: Yeah, yeah, right, but anything that's top secret, you forget. And I had a top secret clearance, and I couldn't even get admitted in the film room— on that morning.

RB: So there is clearance above yours?

W: A "Q" clearance, yeah, sure, which I had no need to (know)—that's the way it went. So, I went on back down range and I really— I really just forgot about it. That's the truth, I forgot about everything.

RB: You mean you went back down range, where did you go to?

W: Back there at Site— Site 4, they call it Golden Cay.

JB: What is a "Q" Clearance?

W: That's Atomic. See, we were tracking— we were tracking what they call the Skipjack, the Atomic Sub, so that was Top Secret.

JB: Right, right.

W: But if she was to fire something, that's "Q" Clearance, and I wasn't even allowed there. I was just (unclear), it's as simple as that.

RB: Really?

W: Right. That's the way it goes.

RB: So you went back up to— (W: Went down.) —went down to—

W: To Site 4— (RB: Yeah) —and I sat there— Now, on the same time, when I spotted this thing, our radar at Site 4 was out and I called Site 6, and their radar went out at the same time! They figured it was a malfunction, cause nobody knew about this thing. I didn't say a word. I'm shootin, but I'm on the intercom. So about a week later, no, three days later, after this happened, the Navy came down—

RB; You were still there, you hadn't been—

W: Oh, no, I was still there. Three days later—

RB: Now, they cancelled the shot for that morning?

W: Yeah, we hadda track the Skipjack, No AZROCs.

RB: That's interesting. But the AZROC firing was cancelled.

W: Yeah. We had all these Brittish ships out there—

RB; Everything was cancelled—

W: Everything was scrubbed.

RB: And they just did a sort of a cover operation, which was tracking the Skipjack?

W: Well, that's what we said, but, uh—

RB: But you can't prove that. (W: No, no.) They— you had to give something with all those people there, cause the news was out—

W: Sure, all the bigwigs— You're darn right, Sarnoff, and the— you haddem. Anyway, about three days later, the Navy sent down a PT Boat to Site 4 and— see, Site 4 is more or less like a round island, off of Golden Cay, and there was only what? Eight of us on there, on this island. And we had some wild goats, which we did, they were just, you know, as pets, and Squib, and one of the fellows brought back one of these weird-looking birds from Avaco— The Navy came down and they said that they were all full of, uh, dangerous diseases, especially the goats, and they hadda be confiscated. So the first one that went was Squib... I noticed that, cause I was up there on the micro-wave tower, and I saw 'em put Squib in a cage. Now the other ones they didn't put in a cage, the goats and the— the other junk we had around there— and the bird —and off they went. And they confiscated 'em.

JB: And, now— did you see anything wrong with them? The animals?

W: With Squib? He just wouldn't eat, because, uh, what a life he had. He hadda life as good as this klutz (his present dog— TB).

RB: But he was off his food for three days?

W: No, he was on his feet—

RB: No, off his <u>food</u>—

W: Oh, food. Yeah, yeah, he wouldn't eat, right. He wouldn't eat, because he— this guy, his name was Armand, he was a cook from, uh, Canada — he used to make him scrambled eggs, or— oh, I'm tellin you — pancakes— an this dog couldn't wait for 4:30 to come, he'd be up, you know, with his nose in the air— come on, cook, get up—

RB: Do you remember Armand's last name?

W: No, no. All I know is he was from Canada, an a good cook. Damn good cook.

JB: But, now, apart from not eating, uh, did you notice anything about the goats or the bird, or Squib, that was unusual?

W: Nothing. The bird was (unclear under Judy)—

JB: The fact that they said they were diseased is—

W: The Navy said that the goats carry a very bad disease, which they could put off on any other animal, no matter what kind it was. And they came down in this PT Boat, they had the crate, but <u>only for Squib</u>.

RB: And they sent a PT Boat.

W: Well that's the only transportation we had. The PTs— or the choppers

RB: And Squib was never—

W: Squib was the only one that was put in the cage. The goats weren't and were just let loose on the back of the boat.

[Note- This was a peculiar turn of events, but certainly not unexpected if the case were real. On the other hand there would be no point in this at all if it were not real. Apparently these wild goats had been there for generations and were no problem until only a few days after a UFO hovered over the island -- and then suddenly they became a danger. That Tracking Station and the goats had been there for years with no problems. Since neither Squib nor the goats were returned (as far as the witness knew) it may be assumed that they are either under observation somewhere or were destroyed in testing. -Publisher]

RB: Was any other mention made by any of the other guys about what had happened? Did anyone else—

W: Yeah, the, uh, radar guy from Site 6, he evidently knew the radar fella from Site 4, and in their log books, they both had it, that their radar went out at the same time; they couldn't understand it.

RB: Same time?

W: Same time, same time. It went kaput cause I was on local, it just wouldn't go, and I went on manuel, and she was dead. And my theodolite, I couldn't move it, only manually. I hadda turn it.

RB: So the gear system failed, too.

W: There was no gear system... (Offers coffee and toast to guests).

(Short digression here, omitted for lack of interest. — TB)

RB: So ho— they'd all logged the radar malfunction at the same time.

W: Yeah. Both of 'em. An I couldn't get the second one—

JB: And the theodolite would only move manually?

W & RB: (In chorus) Manually.

W: Yeah, that's the turret—(unclear).

RB: Normally it moved how?

W: On a switch. I could lock in—

JB: I see, right—

W: They had what they called a lock switch on the bottom—

JB: So it's automatic.

W: Automatic, yeah— but there was no automatic—

RB: Bob was saying that they— that the UFO locked on Squib—

W: Oh, that dog just sat. He went to the end of the, uh, of the dock— he was looking up. That's when I was looking outside of the dome. It was before I got near the camera. And I seen this darn white thing come down, and the dog sat, just the way he sits (his dog - TB), but he was sidewise from where I was lookin, and I know, you know, from lookin at dogs that their tongue goes up and down because a their breathin, or they're excited. That tongue just (stuck?), that was it, an he didn't breathe, I swear to you.

RB: What would you've said the diameter of that was, what would you guess?

W: Of the what?

RB: Of the UFO, the one that sat there. (JB: The main one.) How many feet across would you approximate it?

W: Oh, our dock was what— 20 feet across, and this was double— this hadda be 40 feet... like one end was here, and one end was here, over the dock. (Indicating on drawing.)

RB: Now— how thick was it? One story, a man's height?

W: Oh, no, it was mor'n a man's height, It was BIG. Uh—

RB: The other two were the same size? Did you get a notice?

W: No, they were, like, back, of of 'im, but they were higher. That's how I noticed that damn design. I woulda never noticed that— I put— I woke up yesterday. I put that darn TV set on. Now, I was lookin for a movie an' the first thing I saw when it come on was that design. I figure, oh, AUTEC's finally gonna tell what the hell's goin on. So, I turn up the sound and it's you, talkin to this—whatever—

JB: Hy Gardiner.

W: Hy Gardiner? I dunno. And I sat there an' I start watching, an' that's the only reason I called you, cause I know it's the same design I saw. Well, I thought this was what the Air Force, or somebody, was finally gonna explain to people. what— what the hell was goin' on here, cause I didn't know—

RB: Some guy said to me last night, he called me on the show and said, are you saying that you're accusing the government of secrecy on the—

W: Oh, are you kidding me? Oh, let me tell ya, oh, you'd be surprised at the garbage that they— they hold back. I'm not— I shouldn't tell you that, but—

RB: Um-hum. People don't know what to think. People don't trust their own (vision? -unclear).

W: People don't know because the government don't want the people to know— until they're ready to know. It's as simple as that.

RB: But people keep asking me, but how could so many people keep a secret? But what— how does it work, Bob?

W: You get a nice big fat paycheck, an a trip for you and the wife to, uh, like Paris, all expenses paid, just to keep ya quiet. It's as simple as that, really. I saw it with that laser bit— I saw these guys, aw, I'm tellin ya—

RB: The junkets, the trips that go with it.

W: Yeah, damn right. I don't blame them, because, look: everybody today lives for money, let's face facts. When they make an offer like that, oh— it's the first time in a lifetime, all this. You'r gonna go, that's all, simple as that.

RB: Hmm. People have speculated on a relationship between UFOs and lasers. Have you ever noticed these reports that UFOs go out like a TV tube. They just (pfft), go right down to a— point.

JB: By the way, what year was this?

W: 1966. May 20— May 21, my birthday.

RB & JB: May 21, 1966.

RB: Mine's May 27. How old are you going to be this year?

W: 40 (said with a special chuckel).

RB: I got two on ya. I'll be 42 May 27.

JB: Now, I— you were shooting, I still haven't entirely understood it— Bob was shooting AZROC— shots? What are AZROC shots?

W: (unclear) We had sumpen else there—

RB: There was supposed to have been a test that day.

JB: A test of what?

W: At seven o'clock, an AZROC test.

RB: It's a rocket.

JB: AZROC. I don't know what that is. So, a rocket test?

W: It's a rocket that can— that can be shot off of a boat, or a submarine, from under water, an home in on the tail pipe of a plane.

JB: Right.

RB: It's a heat seeking rocket.

JB: Right, right. Okay.

W; And, uh, if it misses, it comes down on a chute... But they very rarely miss (chuckles).

RB: You retrieve it. I would think it's a very expensive piece of gear and if it doesn't work, you want it back.

W: Yeah, that's what the, uh— the, uh— test—

JB: Now, you think that the brass was there probably not for that test?

RB: Not for the one they finally ran.

W: No, I think the brass— that's what I'm saying. I think the brass including the Chairman of The Board, they were there for the tests because that's the first time I— we— it's the first time we ever had all these bigwigs down there. I'm talking about Australia, New Zealand, West Germans, Italians— that's what struck me as funny, because when I saw that damn insignia, I thought what in the hell are we gonna give this to the Italians for? It should have been like the American flag on th— on the bottom of it, you know, not the Italian— really,—

RB: So, all our NATO allies were present, huh?

W: Yeah, yeah.

JB: To watch the test?

W: I saw the battleships out there.

RB: The battleships were all—

W: Oh, yeah, they blocked off the entire tongue. There were two Australians, two British, and two Germans. They block off that tongue (Tongue of the Ocean, east of Andros— TB)— the mail boats weren't allowed—

RB: What's the tongue?

W: The, uh, Tongue of the Ocean, off of Andros—

RB: Uh-huh. Which comes off of Andros, between and—

W: Well, between Bimini and—

RB: And the whole area was closed to traffic?

W: Oh yeah, cause the mail boats, we had to put up the, uh, red flag the morning before, which means they can't go out—

RB: (over above) which signifies—

W: —because there may be a torpedo goin up their rear end.

(Here's some conversational clutter, deletable)

JB: ...You were inside the...dome. The dome is approx— I don't know—

W: About the size of this room, in width, round, 8 or 10 foot dome,— the top slides back, all the way—

JB: Fine, okay...

RB: And what you've got in there is a (all three) theodolite—

W: And your radar.

JB: Right, Now, you were there, and the—

RB: Was your radar man there with you?

W: I was by myself. By myself. No, our radar guy, who wasn't a (Mod 5) boy, he was downstairs—

RB: Wasn't a what?

W: Mod Vie (??), that's the large radar, from Site 2 and Site 1.

RB: Mod five?

W: Yeah, That's the one with the built-n TV cameras. Gee, if he woulda' been working, he woulda' caught it on TV.

RB: With the TV. (Why wasn't?) he working?

W: I don't know. He was off. He was sleeping. He was gettin ready for the test. The whole thing just happened by accident, cause I was up, loading these damn film cassettes.

JB: But I mean, now, how—how—how tall is this room now (on sketch), I want to get measurements—

W: 9 by 12.

JB: 9 by 12. So the dome would've been about 9 x 12 feet, roughly.

RB: He was down on his knees and suddenly—

W: I was down on my knees below the— see, it's so hard to explain to you—

(RB gives him paper and pencil to draw)

I used to have pictures, and I (mumbles)—

JB: What I wanted to get was the dome, and where the dock was, and, you know, sort of— not the size, obviously, but in— in—

W: The dome was like this (drawing— TB), come up about three feet, then it was like this— (JB: Right.) W: —and this, that part here, slid back— just hit a switch and it slid back—

JB: Right okay, so—

RB: Now the dock is—

W: Coming down straight...(bit of a jumble)—straight to us... Now, here's the long dock... here's the end of the dock, we'll say... from here to here, is from here to the air conditioning unit on the roof. (where they were doing this) (You must be able to interpret all of these indications correctly— TB)

RB: So that's really, uh— really 500 feet, from here to that air conditioner, probably 500 feet.

W: You had water here, an you had water here. This is the dock. The pooch was sittin here. He had come runnin up. I had 'er— the top, she's slid back, right? She's open. Now, down here, over here, you got four lights, what we call ground lights, so you can see what the hell you're doin in there, you know, and, uh, let's see... I was down here, on my knees— in other words, between here and here —cause I was loadin up these here film cassettes, cause I could pull one out an shoot the other one in, an keep, you know, for the test... This, whatever it was (indicating UFO), was sittin right here, on top of the dog— the pooch.

JB: Right. Yeah. And you reckon— and about how high above?

W: He was about, uh— a hundred feet. Maybe even less.... Maybe even less. Here's the doorway, here (mumbles)—

RB: Where do you enter?

W: Well, we get out— I'm a helluva an artist—

RB: Ladder?

W: No, steps. They go right up here. We crawl into a door on the side, over here. The packs were all back over here, the radar was over—

JB: Now, this thing, it was directly over the end of the dock.

W: Right over the pooch, over the end of the dock. That's where the pooch was.

JB: Okay. And the dog had its head up. He was looking at it.

W: Yeah, when I first stuck my head up, and then it (Squib) sat down, the way he does, but he— he turned sidewise. In other words, when I'm standing here (pointing), I'm lookin at him... at his profile, an his tongue is sticking out, an it never went back in— just stuck out. (laughs)

JB: And the other two, what? Came from behind, on the other side?

W: Over here, over here, up top, up top, above— this guy. In other words, one here and one here. That's where I saw those markings with the cross, and I could see, uh, the difference...

JB: Sort of like that?

W: Right, right. But these two were backward, in the back. They had blue— blue and green lights, or blue and red lights. This one (the nearest— TB) had nothin but that white thing (light beam-WS) coming down.

JB: These had blue and red lights?

W: Yeah.

RB: What were the lights doing, Bob? I mean, were they blinking, or were they—

W: No, no. No, it looked like a cop car, when you get a ticket...

JB: And this one was just white...

W: No. Well, yeah, the whole thing was white, but this beam that was comin down over the pooch—

RB: Where was the beam shooting down from?

W: From over here.

RB: Out from under the center?

W: Center.

RB: And focused to a point?

W: On the pooch!

RB: On the pooch. So, the beam began wide, and focused in...

W: Yeah, right. The pooch didn't move!

RB: Do we have beams that can do that?

W: (Laughs) If we did, I couldn't tell you anyway.(Some garble here)

RB: Well were you surprised to see it focus to a point?

W: No, because we were runnin laser tests all month, for God's sake.

RB: But what they had was some sort of concerted— that's fascinating. ...Did other guys see UFOs in the area? Any talk—?

W: (Refers to a tracking of Sputnik re-entry, doesn't say when.) The next day the film was taken away an that was it. We called it garbage... they called it garbage, but I never saw (space) garbage that could go like this, an then like this, like that, and then down. Usually garbage just goes around and around... (tracked from 35,000 to 55,000 feet.)

JB: (Back to the May 21 UFO) And it was there for 20—no, eight minutes. You filmed it for eight, about eight minutes—

W: I ran about 350 feet of film off...

(Some incidental gabble here— TB)

RB: Well, that's terrific. The symbol's come back.

JB: So, it was really exactly like the one in the book, the middle one—

W: This was—

JB: Then the other two—

W: Not this—

JB: No—

W: This is what the other two had, because when they went over, I was still tracking. Now I can't turn my dome that way, I have to swing her around, see (unclear)—

JB: But I mean that was on both sides of it?

W: No, no, just the way you see it, right there. On these two. This one was exactly the way which you have on the one in the book. In other words, I mean— you know— maybe I'm nuts, but this looked like the command ship and these were like two lieutenants. That's what it looked like (laughs).

In June 1967, more than 50 people saw this UFO, with its unusual marking, flying low over San José de Valderas, Spain. Landing marks were found.

This is page 18 of the photo section in the Blum's book BEYOND EARTH, Man's Contact With UFOs, Bantam Edition, April 1974. This page was the one used by the TV station during the interview with Ralph and Judy Blum. The picture was on the TV screed when W. turned his set on that morning. He called the Station to ask about his pictures. That was how the Blums met the witness and discovered his remarkable story.

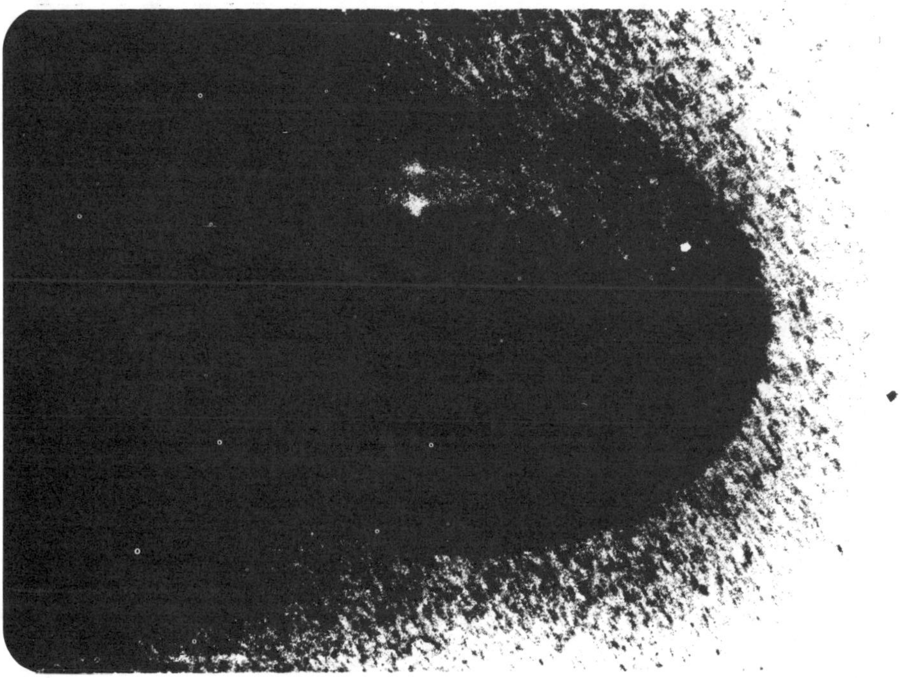

This is actually the image the witness saw on his television screen. The inherent nature of TV studio broadcasting equipment makes it impossible to show the full frame of a vertical format rectangular photo larger than a square without losing the sides to blank space, because of the horizontal rectangular format of all commercial home TV receivers. Therefore the picture from the book had to be "cropped" down to the top horizontal rectangular part enclosing the object image -- which lost all the foreground image data in the Spanish photograph in the process. This resulted in an image very similar to what the witness saw and photographed from the Theodolite cupola at Site 4. This was easily and honestly mistaken for the image the witness filmed with his special camera at Andros Island. Believing, from what he was seeing on his video screen, that his photographs had now been cleared and released (it was 10 years later), he thought the secrecy was over and he called the Blums at the TV Station. As far as we can tell, those theodolite movies have never been made public. The Army and the Air Force officially deny their existence. The important thing is that the Andros Island witness observed a symbol identical to that in the photo taken of an UMMO spacecraft at San Jose de Valderas on 1 June 1967.

JB: Right, right, so—

RB: This was '67, June of '67—

W: '66.

RB: This was '67, this picture. (from Blum book— WS)

W: That was '67???

RB: Mmmmm, In Spain.

* * * * *

RB: And what about photos?

W: Well, they had those there (at W's debriefing— TB).

RB: They did?

W: Yeah, and the photographs that they had clipped outa the film I shot, which was overturned, in other words here's the— face up, an when I walked in, it was that way, face down, but I caught that because I hadda sit right there, when they were asking me these— these questions.

RB: What was it— what was shown on the film? Was it the shots you made?

W: From the two of 'em, yeah, that was in front of me, It was, I— it— uh, when I was— before I walked in, all the shots were face up. When I walked in, they turned 'em over. The Admiral did, so all I saw was, you know, the rear, it was all white, the picture part was down. But I saw that part there (the insignia—TB), which I didn't understand. So I talked to the guy at Site 6, I talked to him about it, which he didn't know what the hell I was talkin about, and I didn't either, to be very frank with you. Well, uh, about a week after Squib was, uh, you know, picked up, they fired the chopper pilot, Dave, who flew down and picked me up—

RB: They what!

W: They fired him.

JB: They fired Dave, the chopper pilot?

W: Yeah. They flew— they fired our radar man, they fired me, and they fired the radar guy at Site 6, and the excuse was that we hadda— a, um— alternative to transfer to Thule, Greenland. Now, who in the hell is gonna transfer from Andros to Thule, Greenland, in their right mind? I got a letter, I was fired!

JB: So the chopper pilot (unclear)—

W: Yeah, Ringo was canned.

JB: And Ringo, too?

W: Yeah, all of us. Yep, anybody that had anything to do with that damn thing was canned, like we never was there, cause as far as the radar guys were concerned, they couldn't see nothin, only on radar, they didn't know what the hell was goin on— so why fire them? And two of the guys, at the time, were married and had a family, and they got canned. And that's no good, when you get canned—

JB: Now wait a minute, you say two of the radar guys. There was the radar guy at Site 4 with you.

W: Yeah, right, who lost track—

RB: The one at Site 4—

JB: So, the Site 5 guy, plus the Site 4 guy—

W: And the one at Site 6 who lost track at the exact same time—

RB: I thought the Site 4 guy was asleep? (Right on Ralphie! TB)

W: No, he wasn't asleep, no, he was on duty— 24 hours—

JB: Yeah, so altogether—

W: Site 2 is the Mod Five. That's the big one with the built-in TV, but they were inoperative—

RB: Right, right—

W: Cause they were waiting for the test to start—

RB: Right, now the (small?) radar at Four was not inoperative?

W: Oh, they're 24 hour air— Site 4, 6, 7—

RB: But it went out?

JB: It went out?

W: It went out—

JB: At the same time?

W: Out at three somethin, and Site 6 went out at the—the exact time, three somethin'. But— and they're the two guys who were fired.... They should never a been—

JB: So that those two guys were fired, the chopper pilot Dave was fired, you were fired, and Ringo was fired...

RB: What happens, what do they say about you when they fired you? Do they give you a recommendation?

W: Naw, they say, tut tut tut, you know, congratulations—

RB: They don't give you— But what if you have to— at your next job, I was— how do you—

W: They gave me a nice recommendation an all that crap—

RB: Did they? They gave you a letter? a nice letter—

W: Yeah,

W: Yeah, over here at the Cape (Kennedy), an when I came back here, all the RCA employees were on strike. Course they're non-union (RB: yeah.), you know. I wound up at the Americana Hotel. Been there now for—what? Ten years? Nine years? Had a good future, right down the damn drain— for what? That's the whole thing, nobody talks to you. You get it all written, everything is written. They had a plane waiting for me at the Andros Airport, and, you know, like, so long Charlie, and that was it. I was shipped out in— what? In three and a half hours. They come down with a special chopper, the man tole me to pack my bags, I packed my bags, I went to site 1, I was debriefed, they took me by Jeep from site 1 right to the airport, and boom! There I was, in Nassau. That was it, as simple as that. One, two, three, out and dried. Ha! So wattaya gonna do? I can't fight them. And the same thing happened to the other guys. Now, as far as Hoot goes, Ringo, I think he— he landed a job down on the, uh, Trinidad Range. I'm not sure though-

RB: Working for another firm, or for the, uh—

W: Oh sure, uh, for the, uh— what they call the, uh, Pan American. They have a range down there... (unclear under RB)

RB: If I wanted to try'n track a guy like Ringo down, how would I set about it?

W: I have no idea, I really don't. I have no idea.

RB: Do guys like that have a home base, or a union they belong to? Does Ringo—

W: No, there's no Union, no. That's— no, no— I wish it were—

JB: How do you spell his name?

W: R-I-N-G-O. Yeah, Hoot, That's his first name, his real first name. H double O-T. (JB repeats) Yeah. He was the down-range manager.

RB: Down range manager for—

W: For AUTEC. (RB repeats) I don't know what he's doin now.

RB: Was he there for quite a while?

W: No, I was there before Hoot. He was there about five to six months I guess—

(AUTEC - Atlantic Underwater Testing Evaluation Center)

RB: Where are they based? Where's their center?

W: Oh, Palm Beach. (RB repeats) Four years ago I flew over there to Andros, to see if any of my old friends were there. They wouldn't even let me on the base—even as a visitor, with a visitor's pass. But I did find out from guys that were coming off the base, in town at the lounge, that all my friends were all gone. All gone. They either quit or — I dunno what happened. All gone.

RB: Did you ever have contact with anyone in the Palm Beach AUTEC (unclear)?

W: Uh, I can't think of— names, they wreck me.

RB: That one'll be a help. (which one? —TB)

W: Yeah, I know, but he wouldn't tell you anything.

JB: Still there? (RB: same)

W: I'm tellin ya, he wouldn't— I'm tellin ya, I went through it...

RB: Well, I'm just wondering if someone who wasn't there anymore—

W: Ever since that morning— the guy said, you forget what you seen, you don't talk about it, and that's the end of it. Course I figured— I'm not kiddin ya— I figured it was something new we had. When I say we, I mean America. That we had, and I was in the wrong place at the wrong time, and I shouldn't never have run film...

RB: You were not (unclear) to see it or photograph it...

W: Right, sure. Sure. But they uh— we didn't have anything like this ...no way in hell. No way...

RB: How do you think the military feels knowing that there's something we can't control?

W: Well, this Air Force guy that accompanied me back to Site 1— he was a— yeah, a two star general—Air Force— Now the Air Force, as far as I know, had no business down there, even for those big tests at all. That's the truth, it was strictly Navy, because it was— it was the English, it was their Navy, The Australians and

Germans— it was all their ships out there, blocking off the tongue, an all that, and they were runnin' all the data on the board up at Site 1. All of a sudden here's this two-star general comes down to the chopper, with Dave, the same pilot, he accompanied me back, like i'm a prisoner of war or something— (laughs).

(JB affirms the AF General came to fetch him— "fetch" amuses W.)

W: If you wanna put it that way, yeah, like the dog. Just give me a collar and a leash, woof! I'll bark...

(JB recaps) (RB recaps)

W: ...it's like, what? Ten years? I lost my Top Secret clearance, I could care less. there is certain things I won't tell you about— I— I— I— can't do it.

RB: Now, where are you gonna be? You gonna be at the Americana?

W: No, I'll be at MGM in Las Vegas (RB repeats). Thank God.

JB: You're sure in your own mind that it wasn't something they were experimenting with?

W: Well, you see, now— that's a toss o' the coin. Now— but wait a minute, if they were experimenting with something, why would they have the same insig— that's the only reason, the same damn insignia!... No, it struck me, it's Italian. I mean, that's where I got that thing from, from old books, or something, you know. It looks like the old Italian markings from the tail of the planes. I figured, what the hell are we gonna give the Italians sompen like this for? An' we don't have it ourselves. So, I start shootin', that's all. An' because o' that I get canned, an' everything else. Which is their business...

(General conversation here; JB shows the Holloman drawing, more gun camera shots, told not to talk)

(W says Dave had spotted some UFOs— background on it, etc.)

W: Why can him (Dave)? What the hell did he do? He didn't do anything. What did I do? All I did was shoot something, you know, that I thought was important— I never seen it before— an then they fire you. It don't make sense!

JB: It's pretty peculiar. It doesn't really make sense, because you'd think that if they'd wanted to insure that you wouldn't talk about it, they'd keep you there and...

(Some garble here as everyone gets into the act)

RB: I got an idea: If they fire you, and you later cause them trouble, they can say this guy was fired for incompetence, if they had to.

W: That's what I was fired for, incompetence! And I had the best damned rate on the whole shot!

RB: What was your rate before you were fired?

W: I was a Tech One. In the Navy, I don't know what it's called. At RCA, you're called a Tech One.

JB: Were they all fired for incompetence?

W: Yeah! Everyone.

RB: Did they give you a letter afterwards?

W: No, they gave me a letter the same day they ushered me out.

RB: What does the letter say?

W: It said Goodbye, nice to have you.

RB: Didn't say anything about competence or incompetence—

W: Incompetence...

RB: (Stunned) It said in the letter, incompetence?

W: Yes. Yes, it did.

JB: Did they specify in what area you were incompetent?

W: No, but Ringo, this guy, who told me that, uh, I was fired because I'm drinking. The guy, uh, the radar fellow at Site 4, was also fired because of drinking. He never drank, as long as I knew him, which was a li'l over a year an' a half. The guy at Site 6 was fired because they wanted him to transfer to Thule, an he refused to, so he got fired for incompetence, and Ringo, I had no idea.

RB: Do you remember the name of the radar guy at Site 4—

W: No, I (unclear)— A polack a big big pole— Jerry Sumpen. Big guy, blond guy. Jerry, uh— matter of fact he still (unclear)—

JB: What's Dave's other name?

(Discussion on Jerry's never drinking; RB on blackened characters)

End Side One...

(Side Two starts off with identification of Sarnoff as RCA boss.)

(RB on why people won't believe the government does this...)

(W on 3½ weeks after sighting he was fired on 15 June 1966)

JB: Did they ask you to swear to this or was it they just told you not to talk, to forget it?

W: He tole me, he says, you will not talk about it, you will forget it, and sign. I said okay. Said, you're being debriefed, and you-'ll be debriefed ina couple of days further. I said okay, fine, so about a week— or maybe two weeks later—

RB: Let me ask you this... were you interrogated about what you saw and its behavior an—

W: Yeah, the very next morning, the day of my damn birthday (Same morning— TB), the day of the shots, because Mike hadda take over for me, cause I was up at Site 1.

RB: How long a debriefing?

W: Three hours. These guys at the table asked me a bunch of questions an I'm tellin 'em exactly what I'm tellin you. They're goin, um-hmm, um-hmm, an' they're goin' pssst, pssst, pssst, so long Mr___, there's a helicopter out at the airport, take him back to Site 4. I said, thank you very kindly, sir, and I walked out. What else could I say? That's why I figured I shot sumpn I shouldna shot. It's as simple as that. I figured— because these guys already knew about this, it was sumpn that belonged to us, America, and until I saw— Well, as a matter of fact, the Air Force guy that took me back down again, I asked him, how come the— on the bottom, she had the Italian insignia? An' he just looked at me like he didn't know what I was talkin' about. And they dropped me off, and that was it. Week and a half later—

RB; So that was the first evidence that you'd got that they didn't know what happened either?

W: From that guy, the Air Force guy. Sure, cause everybody else asked you, you know, the questions— in general, you know, just what you're askin me now, how high was it, how far down the dock was it, where was this, where was that, how much film did you shoot, did you shoot any extra, was it in your locker, because normally, before a test, I shot a test run. I'd take it downstairs to the bathroom. I'd develop it down there to make sure it's— it's clear then I'd okay it upstairs, you know, to— to Mike. He knows that the rest of the film is all right, and the sightings are good, and we shoot.

JB: The what's are good?

W: The, uh— settings. On the theodolite. (RB and JB: Right.) They were really interested about that. So the— when they came back with me, uh— he had a security guard with me— when they came back with me, the security guard went to my locker, opened up all my drawers, went through all my pockets an' clothes, and everything else, an' my foot locker, lookin' for the— just in case I shot extra. Which I didn't! I didn't have time!! (Laughs)..

RB: So there's no way that film was gonna get out of any hands—

W: No way in hell. I wish I had the film, let me tell ya......

JB: The two-star General who accompanied you back, what did he say? He just— he didn't say anything—

W: No, he didn't say anything, he just more or less— him and this security guy accompanied me back, and, uh, I asked him the question about— ...about the Italian— well, to me it looks like the Italian— I don't know...

(RB identifies it as the Fascist Insignia)

...Naw, he looked at me as if he thought I was crazy, so I just shut up. I figure I'm in enough hot water...

RB: How big a Brass meeting was it, were there a lot of officers?

W: Well, I don't know too much about the Navy, but I saw a lot of stuff here, and here, and especially, as I walked in, all of the hats were on the rack, and all I seen was all this stuff on the hats.

RB: About how many guys were at the debriefing?

W: Sarnoff was there... there were four other guys, yeah, they were to the right as you walked in, in plain clothes. But they were sittin with, uh. Sarnoff. And the rest were all military, and then my immediate, uh, boss...

RB: How large a group was it?

W: About 12 people. Oh yeah, (there were) a lot of people there for those shots. We figured it was for the, uh, AZROC shot— and the next morning (same morning— TB) it was scrubbed, all down range. They said it was at 06:30 sharp because of a heavy cloud coverage, an you could stand in the dome an' look up from Site 4, and you wouldn't see a cloud. That's what they told us, and they said start tracking the, uh, Skipjack, which we did, 14 or 15 hours, I forget what it was, that conning tower. I was sick of looking at it. That's the best I can do for you, really......

JB: ...Back to the craft, you know, the thing. You say it was a bright light coming down from it, focusing down. Did you get any idea of the color—I mean, you could see the sign, but did it look black on it, did it— what color—

RB: —Was the sign—

JB: Yes, the sign—

W: What the light?

RB: No, the sign, the symbol, that thing.

W: The symbol? No, to me it looked like it was, uh, blue.

RB: How thick would you've thought the lettering was—

W: It was— It was down, it was over the end of the dock. I mean, to me it looked blue. Now we shoot with all color film. Now what it come out on the film I have no idea.

JB: Right. Now, I wanted to ask you: Now, the whole object, was it bluish, or—

W: No—

JB: It looked—

W: Whitish—

JB: —Whitish.

W: Whitish, but what would you call it? Off-shade white. It wasn't a white like— white white—

RB: It wasn't a metallic silver, it wasn't silver-colored? It was more white than silver—

W: Well, see? I'd have to have the film. I'd have to have...that damn film—

JB: But your impression was off-white, with a beam focusing down very white light—

W: As you looked— as you looked from out here, from right over here, it looked like off white. Off white, and the beam that was on the pooch—

JB: And the symbol on it, the H-thing—

W: It looked like blue—

JB: —It looked like blue.

W: Bluish. (A little overtalk here)

W: Oh yeah, and the next morning, before they scrubbed the test, the Site manager went down to the dock—he didn't know anything about this—there was all the dead barracuda, right off to the sides of the dock. All dead fish. I remember that—small ones, but it was mostly barracuda, because we used to—

RB: How much later? I mean, was this— this was just before the scrubbing? (of the mission -WS)

W: This was about between 06:50 and a quarter to seven, because they scrubbed at— between 06:50 and, uh, 07:00 o'clock.

RB: Who was it went down to the dock?

W: The Site Manager. His name was Roger—I don't know him— ...amd he lives here in Florida, but I don't know— I don't know where... But it was all dead fish. Cause he had a— a small pool off to the right of the dock that we built and when we caught fish, scouba-diving, or even fishin', we'd put 'em in the pool an' feed 'em, an' they were all dead. But even outside the pool where the boats pull up, there was all barracuda, just floatin' on top of the water. They were all dead. I remember that...

(W identified the blue as a dark shade, compares it to something.)

RB: ...Did the other two have lights?

JB: Yeah, they had red and blue lights.

W: In a thodolite— in a theodolite, when you're tracking, your eyes are, like, you know— right into it. You can't see to the right, unless you take your face away. At the time, I was just gettin' ready to track the pooch, cause I could see he wasn't movin'! An' meantime I was shootin' this thing, whatever it was— now, it's gettin' brighter and brighter, and the light's comin' through the sides of the theodolite, where my eyes are. That's when I looked up, over the theodolite— I couldn't see the other two, I was trackin' him— and I saw the other two sittin' there, and with the blue and green lights on—

JB: Blue and red, or blue and gr—

W: Blue an' green, blue and red, whatever the hell it was— but I could only see them with my own eyes, I couldn't track 'em with the (unintelligible) off—

JB: And were those lights flashing at all?

W: No, they were steady, steady. (JB repeats) The only thing was that on or the bottom, it was like a— a— whatta ya callit— it was like a light, like on the other two, but it was like off an on— How can I tell you? It wasn't like taking a light switch an' turn- it off— they never went all the way off, it dimmed, right, the bright, up again, then dim, then bright again— But they never moved, they just sat there. Then the next thing I knew, whooch, right over my head they went.

RB: (Remarks on other reports of the dimming and brightening. Suggests W keep in touch, if something came to mind after reading the book)

(W discusses how the government lies to newsmen during a test.)

W: What happens between the time of the shot and the time it gets to the screen? It's been clipped, clipped, and double clipped again—

(JB rechecks height of dome—12 feet high. From bottom of dome to the ground is another good 12 feet.)

JB: So that's 24 feet in all, so that thing was only about 24 feet above the...pooch, right? Cause it was level with you, practically —level with the dome?

W: No, he was— he was about what this light is...

RB: ...So he's about 30 degrees above you—

W: Oh, yeah— yeah, that's why I couldn't shoot that high.

RB: Is it about a 30 degree angle? a 40 degree angle, above you?

W: Forty, a 40 degree angle, easily.

RB: From 20 to 300 feet away.

W: From here to where that, air conditioner. Yeah, but you see, we had a set-in on the theodolite. We could draw 'im in, draw 'im up. That's what I did.

(all talk at once)

JB: This thing was above you, but was it above the top of the dome?

W: Yeah, about this high— (they reaffirm the angular height)

RB: So you really zoomed in on it.

W: I put it at full power, at 6 power, I put it right in on 'er, and the films musta come out, because otherwise they wouldn't'a sent that—

RB: ...Does your visual come in and show it close up too?

W: Well, see, if I put 6 power on that airconditioner, that'll be as far from where you're sittin to this book.

RB: ...So you could reach out and touch it.

(JB asks about the guys in the film lab—did they get canned too?)

W: No, matter of fact, I never heard any more of it. When they put me up, they said, Bob, you know— They put me on the bus from the heliport, took me— I got my back pay, I couldn't see nobody, right to the airport, and here's this (turkey?) waitin'. Boom, right to, uh, Nassau... I was by myself, and the fellows that were in radar, well, they left three days prior to me. The two guys that were left, left the day after me. Cause I stayed in Nassau about a week, and (unclear) I wanted to talk to 'em...

(re-cap on the pick-up of the animals 3-4 days after)

(The rest is briefly summarized also)

(RB: They can act pretty quickly; no bumbling bureaucracy there.)

(JB: Any headaches or anything afterwards?)

W: The only thing I got was a migraine because it was my birthday and they blew it for me!

(The light wasn't on W, it was on the pooch)

(W: Two guys went sterile because of it—? Tests? Ralph? Tape was restarted in the middle of this.)

(RB: Buck Rogers and the ray guns. W: No joke, that's what we got)

(W: Wrong time and place again. RB: Las Vegas is a good place.)

(They confirm W's LV address; don't use name...)

(W on restrictions around Andros...)

(JB: What was position when fired?)

W: I was a Tech One. It's called a Field Tech. Field Tech One...I was gettin' 260 every two weeks, plus my room and board...

(W describes the little island; recreation at Site 1, once a month —the main Site in Andros Town.)

(RB on folks getting hurt not knowing the truth. W: Nobody's gonna tell 'em the truth, especially not the U.S. Government. And they talk about the Russians—)

(RB: "It couldn't happen here." W: Yeah, it could never happen here. It happens every damn day. That's the truth, every day.)

(The recording ends on this rather desperate note... TB)

ANDROS ISLAND, BAHAMAS
Golden Cay

21 May 1966, 03:00 - 04:00

7 Sites, Main Site in Andros Town, Sites 4 and 6 Involved with UFO. RCA Test scheduled for 07:00 a.m. —Submarine Underwater Rocket Tests. AZROC missile shots from Submarine scheduled for observers.

W was RCA Tech One, Theodolite (angle measureing and tracking instrument with high speed 35mm cine movie camera built in) operator stationed at Site 4.

Dome 9' wide x 12' high

Dock approx 20' across

Many dead barracuda around both sides of the dock

Dog sat on end of dock

Suddenly it was "like the sun came up" — about 40° above the dome— the white concrete dock and the dome lit up with a bright, bright light, which focused on the dog "Squib" who was sitting on the end of the dock, tongue out, immobile as if frozen, some 200 feet away. Dog was a brown and white mongrel. W started filming with the theodolite, which would now only move manually. He shot 350 feet (8 minutes) of high resolution, high speed film of the hovering disc-shaped object.

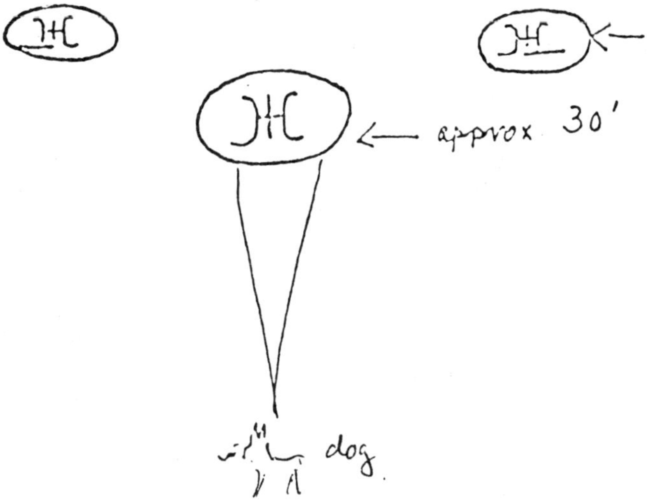

The first object hovered stationary above the dog on the end of the dock, with a cone of white light that focused to a point beam on the paralyzed dog. There was a great hummmm and the first craft was joined by two others that looked identical. They remained higher and farther away, and had two very peculiar symbols clearly visible on the bottom of the ships. The two additional craft had colored lights that pulsed dim and bright. The objects were estimated to be about 40 feet in diameter. The lower ship hovered only about 100 feet above the dog.

COMPARATIVE NOTES

	San Jose de Valderas	**Andros Island**
Color:	White	White
Finish:	Smooth	Smooth
Surface:	unbroken	unbroken
Diameter	40 feet	40 feet
Sound:	Hmmmm	Hmmmm
Symbols	)+(	)+(

This is the official reply from the Department of the Air Force to Richard W. Heiden's Freedom of Information request for documents now clearly over ten years old and theoritically declassified unless they were further upgraded for some reason and remain on the active classified list, an unbelievable move if there was nothing to the situation described by the witness. Even though the Air Force did not have jurisdiction in the Andros Island tests, they were certainly involved and there would have to be communications of some kind, especially since the intruder was an aircraft of some kind.

DEPARTMENT OF THE AIR FORCE
HEADQUARTERS, 1947TH ADMINISTRATIVE SUPPORT GROUP
WASHINGTON, D.C.

16 June 1981

Mr. Richard W. Heiden
7230 W. Capitol Dr., No. 211
Milwaukee, Wis. 53216

Dear Mr. Heiden

This responds to your Freedom of Information Act (FOIA) request dated 9 June 1981.

As you will read in the attached UFO Fact Sheet, the Air Force ended its UFO examinations in December 1969 and all records were transferred to the Archives. Since you state in your letter the Archives does not have the material you want,we're unable to help you further.

Sincerely

ANNE WILKINSON
HQ USAF Freedom of Information
Manager

1 Atch
UFO Fact Sheet

81-483

This official reply from the Department of the Navy in response to a similar Freedom of Information request by Richard W. Heiden was just as unproductive. Please note that this reply was signed by the "Aide/ Administrative Assistant" and "By direction of the Commander", of none other than the Naval Intelligence Command. Please note the careful phrasing to avoid mention of which files were searched or how many, and the following statement that "the files examined disclosed no information of any kind..." This is standard "escape" terminology and allows them to certify that the information sought was not in the file they looked at. Something of that nature would probably not be in the Administrative Files anyway. All other requests were equally unproductive, as was to be expected. We have reason to believe that the event actually happened as described.

DEPARTMENT OF THE NAVY
NAVAL INTELLIGENCE COMMAND
4600 SILVER HILL ROAD
WASHINGTON, D.C. 20389

IN REPLY REFER TO

JUN 26 1981

Mr. Richard W. Heiden
7230 W. Captiol Drive
Milwaukee, Wisconsin 53216

Dear Mr. Heiden:

Reference is made to your letter of 9 June 1981.

Please be advised that a detailed search of files, maintained by this Command, both at the Headquarters level and by subordinate units, has been completed. All available files were checked specifically for any information on, or record of, the three (3) UFO related incidents you cited, e.g., April 20, 1964; January 3, 1965; and, May 21, 1966. The files examined disclosed no information of any kind, in general, and no investigative reports, in particular, concerning the three UFO incidents you listed.

O. J. SAVINO
CWO3, U.S. Navy
Aide/Administrative Assistant
By direction of the Commander

NOT THE FIRST MISSILE INTERFERANCE BY UFOs

All that brass and those officials from RCA had good reason to be concerned about those events of 21 May 1966 at Andros Island, for it was only a little over a year earlier that an event took place which clearly indicated UFO interferance with the launch of one of the newest versions of the ATLAS intercontinental ballistic missiles.

Philippe Piet van Putten, a well known UFO researcher, writing in UFOLOGIA No. 5, published in Campo Grande (MS), Brazil, describes a recent statement released by Dr. Robert Jacobs, Ph.D., assistant professor at the University of Wisconsin, who said that when he was a 1st Lieutenant in the USAF in charge of a photographic instrument at Vandenburg AFB, California, his team was preparing to film the scheduled test launch of an ICBM. On the 8th of January 1965, Jacobs was in charge of a team of 120 technicians filming the test of an ATLAS F aimed out over the Pacific Ocean. On that occasion all had gone very well with the filming guaranteed by radar which guided the equipment very satisfactorily.

From that part of the statement we may conclude that the equipment used was the Askania Cine Theodolite camera system guided by the automatic radar tracking and control system. Those Theodolite movie cameras were mostly 35mm high quality technical systems that used special high density film. We already know from the statement by the RCA technician before that Vandenburg had one of the few in existence. However from there on Jacobs statement gets very interesting in light of what we now know.

Two days after that exercise, Jacobs was called into the office of his superior, one Major Florenz J. Mannsman. Besides the Major there were two men who gave only their first names, and who said they had come from Washington. The Major then projected the film obtained by Lt Jacobs team, and it was then that he came to understand that they had filmed something quite unusual.

At a certain altitude during the filming, an object of circular form, clearly visible, appeared next to the missile and discharged a jet of light at it. The unidentified object changed its course and floated above the missile, whereupon another stronger luminosity was seen. Immediately the UFO circled around the great projectile and shot two more beams of light, from different angles, and then went away. Seconds later, the ATLAS F appeared to function defectively, and was seen to fall hundreds of kilometers away.

Major Mannman asked the Lieutenant what he knew about that unexpected object on the film, and what was his best opinion. They ran the film again several times, and Lt. Jacobs examined the film with a magnifying glass before pronouncing his verdict. "Major it is a UFO!"

The meeting with the two strangers from Washington was concluded with a series of solicitations beginning with, "Until you and I both know what it is, this is only a story, is that not true?"

The film was delivered to the two men, whom Lt. Jacobs now suspected were agents from Intelligence.

Dr. Jacobs had now decided to break his silence because he felt it was not right that this episode should be simply extinguished. In his opinion, "The truth is very important for which it continues to be hidden. The UFOs ARE REAL. I know that they are real, and the Air Force knows that they are real, and the Government knows that they are real. I think that it is time that the Public knows it also."

AN UMMO CALLER RECORDED

When senor Francisco Donis, after receiving a letter from the Ummites, convened a meeting in his home, of members of the so-called "Madrid Group", to read it and discuss the contents of the communication; and the very moment he was reading the letter to the group, a telephone call came in from one of the UMMO expeditionary team members to Sr. Donis.

Senor Rafael Farriols, one of the other contactees present at the time, succeeded in tapping onto the telephone with a simple microphone pick-up, and recorded the end of the brief message before "they" left the line. This did not go unnoticed however, and he was later severely criticised by them for the audacious act.

Several of the Madrid Group members gathered there were direct contactees and had received the by now well known calls from the UMMO visitors, who spoke with a strange voice because of a prosthesis in their throats to make up for a lack of a developed larynx, and after hearing the tape recording played back by Farriols, agreed that the voice sounded like the peculiar UMMO voice known to them.

The Ummites took notice of the fact that Sr. Donis had gathered a meeting of those familiar with the UMMO correspondence, contrary to "their" wishes, with the intention of preparing a series of questions to be put to the UMMO visitors in the course of an effort to put them in touch with another ET visitor called "Atienza" who was in contact with Senor Donis. Donis was hoping for a trade-off of effort.

The UMMO callers asked them not to prepare the list of questions they had in mind.

We have decided to offer the reader an opportunity to hear the unusual voice of an extraterrestrial Ummite expeditionary by impressing that small recording on a thin plastic disc to be bound into the back of this book. The disc may be slit out and played on a 33 rpm turntable or may be transferred to tape as desired.

The recording opens with a statement by The author of this work to introduce the message, which then follows in Spanish. This is followed by a few comments in Spanish by senor Donis himself.

Senor Ribera says the voice sounds "Germanic" to him, speaking as a German speaking Spanish with a strong native accent.

A transcription of the first part of that recording follows:

THE TAPE RECORDING

"Antonio Ribera, author of the book you are reading, UFO CONTACT FROM PLANET UMMO, is speaking to you to introduce the taped voice you are going to hear.

"IT IS NOT A HUMAN VOICE; it belongs to one Ummite who, on the 28th of February 1969, put a call to senor Francisco Donis, who was at the moment at his home in Madrid, Spain, reading a letter received from the Ummites to a gathering of friends. Rafael Farriols succeeded in taping part of the call through a device he applied to a telephone extension in the house. The unknown voice says that the brothers assembled at Donis' home must not put questions to his brothers. It is a monotonous, slow voice, which has been analyzed in several European and American sound laboratories. After their verdict, its frequencies do not correspond to those of a human voice. It is not, then, a HUMAN VOICE, you are going to hear right now:

The maid says to Donis in a very low voice:

Maid: Senor, le llaman al telefono.

Donis takes phone and the voice says:

Voice: ...A mis hermanos...
— No formulen preguntas... preguntas... preguntas...
sus hermanos reunidos en su domicilio a mis hermanos...
— Suplicamos perdon... suplicamos perdon, senor...
— Desconecto comunication, senor desconecto...

Antonio Ribera continues:

"Note the knocks interspersed in the tape every time the Ummite is going to speak. I give you the rest of the cassette with the comments of Donis himself, but I don't know if you want to use them in the reord. It is just for information sake and to give you a background on the whole happening. Note also that the voice is speaking with some difficulty and very slowly."

As we had a very limited time available on this recording disc, we have included only a very small part of the comment by senor Donis.

We invite any other kind of analysis that may be made from this disc recording in any effort to study the dynamics of the sound and to try to arrive at any further scientific analysis that may add to our present knowledge in this respect.

UMMO VOICE RECORDING

We have provided this space for 3½ minute soundsheet reproduction of of the Ummite call to Senor Francisco Donis at his home, by the UMMO visitors technically interrupting and controlling telephone circuits, at the very moment he had convened a meeting of certain members of the "Madrid Group" in the room to discuss a new contact by the mysterious UMMO extraterrestrials. We are trying to solve some technical aspects in time to make this printing. (Unable at this time, sorry)

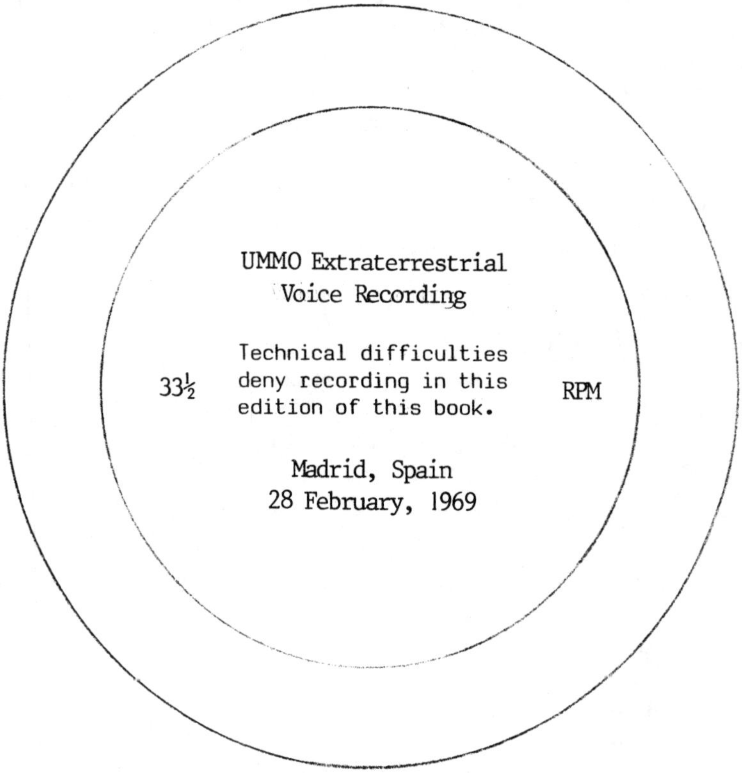

Madrid, Spain, 28 February 1969. The recorded voice of the Ummite man who called Sr. Donis during the meeting. [If no recording is bound in this volume when you receive it, we have failed to get a sufficiently clear and reproducible track transferred to the soundsheet to complete this plan. We apologize. The transcription is on the preceeding page.]

OTHER UFO BOOKS BY THE SAME PUBLISHER

Having perceived a serious shortage of good UFO books in the United States market, and almost a total lack of news media coverage of this most interesting subject in this country, and having extensive files of research material on hand, we have undertaken a small effort to make real case data available to those who seek to study this phenomenon for themselves.

Most of the UFO books published in this country have a small amount of actual case data, and most of that unverifiable, and a whole lot of speculation, attempted explanations, and suggested answers to the perplexing questions raised in them. We offer no such explanations or pat solutions to the enigmatic questions raised, but seek to offer the evidence we have found in as much detail as we can, and at the same time point any researcher who desires to follow up on us and check out anything we have said in the right direction.

We find, contrary to popular belief in this country, that more and more is happening in the UFO field of interest all the time, and that the amount of real case data in existence is massive. We also find that meaningful UFO contacts do not jusr happen and fade away, but that a great many of them actually continue and persist for years and even decades., though this is seldom reported in our media.

We have recently concentrated on the more profound and long-running cirect contact cases, and have prepared and published extensive reports in book form on a few of them.

Other volumes in this series are described and illustrated in more detail in the following pages.

OTHER UFO BOOKS AVAILABLE

UFO CONTACT FROM RETICULUM, Stevens-Herrmann $16.95
416 pages, illustr., hard cover, 2 sets color UFO photos

UFO CONTACT FROM PLANET IARGA, Denaerde-Stevens 15.95
363 pages, illustr., hard cover, 4 color paintings

UFO CONTACT FROM UNDERSEA, Sanchez-Stevens 14.95
190 pages, illustr., hard cover, halftones, sketches and diagrams

UFO CONTACT AT PASCAGOULA, Mendez-Hickson 14.95
174 pages, illustr., hard cover, halftones and sketches

UFOs OVER MODERN CHINA, Stevens-Dong 16.95
352 pages, illustr., hard cover, many chinese paintings

UFO ABDUCTION AT MIRASSOL, Buhler-Pereira-Pires 16.95
416 pages, illustr., hard cover, halftones, sketches and diagrams

UFO CONTACT FROM PLANET KOLDAS, van Vlierden 15.95
305 pages, illustr., hard cover, halftones, sketches and recording

UFO CONTACT FROM PLANET UMMO, Vol. 1, Ribera 16.95
354 pages, illustr., hard cover, sketches and diagrams, halftones

UFO CONTACT FROM ITIBI-RA, Pallmann-Stevens 14.95
286 pages, illustr., hard cover, halftones, sketches

UFO PHOTOGRAPHS AROUND THE WORLD, Vol. 1, Stevens-Roberts 14.95
254 pages, illustr., hard cover, many UFO photos, line drawings

UFO PHOTOGRAPHS AROUND THE WORLD, Vol. 2, Stevens-Roberts 14.95
254 pages, illustr., hard cover, many UFO photos, line drawings

UFO ABDUCTION AT BOTUCATU, Casalleto-Valerio-Stevens 14.95
224 pages, illustr., halftones sketches

UFO CRASH AT AZTEC, Steinman-Stevens 18.95
608 pages, illustr., much documentation

UFO CONTACT FROM PLANET ACART, Berlet 14.95
224 pages, illustr., sketches and diagrams

Above books may be ordered directly from publisher at address below. Add $1.25 for postage, 4th class mail, surface rate each, U.S.A. only. Add $1.75 each for postage, 4th class mail, surface rate only, foreign, plus insurance and airmail extra if desired. Order from:

UFO PHOTO ARCHIVES, P.O. Box 17206, Tucson, Arizona 85710, U.S.A.

UFO abduction at MIRASSOL

An artist's impression of the abducting ET woman of one of the two race-types aboard the spaceship by Chan Johnson

A BIOGENETIC EXPERIMENT

Dr. Walter K. Bühler   Guilherme Pereira

Prof. Ney Matiel Pires

416 Pages, Illustrated, Hard Cover

UFO at MIRASSOL

BUHLER
PIRES
PEREIRA

9 May 1984, 00:15, Sao Paulo, Brazil, Photo of UFO as described in text by witnesses - Amilton Vieira

UFO ABDUCTION AT MIRASSOL

A Biogenetic Experiment

- More than one abduction case -
- Other associated events -
- Many other witnesses -
- Genetic experiment involving Abductee -
- Taken aboard larger mother-ship for this-
- Hi-brid creature produced -
- Electro-magnetic effects -
- Several different spacecraft used -
- UFOnauts return again and again -
- Repeated abductions -
- Witness taken away from home planet -
- Talking balls of light -
- Ray-weapons used -
- Two different race-types aboard -
- Instant healing -
- UFO photographs -

ISBN 0-9608558-8-2

UFO contact from Planet KOLDAS

2 December 1971, 15:00 Punta Norte, Peninsula de Valdez,
Province of Chubut, Argentina, facing Golfo San Matias.

Carl van Vlierden

305 Pages, Illustrated, Hard Cover

23 March 1974, 19:30, Caleta Olivia Province of Santa Cruz, Argentina, facing Golfo San Jorge.

UFO Contact from Planet KOLDAS

UFO CONTACT FROM UNDERSEA

A Report of the Investigation

- 2 Abductions aboard the alien spacecraft —
- First abduction observed by 3 witnesses —
- Elevated aboard in a beam of light —
- Physical examination by the alien beings —
- A trip as guest aboard the alien vessel —
- Several varieties of flying vehicles used —
- A Submarine Base visited by the witness —
- A tour of the alien's Earth facilities —
- Conversatios with the alien beings —
- Hi-technology transciever instruments implanted in the witness's head —
- Other independent unconnected witnesses —
- Police and Authorities involved —
- Line drawings of the spacecraft —
- Photographs of flying discs from undersea —
- Maps of pertinent locations —

ISBN 0-9608558-0-7

UFO Contact from Planet UMMO

1 June 1967, 20:00, San Jose de Valderas, Spain
Photo Y-1, 1st photo by Antonio San Antonio

The Mystery of UMMO

Vol. 1

Antonio Ribera

354 Pages, Illustrated, Hard Cover

1 June 1967, 20:00, San Jose de Valderas
Photo X-2, 2nd photo by Antonio Pardo

UFO CONTACT FROM PLANET UMMO
Vol. I, The Mystery of UMMO

- Ummites coming here for 35 years -
- UMMO contacts with Earth humans for 30 years -
- Over 1,740 pages of UMMO Contact Notes -
- Scores of Earth Contactees -
- UMMO Bases in 8 Countries -
- UMMO Ships photographed 6 times -
- Scores of witnesses to photographing -
- Landing Tracks left on ground -
- Metal artifact recovered at landing site -
- Highly sophisticated technology -
- Faster than light travel -
- UMMO home planet similar to Earth -
- Ummites are Humans also -
- Slight anatomical differences -
- Utilize 10 dimensional frames of reference -
- UMMO Expeditionary Teams change as needed -
- UMMO Ships are self-repairing -

ISBN 0-9608558-5-8

UFO Vol. 1 Contact from Planet UMMO

RIBERA
••
STEVENS

UFO contact from Planet ITIBI-RA

March 1967, 17:30, Yungay, Peru. Sr. Augusto Arranda shot 4 color photos with a 40-year-old box camera.

CANCER PLANET MISSION

Ludwig F. Pallmann
and
Wendelle C. Stevens

286 Pages, Illustrated. Hard Cover

UFO Contact from Planet ITIBI-RA

PALLMANN • STEVENS

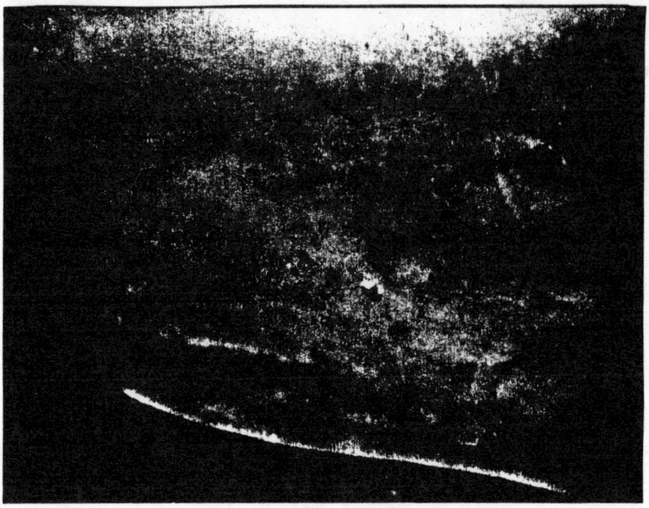

March 1967, Yungay, Peru, These photos of ships as described were made during the height of the plantation activity in the jungles near here.

UFO CONTACT FROM ITIBI-RA

CANCER PLANET MISSION

- Human Extraterrestrial beings -
- Home planet in another Solar System -
- Extraterrestrial plantations on Earth -
- Plant hybridizing experiments -
- Worldwide operations -
- ET society on home planet described -
- Comparison of phylosophy -
- Native aborigines work with ETs -
- Ancient Earth civilizations -
- Abandoned city in jungle -
- Circular spacecraft used -
- Other ET plantations on Earth -
- Other ET activities on Earth -

ISBN 0-934269-04-1

UFO Vol.1

PHOTOGRAPHS

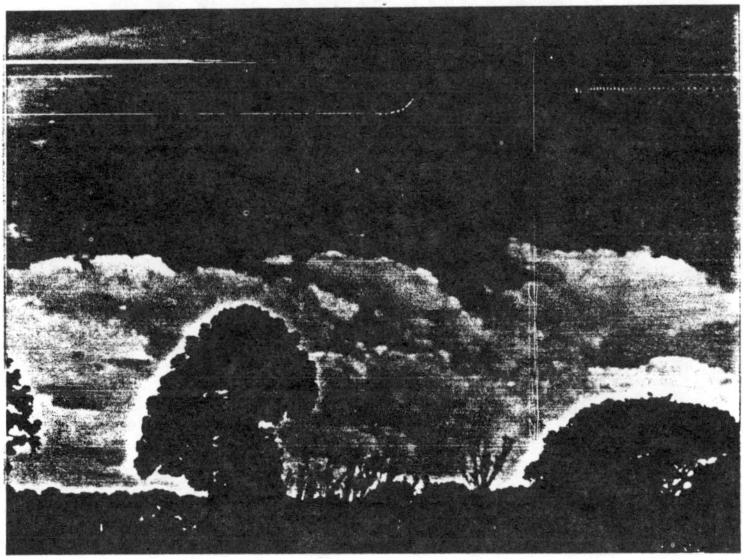

15 November 1978, 16:00, Ipamari, Goyas, Brazil. Sr. Roberto Edilson Perez snapped 4 clear photos of UFO over his estancia.

AROUND THE WORLD

Wendelle Stevens

August Roberts

254 Pages, Illustrated, Hard Cover

UFO Vol. 1 PHOTOGRAPHS

STEVENS
ROBERTS

UFO PHOTOGRAPHS

Around The World
Vol. 1

- Hi-Domed Discs -
- LO-Domed Discs -
- Dark Discs -
- 7 Featurettes -
- 46 UFO Photo Cases -
- 130 UFO Photographs -
- 21 Line Drawings of UFOs -
- Photogrammetric Analysis Techniques -
- Chronology of UFO Photo Cases -
- All Structured Flying Objects -
- Many different Countries Reported -
- Thousands of Witnesses -

ISBN 0-934269-00-9

UFO abduction at BOTUCATU

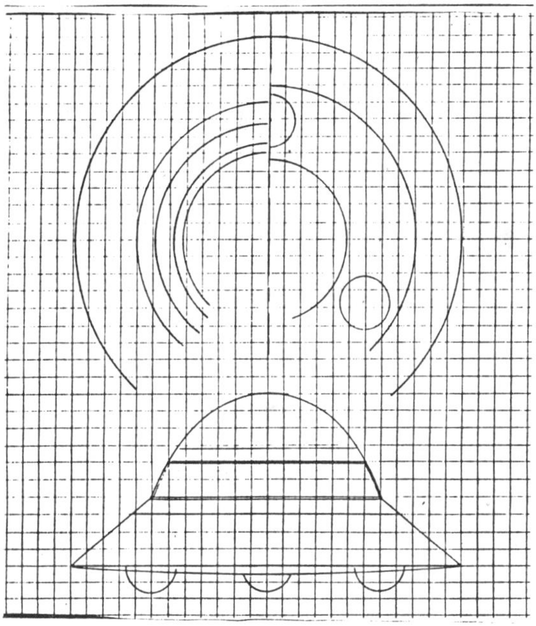

29 November 1982, Botucatu (SP), Brazil. This is the spacecraft used by the alien ETs in at least the first and second abductions of Joao Valerio da Silva of Botucatu. He has since then been taken away from Earth in a ship like this and safely returned.

A Preliminary Report

Rodolfo R. Casellato Joao Valerio da Silva
and
Wendelle C. Stevens

224 Pages, Illustrated, Hard Cover

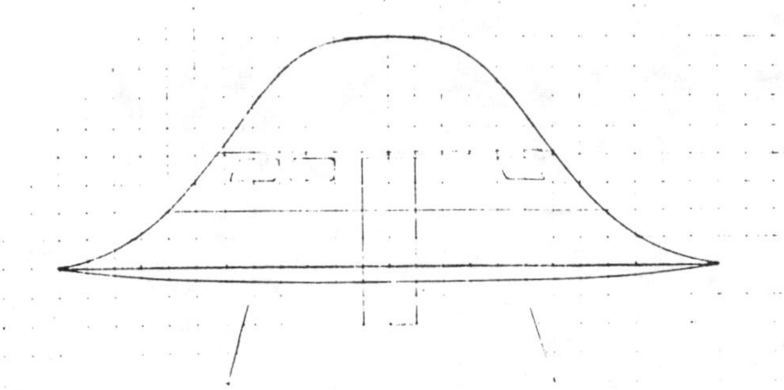

10 May 1978, 23:00 to 01:15, Pelotas, Rio Grande do Sul, Brazil. This alien ET ship abducted Assis Antonio Caetano de Avila from near his home in Pelotas. They wanted to take him someplace else with them, but he refused to go, and was released to go home.

UFO ABDUCTION AT BOTUCATU

A Preliminary Report

- Abducted for biogenetic experiment -
- Other Brazilian man taken aboard twice -
- Different varieties of spacecraft used -
- More than 40 contacts, over 18 aboard ET spacecraft -
- Taken away from Earth more than 4 times -
- Stayed over 18 hours on another planet, 3 days there -
- Took photos there with cheap borrowed camera -
- Unknown language heard, unfamiliar symbol form -
- Artifacts given to abductee -
- An "intelligent" rock performs -
- ET crystal "bleeds" -
- Abductee told he is "one of them" -
- Abductee's oldest son is "one of them" also -
- Abductee develops psychokinetic powers -
- Other psychic faculties develop -
- Six other Earth humans abducted in similar way -

ISBN 0-934269-06-8

UFO at BOTUCATU

CASE-
LLATO
VALÉRIO
STEVENS

UFO CRASH AT AZTEC

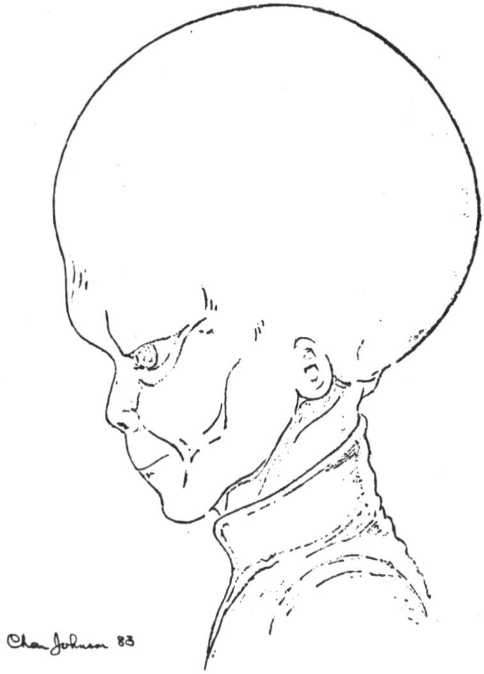

A WELL KEPT SECRET

WILLIAM S. STEINMAN

WENDELLE C. STEVENS

608 Pages, Illustrated, Hard Cover

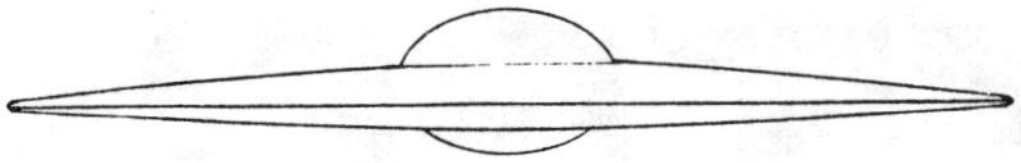

Diameter: 99.9 feet overall — Height: 6.0 feet overall
Cabin: 18.0 feet across — Cabin to rim edge: 41.0 feet
Top of cabin: Raised 45" above the level of the mean plane of the disc
Disc edge: 27" above the saucer base, slightly curved slope upper and lower surface of disc

UFO CRASH AT AZTEC

A Well Kept Secret

- Disc-shaped craft recovered relatively intact -
- Sixteen small human-like bodies aboard -
- Residue and bodies transported away by military team -
- All evidence of crash and recovery destroyed -
- Highest ranking Military and Scientists involved -
- Craft disassembled and studied at secret site -
- Bodies examined and autopsied, some preserved -
- Projects established to duplicate technology -
- Vast development programs launched -
- Super-secret Intelligence within Intelligence -
- Security lid clamped down tight -
- Accidental leaks of information -
- Efforts to plug the leaks, not all successful -
- Dis-information program and smear campaign begun -
- More disabled UFOs come down -
- Special forces set up to handle situation -
- New facilities created to isolate project work -

ISBN 0-934269-05-X

UFO CRASH AT AZTEC

STEINMAN • STEVENS

UFO contact from Planet ACART

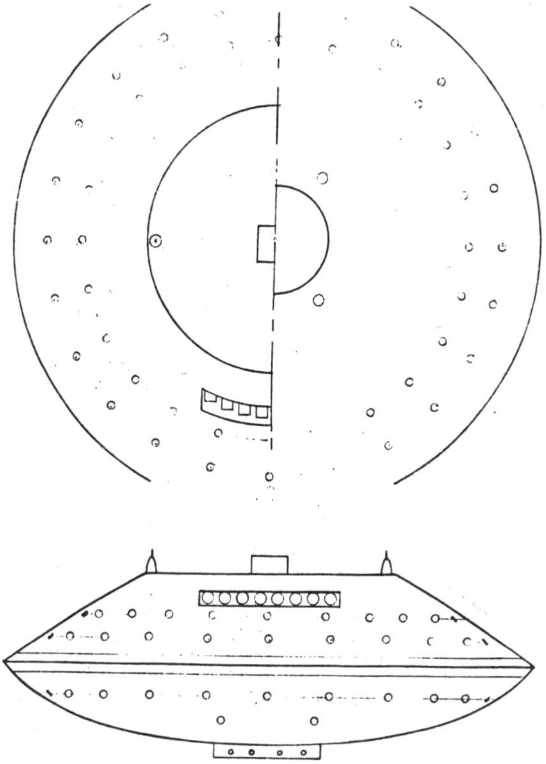

This is a line drawing of the 30 meter diameter interplanetary transport ship from planet Acart used in the abduction and return of Artur Berlet.

FROM UTOPIA TO REALITY

ARTUR BERLET

224 Pages, Illustrated, Hard Cover

UFO from ACART

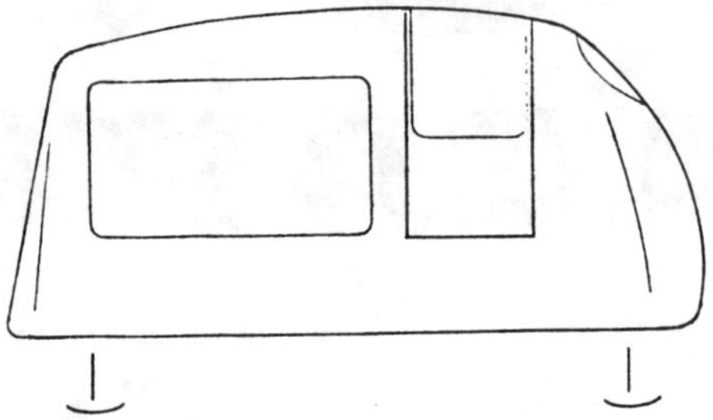

This is a line drawing of the standard personal transport flying machine used by all the citizens of the super-pupolated planet they call Acart.

UFO CONTACT FROM PLANET ACART

From Utopia to Reality

- Human-like extraterrestrial beings -
- Earth man abducted to ET home planet -
- Deep bowl-shaped 30 meter spacecraft -
- Abductee toured the ET planet for 8 days -
- Great ET industrial centers -
- Unique agricultural methods, fish-farming -
- Different cattle, animals, vegetation -
- Huge sities of metallic buildings -
- Super-population of 20 Billion -
- No monetary system -
- No separate nations -
- Different foods and drink -
- Different kind of water -
- ET style and manner of dress -
- Cold ambient temperatures -
- ET vehicles and transportation -
- They observe us regulalrly -

ISBN 0-934269-08-4

ARTUR
BERLET